002 $12

D0087926

BASIC WRITINGS IN THE
HISTORY OF PSYCHOLOGY

BASIC WRITINGS
IN THE HISTORY
OF PSYCHOLOGY

Robert I. Watson, Sr.
UNIVERSITY OF FLORIDA

NEW YORK • OXFORD UNIVERSITY PRESS • 1979

Copyright © 1979 by Oxford University Press, Inc.

Library of Congress Cataloging in Publication Data

Main entry under title:

Basic writings in the history of psychology.

1. Psychology—History—Addresses, essays, lectures.
2. Psychology—Early works to 1850—Addresses, essays, lectures.
I. Watson, Robert Irving, 1909–
BF98.B23   150'.8   78-7274
ISBN 0-19-502443-5
ISBN 0-19-502444-3 pbk.

Printed in the United States of America
9 8 7 6 5

PREFACE

Educational value for students was the prime consideration in preparing this book. What students need are excerpts that common opinion would have it were the most important, the most widely accepted as seminal. They may appear commonplace and conventional to persons already familiar with the history of psychology, but the book is not addressed to them. I have resisted the scholarly impulse to rescue from oblivion heretofore unanthologized documents from our history in favor of those known already to be crucial. It follows that many, if not most, of the excerpts have been used in previous anthologies, for example, those from James Mill on association of ideas and Johannes Müller on specific nerve energies have appeared in at least four earlier books of readings. I make no apology for their repetition here. I consider the overlap on indication of agreement about their significance. It gives me added confidence that I am fulfilling the intent of this book.

The method of selection of those writings also reflects this intent. The contents of several current textbooks in the history of psychology were examined, specifically those listed below:

R. Lowry, *The Evolution of Psychological Theory*. Aldine-Atherton, 1971.

D. N. Robinson, An Intellectual History of Psychology. Macmillan, 1976.

D. P. Schultz, *A History of Modern Psychology*. 2nd ed. Academic Press, 1976.

R. I. Watson, *The Great Psychologists*. 4th ed. Lippincott, 1978.

M. Wertheimer, *A Brief History of Psychology*. Holt, Rinehart and Winston, 1970.

Relatively significant discussion of a particular person's work was found by examining the contents of these texts and their individual and topical sources identified. The results were then compared across texts. The writing selected for inclusion covers persons and topics discussed in at least three, sometimes four, and even in all five of these books. Considerable discussion of these individuals and their writings in these textbooks is an additional reason to feel that the task of understanding them has been made easier for the student. Since only two of the texts, Robinson and Watson, dealt in any serious way with the premodern period, readings earlier than the sixteenth century were precluded.

Learning what eminent contributors to psychology have had to say in their own words about psychological matters is essential for understanding the history of psychology. But it does introduce difficulties. Each was writing for his own time, using the language and thought processes of his times, and most important of all, expressing his particular intentions which certainly did not include making himself easier to understand by contemporary psychology students. This creates a situation in which books of readings may well be confusing to the students. Sometimes an excerpt is thrust upon the student, often without any hint of its significance, often in a strange phraseology and dealing with concepts that the student, to the extent that he or she understands them, feels at a lose to appreciate their significance. The student reads that Descartes held that mind and body are separate and distinct, and yet interrelated. The student is justified in wondering just what this has to do with psychology, as he or she studied it before taking the present course in history. Somewhere a lecture was defined as telling your audience what you are going to talk about, talking about it, and then telling them what you have talked about. A variation of this dictum has been applied to the task at hand. Each excerpt is preceded by a brief statement of the context from which it has been taken and is followed by an examination of its significance often couched in terms of later developments.

As might be expected, the fifty individuals selected for inclusion here are among the most eminent contributors to psychology. Such proved to be the case from a comparative examination of the results of a panel selection study, the judges being contemporary psychologists-historians.[1] A maximum rating of three signifying the highest conviction of eminence that the ratings allowed was given by all nine international judges to thirty-five of the fifty selected for inclusion (along with nineteen more not so selected). Another fifteen individuals had scores ranging from twenty-six, one short of the maximum, down to twenty. Many of these lower scores were obtained by philosophers and physiologists before the time of Wundt. Skinner was unrated because the study had included only deceased psychologists.

The order of presentation is roughly chronological, because the thinking of an individual might well be influenced by that of one's predecessors. To be an accompaniment to the various textbooks, such as those mentioned earlier with their varying thematic divisions, it was considered fairest to present the excerpts in more or less chronological sequence. In

[1]Annin, E. L., Boring, E. G., and Watson, R. I. Important psychologists: 1600–1967. *J. Hist. Behav. Sci.*, 1968, **4**, 303–315.

the opinion of the editor, the variations from chronology that are to be indicated do not inflict any hardship on any of the texts examined. German psychologists being placed just after the German physiologists is an exception, because subsequent readings require one to go back in time to Darwin and the British evolutionists. This is justified by the almost complete disregard on the part of the German psychologists of what was then a contemporary stream of thought. A slight deviation from strict chronology is allowed so as to place the Mills to complete the sequence of Locke, Berkely, Hume, and Hartley.

Gainesville, Florida   Robert I. Watson, Sr.
November 1978

ACKNOWLEDGMENTS

Advice was sought of authors of current textbooks in the history of psychology, with a view toward making this volume of excerpts a suitable accompaniment to their texts. In this endeavor, the help of Richard Lowry, Daniel N. Robinson, Duane Schultz, and Michael Wertheimer is very much appreciated.

Acknowledgments with thanks is made to editors, Heinz and Rowena Ansbacher, David C. Beardslee, Solomon Diamond, Jean and George Mandler, and Michael Wertheimer, who permitted my publishing translations from works edited by them. Heinz and Rowena Ansbacher, as editors of selections from the writings of Alfred Adler, did it so efficiently that it was merely necessary for me to take excerpts from their sequence of his writings to arrive at the order in which they are presented here. General permission to reprint on the part of the one living author, B. F. Skinner, is acknowledged, including specific permission for an article on which he holds copyright (Freedom and the control of man, *American Scholar*, 1955–1956, **25**, 47–65).

To the many publishers and holders of copyright who gave permission to reprint excerpts, acknowledgment is made with gratitude. In many instances, the form is that specified by them, while the remaining are in the form of the references, which are cited on pp. 402–414. Specific pages or sections of excerpts are reported in the references beginning on the same page. These publishers or holders of copyright arranged alphabetically are as follows:

Jung, C. G., *et al. Man and his symbols*. Garden City, N.Y.: Doubleday, 1964. © 1964, Aldus Books, London.

Wundt, W. *Principles of physiological psychology*, 5th ed. New York: Macmillan, 1904. © George Allen and Unwin Ltd.

Thorndike, E. L. A proof of the law of effect. *Science*, 1933. 77, 173–175. Copyright 1933 by the American Association for the Advancement of Science.

Thorndike, E. L. Mental abilities. *Proceedings of the American Philosophical Society*, 1941, *84*, 504–513. Permission granted by the American Philosophical Society.

Angell, J. R. The province of functional psychology. *Psychological Review*, 1907, *14*, 61–91. *Copyright 1907 by the American Psychological Association. Reprinted by permission.*

Cattell, J. McK. Retrospect: Psychology as a profession. *Journal of Consulting Psychology*, 1937, *1*, 1–2. *Copyright 1937 by the American Psychological Association. Reprinted by permission.*

Dewey, J. The reflex arc concept in psychology. *Psychological Review*, 1896, *3*, 357–370. *Copyright 1896 by the American Psychological Association. Reprinted by permission.*

Watson, J. B., & Rayner, R. Conditioned emotional reactions. *Journal of Experimental Psychology*, 1920, *3*, 1–14. *Copyright 1920 by the American Psychological Association. Reprinted by permission.*

Enrenfels, C. v., On Gestalt-qualities. (1932) *Psychological Review*, 1937, *44*, 521–524. *Copyright 1937 by the American Psychological Association. Reprinted by permission.*

Guthrie, E. R. Conditioning as a principle of learning. *Psychological Review*, 1930, *37*, 412–428. *Copyright 1930 by the American Psychological Association. Reprinted by permission.*

Hull, C. L. Mind, mechanism and adaptive behavior. *Psychological Review*, 1937, *44*, 1–32. *Copyright 1937 by the American Psychological Association. Reprinted by permission.*

Thorndike, E. L. Animal Intelligence. *Psychological Review Monograph Supplement*, 1898, No. 2, pp. 1–109. *Copyright 1898 by the American Psychological Association. Reprinted by permission.*

Watson, J. B. Psychology as a behaviorist views it. *Psychological Review*, 1913, *20*, 158–177. *Copyright 1913 by the American Psychological Association. Reprinted by permission.*

Wundt, W. *An introduction to psychology*. 2nd ed. New York: Macmillan, 1912. Reprinted by Arno Press, 1973.

Excerpted from THE INDIVIDUAL PSYCHOLOGY OF ALFRED ADLER: A Systematic Presentation in Selections from His Writings, edited and annotated by Heinz L. Ansbacher, Ph.D. and Rowena R. Ansbacher, Ph.D. © 1956, by Basic Books, Inc., Publishers, New York.

Alder, A. Translations in THE INDIVIDUAL PSYCHOLOGY OF ALFRED ADLER: A systematic presentation in selection from his writings, edited by Heinz L. and Rowena R. Ansbacher © by Basic Books, Inc., Publishers, New York.

Descartes, R. On man. (1662). From THE ROOTS OF PSYCHOLOGY: A Source-book on the History of Ideas, edited by Solomon Diamond, © 1974 by Basic Books, Inc., Publishers, New York.

From Chapter 2, "The Method of Interpreting Dreams: An Analysis of a Speci-men Dream," in THE INTERPRETATION OF DREAMS, by Sigmund Freud, translated from the German and edited by James Strachey, published in the United States by Basic Books, Inc., Publishers, New York, by arrangement with George Allen & Unwin Ltd. and The Hogarth Press Ltd., London.

Bacon, F. Novum organum, (1620) In *The physical and metaphysical works of Lord Bacon, including the advancement of learning and the novum organum.* London: Bell, 1886. Published by Bell & Hyman Limited.

Molesworth, W. ed., *The English works of Thomas Hobbes* Vols. 3, 4. London: Bohn, 1840. Published by Bell and Hyman Limited.

Kant, I. *Metaphysical foundations of natural science.* Trans. J. Ellington. Indi-anapolis, Ind.: Bobbs-Merrill, 1970.

Descartes, R. *The philosophical works of Descartes.* (2 vols.) Trans. by Elizabeth S. Haldane & G. R. T. Ross. London: Cambridge University Press, 1931. Permis-sion granted by Cambridge University Press.

From THE SCIENCE OF LIVING by Alfred Adler. Copyright 1929 by Greenberg Publishers. Reprinted with the permission of the Chilton Book Company, Radnor, Pennsylvania.

McDougall, W. *Physiological psychology.* London: Dent, 1921. Reprinted by per-mission of J. M. Dent and Sons.

Helmholtz, H. v. *On the sensations of tone.* Fourth German ed. New York: Dover, 1954. Permission granted by Dover Publications, Inc.

Lashley, K. *Brain mechanisms and intelligence: A quantitative study of injuries to the brain.* New York: Dover, 1963. Permission granted by Dover Publications, Inc.

Newton, I. *Opticks, or a treatise of the reflections, refractions, inflection & colours of light.* (4th ed.) New York: Dover, 1952. Permission granted by Dover Publications, Inc.

From HEREDITARY GENIUS: AN INQUIRY INTO ITS LAWS AND CONSE-QUENCES by Sir Francis Galton, by permission of the publisher in the United States, E. P. Dutton. An Everyman's Library Edition.

From INQUIRIES INTO HUMAN FACULTY AND ITS DEVELOPMENT by Sir Francis Galton, by permission of the publisher in the United States, E. P. Dutton. An Everyman's Library Edition.

From A TREATISE OF HUMAN NATURE by David Hume, by permission of the publisher in the United States, E. P. Dutton. An Everyman's Library Edition.

From CRITIQUE OF PURE REASON by Immanuel Kant, by permission of the publisher in the United States, E. P. Dutton. An Everyman's Library Edition.

Excerpted by permission of Harcourt Brace Jovanovich, Inc. from PRINCIPLES OF GESTALT PSYCHOLOGY by K. Koffka, copyright, 1935, by Harcourt Brace Jovanovich, Inc.: copyright, 1963, by Elizabeth Koffka.

James, W. *The principles of psychology.* (2 vols.) New York: Holt, 1890. Permission granted by Holt, Rinehart and Winston.

CATS IN A PUZZLE BOX by E. R. Guthrie and G. P. Horton. Copyright 1946 by Rinehart & Company, renewed © 1974 by Edwin R. Guthrie, George P. Horton. Reprinted by permission of Holt, Rinehart and Winston and Edwin R. Guthrie and George P. Horton.

Brentano, F. *Psychology from an empirical standpoint.* (2nd ed.) London: Routlege & Kegan Paul, 1973. Permission granted by Humanities Press, Inc. New Jersey.

Wertheimer, M. The general theoretical situations. (1922) In W. D. Ellis (Ed.), *A souce book of Gestalt psychology.* New York: Harcourt, Brace, 1938. Permission granted by Humanities Press, Inc. New Jersey.

Koffka, K. *The growth of the mind: An introduction to child psychology.* Trans. R. M. Ogden, London: Routledge and Kegan Paul, 1928. Permission granted by Humanities Press Inc. New Jersey.

Galileo, Il saggiatore, (1623), Part 23. As translated in E. A. Burtt, *The metaphysical foundations of modern physical science,* (Rev. ed.) New York: Humanities Press, 1932. Permission granted by Humanities Press, Inc. New Jersey.

From PURPOSIVE BEHAVIOR IN ANIMALS AND MEN by E. C. Tolman. © 1967 by Meredith Publishing Company. Reprinted by permission of Irvington Publishers, Inc.

Müller, J. *Elements of physiology,* Vol. 2. Philadelphia, Pa.: Lea & Blanchard, 1843. Permission granted by Lea & Febiger.

Wertheimer, M. *Principles of perceptual organization.* In D. C. Beardslee, and M[ichael] Wertheimer, Eds. *Readings in perception,* Princeton, N.J.: Van Nostrand, 1958, pp. 115–135. By permission of Litton Educational Publishing.

Reprinted from THE PLACE OF VALUE IN A WORLD OF FACTS by Wolfgang Köhler, with the permission of Liveright Publishing Corporation. Copyright 1938 by Liveright Publishing Corporation. Copyright renewed 1965 by Wolfgang Köhler.

Reprinted from GESTALT PSYCHOLOGY by Dr. Wolfgang Köhler, with the permission of Liveright Publishing Corporation. Copyright 1947 by Liveright Publishing Corporation. Copyright renewed 1975 by Lili Köhler.

Reprinted with permission of Macmillan Publishing Co., Inc. from SCIENCE AND HUMAN BEHAVIOR by B. F. Skinner. Copyright 1953 by Macmillan Publishing Co., Inc.

Tolman, E. C. Principles of purposive behavior. In S. Koch, ed., *Psychology: A study of a science*. Study 1. *Conceptual and systematic*. Vol. 2. *General systematic formulations, learning and special processes*. New York: McGraw-Hill, 1959, pp. 92–147. Used with permission of McGraw-Hill Book Company.

Skinner, B. F. A case history in scientific methods. In S. Koch. ed., *Psychology: a study of a science*. Study 1. *Conceptual and systematic*. Vol. 2. *General systematic formulations, learning, and special processes*. New York: McGraw-Hill, 1959, pp. 359–379. Used with permission of McGraw-Hill Book Company.

Luce, A. A. & T. E. Jessop (eds.), *The Works of George Berkely, Bishop of Cloyne*. (2 vols.) London: Nelson, 1948, 1949. Reprinted by permission of Thomas Nelson and Sons, Limited.

Selection is reprinted from AN OUTLINE OF PSYCHOANALYSIS by Sigmund Freud. Translated by James Strachey. With the permission of W. W. Norton & Company, Inc. Copyright 1949 by W. W. Norton & Company, Inc. Copyright © 1969 by The Intitute of Psychoanalysis and Alix Strachey. Copyright renewed 1976 by Alix S. Strachey.

Selection is reprinted from THE PSYCHOPATHOLOGY OF EVERYDAY LIFE by Sigmund Freud. Translated from the German by Alan Tyson. Edited by James Strachey. Reprinted with the permission of W. W. Norton & Company, Inc. Translation Copyright © 1960 by Alan Tyson. Editorial matter Copyright © 1960, 1965, by James Strachey.

Watson, J. B. *Behaviorism*. (2nd ed.) Chicago: University of Chicago Press, 1939. Permission granted by W. W. Norton and Company, Inc. present publishers.

Helmholtz H. v. *Treatise on physiological optics,* vol. 2. Rochester, N.Y.: Optical Society of America, 1924. Reprinted by permission of the Optical Society of America.

Locke, J. *An essay concerning human understanding*. (2 vols.) by A. C. Fraser, ed., London: Oxford University Press, 1894. By permission of the Oxford University Press.

Hume, D. *Enquiries concerning the human understanding and concerning the principles of morals*. Ed. by L. A. Selby-Bigge. 2nd ed. of 1902. Oxford: Clarendon Press, 1955. By permission of the Oxford University Press.

The Collected Works of C. G. Jung, trans. R. F. C. Hull, Bollingen Series XX. Vol. 2: *Experimental Researches,* copyright © 1973 by Princeton University Press; Vol. 6: *Psychological Types,* copyright © 1971 by Princeton University Press; Vol. 9, *I, The Archetypes and the Collective Unconscious,* copyright © 1959, 1969 by Princeton University Press. Reprinted by permission.

Romanes, G. J. *Animal intelligence*. London: Kegan Paul, Trench, 1882. Permission of Routledge and Kegan Paul.

Newton, I. *Sir Isaac Newton's mathematical principles of natural philosophy and his system of the world*. (2 vols.) (3rd ed.) Trans. by A. Motte & rev. by F.

Cajori. Berkeley, Ca.: University of California Press, 1934. Permission granted by the University of California Press.

Cattell, J. McK. Statistics of American psychologists. *American Journal of Psychology*, 1903, *14*, 310–328. Permission granted by the University of Illinois Press.

Watson, J. B., & Morgan, J. J. B. Emotional reactions and psychological experimentation. *American Journal of Psychology*, 1917, *28*, 163–174. Permission granted by the University of Illinois Press.

Other sources of material were drawn upon that did not request specific acknowledgment in this section. To them also go my thanks. These sources are cited in the reference section, beginning on page 402.

CONTENTS

BASIC WRITINGS IN THE
HISTORY OF PSYCHOLOGY

1

GALILEO ON
THE DIFFERENCE BETWEEN
PHYSICAL AND PSYCHOLOGICAL SCIENCES

GALILEO GALILEI (1564–1642), Italian astronomer-mathematician-physicist, is considered one of the founders of modern science. Although the subject matter of most of his research did not involve psychological problems, he was methodologically important in positive and negative ways. So, too, was his conception of the physical universe subject to mechanical laws. He is best known for his experiments on falling bodies, which laid the foundation for the study of mechanics through his derivation of the law of acceleration and his astronomical discoveries made with the aid of the newly perfected telescope. But he also conducted studies on the speed of the transmission of sound and measured the relative vibration frequencies associated with different pitches of sound. That pitch dependent on the length of the plucked string was known even by the early Greeks. But Galileo was the first to establish experimentally a mathematical relation between pitch as a particular number of physical vibrations and the subject experience. Sound, then, could be approached as a sense experience, and it could be approached as physical vibration.

Significant to psychology was the sharp distinction Galileo made between the objective mechanical world as exemplified by pitch as vibration and the subjective-sensitive world of actually hearing that pitch. He used this distinction as a means of clarifying the boundaries of his scientific task to which he applied himself.

Nevertheless I say, that indeed I feel myself impelled by the necessity, as soon as I conceive a piece of matter or corporeal substance, of conceiving that in its own nature it is bounded and figured in such and such a figure, that in relation to others it is large or small, that it is in this or that place, in this or that time, that it is in motion or remains at rest, that it touches or does not touch another body, that it is single, few, or many; in short by no imagination can a body be separated from such conditions; but that it must be white or red, bitter or sweet, sounding or mute, of a pleasant or unpleasant odour, I do not perceive my mind forced to acknowledge it necessarily accompanied by such conditions; so if the senses were not the escorts, perhaps the reason or the imagination by itself would never have arrived at them. Hence I think that these tastes, odours, colours, etc., on the side of the object in which they seem to exist, are nothing else than mere names, but hold their residence solely in the sensitive body; so that if the animal were removed, every such quality would be abolished and annihilated.[1]

    If the sensing were taken away, secondary qualities, as they were later called, no longer exist. They do not have the same status in physical reality as the primary qualities, and Galileo banished them from the natural world he was investigating. He said that hearing a sound or seeing a color have no reality apart from experience. While the distinction between the object and the percept had been known as long ago as the ancient Greeks, no one before had ruled the percept out of scientific consideration; so Galileo went beyond conventional wisdom and set up a distinction that narrowed the boundaries of psychology, the science to be, so that mechanical laws would not apply. In the interest of methodological objectivity in mechanical matters, he was creating a contentual subjectivity for psychological matters. Moreover, perceptions could not be trusted as sources of information about the world, because they did not necessarily correspond to anything in that world. This stand was to have an effect on later generations, not completely dispelled to this very day. For many individuals, psychological matters are somehow still not as "real" as those with which the physical scientist works.

    On the positive side, his dependence on physical indices of sensory experience, his use of mathematics, and his experimental procedures were to be of inspiration to later workers in the psychological tradition, despite his ruling out the psychological phenomena from the mechanical world he was investigating.

2

BACON ON

FACT COLLECTING, INDUCTION, EXPERIMENT AND THE UTILITARIAN VALUE OF SCIENCE

FRANCIS BACON (1561–1626), English statesman and jurist as well as a philosopher, expressed what was perhaps most characteristic of the dawning modern scientific spirit—the determination to avoid philosophical presuppositions based on authority and tradition. Methodologically, he pleaded eloquently for the collection of facts, the use of induction, and the conduct of experiments. While his methods had obvious flaws (as will be shown), he was to be heralded by later generations as the spokesperson of the new empirical sciences of which psychology became one. But, above all, the potential usefulness of scientific knowledge was his major message. That science serves utilitarian purposes was a novel idea for his time, and he made it a pervasive theme throughout his writings. An aphorism will have to suffice as an excerpt:

3. Human knowledge and human power meet in one; for where the cause is not known the effect cannot be produced. Nature to be commanded must be obeyed; and that which in contemplation is as the cause is in operation as the rule.[1]

In common with other "moderns" of his time, he considered the massive philosophical systems of the Middle Ages to be worse than useless; they were delusory in that they created unreal situations. If one was not very cautious about depending on them, knowledge would not rise higher than the level where Aristotle had left it more than a thousand years earlier. He referred to them as preconceptions that blinded men to the truth, calling them "idols of the theater," since they depicted theatrical worlds created by men, rather than the real one.

44. Lastly, there are Idols which have immigrated into men's minds from the various dogmas of philosophies and also from wrong laws of demonstration. These I call Idols of the Theatre, because in my judgement all the received systems are but so many stage-plays, representing worlds of their own creation after an unreal and scenic fashion. Nor is it only of the systems now in vogue or only of the ancient sects and philoso phies that I speak, for many more plays of the same kind may yet be composed and in like artificial manner set forth, seeing that errors the most widely different have nevertheless causes for the most part alike. Neither again do I mean this only of entire systems, but also of many principles and axioms in science, which by tradition, credulity, and negligence have come to be received.[2]

He would correct these and other errors by new empirical methods of fact collecting, through a new form of induction, and through experimentation.

19. There are and can be only two ways of searching into and discovering truth. The one flies from the senses and particulars to the most general axioms, and from these principles, the truth of which it takes for settled and immoveable, proceeds to judgment and to the discovery of middle axioms. And this way is now in fashion. The other derives axioms from the senses and particulars, rising by a gradual and unbroken ascent, so that it arrives at the most general axioms last of all. This is the true way, but as yet untried. . . .

22. . . . .Both ways set out from the senses and particulars, and rest in the highest generalities; but the difference between them is infinite. For the one just glances at experiment and particulars in passing, the other dwells duly and orderly among them. The one, again, begins at once by establishing certain abstract and useless generalities, the other rises by gradual steps to that which is prior and better known in the order of nature.[3]

Although admitting that the rationalistic approach begins with some scanty evidence from the senses, it but merely "examines experiments and particulars in passing." Bacon proceeded empirically by first seeking more particulars and proceeded gradually. Thus, he was advancing an inductive method but, as he indicates, by finding negative as well as positive instances.

105. In establishing axioms, another form of induction must be devised than has hitherto been employed; and it must be used for proving and discovering not first principles (as they are called) only, but also the lesser axioms, and the middle, and indeed all. For the induction which proceeds by simple enumeration is childish; its conclusions are precarious, and exposed to peril from a contradictory instance; and it generally decides on too small a number of facts, and on those only which are at hand. But the induction which is to be available for the discovery and demonstration of sciences and arts, must analyse nature by proper rejections and exclusions; and then, after a sufficient number of negatives, come to a conclusion on the affirmative instances: which has not yet been done or even attempted, save only by Plato, who does indeed employ this form of induction to a certain extent for the purpose of discussing definitions and ideas. But in order to furnish this induction or demonstration well and duly for its work, very many things are to be provided which no mortal has yet thought of; insomuch that greater labour will have to be spent in it than has hitherto been spent on the syllogism. And this induction must be used not only to discover axioms, but also in the formation of notions. And it is in this induction that our chief hope lies.[4]

We must also proceed empirically, more specifically by experiment.

99. Again, even in the great plenty of mechanical experiments, there is yet a great scarcity of those which are of most use for the information of the understanding. For the mechanic, not troubling himself with the investigation of truth, confines his attention to those things which bear upon his particular work, and will not either raise his mind or stretch out his hand for anything else. But then only will there be good ground of hope for the further advance of knowledge, when there shall be received and gathered together into natural history a variety of experiments, which are of no use in themselves, but simply serve to discover causes and axioms; which I call "*Experimenta lucifera,*" experiments of *light,* to distinguish them from those which I call "*fructifera,*" experiments of *fruit.*

Now experiments of this kind have one admirable property and condition; they never miss or fail. For since they are applied, not for the purpose of producing any particular effect, they answer the end equally well whichever way they turn out; for they settle the question . . .

103. But after this store of particulars has been set out duly and in order before our eyes, we are not to pass at once to the investigation and discovery of new particulars or works; or at any rate if we do so we must not stop there. For although I do not deny that when all the experiments of all the arts shall have been collected and digested, and brought within one man's knowledge and judgment, the mere transferring of the experiments of one art to others may lead, by means of that experience which I term *literate,* to the discovery of many new things of service to the life and state of man, yet it is no great matter that can be hoped from that; but from the new light of axioms, which having been educed from those particulars by a certain method and rule, shall in their turn point out the way again to new particulars, greater things may be looked for. For our road does not lie on a level, but ascends and descends; first ascending to axioms, then descending to works.[5]

Bacon's vaunted inductive method of fact collecting was doomed to be unproductive in terms of useful results. His own patiently collected lists of instances making up the second Book of the *Novum Organum* got nowhere. He was distrustful of the flights into fantasy that marked the generalizations of the "Idols of the Theater," so distrustful that he was blind to the concept of a preliminary hypothesis held while one investigated, by induction, something that was to be accepted as true only if verified as the result of the inductive study. Instead, Bacon held, one must collect facts and more facts and then the truth would be found. He did not realize that by his saying he had no hypothesis, he did not mean that he did not select the facts. His fact collecting was done on the basis of some unstated principle.

Bacon was a persuasive advocate for science, but not a practitioner. He carried out no scientific research of any value. But the methods he would have used, corrected by the specification of the unstated principle being investigated, helped to make science inductive and experimental. It did much to make utilitarian aims an accepted part of scientific endeavor.

3

HARVEY ON
THE HEART
AS A MECHANICAL PUMP

WILLIAM HARVEY (1578–1657), English physiologist and physician to the Royal Court, conclusively demonstrated the circulation of blood by observation, dissection, and quasi measurement and showed that the heart served as a pump, thus explaining a bodily function in terms of mechanical principles. The mechanistic thesis of Galileo was shown to apply to a physiological function, not just to nonanimate motions, thus bringing mechanical demonstrations one step closer to application to psychological functions.

Prior to Harvey's work, Galenic theory of the function and nature of blood had prevailed for more than a thousand years. Galen was a second-century Greek physician of the Roman Empire. In his view, the animal spirits carried by the blood had "life giving " properties and a variety of other equally non-naturalistic entities. On a more mundane level, blood was considered consumed as food, which necessitates a constant new supply. It merely pulsated back and forth in the body; there was no conception of a circuit.

Harvey collected considerable evidence from which he reached the conclusion that the blood circulates.

...when I surveyed my mass of evidence, whether derived from vivisections, and my various reflections on them, or from the ventricles of the heart and the vessels that enter into and issue from them, the symmetry and size of these conduits—for nature doing nothing in vain, would never have given them so large a relative size without a purpose—or from the arrangement and intimate structure of the valves in particular, and of the other parts of the heart in general, with many things besides, I frequently and seriously bethought me, and long revolved in my mind, what might be the quantity of blood which was transmitted, in how short a time its passage might be effected, and the like; and not finding it possible that this could be supplied by the juices of the ingested aliment without the veins on the one hand becoming drained, and the arteries on the other getting ruptured through the excessive charge of blood, unless the blood should somehow find its way from the arteries into the veins, and so return to the right side of the heart; I began to think whether there might not be a MOTION, AS IT WERE, IN A CIRCLE.[1]

One way he confirmed the circulation of the blood was by measurement, or, rather, in this case, assumptions about the amount of blood reaching the heart in a given unit of time.

Let us assume, either arbitrarily or from experiment, the quantity of blood which the left ventricle of the heart will contain when distended to be, say two ounces, three ounces, one ounce and a half—in the dead body I have found it to hold upwards of two ounces. Let us assume further, how much less the heart will hold in the contracted than in the dilated state; and how much blood it will project into the aorta upon each contraction— and all the world allows that with the systole something is always projected, a necessary consequence demonstrated in the third chapter, and obvious from the structure of the valves; and let us suppose as approaching the truth that the fourth, or fifth, or sixth, or even but the eighth part of its charge is thrown into the artery at each contraction; this would give either half an ounce, or three drachms, or one drachm of blood as propelled by the heart at each pulse into the aorta; which quantity, by reason of the valves at the roof of the vessel, can by no means return into the ventricle. Now in the course of half an hour, the heart will have made more than one thousand beats, in some as many as two, three, and even four thousand. Multiplying the number of drachms propelled by the number of pulses, we shall have either one thousand half ounces, or one thousand times three drachms, or a like proportional quantity of blood, according to the amount which we assume as propelled with each stroke of the heart, sent from this organ into the artery; a larger quantity in every case than is contained in the whole body!...

But let it be said that this does not take place in half an hour, but in an hour, or even in a day; any way it is still manifest that more blood passes through the heart in consequence of its action, than can either be supplied by the whole of the ingesta, or than can be contained in the veins at the same moment.[2]

Surely, blood cannot be consumed in the body at this rate, or even contained in the veins. It must be that the same blood supply returns to the heart and then is driven out again.

At first glance, this demonstration may appear irrelevant to psychology. However, Harvey's discovery that the heart was a pump showed that a bodily function was intelligible in mechanical terms without appeal to the soul or to mystical essences or qualities heretofore considered as carried by the blood. Harvey's findings were widely interpreted as heralding that other possible discoveries about the body, especially in the brain, would show that it, too, functioned mechanically. This proved to be the case.

4

DESCARTES ON

RATIONALISM, DUALISM, SUBJECTIVISM. AND MECHANISM

RENÉ DESCARTES (1596–1650), French philosopher, was born shortly after the dawn of modern science and was conversant with the work that had gone before. Although Descartes gave some grudging weight to the influence of experience on our ideas, he was convinced that it was reasoning which gives us ideas that are universally certain, true, and innate.

I have also observed certain laws which God has so established in Nature, and of which He has imprinted such ideas on our minds, that, after having reflected sufficiently upon the matter, we cannot doubt their being accurately observed in all that exists or is done in the world. Further, in considering the sequence of these laws, it seems to me that I have discovered many truths more useful and more important than all that I had formerly learned or even hoped to learn.[1]

Fallability, due to experience, he added, may be corrected by reasoning.

Matter of experience consists of what we perceive by sense, what we hear from the lips of others, and generally whatever reaches our understanding either from external sources or from that contemplation which our mind directs backwards on itself. Here it must be noted that no direct experience can ever deceive the understanding if it restrict its attention accurately to the object presented to it, just as it is given to it either at firsthand or by means of an image; and if it moreover refrain from judging that the imagination faithfully reports the objects of the senses, or that the senses take on the true forms of things, or in fine that external things always are as they appear to be; for in all these judgments we are exposed to error.[2]

Moreover, we are deceived by experience, but this is due to fallability of will, not of reason.

... God has given me for understanding, there is no doubt that all that I understand, I understand as I ought, and it is not possible that I err in this. Whence then come my errors? They come from the sole fact that since the will is much wider in its range and compass than the understanding, I do not restrain it within the same bounds, but extend it also to things which I do not understand: and as the will is of itself indifferent to these, it easily falls into error and sin, and chooses the evil for the good, or the false for the true.[3]

Understanding and reason had characteristically been referred to by Descartes' predecessors as due to the soul.

Thus because probably men in the earliest times did not distinguish in us that principle in virtue of which we are nourished, grow, and perform all those operations which are common to us with the brutes apart from any thought, from that by which we think they called both by the single name *soul*; then, perceiving the distinction between nutrition and thinking, they called that which thinks *mind,* believing also that this was the chief part of the soul. But I, perceiving that the principle by which we are nourished is wholly distinct from that by means of which we think, have declared that the name *soul* when used for both is equivocal; and I say that, when soul is taken to mean *the primary actuality* or *chief essence of man*, it must be understood to apply only to the principle by which we think, and I have called it by the name *mind* as often as possible in order to avoid ambiguity; for I consider the mind not as part of the soul but as the whole of that soul which thinks.[4]

In answering the charge that the word, soul, is ambiguous, the major point he is trying to convey, he seems to acknowledge the correctness of this charge by pointing out that mind is the preferred term. The distinction he was making between soul and mind was accepted by later generations and, hereafter, mind shall be considered the more appropriate term for matters of psychological concern. It is also clear from all of the excerpts that have gone before that Descartes was a rationalist, that is, he believed that reason (understanding) is the major source of knowledge. Thus, he stands in contrast to Galileo, Bacon, and Harvey who were primarily empiricists, in that they looked to information gained from experiment, to inductive collection of facts, and to observation.

Early in life, Descartes had become enamored with the rationalistic beauty of mathematics and tried to find its likeness in other fields for the certainty that he craved. Above all, he wanted to look within himself for those concepts about nature which he could not doubt.

For a long time I had remarked that it is sometimes requisite in common life to follow opinions which one knows to be most uncertain, exactly as though they were indisputable, as has been said above. But because in this case I wished to give myself entirely to the search after Truth, I thought that it was necessary for me to take an apparently opposite course, and to reject as absolutely false everything as to which I could imagine the least ground of doubt, in order to see if afterwards there remained anything in my belief that was entirely certain. Thus, because our senses sometimes deceive us, I wished to suppose that nothing is just as they cause us to imagine it to be; and because there are men who deceive themselves in their reasoning and fall into paralogisms, even concerning the simplest matters of geometry, and judging that I was as subject of error as was any other, I rejected as false all the reasons formerly accepted by me as demonstrations. And since all the same thoughts and conceptions which we have while awake may also come to us in sleep, without any of them being at that time true, I resolved to assume that everything that ever entered into my mind was no more true than the illusions of my dreams. But immediately afterwards I noticed that whilst I thus wished to think all things false, it was absolutely essential that the "I" who thought this should be somewhat, and remarking that this truth *"I think, therefore I am"* was so certain and so assured that all the most extravagant suppositions brought forward by the skeptics were incapable of shaking it, I came to the conclusion that I could receive it without scruple as the first principle of the Philosophy for which I was seeking.

And then, examining attentively that which I was, I saw that I could conceive that I had no body, and that there was no world nor place where I might be; but yet that I could not for all that conceive that I was not. On the contrary, I saw from the very fact that I thought of doubting the truth of other things, it very evidently and certainly followed that I was; on the other hand if I had only ceased from thinking, even if all the rest of what I had ever imagined had really existed, I should have no reason for thinking that I had existed. From that I knew that I was a substance the whole essence or nature of which is to think, and that for its existence there is no need of any place, nor does it depend on any material thing; so that this "me," that is to say, the soul by which I am what I am, is entirely distinct from body, and is even more easy to know than is the latter; and even if body were not, the soul would not cease to be what it is.

After this I considered generally what in a proposition is requisite in order to be true and certain; for since I had just discovered one which I knew to be such, I thought that I ought also to know in what this certainty consisted. And having remarked that there was nothing at all in the statement *"I think, therefore I am"* which assures me of having thereby made a true assertion, excepting that I see very clearly that to think it is necessary to be, I came to the conclusion that I might assume, as a general rule, that the things which we conceive very clearly and distinctly are all true—remembering, however, that there is some difficulty in ascertaining which are those that we distinctly conceive.[5]

In the same discourse in which he established the certainty of his thinking (the mind) and therefore of his existence, he proceeded in successive steps to restore the certainty of the existence of God, and, as a separate step from the restoration of the reality of the existence of the mind, the reality of the existence of body, and then to the restoration of the reality of the rest of the natural world.

Armed with confidence in his ability to use unaided reason to know truth, he established four rules of procedure for himself and others to follow in order to achieve knowledge about which one could be certain.

The first of these was to accept nothing as true which I did not clearly recognise to be so: that is to say, carefully to avoid precipitation and prejudice in judgments, and to accept in them nothing more than what was presented to my mind so clearly and distinctly that I could have no occasion to doubt it.

The second was to divide up each of the difficulties which I examined into as many parts as possible, and as seemed requisite in order that it might be resolved in the best manner possible.

The third was to carry on my reflections in due order, commencing with objects that were the most simple and easy to understand, in order to rise little by little, or by degrees, to knowledge of the most complex, assuming an order, even if a fictitious one, among those which do not follow a natural sequence relatively to one another.

The last was in all cases to make enumerations so complete and reviews so general that I should be certain of having omitted nothing.[6]

Mind and body, although both certain of existence, are separate. His major argument for the separation of mind from body is that he is one that thinks. It will also be remembered that the certainty of body was arrived at as a separate step from the certainty of mind and thus serves as an additional argument for their separation. In still further support of this distinction between mind and body, Descartes happily enlisted the methodological distinction made previously by Galileo.

I observed that nothing at all belonged to the nature or essence of body, except that it was a thing with length, breadth, and depth, admitting of various shapes and various motions. I found also that its shapes and motions were only modes, which no power could make to exist apart from it; and on the other hand that colours, odours, savours, and the rest of such things, were merely sensations existing in my thought, and differing no less from bodies than pain differs from the shape and motion of the instrument which inflicts it. Finally, I saw that gravity, hardness, the power of heating, of attracting, and of purging, and all other qualities which we experience in bodies, consisted solely in motion or its absence, and in the configuration and situation of their parts.[7]

The word "merely" in the quotation carries a wealth of meaning; sensing is relegated to the world of experience, existing only in that experience.

The body is separate and distinct from the mind. It is a form of matter and is to be treated mechanically. Although, he does not mention Galileo by name, Descartes knew his work, and his exposition of the matter is quite in keeping with Galileo's treatment of inanimate matter. In the second paragraph of his treatise, *On Man,* he says that man's body is but a statue, or an earthen machine. This analogy arose from his familiarity with the moving figures in clock towers and statues in the garden estates of the nobility.

In the excerpt that follows in a general setting of the body as a machine, he is concerned with the body's capacity to respond appropriately to external stimulation without conscious direction.

After this, in order to understand how it [the machine] can be incited by external objects which strike the sense organs, so as to move all its members in a thousand other ways, remember that the little threads which I have so often told you come from the inmost part of the brain, and which compose the marrow of the nerves, are so distributed to all the parts which serve as organs that they can very easily be moved by objects of the senses; and when they are moved ever so slightly, they pull at the same instant at the parts of the brain from which they come, and by this means they open the entries of certain pores which are on the internal surface of the brain. Through these the animal spirits which are in the cavities immediately begin to take their course, passing through them into the nerves, and into the muscles, which serve in this machine to perform movements entirely similar to those to which we are naturally incited when our senses are touched in the same manner.

For example, if the fire A is close to the foot B, the small particles of fire, which as you know move very swiftly, are able to move as well the part of the skin which they touch on the foot. In this way, by pulling at the little thread cc, which you see attached there, they at the same instant open e, which is the entry for the pore d, which is where this small thread terminates; just as, by pulling one end of a cord, you ring a bell which hangs at the other end.

Now .when the entry of the pore, or the little tube, de, has thus been opened, the animal spirits flow into it from the cavity F, and through it they are carried partly into the muscles which serve to pull the foot back from the fire, partly into those which serve to turn the eyes and the head to look at it, and partly into those which serve to move the hands forward and to turn the whole body for its defense.[8]

This point of view approaches that which we call reflex behavior. Motion follows predictably from stimulation; mind is not involved. While he did refer to "reflex," what he meant by that term was essentially an analogy with the reflux of water involving a rebound. Moreover, coordinated activities such as walking or carrying a tune were used as illustrations of that to which he referred. On both counts, the modern concept of reflex disagrees. Be that as it may, he was advancing something akin to the reflex as a model of much of the body's behavior.

Animals are similar to machines in the same way as are the bodies of human beings. Humans can nevertheless be distinguished from animals. Commenting on animals, Descartes said:

. . . .we should always have two very certain tests by which to recognise that, for all that, they were not real men. The first is, that they could never use speech or other signs as we do when placing our thoughts on record for the benefit of others. For we can easily understand a machine's being constituted so that it can utter words, and even emit some responses to action on it of a corporeal kind, which brings about a change in its organs; for instance, if it is touched in a particular part it may ask what we wish to say to it; if in another part it may exclaim that it is being hurt, and so on. But it never happens that it arranges its speech in various ways, in order to reply appropriately to everything that may be said in its presence, as even the lowest type of man can do. And the second difference is, that although machines can perform certain things as well as or perhaps better than any of us can do, they infallibly fall short in others, by the which means we may discover that they did not act from knowledge, but only from the disposition of their organs. For while reason is a universal instrument which can serve for all contingencies, these organs have need of some special adaptation for every particular action. From this it follows that it is morally impossible that there should be sufficient diversity in any machine to allow it to act in all the events of life in the same way as our reason causes us to act.

By these two methods we may also recognise the difference that exists between men and brutes. For it is a very remarkable fact that there are none so depraved and stupid, without even excepting idiots, that they cannot arrange different words together, forming of them a statement by which they make known their thoughts; while, on the other hand, there is no other animal, however perfect and fortunately circumstanced it may be, which can do the same. It is not the want of organs that brings this to pass, for it is evident that magpies and parrots are able to utter words just like ourselves, and yet they cannot speak as we do, that is, so as to give evidence that they think of what they say. On the other hand, men who, being born deaf and dumb, are in the same degree, or even more than the brutes, destitute of the organs which serve the others for talking, are in the habit of themselves inventing certain signs by which they make themselves understood by those who, being usually in their company, have leisure to learn their language. And this does not merely show that the brutes have less reason than men, but that they have none at all, since it is clear that very little is required in order to be able to talk.[9]

The body of a human is essentially similar to that of animals, but humans have a reasoning mind which animals lack.

That the mind did interact with the body, despite their separation, constrained him to find a point of interaction and a theory of how this interaction took place.

ARTICLE XXXI.

That there is a small gland in the brain in which the soul exercises its functions more particularly than in the other parts.

It is likewise necessary to know that although the soul is joined to the whole body, there is yet in that a certain part in which it exercises its functions more particularly than in all the others; and it is usually believed that this part is the brain, or possibly the heart: the brain, because it is with it that the organs of sense are connected, and the heart because it is apparently in it that we experience the passions. But, in examining the matter with care, it seems as though I had clearly ascertained that the part of the body in which the soul exercises its functions immediately is in nowise the heart, nor the whole of the brain, but merely the most inward of all its parts, to wit, a certain very small gland which is situated in the middle of its substance and so suspended above the duct whereby the animal spirits in its anterior cavities have communication with those in the posterior, that the slightest movements which take place in it may alter very greatly the course of these spirits; and reciprocally that the smallest changes which occur in the course of the spirits may do much to change the movements of this gland.

ARTICLE XXXII.

How we know that this gland is the main seat of the soul.

The reason which persuades me that the soul cannot have any other seat in all the body than this gland wherein to exercise its functions immediately, is that I reflect that the other parts of our brain are all of them double, just as we have two eyes, two hands, two ears, and finally all the organs of our outside sense are double; and inasmuch as we have but one solitary and simple thought of one particular thing at one and the same moment, it must necessarily be the case that there must somewhere be a place where the two images which come to us by the two eyes, where the two other impressions which proceed from a single object by means of the double organs of the other senses, can unite before arriving at the soul, in order that they may not represent to it two objects instead of one. And it is easy to apprehend how these images or other impressions might unite in this gland by the intermission of the spirits which fill the cavities of the brain; but there is no other place in the body where they can be thus united unless they are so in this gland.[10]

This "very small gland" is the pineal gland, now described as a small, reddish vascular body in the posterior portion of the third ventricle and of no particular physiological importance.

The dualism that Descartes made crystal clear was a matter that numerous predecessors had fully addressed themselves to, so, in itself, dualism was not a novel concept. What was novel about Descartes' dualism was making central that mind, not soul, would heretofore stand in contrast to body for psychological matters. Equally as novel and even more important in the future was his demonstration that acepting or not accepting interactionism could not be ignored in any serious discussion of dualism.

To Descartes, his means of dealing with interaction was not entirely satisfactory, and those who came after him found it to be a fertile source for alternative solutions. Even in his own time, critics pointed out that one all-too-easy solution was to disregard the separation and say that man was *only* a machine and therefore mechanical.

The mind understands through meditation, and possessing freedom of will, stands in sharp contrast to the body studied mechanically and subject to what was later to be referred to as natural law. Subsequently, two very important streams of thought flowed from the work of Descartes—the phenomenological and the mechanical. The former arose primarily from his insistence on the centrality of meditation as a method and from his certainty of being a "thinking thing"; the latter from his insistence on the separation of mind and body which had mechanical action.

In connection with the phenomenological strain, it is important to clear up an apparent contradiction. With Descartes' emphasis on immediate experience, one might question his being designated a rationalist and not an empircist, since it is the latter who insists knowledge comes from experience. The discrepancy is resolved when it is indicated that, unlike German, we do not have words to distinguish between awareness in consciousness, that is, immediate experience, from the effect of cumulative experience. Rationalism and phenomenology are dependent on reflection about immediate experience, empiricism on cumulative experiences.

5

HOBBES ON
PSYCHOLOGY AND THE STATE.
THE IMPORTANCE OF MOTIVATION,
THE SUBJECTIVITY OF PERCEPTION,
AND THE NATURE OF ASSOCIATION

THOMAS HOBBES (1588–1679), English philosopher and minor diplomat, was primarily interested in the advancement of a strong monarchy in support of which he appealed to psychological concepts.

Although older than Descartes by nearly a decade, his contributions relevant to this volume, *Human Nature* and *The Leviathan,* were published in 1650 and 1651 by which time Descartes had published most of his major works. He was influenced by Galileo's conception of motion, not that of Newton, who was less than 10 years of age at the time of his major writings. He is also considered at this point, because he was a direct forebearer of British empiricism and associationism epitomized by Locke, considered shortly. Hobbes is best known as a social philosopher and thus as a precursor of social psychology. His *Leviathan* was so named because he saw the microcosm of man written large in the macrocosm of the state. He stressed studying the behavior of individuals within society as a means of understanding and strengthening the state.

Thus have we considered the nature of man so far as was requisite for the finding out the first and most simple elements wherein the compositions of politic rules and laws are lastly resolved; which was my present purpose.[1]

The dominant, all-pervasive goal of his thinking was a plea that there must be a strong monarchy with a powerful leader. Without this person the natural condition of man prevails—a state of warfare expressed most vividly in the famous line which ends the paragraph about the "life of man" under these conditions:

Whatsoever therefore is consequent to a time of war, where every man is enemy to every man, the same is consequent to the time wherein men live without other security than what their own strength and their own invention shall furnish them withal. In such condition there is no place for industry, because the fruit thereof is uncertain: and consequently no culture of the earth; no navigation, nor use of the commodities that may be imported by sea; no commodious building; no instruments of moving and removing such things as require much force; no knowledge of the face of the earth; no account of time; no arts; no letters; no society; and which is worst of all, continual fear, and danger of violent death; and the life of man, solitary, poor, nasty, brutish, and short.[2]

Hobbes had a cynical view of human nature. Both in leader and follower the basis of human action is desire for power.

So that in the first place, I put for a general inclination of all mankind a perpetual and restless desire of power after power, that ceaseth only in death. And the cause of this is not always that a man hopes for a more intensive delight, than he has already attained to, or that he cannot be content with a moderate power: but because he cannot assure the power and means to live well, which he hath present, without the acquisition of more. And from hence it is that kings, whose power is greatest, turn their endeavours to the assuring it at home by laws, or abroad by wars: and when that is done, there succeedeth a new desire; in some, of fame from new conquest; in others, of ease and sensual pleasure; in others, of admiration, or being flattered for excellence in some art or other ability of the mind.[3]

He goes on to argue that if leaders want power it is better for the sake of mankind that his desire be fulfilled rather than for all to live in a state of war. What was emphasized earlier would today be called motivation. A relatively new note was introduced into psychological thinking by Hobbes.

The seeking of power, moreover, is related, at least implicitly, to the passions, by which Hobbes meant both emotion and motivation expressed in motions akin to those studied by Galileo.

1. ...*conceptions* and apparitions are nothing *really,* but *motion* in some internal substance of the head; which motion *not stopping* there, but proceeding to the *heart,* of necessity must there either *help* or *hinder* the motion which is called vital; when it *helpeth,* it is called *delight, con-*

tentment, or *pleasure,* which is nothing really but motion about the heart as conception is nothing but motion in the head: and the *objects* that cause it are called *pleasant* or *delightful,* or by some name equivalent; the Lations have *jacundum, a juvando,* from helping; and the same delight, with reference to the object, is called *love*: but when such motion *weakeneth* or hindereth the vital motion, then it is called *pain*; and in relation to that which causeth it, hatred, which the Latins express sometimes by *odium,* and sometimes by *taedium.*

2. This motion, in which consisteth *pleasure* or *pain,* is also a *solicitation* or provocation either to draw *near* to the thing that pleaseth, or to *retire* from the thing that displeaseth; and this solicitation is the *endeavor* or internal beginning of *animal* motion, which when the object *delighteth,* is called appetite; when it *displeaseth,* it is called *aversion,* in respect of the displeasure *present*; but in respect of the displeasure *expected, fear.* So that *pleasure, love* and *appetite,* which is also called desire, are *divers* names for divers considerations of the *same thing.*[4]

It would seem that Hobbes was a hedonist—much, if not all, behavior is regulated by appetite, the seeking of pleasure, and by aversion, the avoidance of pain. Equally, if not more important, the selection shows that Hobbes applied the mechanical principles of motion to mental events in the same spirit that Galileo applied them to physical events.

It is now appropriate to turn to other psychological conceptions on which Hobbes expressed himself that were made central to the thinking of later British empiricists and associates—perception and association.

Since the time of the Greeks, two major answers have been given as to what is involved when something is perceived—that we either perceive directly or objectively, in which the perception is a replica of the object or, indirectly or subjectively, in which the perception is known only through the effect it produces in us. Hobbes argued for the latter, using the terms "conception" and "sense" where we would use perception. We shall confine the exerpt to the discussion of vision, although the other senses are discussed in the same place.

Because the *image* in vision consisting of *color* and *shape* is the knowledge we have of the qualities of the object of that sense; it is not hard matter for a man to fall into this opinion, that the same *color* and *shape* are the very *qualities themselves*; and for the same cause, that *sound* and *noise* are the *qualities of the bell,* or of the air. I shall therefore endeavor to make plain these points:

That the subject wherein color and image are inherent, is *not* the *object* or thing seen.

That there is nothing *without us* (really) which we call an *image* or color.

That the said image or color is but an *apparition* unto us of the *motion,* agitation, or alteration, which the *object* worketh in the *brain,* or spirits, or some internal substance of the head. . . .

5. Every man hath so much experience as to have seen the *sun* and the other visible objects by reflection in the *water* and *glasses*; and this alone is sufficient for this conclusion, that *color* and *image* may be there where the *thing seen* is *not.* But because it may be said that notwithstanding the *image* in the water be not in the object, but a thing merely *phantastical,* yet there may be *color* really in the thing itself: I will urge further this experience, that divers times men see directly the *same* object, *double,* as *two candles* for *one,* which may happen from distemper, or otherwise without distemper if a man will, the organs being either in their right temper, or equally distempered; the *colors* and *figures* in two such images of the same thing *cannot be inherent* therein, because the thing seen cannot be in *two places.*

One of these images therefore is *not inherent* in the object: but seeing the organs of the sight are then in equal temper or distemper, the *one* of them is no more inherent than the *other*; and consequently *neither* of them both are in the object; which is the first proposition, mentioned in the precedent number.

6.   Secondly, that the image of any thing by *reflection* in a *glass* or *water* or the like, is *not* any thing *in* or *behind* the glass, or *in* or *under* the water, every man may grant to himself; which is the second proposition.

7. For the third, we are to consider, first that upon every *great agitation* or *concussion* of the *brain* (as it happeneth from a stroke, especially if the stroke be upon the eye) whereby the optic nerve suffereth any great violence, there *appeareth* before the *eyes* a certain light, which light is *nothing without,* but an apparition only, all that is real being the concussion or motion of the parts of that nerve; from which experience we may conclude, that *apparition of light is really nothing but motion* within. If therefore from *lucid bodies* there can be derived *motion,* so as to affect the optic nerve in such manner as is proper thereunto, there will follow an *image* of light somewhere in that line by which the motion was last derived to the eye; that is to say, in the object, if we look directly on it, and in the glass or water, when we look upon it in the line of reflection, which in effect is the third proposition; namely, that image and color is but an apparition to us of that motion, agitation, or alteration which the

object worketh in the brain or spirits, or some *internal* substance in the head.

8. But that *from all lucid,* shining and illuminate bodies, there is a *motion produced* to the eye, and through the eye, to the *optic* nerve, and so into the *brain,* by which that apparition of *light* or *color* is affected is not hard to prove. And first, it is evident that the *fire,* the only lucid body here upon earth, worketh by *motion* equally every way; insomuch as the motion thereof *stopped* or inclosed, it is presently *extinguished,* and no more fire. And further, that that motion, whereby the fire worketh, is *dilation,* and *contraction* of itself *alternately,* commonly called *scintillation* or glowing, is manifest also by experience. From such *motion* in the fire must needs arise a *rejection* or casting from itself of that part of the *medium* which is *contiguous* to it, whereby that part also rejecteth the *next,* and so successively one part beateth back another to the very *eye;* and in the same manner the *exterior* part of the eye presseth the *inte rior,* (the laws of refraction still observed). Now the interior coat of the eye is nothing else but a piece of the *optic* nerve; and therefore the motion is still continued thereby into the *brain,* and by *resistance* or reaction of the brain, is also a *rebound* into the optic nerve again; which we *not conceiving* as motion or rebound from *within,* do think it is *without,* and call it *light;* as hath been already shown by the experience of a stroke. . . .

10. And from hence also it followeth, that *whatsoever accidents* or qualities our senses make us think there be in the *world,* they be *not* there, but are *seeming* and *apparitions* only: the things that really *are* in the world without us, are those *motions* by which these seemings are caused. And this is the *great deception of sense,* which also is to be by sense *corrected:* for as sense telleth me, when I see *directly,* that the color seemeth to be in the object; so also sense telleth me, when I see by *reflection,* that color is not in the object.[5]

Hobbes, then, took the position that the qualities of experience do not inhere in the object but within the experiencing person; what is without are motions and nothing more.

The "orderliness and coherence" of mental activity impressed Hobbes and his dependence on "motions" in the brain, referred to in the previous excerpt, made it relatively easy for him to stress contiguity as accounting for association. As he put it:

2. The *cause* of the *coherence* or consequence of one conception to another, is their first *coherence* or consequence at that *time* when they are produced by sense: as for example, from St. Andrew the mind run-

neth to St. Peter, because their names are read together; from St. Peter to a *stone,* for the same cause; from *stone* to *foundation,* because we see them together; and for the same cause, from foundation to *church,* and from church to *people,* and from people to *tumult*: and according to this example, the mind may run almost from anything to anything. But as in the *sense* the conception of cause and effect may succeed one another; so may they after sense in the *imagination*: and for the most part they do so; the *cause* whereof is the *appetite* of them, *who,* having a conception of the *end,* have next unto it a conception of the next *means* to that end: as, when a man, from a thought of *honor* to which he hath an appetite, cometh to the thought of *wisdom,* which is the next means thereunto; and from thence to the thought of *study,* which is the next means to wisdom.[6]

This "orderliness and coherence" would later find expression in Locke's doctrine of association and in that of others who came after him.

The emphasis that Hobbes placed on motivational and social factors was a corrective to the stress that others had placed on intellectual factors. His mechanistic stand is precisely the one which critics of Descartes predicted might come about. Man, not the body, is a creature of motions, within and without. Mental processes and mechanical notions are inherently similar. Thinking is motion excited in the brain. Interaction of the Cartesian variety was rejected in favor of materialistic monism. (Motion, whether physical or mental, was essentially the same.)

6

NEWTON ON
SCIENTIFIC METHOD,
MECHANICAL FORCES,
AND THE EXPERIMENTAL STUDY OF VISON

The work of Isaac Newton (1642–1727), English astronomer-mathematician, introduces some aspects of modern science (then called natural philosophy) that have influenced psychology. It took two distinguishable forms. One was methdological—his work served to inspire attempts at comparable methodology applied to psychological issues. The other was contentual—the contents of some of his research findings were to be utilized in the psychology to come. First, we will consider his methodology with its emphasis on measurement.

In his book, *Mathematical Principles of Natural Philosophy,* he was concerned with the forces of matter in motion as shown by mathematics. In the preface to its first edition of 1687, he states the way he will proceed:

... therefore I offer this work as the mathematical principles of philosophy, for the whole burden of philosophy seems to consist in this—from the phenomena of motions to investigate the forces of nature, and then from these forces to demonstrate the other phenomena; and to this end the general propositions in the first and second books are directed. In the third book I give an example of this in the explication of the System of the World; for by the propositions mathematically demonstrated in the former books in the third I derive from the celestial phenomena the forces of gravity with which bodies tend to the sun and the several planets. Then from these forces, by other propositions which are also mathematical, I deduce the motions of the planets, the comets, the moon, and the sea. I wish we could derive the rest of the phenomena of Nature by the same kind of reasoning from mechanical principles, for I am induced by many reasons to suspect that they may all depend upon certain forces by which the particles of bodies, by some causes hitherto unknown, are either mutually impelled towards one another, and cohere in regular figures, or are repelled and recede from one another. These forces being unknown, philosophers have hitherto attempted the search of Nature in vain; but I hope the principles here laid down will afford some light either to this or some truer method of philosophy.[1]

An opinion is being expressed in this excerpt that must be reiterated. Newton is led by "many reasons to suspect" that the "phenomena of nature" depend on attractive or repulsive forces. This position modified the already accepted position that motion could be communicated by way of direct contact of one body with another, by adding that mechanical phenomena could be accounted for by forces at a distance from the object in motion. He proved this to be the case in instances extending from planetary motion to the tides. Matter in motion, the basis for the science of mechanics, was being broadened further, and mechanical theories about psychological matters would not be long in coming.

The second source of Newton's influence was the effect of his concern with the composition of matter as shown by experiment. This he carried through in greatest detail in his *Optics*. It is filled with accounts of performed experiments and conclusions drawn not only about the physical basis but also about how color affects one psychologically. Since vision became a contentual concern of the psychologist, his work is relevant on contentual as well as methodological grounds.

Newton first reported in 1672 on his experimental analysis of the spectrum, which provided a solid basis for color theory. Many years and many experiments later, he brought his findings in *Optics*, first published in 1704. He first explains to the reader what he means by color:

And if at any time I speak of light and rays as coloured or endued with colours, I would be understood to speak not philosophically and properly, but grossly, and accordingly to such conceptions as vulgar people in seeing all these experiements would be apt to frame. For the rays to speak properly are not coloured. In them there is nothing else than a certain power and disposition to stir up a sensation of this or that colour. For as sound in a bell or musical string, or other sounding body, is nothing but a trembling motion, and in the air nothing but that motion propagated from the object, and in the sensorium 'tis a sense of that motion under the form of sound; so colours in the object are nothing but a disposition to reflect this or that sort of rays more copiously than the rest; in the rays they are nothing but their dispositions to propagate this or that motion into the sensorium, and in the sensorium they are sensations of those motions under the forms of colours.[2]

Light does not possess color; rather, it can evoke color sensations in us.

His most extensively used experimental device was the prism, a triangular device which, when placed so that a beam of white light enters it, is refracted according to the wave lengths of the light emerging on the other side of the prism where it produces the colors (hues) of the spectrum, better known as the "colors of the rainbow." The very significance of a prism just given owes much to Newton's work. In fact, the well-known mnemonic device of VIBYGOR (violet, indigo, blue, yellow, green, orange, and red) is derived from his work.

By experimental use of prisms, he demonstrated that all grays between white and black are compounds of all primary colors. Today, classroom demonstrations are carried out by the color wheel. Colored papers capable of variation of spatial proportions exposed on different trials are revolved at a speed, such that only one homogenous color is seen per trial. However, Newton used a comb-like instrument drawn across the light source for the same purpose.

Lastly, I made an instrument XY in fashion of a comb, whose teeth being in number sixteen, were about an inch and a half broad, and the intervals of the teeth about two inches wide. Then by interposing successively the teeth of this instrument near the lens, I intercepted part of the colours by the interposed tooth, whilst the rest of them went on through the interval of the teeth to the paper DE, and there pained a round solar image. But the paper I had first placed so, that the image might appear white as often as the comb was taken away; and then the comb being as was said interposed, that whiteness by reason of the intercepted part of the colours at the lens did always change into the colour compounded of those colours which were not intercepted, and that colour was by the motion of the comb perpetually varied so, that in the passing of every tooth over the lens all these colours, red, yellow, green, blue, and purple, did always succeed one another. I caused therefore all the teeth to pass successively over the lens, and when the motion was show, there appeared a perpetual succession of the colours upon the paper: but if I so much accelerated the motion, that the colours by reason of their quick succession could not be distinguished from one another, the appearance of the single colours ceased. There was no red, no yellow, no green, no blue, nor purple to be seen any longer, but from a confusion of them all there arose one uniform white colour. Of the light which now by the mixture of all the colours appeared white, there was no part really white. One part was red, another yellow, a third green, a fourth blue, a fifth purple, and every part retains its proper colour till it strike the sensorium. If the impressions follow one another slowly, so that they may be severally perceived, there is made a distinct sensation of all the colours one after another in a continual succession. But if the impres-

sions follow one another so quickly, that they cannot be severally perceived, there ariseth out of them all one common sensation, which is
neither of this colour alone nor of that alone, but hath it self indifferently
to them all, and this is a sensation of whiteness. By the quickness of the
successions, the impressions of the several colours are confounded in the
sensorium, and out of that confusion ariseth a mixed sensation. If a burning coal be nimbly moved round in a circle with gyrations continually repeated, the whole circle will appear like fire; the reason of which is, that
the sensorium of the coal in the several places of that circle remains impressed on the sensorium, until the coal return again to the same place.
And so in a quick consecution of the colours the impression of every colour
remains in the sensorium, until a revolution of all the colours be completed, and that first colour return again. The impression therefore of all
the successive colours are at once in the sensorium, and jointly stir up a
sensation of them all; and os it is manifest by this experiment, that the
commixed impressions of all the colours do stir up and beget a sensation
of white, that is, that whiteness is compounded of all the colours.[3]

With few exceptions, contemporary and later philosophers interested in scientific matters were profoundly influenced by his conception of science and attempted to work in his spirit, with their particular
problems including those of psychological significance.

7

LOCKE ON
IDEAS AS DEPENDENT
ON EXPERIENCE AND REFLECTION,
AND THE ASSOCIATION OF IDEAS

JOHN LOCKE (1632–1704), English philosopher and minor diplomat, was much taken with Newton's mechanical way. He proceeded to apply mechanical principles to psychological ideas. It was in this spirit that he decided, in *An Essay on Human Understanding,* that he would examine ideas

... which a man observes, and is conscious to himself he has in his mind; and the ways whereby the understanding come to be furnished with them.[1]

Immediately thereafter he takes up what ideas aren't, that they are not innate.

1. *The way shown how we come by any knowledge, sufficient to prove it not innate*—It is an established opinion amongst some men, that there are in the understanding certain *innate principles*; some primary notions, κοιναὶ ἔννοιαι, characters, as it were stamped upon the mind of man, which the soul receives in its very first being, and brings into the world with it. It would be sufficient to convince unprejudiced readers of the falseness of this supposition, if I should only show (as I hope I shall in the following parts of this Discourse) how men, barely by the use of their natural faculties, may attain to all the knowledge they have, without the help of any innate impressions; and may arrive at certainty, without any such original notions or principles. For I imagine any one will easily grant that it would be impertinent to suppose the ideas of colours innate in a

creature to whom God hath given sight, and a power to receive them by the eyes from external objects: and no less unreasonable would it be to attribute several truths to the impressions of nature, and innate characters, when we may observe in ourselves faculties fit to attain as easy and certain knowledge of them as if they were originally imprinted on the mind. . . .

3. *Universal consent proves nothing innate*—This argument, drawn from universal consent, has this misfortune in it, that if it were true in matter of fact, that there were certain truths wherein all mankind agreed, it would not prove them innate, if there can be any other way shown how men may come to that universal agreement, in the things they do consent in, which I presume may be done. . . .

5. *Not on the mind naturally imprinted, because not known to children, idiots, & c*—For, first, it is evident, that all children and idiots have not the least apprehension or thought of them. And the want of that is enough to destroy that universal assent which must needs be the necessary concomitant of all innate truths: it seeming to me near a contradiction to say, that there are truths imprinted on the soul, which it perceives or understands not: imprinting, if it signify anything being nothing else but the making certain truths to be perceived. For to imprint anything on the mind without the mind's perceiving it, seems to me hardly intelligible. If therefore children and idiots have souls, have minds, with those impressions upon them, *they* must unavoidably perceive them, and necessarily know and assent to these truths; which since they do not, it is evident that there are no such impressions. For if they are not notions naturally imprinted, how can they be innate? and if they are notions imprinted, how can they be unknown? To say a notion is imprinted on the mind, and yet at the same time to say that the mind is ignorant of it, and never yet took notice of it, is to make this impression nothing. No proposition can be said to be in the mind which it never yet knew, which it was never yet conscious of. . . .

15. *The steps by which the mind attains several truths*—The senses at first let in particular ideas, and furnish the yet empty cabinet, and the mind by degrees growing familiar with some of them, they are lodged in the memory, and names got to them. Afterwards, the mind proceeding further, abstracts them, and by degrees learns the use of general names. In this manner the mind comes to be furnished with ideas and language, the *materials* about which to exercise its discursive faculty. And the use of reason becomes daily more visible, as these materials that give it employment increase. But though the having of general

ideas and the use of general words and reason usually grow together, yet I
see not how this any way proves them innate. The knowledge of some
truths, I confess, is very early in the mind but in a way that shows them
not to be innate. For, if we will observe, we shall find it still to be about
ideas, not innate, but acquired; it being about those first which are imprinted by external things, with which infants have earliest to do, which
make the most frequent impressions on their senses. In ideas thus got,
the mind discovers that some agree and others differ, probably as soon as
it has any use of memory; as soon as it is able to retain and perceive
distinct ideas. But whether it be then or no, this is certain, it does so long
before it has the use of words; or comes to that which we commonly call
"the use of reason." For a child knows as certainly before it can speak the
difference between the ideas of sweet and bitter (i.e. that sweet is not
bitter), as it knows afterwards (when it comes to speak) that wormwood
and sugarplums are not the same thing.[2]

In taking this stand against innate ideas, Locke was attacking the
rationalistic emphasis of innate ideas that characterized the thinking of
Descartes, although no one is mentioned by name. The reference to the
"yet empty cabinet" was his means of denying the analogy that compared
the mind to a cabinet well-stocked with innate ideas. Instead, he said,
ideas come from sense impression and reflection, thus aligning his views
with the empirical position.

1. *Idea is the object of thinking*—Every man being conscious to
himself that he thinks; and that which his mind is applied about whilst
thinking being the *ideas* that are there, it is past doubt that men have in
their minds several ideas,—such as are those expressed by the words
*whiteness, hardness, sweetness, thinking, motion, man, elephant, army,
drunkenness,* and others: it is in the first place then to be inquired, *How
he comes by them? . . .*

2. *All ideas come from sensation or reflection*—Let us then suppose the mind to be, as we say, white paper, void of all characters, without
any ideas:—How comes it to be furnished? Whence comes it by that vast
store which the busy and boundless fancy of man has painted on it with
an almost endless variety? Whence has it all the *materials* of reason and
knowledge? To this I answer, in one word, from EXPERIENCE. In that
all our knowledge is founded; and from that it ultimately derives itself.
Our observation employed either, about external sensible objects, or
about the internal operations of our minds perceived and reflected on by
ourselves, is that which supplies our understandings with all the mate-

rials of thinking. These two are the fountains of knowledge, from whence all the ideas we have, or can naturally have, do spring.

3. *The objects of sensation one source of ideas*—First, our Senses, conversant about particular sensible objects, do convey into the mind several distinct perceptions of things, according to those various ways wherein those objects do affect them. And thus we come by those *ideas* we have of *yellow, white, heat, cold, soft, hard, bitter, sweet,* and all those which we call sensible qualities; which when I say the senses convey into the mind, I mean, they from external objects convey into the mind what produces there those perceptions. This great source of most of the ideas we have, depending wholly upon our senses, and derived by them to the understanding, I call SENSATION.

4. *The operations of our minds, the other source of them*— Secondly, the other fountain from which experience furnisheth the understanding with ideas is,—the perception of the operations of our own mind within us, as it is employed about the ideas it has got;—which operations, when the soul comes to reflect on and consider, do furnish the understanding with another set of ideas, which could not be had from things without, and such are *perception, thinking, doubting, believing, reasoning, knowing, willing,* and all the different actings of our own minds;—which we being conscious of, and observing in ourselves, do from these receive into our understandings as distinct ideas as we do from bodies affecting our senses. This source of ideas every man has wholly in himself, and though it be not sense, as having nothing to do with external objects, yet it is very like it, and might properly enough be called *internal sense.* But as I call the other SENSATION so I call this REFLECTION, the ideas it affords being such only as the mind gets by reflecting on its own operations within itself. By reflection then, in the following part of this discourse, I would be understood to mean, that notice which the mind takes of its own operations, and the manner of them, by reason whereof there come to be ideas of these operations in the understanding. These two, I say, viz. external material things, as the objects of SENSATION, and the operations of our own minds within, as the objects of REFLECTION are to me the only originals from whence all our ideas take their beginnings. The term *operation* here I use in a large sense, as comprehending not barely the actions of the mind about its ideas, but some sort of passions arising sometimes from them, such as is the satisfaction or uneasiness arising from any thought.

5. *All our ideas are of the one or the other of these*—The understanding seems to me not to have the least glimmering of any ideas which

it doth not receive from one of these two. *External objects* furnish the mind with the ideas of sensible qualities, which are all those different perceptions they produce in us; and *the mind* furnishes the understanding with ideas of its own operations.

These, when we have taken a full survey of them, and their several modes, combinations, and relations, we shall find to contain all our whole stock of ideas; and that we have nothing in our minds which did not come in one of these two ways. Let any one examine his own thoughts, and thoroughly search into his understanding; and then let him tell me, whether all the original ideas he has there, are any other than of the objects of his senses, or of the operations of his mind, considered as objects of his reflection. And how great a mass of knowledge soever he imagines to be lodged there, he will, upon taking a strict view, see that he has not any idea in his mind but what one of these two have imprinted;—though perhaps, with infinite variety compounded and enlarged by the understanding, as we shall see hereafter.[3]

It should be noted that Locke did not insist that ideas come from experience (sense impression) alone; reflection is also active and carries on in our minds an operation of the mind upon itself, in which ideas already supplied by sensory experience give rise to other ideas.

Implicit in what has gone before is a point that must now be made explicit—his conception that ideas are not reality, but rather that which we know.

It is evident the mind knows not things immediately, but only by the intervention of the ideas it has of them. Our knowledge, therefore is real only so far as there is a *conformity* between our ideas and the reality of things.[4]

Knowledge is real only to extent that our ideas conform to the reality of objects. The extent to which sensible qualities do provide information about the reality of objects need explication which Locke supplied.

7. *Ideas in the mind, qualities in bodies*—To discover the nature of our *ideas* the better, and to discourse of them intelligibly, it will be convenient to distinguish them *as they are ideas or perceptions in our minds;* and *as they are modifications of matter in the bodies that cause such perceptions in us*: that so we may not think (as perhaps usually is done) that they are exactly the images and resemblances of something

inherent in the subject; most of those of sensation being in the mind no
more the likeness of something existing without us, than the names that
stand for them are the likeness of our ideas, which yet upon hearing they
are apt to excite in us.

8. *Our ideas and the qualities of bodies*—Whatsoever the mind
perceives *in itself,* or is the immediate object of perception, thought, or
understanding, that I call *idea*; and the power to produce any idea in our
mind, I call *quality* of the subject wherein that power is. Thus a snowball
having the power to produce in us the ideas of white, cold, and round,—
the power to produce those ideas in us, as they are in the snowball, I call
qualities; and as they are sensations or perceptions in our understandings, I call them ideas; which ideas, if I speak of sometimes as in the
things themselves, I would be understood to mean those qualities in the
objects which produce them in us.

9. *Primary qualities of bodies*—Qualities thus considered in
bodies are,

First, such as are utterly inseparable from the body, in what state
soever it be; and such as in all the alterations and changes it suffers, all
the force can be used upon it, it constantly keeps; and such as sense
constantly finds in every particle of matter which has bulk enough to be
perceived; and the mind finds inseparable from every particle of matter,
though less than to make itself singly be perceived by our senses: v.g.
Take a grain of wheat, divide it into two parts; each part has still solidity,
extension, figure, and mobility: divide it again, and it retains still the
same qualities; and so divide it on, till the parts become insensible; they
must retain still each of them all those qualities. For division (which is all
that a mill, or pestle, or any other body, does upon another, in reducing it
to insensible parts) can never take away either solidity, extension, figure,
or mobility from any body, but only makes two or more distinct separate
masses of matter, of that which was but one before; all which distinct
masses, reckoned as so many distinct bodies, after division, make a certain number. These I call *original* or *primary qualities* of body, which I
think we may observe to produce simple ideas in us, viz. solidity, extension, figure, motion or rest, *and* number.

10. *Secondary qualities of bodies*—Secondly, such qualities which
in truth are nothing in the objects themselves but power to produce
various sensations in us by their primary qualities, i.e. by the bulk, figure,
texture, and motion of their insensible parts, as colours, sounds, tastes,
&c. These I call *secondary qualities*. To these might be added a *third*
sort, which are allowed to be barely powers; though they are as much real

qualities in the subject as those which I, to comply with the common way of speaking, call qualities, but for distinction, secondary qualities. For the power in fire to produce a new colour, or consistency, in *wax* or *clay*,—by its primary qualities, is as much a quality in fire, as the power it has to produce in *me* a new idea or sensation of warmth or burning, which I felt not before,—by the same primary qualities, viz. the bulk, texture, and motion of its insensible parts.

11. *How primary qualities produce their ideas*—How bodies produce ideas in us. The next thing to be considered is, how bodies produce ideas in us; and that is manifestly by impulse, the only way which we can conceive bodies to operate in.

12. If then external objects be not united to our minds when they produce ideas therein; and yet we perceive these *original* qualities in such of them as singly fall under our senses, it is evident that some motion must be thence continued by our nerves, or animal spirits, by some parts of our bodies, to the brains or the seat of sensation, there to produce in our minds the particular ideas we have of them. And since the extension, figure, number, and motion of bodies of an observable bigness, may be perceived at a distance by the sight, it is evident some singly imperceptible bodies must come from them to the eyes, and thereby convey to the brain some motion; which produces these ideas which we have of them in us.

13. *How secondary*—After the same manner that the ideas of these original qualities are produced in us, we may conceive that the ideas of *secondary* qualities are also produced, viz. by the operation of insensible particles on our senses. For, it being manifest that there are bodies and good store of bodies, each whereof are so small, that we cannot by any of our senses discover either their bulk, figure, or motion,—as is evident in the particles of the air and water, and others extremely smaller than those; perhaps as much smaller than the particles of air and water, as the particles of air and water are smaller than peas or hail-stones;—let us suppose at present that the different motions and figures, bulk and number, of such particles, affecting the several organs of our senses, produce in us those different sensations which we have from the colours and smells of bodies; v.g. that a violet, by the impulse of such insensible particles of matter, of peculiar figures and bulks, and in different degrees and modifications of their motions, causes the ideas of the blue colour, and sweet scent of that flower to be produced in our minds. It being no more impossible to conceive that God should annex such ideas to such motions, with which they have no similtude, than that he should annex

the idea of pain to the motion of a piece of steel dividing our flesh, with which that idea hath no resemblance.

14. What I have said concerning colours and smells may be understood also of tastes and sounds, and other the like sensible qualities; which, whatever reality we by mistake attribute to them, are in truth nothing in the objects themselves, but powers to produce various sensations in us; and depend on those primary qualities, viz. bulk, figure, texture, and motion of parts as I have said.

15. *Ideas of primary qualities are resemblances; of secondary, not*—From whence I think it easy to draw this observation,—that the ideas of primary qualities of bodies are resemblances of them, and their patterns do really exist in the bodies themselves, but the ideas produced in us by these secondary qualities have no resemblance of them at all. There is nothing like our ideas, existing in the bodies themselves. They are, in the bodies we denominate from them, only a power to produce those sensations in us: and what is sweet, blue, or warm in idea, is but the certain bulk, figure, and motion of the insensible parts, in the bodies themselves, which we call so.

16. Flame is denominated hot and light; snow, white and cold; and manna, white and sweet, from the ideas they produce in us. Which qualities are commonly thought to be the same in those bodies that those ideas are in us, the one the perfect resemblance of the other, as they are in a mirror, and it would by most men be judged very extravagant if one should say otherwise. And yet he that will consider that the same fire that, at one distance produces in us the sensation of warmth, does, at a nearer approach, produce in us the far different sensation of pain, ought to bethink himself what reason he has to say—that this idea of warmth, which was produced in him by the fire, is *actually in the fire*; and his idea of pain, which the same fire produced in him the same way, is *not* in the fire. Why are whiteness and coldness in snow, and pain not, when it produces the one and the other idea in us; and can do neither, but by the bulk, figure, number, and motion of its solid parts?

17. The particular bulk, number, figure, and motion of the parts of fire or snow are really in them,—whether any one's senses perceive them or no: and therefore they may be called *real* qualities, because they really exist in those bodies. But light, heat, whiteness, or coldness, are no more really in them than sickness or pain is in manna. Take away the sensation of them; let not the eyes see light or colours, nor the ears hear sounds; let the palate not taste, nor the nose smell, and all colours, tastes, odours, and sounds, *as they are such particular ideas,* vanish and cease, and are reduced to their causes, i.e. bulk, figure, and motion of parts. . . .[5]

Primary qualities, then, exist in the object whether perceived or not; secondary qualities are not in the object, but in our sensing of them.

In spite of the importance of what has been excerpted up to this point, Locke's most memorable contribution to psychological science came almost as an afterthought. In 1700, in the fourth and last edition of *An Essay on Human Understanding,* he interpolated a chapter bearing the title, "The association of ideas":

1. *Something unreasonable in most men*—There is scarce any one that does not observe something that seems odd to him, and is in itself really extravagant, in the opinions, reasonings, and actions of other men. The least flaw of this kind, if at all different from his own, every one is quicksighted enough to espy in another, and will by the authority of reason forwardly condemn; though he be guilty of much greater unreasonableness in his own tenets and conduct, which he never perceives, and will very hardly, if at all, be convinced of. . . .

3. *Not from education*—This sort of unreasonableness is usually imputed to education and prejudice, and for the most part truly enough, though that reaches not the bottom of the disease, nor shows distinctly enough whence it rises, or wherein it lies. Education is often rightly assigned for the cause, and prejudice is a good general name for the thing itself: but yet, I think, he ought to look a little further, who would trace this sort of madness to the root it springs from, and so explain it, as to show whence this flaw has its original in very sober and rational minds, and wherein it consists.

4. *A degree of madness found in most men*—I shall be pardoned for calling it by so harsh a name as madness, when it is considered that opposition to reason deserves that name, and is really madness; and there is scarce a man so free from it, but that if he should always, on all occasions, argue or do as in some cases he constantly does, would not be thought fitter for Bedlam than civil conversation. I do not here mean when he is under the power of an unruly passion, but in the steady calm course of his life. That which will yet more apologize for this harsh name, and ungrateful imputation on the greatest part of mankind, is, that, inquiring a little by the bye into the nature of madness. . . .

5. *From a wrong connexion of ideas*—Some of our ideas have a *natural* correspondence and connexion one with another: it is the office and excellency of our reason to trace these, and hold them together in that union and correspondence which is founded in their peculiar beings. Besides this, there is another connexion of ideas wholly owing to *chance* or *custom*. Ideas that in themselves are not all of kin, come to be so united in some men's minds, that it is very hard to separate them; they always

keep in company, and the one no sooner at any time comes into the understanding, but its associate appears with it; and if they are more than two which are thus united, the whole gang, always inseparable, show themselves together.

6. *This connexion made by custom*—This strong combination of ideas, not allied by nature, the mind makes in itself either voluntarily or by chance; and hence it comes in different men to be very different, according to their different inclinations, education, interests, &c. *Custom* settles habits of thinking in the understanding, as well as of determining in the will, and of motions in the body: all which seems to be but trains of motions in the animal spirits, which, once set a going, continue in the same steps they have used to; which, by often treading, are worn into a smooth path, and the motion in it becomes easy, and as it were natural. As far as we can comprehend thinking, thus ideas seem to be produced in our minds; or, if they are not, this may serve to explain their following one another in an habitual train, when once they are put into their track, as well as it does to explain such motions of the body. A musician used to any tune will find that, let it but once begin in his head, the ideas of the several notes of it will follow one another orderly in his understanding, without any care or attention, as regularly as his fingers move orderly over the keys of the organ to play out the tune he has begun, though his unattentive thoughts be elsewhere a wandering. Whether the natural cause of these ideas, as well as of that regular dancing of his fingers be the motion of his animal spirits, I will not determine, how probable soever, by this instance, it appears to be so: but this may help us a little to conceive of intellectual habits, and of the tying together of ideas....

9. *Wrong connexion of ideas a great cause of errors*—This wrong connexion in our minds of ideas in themselves loose and independent of one another, has such an influence, and is of so great force to set us awry in our actions, as well moral as natural, passions, reasonings, and notions themselves, that perhaps there is not any one thing that deserves more to be looked after.

10. *An instance*—The ideas of goblins and sprites have really no more to do with darkness than light: yet let but a foolish maid inculcate these often on the mind of a child, and raise them there together, possibly he shall never be able to separate them again so long as he lives, but darkness shall ever afterwards bring with it those frightful ideas, and they shall be so joined, that he can no more bear the one than the other.

11. *Another instance*— man receives a severe injury from another, thinks on the man and that action over and over, and by ruminating on

them strongly, or much, in his mind, so cements those two ideas together, that he makes them almost one; never thinks on the man, but the
pain and displeasure he suffered comes into his mind with it, so that he
scarce distinguishes them, but has as much an aversion for the one as the
other. Thus hatreds are often begotten from slight and innocent occasions, and quarrels propagated and continued in the world.

12. *A third instance*—A man has suffered pain or sickness in any
place; he saw his friend die in such a room: though these have in nature
nothing to do one with another, yet when the idea of the place occurs to
his mind, it brings (the impression being once made) that of the pain and
displeasure with it: he confounds them in his mind, and can as little bear
the one as the other.[6]

From the very first paragraph, Locke was concerned with, as he
put it, "something unreasonable in most men," and the theme of how
wrong associations are formed takes up almost all of the chapter. As the
excerpt shows, he does mention in passing that a musician, once beginning a tune, is able to continue it without further thought. This is an
exception, since the correct associations are being formed. It would seem,
however, that Locke used association primarily to explain its errors.

Inspired by Newton, Locke applied mechanical principles to
psychological problems. His approach was also empirical, in that he rejected innate ideas and depended on molecular ideas obtained through
sense experience and reflection. Ideas, so obtained, combined to form
other and larger combinations of ideas. Only ideas are in the mind, while
qualities of bodies are either primary, that is, existing in the objects
themselves, or secondary, not in the object but produced by our sensing
of them. In his last formulation, association of ideas was incorporated to
help explain how ideas are related to one another but are used primarily
to explain incorrect associations. But those who came after him were to
use them to explain *both* correct and incorrect associations, thus influencing Berkeley (p. 45), Hume (p. 54), Hartley (p. 63), and the Mills
(p. 68).

8

BERKELEY ON
MENTALISM, ASSOCIATION,
AND THE PERCEPTION OF SPACE

GEORGE BERKELEY, (1685–1753), an Irish Anglican clergyman and philosopher, was disturbed by the materialistic emphasis in science and sought, in psychological principles, a defense of religion and refutation of scepticism. It was not science he wished to banish but the belief in the primordial character of matter, which made it possible to be sceptical about, or even to deny, spiritual substance. He raised the question, how are physical objects, whose very existence we do not doubt, known to us? In the first few sections of *A Treatise Concerning the Principles of Human Knowledge,* he states many of the principles fundamental to his point of view concerning this question.

1. It is evident to any one who takes a survey of the *objects* of human knowledge, that they are either ideas actually imprinted on the senses, or else such as are perceived by attending to the passions and operations of the mind, or lastly, ideas formed by help of memory and imagination, either compounding, dividing, or barely representing those originally perceived in the aforesaid ways. By sight I have the ideas of light and colours, with their several degrees and variations. By touch I perceive hard and soft, heat and cold, motion and resistance, and of all these more and less either as to quantity or degree. Smelling furnishes me with odours; the palate with tastes, and hearing conveys sounds to the mind in all their variety of tone and composition. And as several of these are observed to accompany each other, they come to be marked by one name, and so to be reputed as one thing. Thus, for example a certain colour, taste, smell, figure and consistence having been observed to go together, are accounted one distinct thing, signified by the name *apple.*

Other collections of ideas constitute a stone, a tree, a book, and the like sensible things—which as they are pleasing or disagreeable, excite the passions of love, hatred, joy, grief, and so forth.[1]

Mind is the immediate reality; what we know is a collection of sensory impressions that we call ideas. He goes on in the next section:

2. But, besides all that endless variety of ideas or objects of knowledge, there is likewise something which knows or perceives them, and exercises divers operations, as willing, imagining, remembering, about them. This perceiving, active being is what I call *mind, spirit, soul,* or *myself.* By which words I do not denote any one of my ideas, but a thing entirely distinct from them, wherein, they exist, or, which is the same thing, whereby they are perceived; for the existence of an idea consists in being perceived.[2]

Mind is the means of perceiving these experiences, a concept that firmly established him as an empiricist. And, in the following section:

13. That neither our thoughts, nor passions, nor ideas formed by the imagination, exist without the mind, is what everybody will allow. And it seems no less evident that the various sensations or ideas imprinted on the sense, however blended or combined together (that is, whatever objects they compose), cannot exist otherwise than in a mind perceiving them—I think an intuitive knowledge may be obtained of this by any one that shall attend to what is meant by the term *exists,* when applied to sensible things. The table I write on, I say exists, that is, I see and feel it; and if I were out of my study I should say it existed, meaning thereby that if I was in my study I might perceive it, or that some other spirit actually does perceive it. There was an odour, that is, it was smelled; there was a sound, that is to say, it was heard; a colour or figure, and it was perceived by sight or touch. This is all that I can understand by these and the like expressions. For as to what is said of the absolute existence of unthinking things without any relation to their being perceived, that seems perfectly unintelligible. Their *esse* is *percipi,* nor is it possible they should have any existence out of the minds or thinking things which perceive them.[3]

The world's phenomena are real enough, their *esse* is *percipi.* Perception *is* the reality; what is denied is the primacy of "matter" about which earlier philosophers had been so concerned. This view that the mental aspects of life are paramount has been called "mentalism," to distinguish it from "subjective idealism" which denies the physical reality of matter.

It should be remembered that both Galileo and Locke had raised the question of primary and secondary qualities, the former residing in the material object, the latter being the same that Berkeley was now saying all reality consisted of. A few sections later, he abolished this distinction entirely.

9. Some there are who make a distinction betwixt *primary* and *secondary* qualities. By the former they mean extension, figure, motion, rest, solidity or impenetrability, and number; by the latter they denote all other sensible qualities, as colours, sounds, tastes, and so forth. The ideas we have of these they acknowledge not to be the resemblances of anything existing without the mind, or unperceived, but they will have our ideas of the primary qualities to be patterns or images of things which exist without the mind, in an unthinking substance which they call matter. By matter, therefore, we are to understand an inert, senseless substance, in which extension, figure, and motion do actually subsist. But it is evident from what we have already shewn, that extension, figure, and motion are only ideas existing in the mind, and that an idea can be like nothing but another idea, and that consequently neither they nor their archetypes can exist in an unperceiving substance. Hence, it is plain that that the very notion of what is called *Matter* or *corporeal substance,* involves a contradiction in it.

10. They who assert that figure, motion, and the rest of the primary or original qualities do exist without the mind in unthinking substances, do at the same time acknowledge that colours, sounds, heat, cold, and suchlike secondary qualities, do not, which they tell us are sensations existing in the mind alone, that depend on and are occasioned by the different size, texture, and motion of the minute particles of matter. This they take for an undoubted truth, which they can demonstrate beyond all exception. Now, if it be certain that those original qualities are inseparably united with the other sensible qualities, and not, even in thought, capable of being abstracted from them, it plainly follows that they exist only in the mind. But I desire any one to reflect and try whether he can, by any abstraction of thought, conceive the extension and motion of a body without all other sensible qualities. For my own part, I see evidently that it is not in my power to frame an idea of a body extended and moving, but I must withal give it some colour or other sensible

quality which is acknowledged to exist only in the mind. In short, extension, figure, and motion, abstracted from all other qualities, are inconceivable. Where therefore the other sensible qualities are, there must these be also, to wit, in the mind and nowhere else.[4]

How could Locke and the others know from experience that some qualities were primary and some not, since they both were known only from experience? The same argument cogent to secondary qualities applied with equal force to so-called primary qualities. Qualities incorrectly divided in the past into primary and second qualities are both known through the mind and do not reside in the object. Hence, what we know, the objects of human knowledge, are mental and not material. This was the basis on which he would refute materialism by demonstrating that all we know is mental—that is to say, it is spiritual, not material. To Berkeley, however, there was no question but that nature was real. The active cause of the permanence of objects was God, the permanent perceiver, and what makes for the unity of man's experience was one's immortal soul.

In a few pages, Berkeley had stated many of his fundamental principles. There are other matters about which he wrote that psychologists find very important. One is his systematic specification of various forms of association. One of these forms, that for simultaneous association, has already been excerpted. On rereading the first excerpt (page 42), it can be noted that this was his way of phrasing the nature of simultaneous association. Complex ideas are formed by a "colour taste, smell, figure and consistence" going together which consequently are considered "one distinct" thing to which we give "the name apple." Contiguity of sensation is the basis for simultaneous association.

For examination of the other important issue, we must turn to his second major publication. *An Essay Toward a New Theory of Vision.* Berkeley had found that an argument seriously advanced against his view was the contention that we "see" objects spread out before us and they seem at a distance from ourselves. Therefore, we judge them as existing independently of mind. Accordingly, he embarked on what is presumed to be psychology's first topical monograph—one on space perception. His major problem was to show how tridemensional space may be perceived by a bidimensional perceiving organ, the retina of the eye. He dealt with both distance and magnitude; the excerpt that follows is confined to the former.

1. My design is to shew the manner wherein we perceive by sight the distance, magnitude, and situation of objects. Also to consider the difference there is betwixt the ideas of sight and touch, and whether there be any idea common to both senses.

2. It is, I think, agreed by all that distance, of itself and immediately, cannot be seen. For distance being a line directed end-wise to the eye, it projects only one point in the fund of the eye, which point remains invariably the same, whether the distance be longer or shorter.

3. I find it also acknowledged that the estimate we make of the distance of objects considerably remote is rather an act of judgment grounded on experience than of sense. For example, when I perceive a great number of intermediate objects, such as houses, fields, rivers, and the like, which I have experienced to take up a considerable space, I thence form a judgment or conclusion that the object I see beyond them is at a great distance. Again, when an object appears faint and small, which at a near distance I have experienced to make a vigorous and large appearance, I instantly conclude it to be far off: And this, 'Tis evident, is the result of experience; without which, from the faintness and littleness I should not have inferred any thing concerning the distance of objects.

4. But when an object is placed at so near a distance as that the interval between the eyes bears any sensible proportion to it, the opinion of speculative men is that the two optic axes (the fancy that we see only with one eye at once being exploded) concurring at the object do there make an angle, by means of which, according as it is greater or lesser, the object is perceived to be nearer or farther off.

5. Betwixt which and the foregoing manner of estimating distance there is this remarkable difference: That whereas there was no apparent, necessary connexion between small distance and a large and strong appearance, or between great distance and a little and faint appearance, there appears a very necessary connexion between an obtuse angle and near distance, and an acute angle and farther distance. It does not in the least depend upon experience, but may be evidently known by any one before he had experienced it, that the nearer the concurrence of the optic, axes, the greater the angle, and the remoter their concurrence is, the lesser will be the angle comprehended by them.

6. There is another way mentioned by optic writers, whereby they will have us judge of those distances, in respect of which the breadth of the pupil hath any sensible bigness: And that is the greater or lesser divergency of the rays, which issuing from the visible point do fall on the pupil, that point being judged nearest which is seen by most diverging rays, and that remoter which is seen by less diverging rays: And so on, the apparent distance still increasing, as the divergency of the rays decreases, till at length it becomes infinite, when the rays that fall on the pupil are to

sense parallel. And after this manner it is said we perceive distance when we look only with one eye.

7. In this case also it is plain we are not beholding to experience: It being a certain, necessary truth that the nearer the direct rays falling on the eye approach to a parallelism, the farther off is the point of their intersection, or the visible point from whence they flow.

8. Now though the accounts here given of perceiving near distance by sight are received for true, and accordingly made use of in determining the apparent places of objects, they do nevertheless seem very unsatisfactory: And that for these following reasons.

9. It is evident that when the mind perceives any idea, not immediately and of it self, it must be by the means of some other idea. Thus, for instance, the passions which are in the mind of another are of themselves to me invisible. I may nevertheless perceive them by sight, though not immediately, yet by means of the colours they produce in the countenance. We often see shame or fear in the looks of a man, by perceiving the changes of his countenance to red or pale.

10. Moreover it is evident that no idea which is not it self perceived can be the means of perceiving any other idea. If I do not perceive the redness or paleness of a man's face themselves, it is impossible I should perceive by them the passions which are in his mind.

11. Now from sect. 2 it is plain that distance is in its own nature imperceptible, and yet it is perceived by sight. It remains, therefore, that it be brought into view by means of some other idea that is it self immediately perceived in the act of vision.

12. But those lines and angles, by means whereof some men pretend to explain the perception of distance, are themselves not at all perceived, nor are they in truth ever thought of by those unskilful in optics. I appeal to any one's experience whether upon sight of an object he computes its distance by the bigness of the angle made by the meeting of the two optic axes? Or whether he ever thinks of the greater or lesser divergency of the rays, which arrive from any point to his pupil? Every one is himself the best judge of what he perceives, and what not. In vain shall any man tell me that I perceive certain lines and angles which introduce into my mind the various ideas of distance, so long as I my self am conscious of no such thing.

13. Since, therefore, those angles and lines are not themselves perceived by sight, it follows from sect. 10 that the mind doth not by them judge of the distance of objects.

14. The truth of this assertion will be yet farther evident to any one that considers those lines and angles have no real existence in nature, being only an hypothesis framed by the mathematicians, and by them introduced into optics, that they might treat of that science in a geometrical way.

15. The last reason I shall give for rejecting that doctrine is, that though we should grant the real existence of those optic angles, etc., and that it was possible for the mind to perceive them, yet these principles would not be found sufficient to explain the phænomena of distance, as shall be shewn hereafter.

16. Now, it being already shewn that distance is suggested to the mind by the mediation of some other idea which is it self perceived in the act of seeing, it remains that we inquire what ideas or sensations there be that attend vision, unto which we may suppose the ideas of distance are connected and by which they are introduced into the mind. And *first,* It is certain by experience that when we look at a near object with both eyes, according as it approaches or recedes from us, we alter the disposition of our eyes, by lessening or widening the interval between the pupils. This disposition or turn of the eyes is attended with a sensation, which seems to me to be that which in this case beings the idea of greater or lesser distance into the mind.

17. Not that there is any natural or necessary connexion between the sensation we perceive by the turn of the eyes and greater or lesser distance, but because the mind has by constant experience found the different sensations corresponding to the different dispositions of the eyes to be attended each with a different degree of distance in the object, there has grown an habitual or customary connexion between those two sorts of ideas, so that the mind no sooner perceives the sensation arising from the different turn it gives the eyes, in order to bring the pupils nearer or farther asunder, but it withal perceives the different idea of stance which was wont to be connected with that sensation; just as upon hearing a certain sound, the idea is immediately suggested to the understanding which custom had united with it. . . .

20. From all which it follows that the judgment we make of the distance of an object, viewed with both eyes, is entirely the result of experience. If we had not constantly found certain sensations arising from the various disposition of the eyes, attended with certain degrees of distance, we should never make those sudden judgments from them concerning the distance of objects; no more than we would pretend to

judge of a man's thoughts by his pronouncing words we had never heard before.

21. *Secondly,* An object placed at a certain distance from the eye, to which the breadth of the pupil bears a considerable proportion, being made to approach, is seen more confusedly: And the nearer it is brought the more confused appearance it makes. And this being found constantly to be so, there ariseth in the mind an habitual connexion between the several degrees of confusion and distance; the greater confusion still implying the lesser distance, and the lesser confusion the greater distance of the object.

22. This confused appearance of the object doth therefore seem to be the medium whereby the mind judgeth of distance in those cases wherein the most approved writers of optics will have it judge by the different divergency with which the rays flowing from the radiating point fall on the pupil. No man, I believe, will pretend to see or feel those imaginary angles that the rays are supposed to form according to their various inclinations on his eye. But he cannot choose seeing whether the object appear more or less confused. It is therefore a manifest consequence from what hath been demonstrated that instead of the greater or lesser divergency of the rays, the mind makes use of the greater or lesser confusedness of the appearance, thereby to determine the apparent place of an object. . . .

27. *Thirdly,* An object being placed at the distance above specified, and brought nearer to the eye, we may nevertheless prevent, at least for some time, the appearances growing more confused, by straining the eye. In which case that sensation supplies the place of confused vision in aiding the mind to judge of the distance of the object; it being esteemed so much the nearer by how much the effort or straining of the eye in order to distinct vision is greater.

28. I have here set down those sensations or ideas that seem to be the constant and general occasions of introducing into the mind the different ideas of near distance. It is true in most cases that divers other circumstances contribute to frame our idea of distance, to wit, the particular number, size, kind, etc., of the things seen. Concerning which, as well as all other the forementioned occasions which suggest distance, I shall only observe they have none of them, in their own nature, any relation or connexion with it: Nor is it possible they should ever signify the various degrees thereof, otherwise than as by experience they have been found to be connected with them.[5]

Berkeley had demonstrated, to his satisfaction, that knowledge of distance is a learned and supplementary aspect of vision and not a given property of nature. By stating that perception of distance (and magnitude) was capable of reduction into simpler elements, he was encouraging those who came after him to analyze other perceptional experiences into more simple elements. Above all, he had shown that the problem of knowledge of space is not only a philosophical issue but a psychological problem.

9

HUME ON

THE EMPIRICAL ORIGIN OF IDEAS AND ASSOCIATION, INCLUDING CAUSALITY, AND SELF

DAVID HUME (1711–1776), Scottish writer, philosopher, civil servant, and frustrated would-be professor, was severely critical of the conclusions reached by his predecessors, Berkeley and Locke, who were held in high esteem among academicians of his time, although he shared their conviction that knowledge arises from experience.

His reasons for trying to advance the study of human nature by empirical means was expressed in the introduction to *A Treatise of Human Nature,* first published in 1739:

It is evident, that all the sciences have a relation, greater or less, to human nature; and that, however wide any of them may seem to run from it, they still return back by one passage or another. Even *Mathematics, Natural Philosophy,* and *Natural Religion,* are in some measure dependent on the science of MAN; since they lie under the cognisance of men, and are judged of by their powers and faculties. It is impossible to tell what changes and improvements we might make in these sciences were we thoroughly acquainted with the extent and force of human understanding, and could explain the nature of the ideas we employ, and of the operations we perform in our reasonings. And these improvements are the more to be hoped for in natural religion, as it is not content with instructing us in the nature of superior powers, but carries its views further, to their disposition towards us, and our duties towards them; and consequently, we ourselves are not only the beings that reason, but also one of the objects concerning which we reason.

If, therefore, the sciences of mathematics, natural philosophy, and natural religion, have such a dependence on the knowledge of man, what may be expected in the other sciences, whose connection with human nature is more close and intimate? The sole end of logic is to explain the principles and operations of our reasoning faculty, and the nature of our ideas; morals and criticism regard our tastes and sentiments; and politics consider men as united in society, and dependent on each other. In these four sciences of *Logic, Morals, Criticism,* and *Politics,* is comprehended almost everything which it can anyway import us to be acquainted with, or which can tend either to the improvement or ornament of the human mind. . . .

And, as the science of man is the only solid foundation for the other sciences, so, the only solid foundation we can give to this science itself must be laid on experience and observation.[1]

The empirical science of psychology, then, is the foundation for the other sciences and, as a science, it is taken out of the realm of philosophy. Both of these assertions were to be reiterated often in the future. The second contention became the basic distinction between psychology as a branch of philosophy and psychology as a science (see Wundt, p. 128).

Just as Locke and Berkeley did before him, Hume plunged immediately into demonstration of the empirical origin of our ideas.

All the perceptions of the human mind resolve themselves into two distinct kinds, which I shall call *impressions* and *ideas.* The difference betwixt these consists in the degrees of force and liveliness, with which they strike upon the mind, and make their way into our thought or consciousness. Those perceptions which enter with most force and violence, we may name *impressions*; and, under this name, I comprehend all our sensations, passions, and emotions, as they make their first appearance in the soul. By *ideas,* I mean the faint images of these in thinking and reasoning; such as, for instance, are all the perceptions excited by the present discourse, excepting only those which arise from the sight and touch, and excepting the immediate pleasure or uneasiness it may occasion. I believe it will not be very necessary to employ many words in explaining this distinction. Every one of himself will readily perceive the difference betwixt feeling and thinking. The common degrees of these are easily distinguished; though it is not impossible but, in particular instances, they may very nearly approach to each other. Thus, in sleep, in a fever, in madness, or in any very violent emotions of soul, our ideas may approach to our impressions: as, on the other hand, it sometimes happens, that our impressions are so faint and low, that we cannot distinguish them from our ideas. But, notwithstanding this near resemblance in a few instances, they are in general so very different, that no one can make a scruple to rank them under distinct heads and assign to each a peculiar name to mark the difference.*

There is another division of our perceptions, which it will be convenient to observe, and which extends itself both to our impressions and ideas. This division is into *simple* and *complex*. Simple perceptions, or impressions and ideas, are such as admit of no distinction nor separation. The complex are the contrary to these, and may be distinguished into parts. Though a particular colour, taste, and smell, are qualities all united together in this apple, it is easy to perceive they are not the same, but are at least distinguishable from each other.

Having, by these divisions, given an order and arrangement to our objects, we may now apply ourselves to consider, with the more accuracy, their qualities and relations. The first circumstance that strikes my eye, is the great resemblance betwixt our impressions and ideas in every other particular, except their degree of force and vivacity. The one seems to be, in a manner, the reflection of the other; so that all the perceptions of the mind are double, and appear both as impressions and ideas. When I shut my eyes, and think of my chamber, the ideas I form are exact representations of the impressions I felt; nor is there any circumstance of the one, which is not to be found in the other. In running over my other perceptions, I find still the same resemblance and representation. Ideas and impressions appear always to correspond to each other. This circumstance seems to me remarkable, and engages my attention for a moment.

Upon a more accurate survey I find I have been carried away too far by the first appearance, and that I must make use of the distinction of perceptions into *simple* and *complex,* to limit this general decision, *that all our ideas and impressions are resembling*. I observe that many of our complex ideas never had impressions that corresponded to them, and that many of our complex impressions never are exactly copied in ideas. I can

---

*I here make use of these terms, *impression* and *idea*, in a sense different from what is usual, and I hope this liberty will be allowed me. Perhaps I rather restore the word idea to its original sense, from which Mr. Locke had perverted it, in making it stand for all our perceptions. By the term of impression, I would not be understood to express the manner in which our lively perceptions are produced in the soul, but merely the perceptions themselves; for which there is no particular name, either in the English or any other language that I know of.

imagine to myself such a city as the New Jerusalem, whose pavement is gold, and walls are rubies, though I never saw any such. I have seen Paris; but shall I affirm I can form such an idea of that city, as will perfectly represent all its streets and houses in their real and just proportions?

I perceive, therefore, that though there is, in general, a great resemblance betwixt our *complex* impressions and ideas, yet the rule is not universally true, that they are exact copies of each other. We may next consider how the case stands with our *simple* perceptions. After the most accurate examination of which I am capable, I venture to affirm, that the rule here holds without any exception, and that every simple idea has a simple impression, which resembles it, and every simple impression a correspondent idea. That idea of red, which we form in the dark, and that impression which strikes our eyes in sunshine, differ only in degree, not in nature. That the case is the same with all our simple impressions and ideas, it is impossible to prove by a particular enumeration of them. Every one may satisfy himself in this point by running over as many as he pleases. But if any one should deny this universal resemblance, I know no way of convincing him, but by desiring him to show a simple impression that has not a correspondent idea, or a simple idea that has not a correspondent impression. If he does not answer this challenge, as it is certain he cannot, we may, from his silence and our own observation, establish our conclusion.

Thus we find, hat all simple ideas and impressions resemble each other; and, as the complex are formed from them, we may affirm in general, that these two species of perception are exactly correspondent. Having discovered this relation, which requires no further examination, I am curious to find some other of their qualities. Let us consider, how they stand with regard to their existence, and which of the impressions and ideas are causes, and which effects.

The full examination of this question is the subject of the present treatise; and, therefore, we shall here content ourselves with establishing one general proposition, *That all our simple ideas in their first appearance, are derived from simple impressions, which are correspondent to them, and which they exactly represent.*[2]

The major proposition is so effectively summarized in the last sentence that no further comment is necessary.

He also considered the association of ideas:

...To me, there appear to be only three principles of connexion among ideas, namely, *Resemblance, Contiguity* in time or place, and *Cause* or *Effect*.

That these principles serve to connect ideas will not, I believe, be much doubted. A picture naturally leads our thoughts to the original; the mention of one apartment in a building naturally introduces an enquiry or discourse concerning the others: and if we think of a wound, we can scarcely forbear reflecting on the pain which follows it. But that this enumeration is complete, and that there are no other principles of association except these, may be difficult to prove to the satisfaction of the reader, or even to a man's own satisfaction. All we can do, in such cases, is to run over several instances, and examine carefully the principle which binds the different thoughts to each other, never stopping till we render the principle as general as possible. The more instances we examine, and the more care we employ, the more assurance shall we acquire, that the enumeration, which we form from the whole, is complete and entire.[3]

Of the three forms of association just discussed, cause and effect rated special scrutiny and is excerpted here because of its significance and because of the startling sceptical conclusion about it which Hume reached.

22. All reasonings concerning matter of fact seem to be founded on the relation of *Cause and Effect*. By means of that relation alone we can go beyond the evidence of our memory and senses. If you were to ask a man, why he believes any matter of fact, which is absent; for instance, that his friend is in the country, or in France; he would give you a reason; and this reason would be some other fact; as a letter received from him, or the knowledge of his former resolutions and promises. A man finding a watch or any other machine in a desert island, would conclude that there had once been men in that island. All our reasonings concerning fact are of the same nature. And here it is constantly supposed that there is a connexion between the present fact and that which is inferred from it. Were there nothing to bind them together, the inference would be entirely precarious. The hearing of an articulate voice and rational discourse in the dark assures us of the presence of some person: Why? because these are the effects of the human make and fabric, and closely connected with it. If we anatomize all the other reasonings of this nature, we

shall find that they are founded on the relation of cause and effect, and that this relation is either near or remote, direct or collateral. Heat and light are collateral effects of fire, and the one effect may justly be inferred from the other.

23. If we would satisfy ourselves, therefore, concerning the nature of that evidence, which assures us of matters of fact, we must enquire how we arrive at the knowledge of cause and effect.

I shall venture to affirm, as a general proposition, which admits of no exception, that the knowledge of this relation is not, in any instance, attained by reasonings *a priori;* but arises entirely from experience, when we find that any particular objects are constantly conjoined with each other. Let an object be presented to a man of ever so strong natural reason and abilities; if that object be entirely new to him, he will not be able, by the most accurate examination of its sensible qualities, to discover any of its causes or effects. Adam, though his rational faculties be supposed, at the very first, entirely perfect, could not have inferred from the fluidity and transparency of water that it would suffocate him, or from the light and warmth of fire that it would consume him. No object ever discovers, by the qualities which appear to the senses, either the causes which produced it, or the effects which will arise from it; nor can our reason, unassisted by experience, ever draw any inference concerning real existence and matter of fact.

24. This proposition, *that causes and effects are discoverable, not by reason but by experience,* will readily be admitted with regard to such objects, as we remember to have once been altogether unknown to us; since we must be conscious of the utter inability, which we then lay under, of foretelling what would arise from them. Present two smooth pieces of marble to a man who has no tincture of natural philosophy; he will never discover that they will adhere together in such a manner as to require great force to separate them in a direct line, while they make so small a resistance to a lateral pressure. Such events, as bear little analogy to the common course of nature, are also readily confessed to be known only by experience; nor does any man imagine that the explosion of gunpowder, or the attraction of a loadstone, could ever be discovered by arguments *a priori.* In like manner, when an effect is supposed to depend upon an intricate machinery or secret structure of parts, we make no difficulty in attributing all our knowledge of it to experience. Who will assert that he can give the ultimate reason, why milk or bread is proper nourishment for a man, not for a lion or a tiger?

But the same truth may not appear, at first sight, to have the same evidence with regard to events, which have become familiar to us from our first appearance in the world, which bear a close analogy to the whole course of nature, and which are supposed to depend on the simple qualities of objects, without any secret structure of parts. We are apt to imagine that we could discover these effects by the mere operation of our reason, without experience. We fancy, that were we brought on a sudden into this world, we could at first have inferred that one billiardball would communicate motion to another upon impulse; and that we needed not to have waited for the event, in order to pronounce with certainty concerning it. Such is the influence of custom, that, where it is strongest, it not only covers our natural ignorance, but even conceals itself, and seems not to take place, merely because it is found in the highest degree.

25. But to convince us that all the laws of nature, and all the operations of bodies without exception, are known only by experience, the following reflections may, perhaps, suffice. Were any object presented to us, and were we required to pronounce concerning the effect, which will result from it, without consulting past observation; after what manner, I beseech you, must the mind proceed in this operation? It must invent or imagine some event, which it ascribes to the object as its effect; and it is plain that this invention must be entirely arbitrary. The mind can never possibly find the effect in the supposed cause, by the most accurate scrutiny and examination. For the effect is totally different from the cause, and consequently can never be discovered in it. Motion in the second billardball is a quite distinct event from motion in the first; nor is there anything in the one to suggest the smallest hint of the other. A stone or piece of metal raised into the air, and left without any support, immediately falls: but to consider the matter *a priori,* is there anything we discover in this situation which can beget the idea of a downward, rather than an upward, or any other motion, in the stone or metal?

And as the first imagination or invention of a particular effect, in all natural operations, is arbitrary, where we consult not experience; so must we also esteem the supposed tie or connexion between the cause and effect, which binds them together, and renders it impossible that any other effect could result from the operation of that cause. When I see, for instance, a billiardball moving a straight line towards another; even suppose motion in the second ball should by accident be suggested to me, as the result of their contact or impulse; may I not conceive, that a hundred different events might as well follow from that cause? May not both these balls remain at absolute rest? May not the first ball return in a straight line, or leap off from the second in any line or direction? All these suppositions are consistent and conceivable. Why then should we give the preference to one, which is no more consistent or conceivable than the rest? All our reasonings *a priori* will never be able to show us any foundation for this preference.

In a word, then, every effect is a distinct event from its cause. It could not, therefore, be discovered in the cause, and the first invention or conception of it, *a priori,* must be entirely arbitrary. And even after it is suggested, the conjunction of it with the cause must appear equally arbitrary; since there are always many other effects, which, to reason, must seem fully as consistent and natural. In vain, therefore, should we pretend to determine any single event, or infer any cause or effect, without the assistance of observation and experience.

26. Hence, we may discover the reason why no philosopher, who is rational and modest, has ever pretended to assign the ultimate cause of any natural operation, or to show distinctly the action of that power, which produces any single effect in the universe. It is confessed, that the utmost effort of human reason is to reduce the principles, productive of natural phenomena, to a greater simplicity, and to resolve the many particular effects into a few general causes, by means of reasonings from analogy, experience, and observation. But as to the causes of these general causes, we should in vain attempt their discovery; nor shall we ever be able to satisfy ourselves, by any particular explication of them. These ultimate springs and principles are totally shut up from human curiosity and enquiry. Elasticity, gravity, cohesion of parts, communication of motion by impulse; these are probably the ultimate causes and principles which we shall ever discover in nature; and we may esteem ourselves sufficiently happy, if, by accurate enquiry and reasoning, we can trace up the particular phenomena to, or near to, these general principles. The most perfect philosophy of the natural kind only staves off our ignorance a little longer: as perhaps the most perfect philosophy of the moral or metaphysical kind serves only to discover larger portions of it. Thus the observation of human blindness and weakness is the result of all philosophy, and meets us at every turn, in spite of our endeavours to elude or avoid it.

27. Nor is geometry, when taken into the assistance of natural philosophy, ever able to remedy this defect, or lead us into the knowledge of ultimate causes, by all that accuracy of reasoning for which it is so justly celebrated. Every part of mixed mathematics proceeds upon the

supposition that certain laws are established by nature in her operations; and abstract reasonings are employed, either to assist experience in the discovery of these laws, or to determine their influence in particular instances, where it depends upon any precise degree of distance and quantity. Thus, it is a law of motion, discovered by experience, that the moment or force of any body in motion is in the compound ratio or proportion of its solid contents and its velocity; and consequently, that a small force may remove the greatest obstacle or raise the greatest weight, if, by any contrivance or machinery, we can increase the velocity of that force, so as to make it an overmatch for its antagonist. Geometry assists us in the application of this law, by giving us the just dimensions of all the parts and figures which can enter into any species of machine; but still the discovery of the law itself is owing merely to experience, and all the abstract reasonings in the world could never lead us one step towards the knowledge of it. When we reason *a priori,* and consider merely any object or cause, as it appears to the mind, independent of all observation, it never could suggest to us the notion of any distinct object, such as its effect; much less show us the inseparable and inviolable connexion between them. A man must be very sagacious who could discover by reasoning that crystal is the effect of heat, and ice of cold, without being previously acquainted with the operation of these qualities.[4]

Causality is nothing more than recurrent concommitance; a habit of mind originating in experience which leads us to expect the sequence of events. But, beyond this, there is no evidence that causality exists anywhere except in the mind, not in objects. This was a conclusion that Kant tried to dispel some thirty years later (p. 87).

Hume was similarly sceptical about the reality of mind or self, a position that Berkeley had defended.

There are some philosophers who imagine we are every moment intimately conscious of what we call our *self*; that we feel its existence and its continuance in existence; and are certain, beyond the evidence of a demonstration, both of its perfect identity and simplicity. . . .For my part, when I enter most intimately into what I call *myself*, I always stumble on some particular perception or other, of heat or cold, light or shade, love or hatred, pain or pleasure. I never can catch *myself* at any time without a perception, and never can observe anything but the perception. When my perceptions are removed for any time, as by sound sleep, so long am I insensible of *myself,* and may truly be said not to exist. And were all my perceptions removed by death, and could I neither think, nor feel, nor see, nor love, nor hate, after the dissolution of my body, I should be entirely annihilated, nor do I conceive what is further requisite to make me a perfect nonentity. If any one, upon serious and unprejudiced reflection, thinks he has a different notion of *himself,* I must confess I can reason no longer with him. All I can allow him is, that he may be in the right as well as I, and that we are essentially different in this particular. He may, perhaps, perceive something simple and continued, which he calls *himself*; though I am certain there is no such principle in me.

But setting aside some metaphysicians of this kind, I may venture to affirm of the rest of mankind, that they are nothing but a bundle or collection of different perceptions, which succeed each other with an inconceivable rapidity, and are in a perpetual flux and movement. Our eyes cannot turn in their sockets without varying our perceptions. Our thought is still more variable than our sight; and all our other senses and faculties contribute to this change; nor is there any single power of the soul, which remains unalterably the same, perhaps for one moment. The mind is a kind of theatre, where several perceptions successively make their appearance; pass, repass, glide away, and mingle in an infinite variety of postures and situations. There is properly no *simplicity* in it at one time, nor *identity* in different, whatever natural propension we may have to imagine that simplicity and identity. The comparison of the theatre must not mislead us. They are the successive perceptions only, that constitute the mind; nor have we the most distant notion of the place where these scenes are represented, or of the materials of which it is composed.

What then gives us so great a propension to ascribe an identity to these successive perceptions, and to suppose ourselves possessed of an invariable and uninterrupted existence through the whole course of our lives? In order to answer this question we must distinguish betwixt personal identity, as it regards our thought or imagination, and as it regards our passions or the concern we take in ourselves. The first is our present subject; and to explain it perfectly we must take the matter pretty deep, and account for that identity, which we attribute to plants and animals; there being a great analogy betwixt it and the identity of a self or person.

We have a distinct idea of an object that remains invariable and uninterrupted through a supposed variation of time; and this idea we call that of *identity* or *sameness.* We have also a distinct idea of several different objects existing in succession, and connected together by a close relation; and this to an accurate view affords as perfect a notion of *diversity* as if there was no manner of relation among the objects. But though these two ideas of identity, and a succession of related objects, be in themselves perfectly distinct, and even contrary, yet it is certain that, in our common way of thinking, they are generally confounded with each other. That action of the imagination, by which we consider the uninterrupted and invariable object, and that by which we reflect on the succession of related objects, are almost the same to the feeling; nor is there much more effort of thought required in the latter case than in the former. The relation facilitates the transition of the mind from one object to another, and renders its passage as smooth as if it contemplated one continued object. This resemblance is the cause of the confusion and mistake, and makes us substitute the notion of identity, instead of that of related objects. However at one instant we may consider the related succession as variable or interrupted, we are sure the next to ascribe to it a perfect identity, and regard it as invariable and uninterrupted. Our propensity to this mistake is so great from the resemblance above mentioned, that we fall into it before we are aware; and though we incessantly correct ourselves by reflection, and return to a more accurate method of thinking, yet we cannot long sustain our philosophy, or take off this bias from the imagination. Our last resource is to yield to it, and boldly assert that these different related objects are in effect the same, however interrupted and variable. In order to justify to ourselves this absurdity, we often feign some new and unintelligible principle, that connects the objects together, and prevents their interruption or variation. Thus we feign the continued existence of the perceptions of our senses, to remove the interruption; and run into the notion of a soul, and self, and substance, to disguise the variation. But, we may further observe, that where we do not give rise to such a fiction, our propension to confound identity with relation is so great, that we are apt to imagine something unknown and mysterious, connecting the parts, beside their relation; and this I take to be the case with regard to the identity we ascribe to plants and vegetables. And even when this does not take place, we still feel a propensity to confound these ideas, though we are not able fully to satisfy ourselves in that particular, nor find anything invariable and uninterrupted to justify our notion of identity. . . .It is evident that the identity which we attribute to the human mind, however perfect we may imagine it to be, is not able to run the several different perceptions into one, and make them lose their characters of distinction and difference, which are essential to them. It is still true that every distinct perception which enters into the composition of the mind, is a distinct existence, and is different, and distinguishable, and separable from every other perception, either contemporary or successive. But as, notwithstanding this distinction and separability, we suppose the whole train of perceptions to be united by identity, a question naturally arises concerning this relation of identity, whether it be something that really binds our several perceptions together, or only associates their ideas in the imagination; that is, in other words, whether, in pronouncing concerning the identity of a person, we observe some real bond among his perceptions, or only feel one among the ideas we form of them. This question we might easily decide, if we would recollect what has been already proved at large, that the understanding never observes any real connection among objects, and that even the union of cause and effect, when strictly examined, resolves itself into a customary association of ideas. For from thence it evidently follows, that identity is nothing really belonging to these different perceptions, and uniting them together, but is merely a quality which we attribute to them, because of the union of their ideas in the imagination when we reflect upon them.[5]

Berkeley had found in the self or mind an entity that knows the objects of sense (p. 43). Hume denied that there was any entity to be found. Mind and self are a collection of impressions, nothing more. He thus completed the progression of thought on the nature of experience that had started with Locke's blithe assertion that experience arose from sense impression but did not question the existence of the independence of objects. Berkeley, while denying we could know the existence of objects from experience as such, but God, the "permanent perceiver," gave us the assurance of their presence through the soul, which unified our experiences. Hume denied this last step by denying that the mind was more than a collection of impressions from which all else begins.

10

HARTLEY ON
ASSOCIATIONS OF THE MIND
AND VIBRATIONS OF THE BODY

DAVID HARTLEY (1707–1757), English philosopher-physician, developed a Newtonian inspired psychological model, by adding an underlying physiological substratum which Locke deliberately had foregone. He wanted to explain the operation of the human body as well as the mind in mechanical terms. Before him, Descartes had done so for the body, but Hartley would unite a mechanical view of body with a mechanical view of the human mind. He introduced his major work in 1749, *Observations of Man,* with the forthright statement, "Man consists of two parts, body and mind."

The beginning of the first chapter states his purpose and his sources:

My chief design in the following chapter, is, briefly, to explain, establish, and apply the doctrines of vibrations and association. The first of these doctrines is taken from the hints concerning the performance of sensation and motion, which Sir Isaac Newton has given at the end of his *Principia,* and in the questions annexed to his *Optics*; the last, from what Mr. Locke, and other ingenious persons since his time, have delivered concerning the influence of association over our opinions and affections, and its use in explaining those things in an accurate and precise way, which are commonly referred to the power of habit and custom, in a general and indeterminate one.

The doctrine of vibrations may appear at first sight to have no connection with that of association; however, if these doctrines be found in fact to contain the laws of the bodily and mental powers respectively, they must be related to each other, since the body and mind are. One may expect, that vibrations should infer association as their effect- and association point to vibrations as its cause.[1]

This excerpt is followed by an explanation of how physical vibrations and sensations are related. External physical vibrations set in motion the white medullary substance of the brain with which sensations are associated.

The evidence which he presented drew upon whatever physiological and medical information was then available, which meant that it could not be couched in terms of nerves or neural impulses. Representative is his account of the reaction between simultaneous and successive association in the mind and vibrations in the brain and is given in successive propositions:

Prop. 10. Any sensations A,B,C, etc. by being associated with one another a sufficient number of times, get such a power over the corresponding ideas a,b,c, etc. that any one of the sensations A, when impressed alone, shall be able to excite in the mind, b, c, etc. the ideas of the rest.

Sensations may be said to be associated together, when their impressions are either made precisely at the same instant of time, or in the contiguous successive instants. We may therefore distinguish association into two sorts, the synchronous, and the successive.

This proposition, or first and simplest case of association, is manifest from innumerable common observations. Thus the names, smells, tastes, and tangible qualities of natural bodies, suggest their visible appearances to the fancy, i.e. excite their visible ideas; and, vice versa, their visible appearances impressed on the eye raise up those powers of reconnoitering their names, smells, tastes, and tangible qualities, which may not improperly be called their ideas, as above noted; and in some case raise up ideas, which may be compared with visible ones, in respect of vividness. All which is plainly owing to the association of the several sensible qualities of bodies with their names, and with each other. It is remarkable, however, as being agreeable to the superior vividness of visible and audible ideas before taken notice of, that the suggestion of the visible appearance from the name, is the most ready of any other; and, next to this, that of the name from the visible appearance; in which last case, the reality of the audible idea, when not evident to the fancy, may be inferred from the ready pronunication of the name. For it will be shown hereafter, that the audible idea is most commonly a previous requisite to pronunciation. Other instances of the power of association may be taken from compound visible and audible impressions. Thus the sight of part of a large building suggests the idea of the rest instantaneously; and the sound of the words which begin a familiar sentence, brings the remaining part to our memories in order, the association of the parts being synchronous in the first case, and successive in the last.

It is to be observed, that, in successive associations, the power of raising the ideas in only exerted according to the order in which the association is made. Thus, if the impressions, A, B, C, be always made in the order of the alphabet, B impressed alone will not raise a, but c only. Agreeably to which, it is easy to repeat familiar sentences in the order in which they always occur, but impossible to do it readily in an inverted one. The reason of this is, that the compound idea, c, b, a corresponds to the compound sensation, C, B, A; and therefore requires the impression of C, B, A, in the same manner as a, b, c, does that of A, B, C. This will, however, be more evident, when we come to consider the associations of vibratory motions, in the next proposition. . . .

Prop. 11. Any vibrations, A, B, C, etc. by being associated together a sufficient number of times, get such a power over a, b, c, etc. the corresponding miniature vibrations, that any of the vibrations A, when impressed alone, shall be able to excite b, c, etc. the miniatures of the rest. . . .it seems . . .deducible from the nature of vibrations, and of an animal body. Let A and B be two vibrations, associated synchronically. Now, it is evident, that the vibration A (for I will, in this proposition, speak of A and B in the singular number, for the sake of greater clearness) will, by endeavouring to diffuse itself into those parts of the medullary substance which are affected primarily by the vibration B, in some measure modify and change, B, so as to make B a little different from what it would be, if impressed along. For the same reasons the vibration A will be a little affected, even in its primary seat, by the endeavour of B to diffuse itself all over the medullary substance. Suppose now the vibrations A and B to be impressed at the same instant, for a thousand times; it follows, from the ninth proposition, that they will first overcome the disposition to the natural vibrations N, and then leave a tendency to themselves, which will now occupy the place of the original natural tendency to vibrations. When therefore the vibration A is impressed alone, it cannot be entirely such as the object would excite of itself, but must lean, even in its primary seat, to the modifications and changes induced by B, during their thousand joint impressions; and therefore much more, in receding from this primary seat, will it lean that way; and when it comes to the seat of B, it will excite B's miniature a little modified and changed by itself.

Or thus: When A is impressed alone, some vibration must take place in the primary seat of B, both on account of the heat and pulsation of the arteries, and because A will endeavour to diffuse itself over the whole medullary substance. This cannot be that part of the natural vibrations N, which belongs to this region, because it is supposed to be over-ruled already. It cannot be that which A impressed alone would have propagated into this region, because that has always hitherto been over-ruled, and converted into B; and therefore cannot have begotten a tendency to itself. It cannot be any full vivid vibration, such as B, C, D, etc. belonging to this region, because all full vibrations require the actual impression of an object upon the corresponding external organ. And of miniature vibrations belonging to this region, such as b, c, d, etc. it is evident, that b has the preference, since A leans to it a little, even in its own primary seat, more and more, in receding from this, and almost entirely, when it comes to the primary seat of B. For the same reasons B impressed alone will excite a; and, in general, if A, B, C, etc. be vibrations synchronically impressed on different regions of the medullary substance, A impressed alone will, at last, excite b, c, etc. according to the proposition.

If A and B be vibrations impressed successively, then will the latter part of A, vis, that part which, according to the their and fourth proposition, remains, after the impression of the object ceases, be modified and altered by B, at the same time that it will a little modify and alter, it, till at last it be quite overpowered by it, and end in it. It follows therefore, by a like method of reasoning, that the successive impression of A and B, sufficiently repeated, will so alter the medullary substance, as that when A is impressed alone, its latter part shall not be such as the sole impression of A requires, but lean towards B, and end in b at last. But B will not excite a in a retrograde order, by supposition, the latter part of B was not modified and altered by A, but by some other vibration, such as C or D. And as B, by being followed by C, may at last raise c, so b, when raised by A, in the method here proposed, may be also sufficient to raise c, inasmuch as the minature c being a feeble motion, not stronger, perhaps, than the natural vibrations N, requires only to have its kind, place, and line of direction, determined by association, the heat and arterial pulsation conveying to it the requisite degree of strength. And thus associations, as well as in synchronous ones, according to the proposition.[2]

Several significant achievements drawn from these excerpts may be credited to Hartley. He had "created" a relationship, plausible for his time, between bodily function and mental processes neglected by Locke because of his lack of interest, by Berkeley because of his mentalistic stance, and by Hume because of his scepticism. Hartley restored the body as the physical basis for mental interconnections including motor activities; ideas are associated with movements. He formalized the doctrine of association by making it central to his writings and used it to explain all mental life, rather than making it incidental to other concerns and other principles as had his predecessors. And, he made contiguity the fundamental law of association.

11

THE MILLS

ON ASSOCIATION
AND MENTAL CHEMISTRY

JAMES MILL (1773–1836), and John Stuart Mill (1806–1873) his son, were philosophers who contributed significantly to social theory and to economics. James was a leader of the utilitarian movement, a theory first promulgated by his friend, Jeremy Bentham, which stressed the socioeconomic principle of utility,—that people are ruled by self-interest—and popularized the slogan, "the greatest good for the greatest number." James Mill, led by this interest, turned to psychological matters in the associationist tradition. John Stuart Mill, while sympathetic to utilitarianism, directed his attention primarily to logic and the philosophy of the scientific method.

James Mill's *Analysis of the Phenomena of the Human Mind,* originally appearing in 1829, was revised under the editorship of his son in 1869. It is this edition that is excerpted here.

In an effort to find its simplest elements, James Mill applied a reductive procedure to the association doctrines of Hartley and Hume, both to reduce the number of laws of association and the causes of variation in the strength of associations.

Thought succeeds thought; idea follows idea, incessantly. If our senses are awake, we are continually receiving sensations, of the eye, the ear, the touch, and so forth; but not sensations alone. After sensations, ideas are perpetually excited of sensations formerly received; after those ideas, other ideas: and during the whole of our lives, a series of those two states of consciousness, called sensations, and ideas, is constantly going on. I see a horse: that is a sensation. Immediately I think of his master: that is an idea. The idea of his master makes me think of his office; he is a minister of state: that is another idea. The idea of a minister of state makes me think of public affairs; and I am led into a train of political ideas; when I am summoned to dinner. This is a new sensation, followed by the idea of dinner, and of the company with whom I am to partake it. The sight of the company and of the food are other sensations; these suggest ideas without end; other sensations perpetually intervene, suggesting other ideas: and so the process goes on.

In contemplating this train of feelings, of which our lives consist, it first of all strikes the contemplator, as of importance to ascertain, whether they occur casually and irregularly, or according to a certain order.

With respect to the SENSATIONS, it is obvious enough that they occur, according to the order established among what we call the objects of nature, whatever those objects are; to ascertain more and more of which order is the business of physical philosophy in all its branches.

Of the order established among the objects of nature, by which we mean the objects of our senses, two remarkable cases are all which here we are called upon to notice; the SYNCHRONOUS ORDER and the SUCCESSIVE ORDER. The synchronous order, or order of simultaneous existence, is the order in space; the successive order, or order of antecedent and consequent existence, is the order in time. Thus the various objects in my room, the chairs, the tables, the books, have the synchronous order, or order in space. The falling of the spark, and the explosion of the gunpowder, have the successive order, or order in time.

According to this order, in the objects of sense, there is a synchronous, and a successive, order of our sensations. I have SYNCHRONICALLY, or at the same instant, the sight of a great variety of objects; touch of all the objects with which my body is in contact; hearing of all the sounds which are reaching my ears; smelling of all the smells which are reaching my nostrils; taste of the apple which I am eating; the sensation of resistance both from the apple which is in my mouth, and the ground on which I stand; with the sensation of motion from the act of walking. I have SUCCESSIVELY the sight of the flash from the mortar fired at a distance, the hearing of the report, the sight of the bomb, and of its motion in the air, the sight of its fall, the sight and hearing of its explosion, and lastly, the sight of all the effects of that explosion.

Among the objects which I have thus observed synchronically, or successively; that is, from which I have had synchronical or successive sensations; there are some which I have so observed frequently; others which I have so observed not frequently: in other words, of my sensations some have been frequently synchronical, others not frequently; some frequently successive, others not frequently. Thus, my sight of roast beef, and my taste of roast beef, have been frequently SYNCHRONICAL, my smell of a rose, and my sight and touch of a rose, have been frequently synchronical; my sight of a stone, and my sensations of its hardness, and weight, have been frequently synchronical. Others of my sensations have not been frequently synchronical: my sight of a lion, and the hearing of his roar; my sight of a knife, and its stabbing a man. My sight of the flash of lightning, and my hearing of the thunder, have been often SUCCESSIVE; the pain of cold, and the pleasure of heat, have been often successive; the sight of a trumpet, and the sound of a trumpet, have been often successive. On the other hand, my sight of hemlock, and my taste of hemlock, have not been often successive: and so on.

It so happens, that, of the objects from which we derive the greatest part of our sensations, most of those which are observed synchronically, are frequently observed synchronically; most of those which are observed successively, are frequently observed successively. In other words, most of our synchronical sensations, have been frequently synchronical; most of our successive sensations, have been frequently successive. Thus, most of our synchronical sensations are derived from the objects around us, the objects which we have the most frequent occasion to hear and see; the members of our family; the furniture of our houses; our food; the instruments of our occupations or amusements. In like manner, of those sensations which we have had in succession, we have had the greatest number repeatedly in succession; the sight of fire, and its warmth; the touch of snow, and its cold; the sight of food, and its taste.

Thus much with regard to the order of SENSATIONS; next with regard to the order of IDEAS.

As ideas are not derived from objects, we should not expect their order to be derived from the order of objects; but as they are derived from sensations, we might by analogy expect, that they would derive their order from that of the sensations; and this to a great extent is the case.

Our ideas spring up, or exist, in the order in which the sensations existed, of which they are the copies.

This is the general law of the "Association of Ideas"; by which term, let it be remembered, nothing is here meant to be expressed, but the order of occurrence.

In this law, the following things are to be carefully observed.

1. Of those sensations which occurred synchronically, the ideas also spring up synchronically. I have seen a violin, and heard the tones of the violin, synchronically. If I think of the tones of the violin, the visible

appearance of the violin at the same time occurs to me. I have seen the sun, and the sky in which it is placed, synchronically. If I think of the one, I think of the other at the same time. One of the cases of synchronical sensation, which deserves the most particular attention, is, that of the several sensations derived from one and the same object; a stone, for example, a flower, a table, a chair, a horse, a man.

From a stone I have had, synchronically, the sensation of colour, the sensation of hardness, the sensations of shape, and size, the sensation of weight. When the idea of one of these sensations occurs, the ideas of all of them occur. They exist in my mind synchronically; and their synchronical existence is called the idea of the stone; which, it is thus plain, is not a single idea, but a number of ideas in a particular state of combination.

Thus, again, I have smelt a rose, and looked at, and handled a rose, synchronically; accordingly the name rose suggests to me all those ideas synchronically; and this combination of those simple ideas is called my idea of the rose.

My idea of an animal is still more complex. The word thrush, for example, not only suggests an idea of a particular colour and shape, and size, but of song, and flight, and nestling, and eggs, and callow young, and others.

My idea of a man is the most complex of all; including not only colour, and shape, and voice, but the whole class of events in which I have observed him either the agent or the patient.

2. As the ideas of the sensations which occurred synchronically, rise synchronically, so the ideas of the sensations which occurred successively, rise successively.

Of this important case of association, or of the successive order of our ideas, many remarkable instances might be adduced. Of these none seems better adapted to the learner than the repetition of any passage, or words; the Lord's Prayer, for example, committed to memory. In learning the passage, we repeat it; that is, we pronounce the words, in successive order, from the beginning to the end. The order of the sensations is successive. When we proceed to repeat the passage, the ideas of the words also rise in succession, the preceding always suggesting the succeeding, and no other. *Our* suggests *Father, Father* suggests *which, which* suggests *art*; and so on, to the end. How remarkably this is the case, any one may convince himself, by trying to repeat backwards, even a passage with which he is as familiar as the Lord's Prayer. The case is the same with numbers. A man can go on with the numbers in the progressive order, one, two, three, &c. scarcely thinking of his act; and though it is possible for him to repeat them backward, because he is accustomed to subtraction of numbers, he cannot do so without an effort.

Of witnesses in courts of justice it has been remarked, that eye-witnesses, and ear-witnesses, always tell their story in the chronological order; in other words, the ideas occur to them in the order in which the sensations occurred; on the other hand, that witnesaes, who are inventing, rarely adhere to the chronological order.

3. A far greater number of our sensations are received in the successive, than in the synchronical order. Of our ideas, also, the number is infinitely greater that rise in the successive than the synchronical order.

4. In the successive order of ideas, that which precedes, is sometimes called the suggesting, that which succeeds, the suggested idea; not that any power is supposed to reside in the antecedent over the consequent; suggesting, and suggested, mean only antecedent and consequent, with the additional idea, that such order is not casual, but, to a certain degree, permanent.

5. Of the antecedent and consequent feelings, or the suggesting, and suggested; the antecedent may be either sensations or ideas; the consequent are always ideas. An idea may be excited either by a sensation or an idea. The sight of the dog of my friend is a sensation, and it excites the idea of my friend. The idea of Professor Dugald Stewart delivery a lecture, recalls the idea of the delight with which I heard him; that, the idea of the studies in which it engaged me; that, the trains of thought which succeeded; and each epoch of my mental history, the succeeding one, till the present moment; in which I am endeavouring to present to others what appears to me valuable among the innumerable ideas of which this lengthened train has been composed.

6. As there are degrees in sensations, and degrees in ideas; for one sensation is more vivid than another sensation, one idea more vivid than another idea; so there are degrees in association. One association, we say, is stronger than another: First, when it is more permanent than another: Secondly, when it is performed with more certainty: Thirdly, when it is performed with more facility. It is well known, that some associations are very transient, others very permanent. The case which we formerly mentioned, that of repeating words committed to memory, affords an apt illustration. In some cases, we can perform the repetition, when a few hours, or a few days have elapsed; but not after a longer period. In others, we can perform it after the lapse of many years. There are few children in whose minds some association has not been formed between darkness

and ghosts. In some this association is soon dissolved; in some it continues for life.

In some cases the association takes place with less, in some with greater certainty. Thus, in repeating words, I am not sure that I shall not commit mistakes, if they are imperfectly got; and I may at one trial repeat them right, at another wrong: I am sure of always repeating those correctly, which I have got perfectly. Thus, in my native language, the association between the name and the thing is certain; in a language with which I am imperfectly acquainted, not certain. In expressing myself in my own language, the idea of the thing suggests the idea of the name with certainty. In speaking a language with which I am imperfectly acquainted, the idea of the thing does not with certainty suggest the idea of the name; at one time it may, at another not.

That ideas are associated in some cases with more, in some with less facility, is strikingly illustrated by the same instance, of a language with which we are well, and a language with which we are imperfectly, acquainted. In speaking our own language, we are not conscious of any effort; the associations between the words and the ideas appear spontaneous. In endeavouring to speak a language with which we are imperfectly acquainted, we are sensible of a painful effort: the associations between the words and ideas being not ready, or immediate.

7. The causes of strength in association seem all to be resolvable into two; the vividness of the associated feelings; and the frequency of the association.

In general, we convey not a very precise meaning, when we speak of the vividness of sensations and ideas. We may be understood when we say that, generally speaking, the sensation is more vivid than the idea; or the primary, than the secondary feeling; though in dreams, and in delirium, ideas are mistaken for sensations. But when we say that one sensation is more vivid than another, there is much more uncertainty. We can distinguish those sensations which are pleasurable, and those which are painful, from such as are not so; and when we call the pleasurable and painful more vivid, than those which are not so, we speak intelligibly. We can also distinguish degrees of pleasure, and of pain; and when we call the sensation of the higher degree more vivid than the sensation of the lower degree, we may again be considered as expressing a meaning tolerably precise.

In calling one IDEA more vivid than another, if we confine the appellation to the ideas of such SENSATIONS as may with precision be called more or less vivid; the sensations of pleasure and pain, in their various degrees, compared with sensations which we do not call either pleasurable or painful; our language will still have a certain degree of precision. But what is the meaning which I annex to my words, when I say, that my idea of the taste of the pine-apple which I tasted yesterday is vivid; my idea of the taste of the foreign fruit which I never tasted but once in early life, is not vivid? If I mean that I can more certainly distinguish the more recent, than the more distant sensation, there is still some precision in my language; because it seems true of all my senses, that if I compare a distant sensation with the present, I am less sure of its being or not being a repetition of the same, than if I compare a recent sensation with a present one. Thus, if I yesterday had a smell of a very peculiar kind, and compare it with a present smell, I can judge more accurately of the agreement or disagreement of the two sensations, than if I compared the present with one much more remote. The same is the case with colours, with sounds, with feelings of touch, and of resistance. It is therefore sufficiently certain, that the idea of the more recent sensation affords the means of a more accurate comparison, generally, than the idea of the more remote sensation. And thus we have three cases of vividness, of which we can speak with some precision: the case of sensations, as compared with ideas; the case of pleasurable and painful sensations, and their ideas as compared with those which are not pleasurable or painful; and the case of the more recent, compared with the more remote.

That the association of two ideas, but for once, does, in some cases, give them a very strong connection, is within the sphere of every man's experience. The most remarkable cases are probably those of pain and pleasure. Some persons who have experienced a very painful surgical operation, can never afterwards bear the sight of the operator, however strong the gratitude which they may actually feel towards him. . . .

So much with regard to vividness, as a cause of strong associations. Next, we have to consider frequency or repetition; which is the most remarkable and important cause of the strength of our associations.

Of any two sensations, frequently perceived together, the ideas are associated. Thus, at least, in the minds of Englishmen, the idea of a soldier, and the idea of a red coat are associated; the idea of a clergyman, and the idea of a black coat; the idea of a quaker, and of a broad-brimmed hat; the idea of a woman and the idea of petticoats. A peculiar taste suggests the idea of an apple; a peculiar smell the idea of a rose. If I have heard a particular air frequently sung by a particular person, the hearing of the air suggests the idea of the person.

The most remarkable exemplification of the effect of degrees of frequency, in producing degrees of strength in the associations, is to be found in the cases in which the association is purposely and studiously contracted; the cases in which we learn something; the use of words, for example. . . .

Learning to play on a musical instrument is another remarkable illustration of the effect of repetition in strengthening associations, in rendering those sequences, which, at first, are slow, and difficult, afterwards, rapid and easy. At first, the learner, after thinking of each successive note, as it stands in his book, has each time to look out with care for the key or the string which he is to touch, and the finger he is to touch it with, and is every moment committing mistakes. Repetition is well known to be the only means of overcoming these difficulties. As the repetition goes on, the sight of the note, or even the idea of the note, becomes associated with the place of the key or the string; and that of the key or the string with the proper finger. The association for a time is imperfect, but at last becomes so strong, that it is performed with the greatest rapidity, without an effort, and almost without consciousness.

8. Where two or more ideas have been often repeated together, and the association has become very strong, they sometimes spring up in such close combination as not to be distinguishable. Some cases of sensation are analogous. For example; when a wheel, on the seven parts of which the seven prismatic colours are respectively painted, is made to revolve rapidly, it appears not of seven colours, but of one uniform colour, white. By the rapidity of the succession, the several sensations cease to be distinguishable; they run, as it were, together, and a new sensation, compounded of all the seven, but apparently a simple one, is the result. Ideas, also, which have been so often conjoined, that whenever one exists in the mind, the others immediately exist along with it, seem to run into one another, to coalesce, as it were, and out of many to form one idea; which idea, however in reality complex, appears to be no less simple, than any one of those of which it is compounded. . . .

11. Mr. Hume, and after him other philosophers, have said that our ideas are associated according to three principles; Contiguity in time and place, Causation, and Resemblance. The Contiguity in time and place, must mean, that of the sensations; and so far it is affirmed, that the order of the ideas follows that of the sensations. Contiguity of two sensations in time, means the successive order. Contiguity of two sensations in place, means the synchronous order. We have explained the mode in

which ideas are associated, in the synchronous, as well as the successive order, and have traced the principle of contiguity to its proper source.

Causation, the second of Mr. Hume's principles, is the same with contiguity in time, or the order of succession. Causation is only a name for the order established between an antecedent and a consequent; that is, the established or constant antecedence of the one, and consequence of the other. Resemblance only remains, as an alleged principle of association, and it is necessary to inquire whether it is included in the laws which have been above expounded. I believe it will be found that we are accustomed to see like things together. When we see a tree, we generally see more trees than one; when we see an ox, we generally see more oxen than one; a sheep, more sheep than one; a man, more men than one. From this observation, I think, we may refer resemblance to the law of frequency, of which it seems to form only a particular case.

Mr. Hume makes contrast a principle of association, but not a separate one, as he thinks it is compounded of Resemblance and Causation. It is not necessary for us to show that this is an unsatisfactory account of contrast. It is only necessary to observe, that, as a case of association, it is not distinct from those which we have above explained.

A dwarf suggests the idea of a giant. How? We call a dwarf a dwarf, because he departs from a certain standard. We call a giant a giant, because he departs from the same standard. This is a case, therefore, of resemblance, that is, of frequency.

Pain is said to make us think of pleasure; and this is considered a case of association by contrast. There is no doubt that pain makes us think of relief from it; because they have been conjoined, and the great vividness of the sensations makes the association strong. Relief from pain is a species of pleasure; and one pleasure leads to think of another, from the resemblance. This is a compound case, therefore, of vividness and frequency. All other cases of contrast, I believe, may be expounded in a similar manner.

I have not thought it necessary to be tedious in expounding the observations which I have thus stated; for whether the reader supposes that resemblance is, or is not, an original principle of association, will not affect our future investigations.

12. Not only do simple ideas, by strong association, run together, and form complex ideas: but a complex idea, when the simple ideas which compose it have become so consolidated that it always appears as one, is capable of entering into combinations with other ideas, both simple and complex. Thus two complex ideas may be united together, by a

strong association, and coalesce into one, in the same manner as two or more simple ideas coalesce into one. This union of two complex ideas into one, Dr. Hartley has called a duplex idea. Two also of these duplex, or doubly compounded ideas, may unite into one; and these again into other compounds, without end. It is hardly necessary to mention, that as two complex ideas unite to form a duplex one, not only two, but more than two may so unite; and what he calls a duplex idea may be compounded of two, three, four, or any number of complex ideas.

Some of the most familiar objects with which we are acquainted furnish instances of these unions of complex and duplex ideas.

Brick is one complex idea, mortar is another complex idea; these ideas, with ideas of position and quantity, compose my idea of a wall. My idea of a plank is a complex idea, my idea of a rafter is a complex idea, my idea of a nail is a complex idea.

These, united with the same ideas of position and quantity, compose my duplex idea of a floor. In the same manner my complex idea of glass, and wood, and others, compose my duplex idea of a window; and these duplex ideas, united together, compose my idea of a house, which is made up of various duplex ideas. How many complex, or duplex ideas, are all united in the idea of furniture? How many more in the idea of merchandise? How many more in the idea called Every Thing?[1]

All association was reduced by James Mill to contiguity (togetherness) in time or place either expressed in synchronous association (the objects in a room) or in successive association (the words of a poem). But since ideas merely follow the order of sensations, even the law of contiguity reduces to his more fundamental condition of frequency, although vividness also plays a part in strength of association. Moreover, no matter how complex the ideas, the process is the same, even when, as the last sentence suggests "the idea [is that] called Every Thing." There is no need for any unification or organization of the total idea. Mind is a passive process; mind has no creative function; synthesis is unnecessary.

John Stuart Mill, however, emancipated himself from the atomistic associationism of his father, both in the notes appended to his father's work and in the following excerpt:

These simple or elementary Laws of Mind have been ascertained by the ordinary methods of experimental inquiry; nor could they have been ascertained in any other manner. But a certain number of elementary laws having thus been obtained, it is a fair subject of scientific inquiry how far those laws can be made to go in explaining the actual phenomena. It is obvious that complex laws of thought and feeling not only may, but must, be generated from these simple laws. And it is to be remarked, that the case is not always one of Composition of Causes: the effect of concurring causes is not always precisely the sum of the effects of those causes when separate, nor even always an effect of the same kind with them. Reverting to the distinction which occupies so prominent a place in the theory of induction, the laws of the phenomena of mind are sometimes analogous to mechanical, but sometimes also to chemical laws. When many impressions or ideas are operating in the mind together, there sometimes takes place a process of a similar kind to chemical combination. When impressions have been so often experienced in conjunction, that each of them calls up readily and instantaneously the ideas of the whole group, those ideas sometimes melt and coalesce into one another, and appear not several ideas, but one; in the same manner as, when the seven prismatic colors are presented to the eye in rapid succession, the sensation produced is that of white. But as in this last case it is correct to say that the seven colors when they rapidly follow one another *generate* white, but not that they actually *are* white; so it appears to me that the Complex Idea, formed by the blending together of several simpler ones, should, when it really appears simple (that is, when the separate elements are not consciously distinguishable in it), be said to *result from,* or *be generated by,* the simple ideas, not to *consist* of them. Our idea of an orange really *consists* of the simple ideas of a certain color, a certain form, a certain taste and smell, etc., because we can, by interrogating our consciousness, perceive all these elements in the idea. But we can not perceive, in so apparently simple a feeling as our perception of the shape of an object by the eye, all that multitude of ideas derived from other senses, without which it is well ascertained that no such visual perception would ever have had existence; nor, in our idea of Extension, can we discover those elementary ideas of resistance, derived from our muscular frame, in which it has been conclusively shown that the idea originates. These, therefore, are cases of mental chemistry; in which it is proper to say that the simple ideas generate, rather than that they compose, the complex ones.

With respect to all the other constituents of the mind, its beliefs, its abstruser conceptions, its sentiments, emotions, and volitions, there are some (among whom are Hartley and the author of the *Analysis*) who think that the whole of these are generated from simple ideas of sensation, by a chemistry similar to that which we have just exemplified. These philosophers have made out a great part of their case, but I am not satisfied that they have established the whole of it.[2]

The combination of mental elements in their interactive effects gives rise to something new in the experience, not present in the original elements.

The various so-called causes of variation in the strength, for example, frequency of associations, were to be submitted to experimental scrutiny only during a later period in psychology (see pages 142, 255, 382).

12

KANT ON
THE NATIVISTIC,
ACTIVE STRUCTURING OF EXPERIENCE,
AND THE IMPOSSIBILITY
OF A SCIENCE OF PSYCHOLOGY

IMMANUEL KANT (1724–1804), German philosopher, was the most influential of all thinkers in his field for the period from the last decades of the eighteenth century through several decades of the nineteenth century. He saw his task as that of critically analyzing the philosophy of the past, which led him to call his system the "critical philosophy." The task of philosophers who came after him was to adopt, oppose, or reinterpret Kant: they could not ignore him. In part, this was because of the sheer breadth of his views, touching as they do on almost all issues of philosophy. In short compass, we will deal only with those two or three issues most pertinent to psychology. From the perspective of present interests, he offers a systematic inventory of the powers and contents of the human mind with a view of achieving theoretical certainty. He took a stand on empiricism that was both original and disconcerting.

That all our knowledge begins with experience there can be no doubt. For how is it possible that the faculty of cognition should be awakened into exercise otherwise than by means of objects which affect our senses, and partly of themselves produce representations, partly rouse our powers of understanding into activity, to compare, to connect, or to separate these, and so to convert the raw material of our sensuous impressions into a knowledge of objects, which is called experience? In respect of time, therefore, no knowledge of ours is antecedent to experience, but begins with it.

But, though all our knowledge begins with experience, it by no means follows that all arises out of experience. For, on the contrary, it is quite possible that our empirical knowledge is a compound of that which we receive through impressions, and that which the faculty of cognition supplies from itself (sensuous impressions giving merely the *occasion*), an addition which we cannot distinguish from the original element given by sense, till long practice has made us attentive to, and skillful in separating it. It is, therefore, a question which requires close investigation, and not to be answered at first sight, whether there exists a knowledge altogether independent of experience, and even of all sensuous impressions? Knowledge of this kind is called *a priori,* in centradistinction to empirical knowledge, which has its sources *a posteriori,* that is, in experience.

But the expression, *"a priori,"* is not as yet definite enough adequately to indicate the whole meaning of the question above started. For, in speaking of knowledge which has its sources in experience, we are wont to say, that this or that may be known *a priori,* because we do not derive this knowledge immediately from experience, but from a general rule, which, however, we have itself borrowed from experience. Thus, if a man undermined his house, we say, "he might know *a priori* that it would have fallen"; that is, he needed not to have waited for the experience that it did actually fall. But still, *a priori,* he could not know even this much. For, that bodies are heavy, and, consequently, that they fall when their supports are taken away, must have been known to him previously, by means of experience.

By the term "knowledge *a priori,*" therefore, we shall in the sequel understand, not such as is independent of this or that kind of experience, but such as is absolutely so of *all* experience. Opposed to this is empirical knowledge, or that which is possible only *a posteriori,* that is, through experience. Knowledge *a priori* is either pure or impure. Pure knowledge *a priori* is that with which no empirical element is mixed up. For example, the proposition, "Every change has a cause," is a proposition *a priori,* but impure, because change is a conception which can only be derived from experience.[1]

Implicitly, Kant was saying that he agreed with Locke and the other empiricists that all knowledge begins with experience, but added that it does not necessarily follow that all knowledge *arises* from experience. The mind itself supplies some of this knowledge, *a priori.* There were *a priori* elements in all experiences.

Now that he stated his general position, Kant proceeded to analyze space in these terms. In the next excerpt, the term "transcendental" refers to that which was not in experience but implied by experience, while "aesthetics" is used, not for beauty or related concepts, but for knowledge that is immediate and based on sensory experience.

In whatsoever mode, or by whatsoever means, our knowledge may relate to objects, it is at least quite clear that the only manner in which it immediately relates to them is by means of an intuition. To this as the indispensable groundwork, all thought points. But an intuition can take place only in so far as the object is given to us. This, again, is only possible, to man at least, on condition that the object affect the mind in a certain manner. The capacity for receiving representations (receptivity) through the mode in which we are affected by objects, is called *sensibility*. By means of sensibility, therefore, objects are given to us, and it alone furnishes us with intuitions; by the understanding they are *thought,* and from it arise conceptions. But all thought must directly, or indirectly, by means of certain signs, relate ultimately to intuitions; consequently, with us, to sensibility, because in no other way can an object be given to us.

The effect of an object upon the faculty of representation, so far as we are affected by the said object, is sensation. That sort of intuition which relates to an object by means of sensation is called an empirical intuition. The undetermined object of an empirical intuition is called *phenomenon.* That which in the phenomenon corresponds to the sensation, I term its *matter*; but that which effects that the content of the phenomenon can be arranged under certain relations, I call its *form.* But that in which our sensations are merely arranged, and by which they are susceptible of assuming a certain form, cannot be itself sensation. It is, then, the matter of all phenomena that is given to us *a posteriori*; the form must lie ready *a priori* for them in the mind, and consequently can be regarded separately from all sensation.

I call all representations *pure,* in the transcendental meaning of the word, wherein nothing is met with that belongs to sensation. And accordingly we find existing in the mind *a priori,* the pure form of sensuous intuitions in general, in which all the manifold content of the phenomenal world is arranged and viewed under certain relations. This pure form of sensibility I shall call *pure intuition.* Thus, if I take away from our representation of a body all that the understanding thinks as belonging to it, as substance, force, divisibility, etc., and also whatever belongs to sensation, as impenetrability, hardness, colour, etc.; yet there is still something left us from this empirical intuition, namely, extension and shape. These belong to pure intuition, which exists *a priori* in the mind, as a mere form of sensibility, and without any real object of the senses or any sensation.

The science of all the principles of sensibility *a priori,* I call *transcendental aesthetic.* There must, then, be such a science forming the first part of the transcendental doctrine of elements, in contradistinction to that part which contains the principles of pure thought, and which is called *transcendental logic*.

In the science of transcendental aesthetic accordingly, we shall first isolate sensibility or the sensuous faculty, by separating from it all that is annexed to its perceptions by the conceptions of understanding, so that nothing be left but empirical intuition. In the next place we shall take away from this intuition all that belongs to sensation, so that nothing may remain but pure intuition, and the mere form of phenomena, which is all that the sensibility can afford *a priori*. From this investigation it will be found that there are two pure forms of sensuous intuition, as principles of knowledge *a priori*, namely, space and time. To the consideration of these we shall now proceed.

SECTION I. OF SPACE

2. *Metaphysical Exposition of this Conception*

By means of the external sense (a property of the mind), we represent to ourselves objects as without us, and these all in space. Therein alone are their shape, dimensions, and relations to each other determined or determinable. The internal sense, by means of which the mind contemplates itself or its internal state, gives, indeed, no intuition of the soul as an object; yet there is nevertheless a determinate form, under which alone the contemplation of our internal state is possible, so that all which relates to the inward determinations of the mind is represented in relations of time. Of time we cannot have any external intuition, any more than we can have an internal intuition of space. What then are time and space? Are they real existences? Or, are they merely relations or determinations of things, such, however, as would equally belong to these things in themselves, though they should never become objects of intuition; or, are they such as belong only to the form of intuition, and consequently to the subjective constitution of the mind, without which these predicates of time and space could not be attached to any object? In order to become informed on these points, we shall first give an exposition of the conception of space. By exposition, I mean the clear, though not detailed, representation of that which belongs to a conception; and an exposition is metaphysical when it contains that which represents the conception as given *a priori*.

1.   Space is not a conception which has been derived from outward experiences. For, in order that certain sensations may relate to something without me (that is, to something which occupies a different part of space from that in which I am); in like manner, in order that I may

present them not merely as without, of, or near to each other, but also in separate places, the representation of space must already exist as a foundation. Consequently, the representation of space cannot be borrowed from the relations of external phenomena through experience; but, on the contrary, this external experience is itself only possible through the said antecedent representation.

2.   Space is a necessary representation *a priori,* which serves for the foundation of all external intuitions. We never can imagine or make a representation to ourselves of the non-existence of space, though we may easily enough think that no objects are found in it. It must, therefore, be considered as the condition of the possibility of phenomena, and by no means as a determination dependent on them, and is a representation *a priori,* which necessarily supplies the basis for external phenomena.

3.   Space is no discursive, or as we say, general conception of the relations of things, but a pure intuition. For, in the first place, we can only represent to ourselves one space, and, when we talk of divers spaces, we mean only parts of one and the same space. Moreover, these parts cannot antecede this one all-embracing space, as the component parts from which the aggregrate can be made up, but can be cogitated only as existing in it. Space is essentially one, and multiplicity in it, consequently the general notion of spaces, of this or that space, depends solely upon limitations. Hence it follows that an *a priori* intuition (which is not empirical) lies at the root of all our conceptions of space. Thus, moreover, the principles of geometry—for example, that "in a triangle, two sides together are greater than the third," are never deduced from general conceptions of line and triangle, but from intuition, and this is *a priori,* with apodeictic certainty.

4.   Space is represented as an infinite given quantity. Now every conception must indeed be considered as a representation which is contained in an infinite multitude of different possible representations. Which, therefore, comprises these under itself; but no conception, as such, can be so conceived, as if it contained within itself an infinite multitude of representations. Nevertheless, space is so conceived of, for all parts of space are equally capable of being produced to infinity. Consequently, the original representation of space is an intuition *a priori,* and not a conception.

3. *Transcendental Exposition of the Conception of Space*

By a transcendental exposition, I mean the explanation of a conception, as a principle, whence can be discerned the possibility of other synthetical *a priori* cognitions. For this purpose, it is requisite, firstly, that such cognitions do really flow from the given conception; and, secondly, that the said cognitions are only possible under the presupposition of a given mode of explaining this conception.

Geometry is a science which determines the properties of space synthetically, and yet *a priori*. What, then, must be our representation of space, in order that such a cognition of it may be possible? It must be originally intuition, for from a mere conception, no propositions can be deduced which go out beyond the conception, and yet this happens in geometry. (Introd. V.) But this intuition must be found in the mind *a priori*, that is, before any perception of objects, consequently must be pure, not empirical, intuition. For geometrical principles are always apodeictic, that is, united with the consciousness of their necessity, as: "Space has only three dimensions." But propositions of this kind cannot be empirical judgments, nor conclusions from them. (Introd. II.) Now, how can an external intuition anterior to objects themselves, and in which our conception of objects can be determined *a priori*, exist in the human mind? Obviously not otherwise than in so far as it has its seat in the subject only, as the *formal* capacity of the subject's being affected by objects, and thereby of obtaining immediate representation, that is, intuition; consequently, only as the *form of the external sense* in general.

Thus it is only by means of our explanation that the possibility of geometry, as a synthetical science *a priori,* becomes comprehensible. Every mode of explanation which does not show us this possibility, although in appearance it may be similar to ours, can with the utmost certainty be distinguished from it by these marks.

4. *Conclusions from the foregoing Conceptions*

(a) Space does not represent any property of objects as things in themselves, nor does it represent them in their relations to each other; in other words, space does not represent to us any determination of objects such as attaches to the objects themselves, and would remain, even though all subjective conditions of the intuition were abstracted. For neither absolute nor relative determinations of objects can be intuited prior to the existence of the things to which they belong, and therefore no *a priori*.

(b) Space is nothing else than the form of all phenomena of the external sense, that is, the subjective condition of the sensibility, under which alone external intuition is possible. Now, because the receptivity or capacity of the subject to be affected by objects necessarily antecedes all intuitions of these objects, it is easily understood how the form of all phenomena can be given in the mind previous to all actual perceptions, therefore *a priori,* and how it, as a pure intuition, in which all objects must be determined, can contain principles of the relations of these objects prior to all experience.

It is therefore from the human point of view only that we can speak of space, extended objects, etc. If we depart from the subjective condition, under which alone we can obtain external intuition, or, in other words, by means of which we are affected by objects, the representation of space has no meaning whatsoever. This predicate is only applicable to things in so far as they appear to us, that is, are objects of sensibility. The constant form of this receptivity, which we call sensibility, is a necessary condition of all relations in which objects can be intuited as existing without us, and when abstraction of these objects is made, is a pure intuition, to which we give the name of space. It is clear that we cannot make the special conditions of sensibility into conditions of the possibility of things, but only of the possibility of their existence as far as they are phenomena. And so we may correctly say that space contains all which can appear to us externally, but not all things considered as things in themselves, be they intuited or not, or by whatsoever subject one will. As to the intuitions of other thinking beings, we cannot judge whether they are or are not bound by the same conditions which jimit our own intuition, and which for us are universally valid. If we join the limitation of a judgment to the conception of the subject, then the judgement will possess unconditioned validity. For example, the proposition, "All objects are beside each other in space," is valid only under the limitation that these things are taken as objects of our sensuous intuition. But if I join the condition to the conception and say, "All things, as external phenomena, are beside each other in space," then the rule is valid universally, and without any limitation. Our expositions, consequently, teach the *reality* (i.e., the objective validity) of space in regard of all which can be presented to us externally as object, and at the same time also the *ideality* of space in regard to objects when they are considered by means of reason as things in themselves, that is, without reference to the constitution of our sensibility. We maintain, therefore, the *empirical reality* of space in regard to all possible external experience, although we must admit its *transcendental ideality*; in other words, that it is nothing, so soon as we withdraw the condition upon which the possibility of all experience depends and look upon space as something that belongs to things in themselves.[2]

He followed with a parallel discussion of time, again arguing that just as with space, time does not inhere in reality but is a subjective pattern of pure perception. Primary qualities were again reduced to subjective phenomena. Thus, he provides the basis for nativistic psychological theories of perception or modifications thereof, such as those found in modern Gestalt theory (p. 305).

He was not advocating Cartesian innate ideas, but, rather, the view that the individual is born with the active ability to order the experience of space. He was also opposing the view of the British empiricists, particularly Hume and Hartley, that the mind is composed of elements mechanically linked together by the process of association. To Kant, the mind actively organizes the raw data of experience.

Kant saw part of his task as providing an alternative to Hume's conclusions that causality was neither self-evident nor capable of logical demonstration and that neither self identity nor physical objects could be demonstrated to exist. His solution was to demonstrate independent *a priori* rational principles that, once established, would make it possible to arrive inductively at general laws that Hume had argued was impossible.

This was done in a discussion of the implicit principles that underlie experience, the "categories." Too long and detailed to make excerpting possible, a summary will have to suffice. The categories are universal, necessary, and independent of sense experience and include unity, reality, totality and, most relevant to present discussion, causality. While causality is not impirically derivable as Hume had argued, it can be demonstrated on *a priori* principles.

In view of the tremendous influence of his views, both during the age in which he lived and for years thereafter, it is important to isolate what he thought about the possibility of a science of psychology. He did this in a setting which simultaneously posed the same question for chemistry, that, at time of writing (1786), was only at its beginnings, resembling more a collection of recipes useful in practical work than it did the science that it was to become.

But the empirical doctrine of the soul must always remain yet even further removed than chemistry from the rank of what may be called a natural science proper. This is because mathematics is inapplicable to the phenomena of the internal sense and their laws, unless one might want to take into consideration merely the law of continuity in the flow of this sense's internal changes. But the extension of cognition so attained would bear much the same relation to the extension of cognition which mathematics provides for the doctrine of body, as the doctrine of the properties of the straight line bears to the whole of geometry. The reason for the limitation on this extension of cognition lies in the fact that the pure internal intuition in which the soul's phenomena are to be constructed is time, which has only one dimension. But not even as a systematic art of analysis or as an experimental doctrine can the empirical doctrine of the soul ever approach chemistry, because in it the manifold of internal observation is separated only by mere thought, but cannot be kept separate and be connected again at will; still less does another thinking subject submit to our investigations in such a way as to be conformable to our purposes, and even the observation itself alters and distorts the state of the object observed. It can, therefore, never become anything more than a historical (and as such, as much as possible) systematic natural doctrine of the internal sense, i.e., a natural description of the soul, but not a science of the soul, nor even a psychological experimental doctrine.[3]

Psychology, he was saying, lacked a mathematical base that is essential for all sciences. While it has the dimension of time, it has no spatial dimension, since mind is not spatial. And experiment is not possible without both dimensions. While still a part of philosophy, psychology could not hope to be a separate science. In denying the possibility of the experiments and the use of mathematics in the study of the mind, Kant's pronouncement effectively helped to delay the appearance of psychology as an experimental science.

13

HERBART ON

IDEAS AS FORCES,
THE THRESHOLD OF CONSCIOUSNESS,
THE ESSENTIAL NATURE OF MATHEMATICS,
AND THE SIGNIFICANCE OF APPERCEPTION

JOHANN FRIEDRICH HERBART (1776–1841), German philosopher, was led by his metaphysical assumptions to regard the philosophy of mind as the mechanics of the mind. Emerging from this analogy was the view that concepts, that is, actions or ideas as we would call them, are forces, that there is a threshold, at which level ideas appear in consciousness, and that the study of mind necessitates mathematical treatment.

Many of his most important contributions to psychological thinking were given preliminary discussion in the opening chapters of his *Textbook of Psychology,* first published in 1816:

10. Concepts become forces when they resist one another. This resistance occurs when two or more opposed concepts encounter one another.

At first let us take this proposition as simply as possible. In this connection, therefore, we shall not think of complex nor of compound concepts of any kind whatever; nor of such as indicate an object with several characteristics, neither of anything in time nor space, but of entirely simple concepts or sensations—e.g., red, blue, sour, sweet, etc. It is not our purpose to consider the general notions of the above-mentioned sensations, but to consider such representations as may result from an instantaneous act of sense-perception.

Again, the question concerning the origin of the sensations mentioned does not belong here, much less has the discussion to do with the consideration of anything else that might have previously existed or occurred in the soul.

The proposition as it stands is that opposed concepts resist one another. Concepts that are not opposed—e.g., a tone and a color—may exist, in which case it will be assumed that such concepts offer no resistance to one another. (Exceptions to this latter proposition may occur, of which more hereafter.)

Resistance is an expression of force. To the resisting concept, however, its action is quite accidental; it adjusts itself to the attack which is mutual among concepts, and which is determined by the degree of opposition existing between them. This opposition may be regarded as that by which they are affected collectively. In themselves, however, concepts are not forces.

11. Now, what is the result of the resistance mentioned?

Do concepts partially or wholly destroy one another, or not withstanding the resistance, do they remain unchanged?

Destroyed concepts are the same as none at all. However, if notwithstanding the mutual attack, concepts remain unchanged, then one could not be removed or suppressed by another (as we see every moment that they are). Finally, if all that is conceived of each concept were changed by the contest, then this would signify nothing more than, at the beginning, quite another concept had been present in consciousness.

The presentation (concept), then, must yield without being destroyed—i.e., the real concept is changed into an effort to present itself.

Here it is in effect stated that, as soon as the hindrance yields, the concept by its own effort will again make its appearance in consciousness. In this lies the possibility (although not for all cases the only ground) of reproduction.

12. When a concept becomes not entirely, but only in part, transformed into an effort, we must guard against considering this part as a severed portion of the whole concept. It has certainly a definite magnitude (upon the knowledge of which much depends), but this magnitude indicates only a degree of the obscuration of the whole concept. If the question be in regard to several parts of one and the same concept, these parts must not be regarded as different, severed portions, but the smaller divisions may be regarded as being contained in the larger. The same is true of the remainders after the collisions—i.e., of those parts of a concept which remain unobscured, for those parts are also degrees of the real concept.

13. When a sufficiency of opposition exists between concepts, the latter are in equilibrium. They come only gradually to this point. The continuous change of their degree of obscuration may be called their movement.

The statics and mechanics of the mind have to do with the calculation of the equilibrium and movement of the concepts.

14. All investigations into the statics of the mind begin with two different quantitative factors, viz., the sum (or the aggregate amount) of the resistances and the ratio of their limitation. The former is the quantity which rises from their encounter, to be divided between the opposing concepts. If one knows how to state it, and knows also the ratio in which the different concepts yield in the encounter, then, by a simple calculation in proportion, the statical point of each concept—i.e., the degree of its obscuration in equilibrium—may be found.

15. The sum as well as the ratio of the mutual limitation depends upon the strength of each individual concept which is affected in inverse ratio to its strength, and upon the degree of opposition between the two concepts. For their influence upon each other stands in direct ratio to the strength of each.

The principle determining the sum of the mutual limitation is, that it shall be considered as small as possible, because all concepts strive against suppression, and certainly submit to no more of it than is absolutely necessary.

16. By actual calculation, the remarkable result is obtained that, in the case of the two concepts, the one never entirely obscures the other, but, in the case of three or more, one is very easily obscured, and can be made as ineffective—notwithstanding its continuous struggle—as if it were not present at all. Indeed, this obscuration may happen to a large number of concepts as well as to one, and may be effected through the agency of two, and even through the combined influence of concepts less strong than those which are suppressed.

Here the expression "threshold of consciousness" must be explained, as we shall have occasion to use it. A concept is in consciousness in so far as it is not suppressed, but is an actual representation. When it rises out of a condition of complete suppression, it enters into consciousness. Here, then, it is on the threshold of consciousness. It is very important to determine by calculation the degree of strength which a concept must attain in order to be able to stand beside two or more stronger ones exactly on the threshold of consciousness, so that, at the slightest yielding of the hindrance, it would begin to rise into consciousness. . . .

17. Among the many, and, for the most part, very complicated laws underlying the movement of concepts, the following is the simplest:

While the arrested portion (*Hemmungssumme*) of the concept sinks, the sinking part is at every moment proportional to the part unsuppressed.

By this it is possible to calculate the whole course of the sinking even to the statical point.

NOTE.—Mathematically, the above law may be expressed: $\sigma = S_{(1-e^{-t})}$ in which S= the aggregate amount suppressed, $t =$ the time elapsed during the encounter, $\sigma =$ the suppressed portion of all the concepts in the time indicated by t.

As the latter quantity is apportioned among the individual concepts, it is found that those which fall directly beneath the statical threshold (16) are very quickly driven thence, while the rest do not reach exactly their statical point in any given finite time. On account of this latter circumstance, the concepts in the mind of a man of most equable temperament are, while he is awake, always in a state of gentle motion. This is also the primary reason why the inner perception never meets an object which holds it quite motionless.

18. When to several concepts already near equilibrium a new one comes, a movement arises which causes them to sink for a short time beneath their statical point, after which they quickly and entirely of themselves rise again—something as a liquid, when an object is thrown into it, first sinks and then rises. In this connection several remarkable circumstances occur:

19. First, upon an occasion of this kind, one of the older concepts may be removed entirely out of consciousness even by a new concept that is much weaker than itself. In this case, however, the striving of the suppressed concept is not to be considered wholly ineffective, as shown above (see 16); it works with all its force against the concepts in consciousness. Although its object is not conceived, it produces a certain condition of consciousness. The way in which these concepts are removed out of consciousness and yet are effective therein may be indicated by the expression, "They are on the mechanical threshold." The threshold mentioned above (16) is called for the sake of distinction the statical threshold.

20. Second, the time during which one or more concepts linger upon the mechanical threshold can be extended if a series of new, although weaker, concepts come in succession to them.

Every employment to which we are unaccustomed puts us in this condition. The earlier concepts are pressed back of the later ones. The former, however, because they are the stronger, remain tense, affect the physical organism more and more, and finally make it necessary that the employment cease, when the old concepts immediately rise, and we experience what is called a feeling of relief which depends in part upon the physical organism, although the first cause is purely psychological.

21. Third, when several concepts are driven in succession to the mechanical threshold, several sudden successive changes in the laws of reciprocal movements arise.

In this way is to be explained the fact that the course of our thoughts is so often inconsequent, abrupt, and apparently irregular. This appearance deceives in the same way as the wandering of the planets. The conformity to law in the human mind resembles exactly that in the firmament. . . .

22. The easily conceivable metaphysical reason why opposed concepts resist one another is the *unity of the soul, of which they are the self-preservations*. This reason explains without difficulty the combination of our concepts (which combination is known to exist). If, on account of their opposition, they did not suppress one another, all concepts would compose but one act of one soul; and, indeed, in so far as they are not divided into a manifold by any kind of arrests whatever, they really constitute but one act. Concepts that are on the threshold of consciousness can not enter into combination with others, as they are completely transformed into effort directed against other definite concepts, and are thereby, as it were, isolated. In consciousness, however, concepts combine in two ways: First, concepts which are not opposed or contrasted with one another (as a tone and a color) so *far as they meet unhindered, form a complex*; second, *contrasted concepts* [e.g., red and yellow], in so far as they are effected neither by accidental foreign concepts nor by unavoidable opposition, become blended *(fused)*.

Complexes may be complete; blendings (fusions) from their nature must always be (more or less) incomplete.

NOTE.—Of such complexes as are partially or almost complete, we have remarkable instances in the concepts of things with several characteristics and of words used as signs of thoughts. In the mother-tongue the latter, words and thoughts, are so closely connected that it would appear that we think by means of words. (Concerning both examples more hereafter.) Among the blendings are especially remarkable, partly those which include in themselves an aesthetic relation (which, taken psychologically, is created at the same time with the blending), partly those which involve succession, in which serial forms have their origin.

23. That which is complicated or blended out of several concepts furnishes an aggregate of force, and for this reason works according to quite other statical and mechanical laws than those according to which

the individual concepts would have acted. Also the thresholds of consciousness change according to the complex or blending (fusion), so that on account of a combination a concept of the very weakest kind may be able to remain and exert an influence in consciousness.[1]

With the very first sentence of this excerpt, a distinctive and important addition is being made to the earlier, rather passive British associationism. Concepts (ideas) are forces that resist one another. Herbart also considers attraction of ideas and ideas that neither resist nor attract. Ideas may be suppressed. Ideas, once in consciousness, may no longer be available, but by shifts in the patterns of ideas, return to consciousness. This return to consciousness results in introducing the concept of a threshold to conscious experience which he expresses in the formula in the excerpt (p. 92). However, there are many others throughout the rest of the work. It is important to realize that these formulas, while mathematical, were not made quantitative by use of actual data. They were expressions of the way Herbart *thought* the factors considered would relate to one another. Nevertheless, Herbart was insisting that mathematics is essential to the science of psychology in the face of the very formidable and contrary position of Kant (p. 87).

Early in life, he had been influenced by the teachings of Johann Pestalozzi, a prominent Swiss educator of the late eighteenth century. They became one of the themes of his thinking. Most noteworthy was his promulgation of the concept of apperceptive mass.

39. From the foregoing, it may, in a way, be perceived that after a considerable number of concepts in all kinds of combinations is present, every new act of perception must work as an excitant by which some will be arrested, others called forward and strengthened, progressing series interrupted or set again in motion, and this or that mental state occasioned. These manifestations must become more complex if, as is usual, the concept received by the new act of perception contains in itself a multiplicity or variety, that at the same time enables it to hold its place in several combinations and series, and gives them a fresh impulse which brings them into new relations of opposition or blending with one another. By this, the concepts brought by the new act of perception are assimilated to the older concepts in such a way as to suffer somewhat after the first excitation has worked to the extent of its power, because the old concepts—on account of their combinations with one another—are much stronger than the new individuals which are added.

40. If, however, already very strong complexes and blendings with many members have been formed, then the same relation which existed between the old and the new concepts may be repeated within between

the old concepts. Weaker concepts, which, according to any kind of law, enter into consciousness, act as excitants upon those masses before mentioned, and are received and appropriated by them (apperceived) just as in the case of a new sense-impression; hence *the inner perception* is analogous to the outer. Self-consciousness is not the subject of discussion here, although it is very often combined with the above.

41. In what has been said, lies that which experience confirms, viz., that the inner perception is never a passive apprehension, but always (even against the will) active. The apperceived concepts do not continue rising or sinking according to their own laws, but they are interrupted in their movements by the more powerful masses which drive back whatever is opposed to them although it is inclined to rise; and in the case of that which is similar to them although it is on the point of sinking, they take hold of it and blend it with themselves.

42. It is worth the trouble to indicate how far this difference among concepts—which we might be inclined to divide into dead and living—may be carried.

Let us recall the concepts on the statical threshold (16). These are, indeed, in effect nothing less than dead; for, in the condition of arrest in which they stand, they are not able by their own effort to effect anything whatever [toward rising into consciousness]. Nevertheless, through the combination in which they stand, they may be reproduced, and, besides, they will often be driven back in whole heaps and series by those more powerful masses, as when the leaves of a book are turned hurriedly.

43. If the apperceived concepts—or at least some of them—are not on the statical threshold, then the apperceiving concepts suffer some violence from them; also the latter may be subject to arrest from another side, in which case the inner perception is interrupted; through this, uncertainty and irresolution may be explained.[2]

He is saying that information is acquired most easily when it is introduced through articulation within an already familiar pattern of ideas. Lesson planning on this basis has become a standard educational practice to this very day.

Turning to his overall significance, despite the lack of actual measurement, his endorsement of mathematics applied to psychological problems did serve as an object lesson to later model builders and, more specifically, encouraged Fechner in his combination of mathematics and experience (p. 107).

14

MÜLLER ON
VITALISM AND
THE SPECIFIC ENERGY OF NERVES

JOHANNES MÜLLER (1801–1858), German physiologist, was one of its founders as a modern, independent field of science in the sense that he was appointed to the first professorship of physiology in 1833 at the University of Berlin. Between 1834 and 1840, he labored over his monumental *Handbuch der Physiologie des Menschen für Vorlesungen* which systematized the field. In the early nineteenth century, physiological processes were no longer conceived as demanding that there be an immaterial soul directing bodily processes. But it was still possible to argue, as did Müller, that properties of living things require a life force. The excerpt that follows had been preceded by a contrary statement, advanced by Reil, who argued that physical factors are sufficient to account for life's composition and form.

Reil refers organic phenomena to original difference in the composition and form of organic bodies. Differences in composition and form are, according to his theory, the cause of all the variety in organised bodies, and in their endowments. But if these two principles be admitted, still the problem remains unsolved; it may still be asked, how the elementary combination acquired its form, and how the form acquired its elementary combination. Into the composition of the organic matter of the living body there must enter an unknown (according to Reil's theory, subtile material) principle, or the organic matter must retain its properties by the operation of some unknown forces. Whether this principle is to be regarded as an imponderable matter, or as a force or energy, is just as uncertain as the same question is in reference to several important phenomena in physics; physiology in this case is not behind the other natural scienes, for the properties of this principle, as displayed in the functions of the nerves, are nearly as well known as those of light, caloric, and electricity, in physics. . . .

We have thus seen that organic bodies consist of matters which present a peculiar combination of their component elements—a combination of three, four, or more to form one compound, which is observed only in organic bodies, and in them only during life. Organised bodies moreover are constituted of organs,—that is, of essential members of one whole,—each member having a separate function, and each deriving its existence from the whole: and they not merely consist of these organs, but by virtue of an innate power they form them within themselves. Life, therefore, is not simply the result of the harmony and reciprocal action of these parts; but it is first manifested in a principle, or imponderable matter which is in action in the substance of the germ, enters into the composition of the matter of this germ, and imparts to organic combinations properties which cease at death.[1]

Müller's was almost the last major call for interpreting physiological mechanisms in terms of a life principle. Nevertheless, it is worth mentioning, because this doctrine of vitalism had held sway in most previous physiological thinking, but the mid-decades of the nineteenth century were to see a strong upsurge in the mechanistic point of view in physiology, epitomized in the work of Helmholtz (p. 114).

The major research contribution of Müller was in the area of the so-called specific energy of nerves—that the sensory quality experienced is primarily determined by its neural mechanisms once the sense organ is activated, no matter what the source of that stimulation.

The senses, by virtue of the peculiar properties of their several nerves, make us acquainted with the states of our own body, and they also inform us of the qualities and changes of external nature, as far as these give rise to changes in the condition of the nerves. Sensation is a property common to all the senses; but the kind (*"modus,"*) of sensation is different in each: thus we have the sensations of light, of sound, of taste, of smell, and of feeling, or touch. By feeling, or touch, we understand the peculiar kind of sensation of which the ordinary sensitive nerves generally—as, the nervus trigeminus, vagus, glossopharyngeus, and the spinal nerves,—are susceptible; the sensations of itching, of pleasure and pain, of heat and cold, and those excited by the act of touch in its more limited sense, are varieties of this mode of sensation. That which through the medium of our senses is actually perceived by the sensorium, is indeed merely a property or change of condition of our nerves; but the imagination and reason are ready to interpret the modifications in the state of the nerves produced by external influences as properties of the external bodies themselves. This mode of regarding sensations has become so habitual in the case of the senses which are more rarely affected by internal causes, that it is only on reflection that we perceive it to be erroneous. In the case of the sense of feeling or touch, on the contrary, where the peculiar sensations of the nerves perceived by the sensorium are excited as frequently by internal as by external causes, it is easily conceived that the feeling of pain or pleasure, for example, is a condition of the nerves, and not a property of the things which excite it. This leads us to the consideration of some general laws, a knowledge of which is necessary before entering on the physiology of the separate senses.

    I. In the first place, it must be kept in mind that *external agencies can give rise to no kind of sensation which cannot also be produced by internal causes, exciting changes in the condition of our nerves.*

In the case of the sense of touch, this is at once evident. The sensations of the nerves of touch (or common sensibility) are those of cold and heat, pain and pleasure, and innumerable modifications of these, which are neither painful nor pleasurable, but yet have the same kind of sensation as their element, though not in an extreme degree. All these sensations are constantly being produced by internal causes in all parts of our body endowed with sensitive nerves; they may also be excited by causes acting from without, but external agencies are not capable of adding any new element to their nature. The sensations of the nerves of touch are therefore states or qualities proper to themselves, and merely rendered manifest by exciting causes external or internal. The sensation of smell also may be perceived independently of the application of any odorous substance from without, the nerve of smell being thrown by an internal cause into the condition requisite for the production of the sensation. This perception of the sensation of odours without an external exciting cause, though not of frequent occurrence, has been many times observed in persons of an irritable nervous system; and the sense of taste is probably subject to the same affection, although it would always be difficult to determine whether the taste might not be owing to a change in the qualities of the saliva or mucus of the mouth; the sensation of nausea, however, which belongs to the sensations of taste, is certainly very often perceived as the result of a merely internal affection of the nerves. The sensations of the sense of vision, namely, colour, light, and darkness, are also perceived independently of all external exciting cause. In the state of the most perfect freedom from excitement, the optic nerve has no other sensation than that of darkness. The excited condition of the nerve is manifested, even while the eyes are closed, by the appearance of light, or luminous flashes, which are mere sensations of the nerve, and not owing to the presence of any matter of light, and consequently are not capable of illuminating any surrounding objects. Every one is aware how common it is to see bright colours while the eyes are closed, particularly in the morning when the irritability of the nerves is still considerable. . . .

The sensations of hearing also are excited as well by internal as by external causes; for, whenever the auditory nerve is in a state of excitement, the sensations peculiar to it, as the sounds of ringing, humming, &c. are perceived. It is by such sensations that the diseases of the auditory nerve manifest themselves; and, even in less grave, transient affections of the nervous system, the sensations of humming and ringing in the ears afford evidence that the sense of hearing participates in the disturbance.

No further proof is wanting to show, that external influences give rise in our senses to no other sensations, than those which may be excited in the corresponding nerves by internal causes.

II. *The same internal cause excites in the different senses different sensations;—in each sense the sensations peculiar to it.*

One uniform internal cause acting on all the nerves of the senses in the same manner, is the accumulation of blood in the capillary vessels of the nerve, as in congestion and inflammation. This uniform cause excites in the retina, while the eyes are closed, the sensation of light and luminous flashes; in the auditory nerve, humming and ringing sounds; and in the nerves of feeling, the sensation of pain. In the same way, also, a narcotic substance introduced into the blood excites in the nerves of each sense peculiar symptoms; in the optic nerves the appearance of luminous sparks before the eyes; in the auditory nerves, "tinnitus aurium;" and in the common sensitive nerves the sensation of ants creeping over the surface.

III. *The same external cause also gives rise to different sensations in each sense, according to the special endowments of its nerve.*

The mechanical influence of a blow, concussion, or pressure excites, for example, in the eye the sensation of light and colours. It is well known that by exerting pressure upon the eye, when the eyelids are closed, we can give rise to the appearance of a luminous circle; by more gentle pressure the appearance of colours may be produced, and one colour may be made to change to another. Children, waking from sleep before daylight, frequently amuse themselves with these phenomena. The light thus produced has no existence external to the optic nerve, it is merely a sensation excited in it. However strongly we press upon the eye in the dark, so as to give rise to the appearance of luminous flashes, these flashes, being merely sensations, are incapable of illuminating external objects. Of this any one may easily convince himself by experiment. I have in repeated trials never been able, by means of these luminous flashes in the eye, to recognise in the dark the nearest objects, or to see them better than before; nor could another person, while I produced by pressure on my eye the appearance of brilliant flashes, perceive in it the slightest trace of real light. . . .

IV. *The peculiar sensations of each nerve of sense can be excited by several distinct causes internal and external.*

The facts on which this statement is founded have been already mentioned; for we have seen that the sensation of light in the eye is excited:

1. By the undulations or emanations which from their action on the eye are called light, although they have many other actions than this; for instance, they effect chemical changes, and are the means of maintaining the organic processes in plants.
2. By mechanical influences; as concussion, or a blow.
3. By electricity.
4. By chemical agents, such as narcotics, digitalis, &c. which, being absorbed into the blood, give rise to the appearance of luminous sparks, &c. before the eyes independently of any external cause.
5. By the stimulus of the blood in the state of congestion.

The sensation of sound may be excited in the auditory nerve:

1. By mechanical influences, namely, by the vibrations of sonorous bodies imparted to the organ of hearing through the intervention of media capable of propagating them.
2. By electricity.

3. By chemical influences taken into the circulation; such as the narcotics, or alterantia nervina.
4. By the stimulus of the blood.

The sensation of odours may be excited in the olfactory nerves:

1. By chemical influences of a volatile nature,—odorous substances.
2. By electricity.

The sensation of taste may be produced:

1. By chemical influences acting on the gustatory nerves either from without or through the medium of the blood; for, according to Magendie, dogs taste milk injected into their blood-vessels, and begin to lap with their tongue.
2. By electricity.
3. By mechanical influences; for we must refer to taste the sensation of nausea produced by mechanically irritating the velum palati, epiglottis, and root of the tongue.

The sensations of the nerves of touch or feeling are excited:

1. By mechanical influences; as sonorous vibrations, and contact of any kind.
2. By chemical influences.
3. By heat.
4. By electricity.
5. By the stimulus of the blood.

V. *Sensation consists in the sensorium receiving through the medium of the nerves, and as the result of the action of an external cause, a knowledge of certain qualities or conditions, not of external bodies, but of the nerves of sense themselves; and these qualities of the nerves of sense are in all different, the nerve of each sense having its own peculiar quality or energy.*

The special susceptibility of the different nerves of sense for certain influences,—as of the optic nerve for light, of the auditory nerve for vibrations, and so on,—was formerly attributed to these nerves having each a specific irritability. But this hypothesis is evidently insufficient to explain all the facts. The nerves of the senses have assuredly a specific irritability for certain influences; for many stimuli, which exert a violent action upon one organ of sense, have little or no effect upon another: for example, light, or vibrations so infintely rapid as those of light, act only on the nerves of vision and common sensation; slower vibrations, on the nerves of hearing and common sensation, but not upon those of vision; odorous substances only upon the olfactory nerves. The external stimuli must therefore be adapted to the organ of sense—must be "homogeneous:" thus light is the stimulus adapted to the nerve of vision; while vibrations of less rapidity, which act upon the auditory nerve, are not adapted to the optic nerve, or are indifferent to it; for if the eye be touched with a tuning-fork while vibrating, a sensation of tremours is excited in the conjunctiva, but no sensation of light. We have seen, however, that one and the same stimulus, as electricity, will produce different sensations in the different nerves of the senses; all the nerves are susceptible of its action, but the sensations in all are different. The same is the case with other stimuli, as chemical and mechanical influences. The hypothesis of a specific irritability of the nerves of the senses for certain stimuli, is therefore insufficient; and we are compelled to ascribe, with Aristotle, peculiar energies to each nerve,—energies which are vital qualities of the nerve, just as contractility is the vital property of muscle. . . .

The sensation of sound, therefore, is the peculiar "energy" or "quality" of the auditory nerve; the sensation of light and colours that of the optic nerve; and so of the other nerves of sense. . . .

VI. *The nerve of each sense seems to be capable of one determinate kind of sensation only, and not of those proper to the other organs of sense; hence one nerve of sense cannot take the place and perform the function of the nerve of another sense.*

The sensation of each organ of sense may be increased in intensity till it becomes pleasurable, or till it becomes disagreeable, without the specific nature of the sensation being altered, or converted into that of another organ of sense. The sensation of dazzling light is an unpleasant sensation of the organ of vision; harmony of colours, an agreeable one. Harmonious and discordant sounds are agreeable and disagreeable sensations of the organ of hearing. The organs of taste and smell have their pleasant and unpleasant tastes and odours; the organ of touch its pleasurable and painful feelings. It appears, therefore, that, even in the most excited condition of an organ of sense, the sensation preserves its specific character. . . .

VII. *It is not known whether the essential cause of the peculiar "energy" of each nerve of sense is seated in the nerve itself, or in the parts of the brain and spinal cord with which it is connected; but it is certain that the central portion of the nerves included in the encephalon are susceptible of their peculiar sensations, independently of the more peripheral portion of the nervous cords which form the means of communication with the external organs of sense.*

The specific sensibility of the individual senses to particular stimuli,—owing to which vibrations of such rapidity or length as to produce sound are perceived, only by the senses of hearing and touch, and mere mechanical influences, scarcely at all by the sense of taste,—must be a property of the nerves themselves; but the peculiar mode of reaction of each sense, after the excitement of its nerve, may be due to either of two conditions. Either the nerves themselves may communicate impressions different in quality to the sensorium, which in every instance remains the same; or the vibrations of the nervous principle may in every nerve be the same and yet give rise to the perception of different sensations in the sensorium, owing to the parts of the latter with which the nerves are connected having different properties. The proof of either of these propositions I regard as at present impossible....

VIII. *The immediate objects of the perception of our senses are merely particular states induced in the nerves, and felt as sensations either by the nerves themselves or by the sensorium; but inasmuch as the nerves of the senses are material bodies, and therefore participate in the properties of matter generally occupying space, being susceptible of vibratory motion, and capable of being changed chemically as well as by the action of heat and electricity, they make known to the sensorium, by virtue of the changes thus produced in them by external causes, not merely their own condition, but also properties and changes of condition of external bodies. The information thus obtained by the senses concerning external nature, varies in each sense, having a relation to the qualities or energies of the nerve.*

Qualities which are to be regarded rather as sensations or modes of reaction of the nerves of sense, are light, colour, the bitter and sweet tastes, pleasant and unpleasant odours, painful and pleasant impressions on the nerves of touch, cold and warmth: properties which may belong wholly to external nature are "extension," progressive and tremulous motion, and chemical change.

All the senses are not equally adapted to impart the idea of "extension" to the sensorium. The nerve of vision and the nerve of touch, being capable of an exact perception of this property in themselves, make us acquainted with it in external bodies. In the nerves of taste, the sensation of extension is less distinct, but is not altogether deficient; thus we are capable of distinguishing whether the seat of a bitter or sweet taste be the tongue, the palate, or the fauces. In the sense of touch and sight, however, the perception of space is most acute. The retina of the optic nerve has a structure especially adapted for this perception; for the ends of the nervous fibres in the retina are, as Treviranus discovered, so arranged as to be at last perpendicular to its inner surface, and by their papillar extremities form a pavement-like composite membrane. On the great number of these terminal fibrils depends the delicate power of discriminating the position of bodies in space possessed by the sense of vision; for each fibre represents a greater or less field of the visible world, and imparts the impression of it to the sensorium.[2]

However stimulated, each sensory nerve gives rise to its particular type of sensory process, and no other. It is not the nature of the stimulus but rather the particular nerve that is stimulated that decides the sensory experience. In an earlier publication, he made clear that a particular brain center is also involved. Modern research finds the center, not the nerve, to be the decisive source.

This doctrine did much to focus the research interests of physiologists on the nature of the observing organism. Perception, it would seem, not only depends on what is being perceived, but it also depends on the nature of the organism; the perceiving organism is certainly a matter with which psychologists were very much concerned later on.

Müller saw his doctrine as supporting the nativistic views of Kant about that which we perceive (p. 80). After all, what is more innate than the nervous system itself? The views of Kant and Müller were to be challenged by Helmholtz (p. 125).

15

WEBER AND FECHNER ON
MEASUREMENT AND PSYCHOPHYSICS

The research and theory of ERNST HEINRICH WEBER (1795–1878), German physiologist, and GUSTAV THEODOR FECHNER (1801–1887), German philosopher and physicist, are so intertwined as to make their joint treatment advisable. The earlier chronological research of Weber took on a different significance when interpreted by Fechner in a larger framework.

The specific research problem that Weber investigated was a comparison of the relative sensitivity of touch compared to that of "common feeling" (muscle sense). To put it in terms of what he was measuring, it was the ability to discriminate the heavier of two weights resting on the skin by touch alone, as compared to discrimination when "hefting" or lifting the weights (touch *and* muscular exertion). For each trial, the subjects reported one weight heavier than the other when they could; but, if they were unable to discriminate between them, the subjects called them equal. Very small differences in weight resulted in the judgment that they were the same; large differences were obvious. By using different levels of weight and a sufficient number of trials, ratios could be calculated in terms of fineness of discrimination. Finding the "just noticeable difference" of which his subjects could discriminate, each of the two tasks gave him the answer to his original problem.

The results for weight perception under the two conditions and extensions of the same procedure to other sense modalities is reported in the following excerpt.

The smallest perceptible difference between two weights, which we can distinguish by the feeling of muscular exertion, appears according to my experiments to be that between weights which stand approximately in the relation of 39 to 40: that is to say, of which one is about 1–40 heavier than the other. By means of the feeling of pressure, which two weights make upon our skin, all we are able to distinguish is a difference of weight that amounts to only 1–30, so that the weights accordingly stand in the relation of 29 to 30.

If we look at one line after another, any one who possesses a very exceptional visual discrimination can according to my experiments discover a difference between two lines whose lengths are related as 50:51, or even as 100 = 101. Those who have a less delicate visual discrimination distinguish lines, which are separated from one another by 1–25 of their length. The smallest perceptible difference of the pitch of two tones, (which are really in unison), that a musician perceives, if he hears two tones successively, is according to Delezenne 1–4 *Komma* (81–80) 1–4. A lover of music according to him distinguishes only about 1–2 *Komma* (81–80) 1–2. If the tones are heard simultaneously we cannot, according to Delezenne's experiments, perceive such small tonal differences. 1–4 *Komma* is nearly the relation of 321:322, but 1–2 *Komma* is nearly the relation of 160:161.

I have shown that the result in the determinations of weight is the same, whether one takes ounces or half ounces; for it does not depend upon the number of grains that form the increment of weight, but depends on the fact that this increment makes up the thirtieth or fiftieth [should be fortieth] part of the weight which we are comparing with the second weight. This likewise holds true of the comparison of the length of two lines and of the pitch of two tones. It makes no difference whether we compare lines that are, say, two inches or one inch long, if we examine them successively, and can see them lying parallel to each other; and yet the extent by which the one line exceeds the other is in the former case twice as great as in the latter. To be sure, if both lines lie close together and parallel, we compare only the ends of the lines to discover how much the one line exceeds the other; and in this test the question is only how great that length of line which overlaps the other really is, and how near the two lines lie to one another.

So too in the comparison of the pitch of two tones, it does not matter whether the two tones are seven tonal stops [i.e. an octave] higher or lower, provided only they do not lie at the end of the tonal series, where the exact discrimination of small tonal differences becomes more difficult.[1]

Fechner, who was not only a philosopher but also a mystic and a physicist, saw these results as supplying a method by which to approach a larger problem he was already grappling with—the very nature of the relationship between the spiritual and material worlds. Fechner had had a mystical experience during which, on the morning of October 22, 1850, "before getting out of bed," he conceived that a law of the connection between body and mind was to be found on a statement of the quantitative relation between mental sensation and bodily stimulus, not in simple proportion, but such that increases in the former correspond to proportional changes in the latter. Ten years after that morning in 1850, his *Elements of Psychophysics* appeared, utilizing Weber's methodology with Fechnerian variations. This excerpt opens with his interpretation of the significance of Weber's law:

Weber's law, that equal relative increments of stimuli are proportional to equal increments of sensation, is, in consideration of its generality and the wide limits within which it is absolutely or approximately valid, to be considered fundamental for psychic measurement. . . .

    Although not as yet having a measurement for sensation, still one can combine in an exact formula the relation expressed in Weber's law,—that the sensation difference remains constant when the relative stimulus difference remains constant,—with the law, established by the mathematical auxiliary principle, that small sensation increments are proportional to stimulus increments. Let us suppose, as has generally been done in the attempts to preserve Weber's law, that the difference between two stimuli, or, what is the same, the increase in one stimulus, is very small in proportion to the stimulus itself. Let the stimulus which is increased be called β, the small increase $d\beta$, where the letter d is to be considered not as a special magnitude, but simply as a sign that $d\beta$ is the small increment of β. This already suggests the differential sign. The relative stimulus increase therefore is $d\beta/\beta$. On the other hand, let the sensation which is dependent upon the stimulus β be called γ, and let the small increment of the sensation which results from the increase of the stimulus by $d\beta$ be called $d\gamma$, where d again simply expresses the small increment. The terms $d\beta$ and $d\gamma$ are each to be considered as referring to an arbitrary unit of their own nature.

    According to the empirical Weber's law, $d\gamma$ remains constant when $d\beta/\beta$ remains constant, no matter what absolute values $d\beta$ and β take; and according to the *a priori* mathematical auxiliary principle the changes $d\gamma$ and $d\beta$ remain proportional to one another so long as they remain very small. The two relations may be expressed together in the following equation:

$$d\gamma = Kd\beta/\beta \qquad (1)$$

where k is a constant (dependent upon the units selected for γ and β). In fact, if one multiplies βd and β by any number, so long as it is the same number for both, the proportion remains constant, and with it also the sensation difference $d\gamma$. This is Weber's law. If one doubles or triples the value of the variation $d\beta$ without changing the initial value β, then the value of the change $d\gamma$ is also doubled or tripled. This is the mathematical principle. The equation $d\gamma = Kd\beta/\beta$ therefore entirely satisfies both Weber's law and this principle; and no other equation satisfies both together. This is to be called the *fundamental formula,* in that the deduction of all consequent formulas will be based upon it.

The fundamental formula does not presuppose the measurement of sensation, nor does it establish any; it simply expresses the relation holding between small relative stimulus increments and sensation increments. In short, it is nothing more than Weber's law and the mathematical auxiliary principle united and expressed in mathematical symbols.

There is, however, another formula connected with this formula by infinitesimal calculus, which expresses a general quantitative relation between the stimulus magnitude as a summation of stimulus increments, and the sensation magnitude as a summation of sensation increments, in such a way, that with the validity of the first formula, together with the assumption of the fact of limen, the validity of this latter formula is also given. . . .

One can readily see, that the relation between the increments $d\gamma$ and $d\beta$ in the fundamental formula corresponds to the relation between the increments of a logarithm and the increments of the corresponding number. For as one can easily convince oneself, either from theory or from the table, the logarithm does not increase by equal increments when the corresponding number increases by equal increments, but rather when the latter increases by equal relative amounts; in other words, the increases in the logarithms remain equal, when the relative increases of the numbers remain equal. Thus, for example, the following numbers and logarithms belong together:

NUMBER	LOGARITHM
10	1.000000
11	1.0413927
100	2.000000
110	2.0413927
1000	3.000000
1100	3.0413927

where an increase of the number 10 by 1 brings with it just as great an increase in the corresponding logarithm, as the increase of the number 100 by 10 or 1000 by 100. In each instance the increase in the logarithm is 0.0413927. Further, as was already shown in explaining the mathematical auxiliary principle, the increases in the logarithms are proportional to the increases of the numbers, so long as they remain very small. Therefore one can say, that Weber's law and the mathematical auxiliary principle are just as valid for the increases of logarithms and numbers in their relation to one another, as they are for the increases of sensation and stimulus.

The fact of the threshold appears just as much in the relation of a logarithm to its number as in the relation of sensation to stimulus. The sensation begins with values above zero, not with zero, but with a finite value of the stimulus—the threshold; and so does the logarithm begin with values above zero, not with a zero value of the number, but with a finite value of the number, the value 1, inasmuch as the logarithm of 1 is equal to zero.

If now, as was shown above, the increase of sensation and stimulus stands in a relation similar to that of the increase of logarithm and number, and, the point at which the sensation begins to assume a noticeable value stands in a relation to the stimulus similar to that which the point at which the logarithm attains positive value stands to the number, then one may also expect that sensation and stimulus themselves stand in a relation to one another similar to that of logarithm to number, which, just as the former (sensation and stimulus) may be regarded as made up of a sum of successive increments.

Accordingly the simplest relation between the two that we can write is $\gamma = \log \beta$.

In fact it will soon be shown that, provided suitable units of sensation and stimulus are chosen, the functional relation between both reduces to this very simple formula. Meanwhile it is not the most general formula that can be derived, but one which is only valid under the supposition of particular units of sensation and stimulus, and we still need a direct and absolute deduction instead of the indirect and approximate one.

The specialist sees at once how this may be attained, namely, by treating the fundamental formula as a differential formula and integrating it. In the following chapter one will find this done. Here it must be supposed already carried out, and those who are not able to follow the simple infinitesimal deduction, must be asked to consider the result as a mathematical fact. This result is the following functional formula between stimulus and sensation, which goes by the name of the measurement formula and which will now be further discussed:

$$\gamma = x(\log \beta - \log b) \qquad (2)$$

In this formula x again stands for a constant, dependent upon the unit selected and also the logarithmic system, and b a second constant which stands for the threshold value of the stimulus, at which the sensation γ begins and disappears.

According to the rule, that the logarithm of a quotient of two numbers may be substituted for the difference of their logarithms, . . . one can substitute for the above form of the measurement formula the following, which is more convenient for making deductions.

$$\gamma = x \log \beta/b \qquad (3)$$

From this equation it follows that the sensation magnitude γ is not to be considered as a simple function of the stimulus value β, but of its relation to the threshold value b, where the sensation begins and disappears. This relative stimulus value, β/b is for the future to be called the fundamental stimulus value, or the fundamental value of the stimulus.

Translated in words, the measurement formula reads:

The magnitude of the sensation (γ) is not proportional to the absolute value of the stimulus (β), but rather to the logarithm of the magnitude of the stimulus, when this last is expressed in terms of its threshold value (b), i.e. that magnitude considered as unit at which the sensation begins and disappears. In short, it is proportional to the logarithm of the fundamental stimulus value.

Before we proceed further, let us hasten to show that that relation between stimulus and sensation, from which the measurement formula is derived, may be correctly deduced in turn from it, and that this latter thus finds its verification in so far as these relations are found empirically. We have here at the same time the simplest examples of the application of the measurement formula.

The measurement formula is founded upon Weber's law and the fact of the stimulus threshold; and both must follow in turn from it.

Now as to Weber's law. In the form that equal increments of sensation are proportional to relative stimulus increments, it may be obtained by differentiating the measurement formula, inasmuch as in this way one returns to the fundamental formula, which contains the expression of the law in this form.

In the form, that equal sensation differences correspond to equal relations of stimulus, the law may be deduced in quite an elementary manner as follows.

Let two sensations, whose difference is to be considered, be called γ and γ', and the corresponding stimuli β and β'. Then according to the measurement formula

$$\gamma = x(\log \beta - \log b)$$
$$\gamma' = x(\log \beta' - \log b)$$

and likewise for the sensation difference

$$\gamma - \gamma' = x(\log \beta - \log \beta')$$

or, since $\log \beta - \log \beta' = \log \beta/\beta'$

$$\gamma - \gamma' = x \log \beta/\beta'$$

From this formula it follows, that the sensation difference $\gamma - \gamma'$ is a function of the stimulus relation β/β', and remains the same no matter what values β, β' may take, so long as the relation remains unchanged, which is the statement of Weber's law.

In a later chapter we shall return to the above formula under the name of the difference formula, as one of the simplest consequences of the measurement formula.

As for the fact of the threshold, which is caused by the sensation having zero value not at zero but at a finite value of the stimulus, from which point it first begins to obtain noticeable values with increasing values of stimulus, it is so far contained in the measurement formula as γ does not, according to this formula, have the value zero when $\beta = o$, but when β is equal to a finite value b. This follows as well from equation (2) as (3) of the measurement formula, directly from (2), and from (3) with the additional consideration of the fact, that when β equals b, $\log \beta/b$ equals $\log 1$, and $\log 1 = 0$.

Naturally all deduction from Weber's law and the fact of the threshold will also be deductions from our measurement formula.

It follows from the former law, that every given increment of stimulus causes an ever decreasing increment in sensation in proportion as the stimulus grows larger, and that at high values of the stimulus it is no longer sensed, while on the other hand, at low values it may appear exceptionally strong.

In fact the increase of a larger number β by a given amount is accompanied by a considerably smaller increase in the corresponding logarithm γ, than the increase of a small number β by the same amount. When the number 10 is increased by 10, (that is, reaches 20), the logarithm corresponding to 10, which is 1, is increased to 1.3010. When, however, the number 1000 is increased by 10, the logarithm corresponding to 1000, namely 3, is only increased to 3.0043. In the first case the logarithm is increased by 1–3 of its amount, in the latter case by about 1–700.

In connection with the fact of the threshold belongs the deduction, that a sensation is further from the perception threshold the more the stimulus sinks under its threshold value. This distance of a sensation from the threshold, is represented in the same manner by the negative values of γ, according to our measurement formula, as the increase above the threshold is represented by the positive values.

In fact one sees directly from equation (2), that when β is smaller than b and with it log β smaller than log b, the sensation takes on negative values, and the same deduction follows in equation (3), in that β/b' becomes a proper fraction when $\beta < b$, and the logarithm of a proper fraction is negative.

In so far as sensations, which are caused by a stimulus which is not sufficient to raise them to consciousness, are called unconscious, and those which affect consciousness are called conscious, we may say that the unconscious sensations are represented in our formula by negative, the conscious by positive values. We will return to this statement in a special chapter ... since it is of great importance, and perhaps not directly evident to everyone. For the present I shall not let it detain me longer.

According to the foregoing our measurement formula corresponds to experience:

1. In the cases of equality, where a sensation difference remains the same when the absolute intensity of the stimulus is altered (Weber's law).
2. In the cases of the thresholds, where the sensation itself ceases, and where its change becomes either imperceptible or barely perceptible. In the former case, when the sensation reaches its lower threshold; in the latter case, when it becomes so great that a given stimulus increase is barely noticed.
3. In the contrasting cases, between sensations which rise above the threshold of consciousness and those that do not reach

it,—in short, conscious and unconscious sensations. From the above measurement formula may be considered well founded.

In the measurement formula one has a general dependent relation between the size of the fundamental stimulus and the size of the corresponding sensation and not one which is valid only for the cases of equal sensations. This permits the amount of sensation to be calculated from the relative amounts of the fundamental stimulus and thus we have a measurement of sensation.[2]

The excerpt above is a part of Fechner's summarization and, because of its brevity, does not do justice to the many, many research investigations on which it is based.

Fechner held that these results demonstrated that one could measure sensation as well as the sensory stimulus, and could state their relation in the form of an equation. To put it in simplest terms, the psychic aspect (the sensation) increases arithmetically by a constant difference when the physical aspect (the stimulus) increases geometrically by a constant multiple. This sort of relationship is mathematically known as logarithmic. Hence, a sensation equals a constant multiplied by the logarithm of the stimulus.

The very procedure Weber and Fechner had developed reflected a significant lesson: a series of repeated measurements yielded data subject to reduction to a principle or law of measurement. A psychological process had been measured and the results expressed in a mathematical equation.

Research in sensory psychology was put on a quantitative basis by their research. Their methods proved to be very fruitful and are still serviceable and fundamental to sensory measurement today.

16

HELMHOLTZ ON

SPEED OF NEURAL IMPULSE,
THE TRIPARTITE THEORY OF COLOR VISION,
THE PLACE THEORY OF AUDITION,
AND THE EMPIRICAL THEORY
OF SPACE PERCEPTION

HERMANN VON HELMHOLTZ (1821–1894), German physiologist, was an extremely versatile individual who made many important contributions to physiological problems directly relevant to psychology.

At the age of twenty-nine, he published a report on what to those before him had seemed to be an insoluble problem—the rate of the transmission of the neural impulse. The prevailing opinion had been that it was instantaneous, or, at least, too fast to be measured. With a nerve-muscle preparation of a frog's leg, he did what others believed to be impossible.

I have found that there is a measurable period of time during which the effect of a stimulus consisting of a momentary electrical current applied to the iliac plexus of a frog is transmitted to the calf muscles at the entrance of the crural nerve. In the case of large frogs with nerves 50–60 mm. in length, which I preserved at a temperature of 2–6° C. while the temperature of the observation chamber was 11–15°, this period of time amounted to 0.0014 to 0.0020 of a second.

The stimulation of the nerve was given by means of an induction coil. By means of a special mechanical device, a second electrical current was transmitted to a galvanometer at the moment the original current was transmitted to the induction coil. I convinced myself that the error of measurement amounted to considerably less than 1/10 of the period of time with which we are here concerned. The current flowed through the induction coil until the stimulated gastrocnemius muscle had contracted sufficiently to lift a weight which was suspended by a platinum point on a gold-plated support. The lifting of the weight interrupted the current to the induction coil and to the galvanometer. The duration of the current, therefore, was exactly equal to the period elapsing from the application of the stimulation to the nerve to the commencement of the mechanical reaction of the muscle. The effect produced by the current on the galvanometer is proportional to the duration of the current. The time period may be calculated from the oscillation of the galvanometer when the oscillation which would result from known current is also known. I measured the deviation with mirror and telescope. In its essentials the procedure coincides with that of Pouillet for measurements of short periods of time.[1]

He went on to other equally important research studies, including the problem of the physiological basis for color vision. As early as 1802, Thomas Young (1773-1829), an English student of vision, had hypothesized that three simple sensations—red, green, and violet—when combined in various ways, gave a variety of colors "beyond all calculations." The then current knowledge of physiology led him to speak vaguely of "particles" of the retina as the basis of color vision. Helmholtz demonstrated a specific physiological base for this hypothesis. A summary he offered is included in the next excerpt:

If we confine our assumptions concerning the development of a theory of color vision to the properties belonging with certainty to the nerves, there is present in fairly secure outline the theory of Thomas Young.

The sensation of dark corresponds to the state of rest of the optic nerve, that of colored or white light to an excitement of it. The three simple sensations which correspond to the excitement only of a single one of the three nerve systems, and from which all the others can be composed, must correspond in the table of colors to the three angles of the color triangle.

In order to assume the finest possible color sensation not demonstrable by objective stimulus, it appears appropriate so to select the angles of the color triangle that its sides include in the closest possible way the curves of the colors of the spectrum.

Thomas Young has therefore assumed:

1. There are in the eye three kinds of nerve fibres. The excitation of the first produces the sensation of red; the excitation of the second, the sensation of green; the excitation of the third, the sensation of violet.
2. Objective homogeneous light excites these three kinds of fibres with an intensity which varies according to the length of

the wave. The fibres sensitive to red are excited most strongly by light of the greatest wave-length; and those sensitive to violet by light of the smallest wave-length. Nevertheless, it is not precluded, but rather to be assumed, for the explanation of a series of phenomena, that each color of the spectrum excites all the kinds of fibres, but with different intensity. If we suppose in Fig. 1 the spectrum colors placed horizontally and in their natural order, beginning from red R up to violet V, the three curves may represent more or less exactly the strength of the excitation of the three kinds of fibres: no. 1 those sensitive to red; no. 2 those sensitive to green; and no. 3 those sensitive to violet.

The simple red excites strongly the fibres sensitive to red, and weakly the two other kinds of fibres; sensation: red.

The simple yellow excites moderately the fibres sensitive to red and green, weakly the violet; sensation: yellow.

The simple green excites strongly the fibres sensitive to green, much more weakly the two other kinds; sensation: green.

The simple blue excites moderately the fibres sensitive to green and violet, weakly the red; sensation: blue.

The simple violet excites strongly the fibres which belong to it, and weakly the others; sensation: violet.

The excitation of all the fibres of nearly equal strength gives the sensation of white, or of whitish colors.

Perhaps it may be objected at first view to this hypothesis, that three times the number of nerve fibres and nerve endings must be presumed than in the older assumption, according to which each separate nerve fibre was thought capable of transmitting all kinds of chromatic excitations. But I do not believe, that in this connection the supposition of Young is in contradiction with the anatomical facts. An hypothesis was previously discussed, which explains the accuracy of sight by the aid of much smaller number of visual nerve fibres, than the number of distinguishable places in the field of vision.

The choice of the three fundamental colors seems at first, as we have observed, somewhat arbitrary. Any other three colors might be chosen from which white can be composed. Young was guided probably by the consideration that the colors at the end of the spectrum appear to claim a privileged position. If we were not to select these it would be necessary to take for one of the fundamental colors a purple shade, and the curve which corresponds to it in the [following] figure (Fig. 1), would have two maxima: one in red, and the other in violet.

The single circumstance, which is of direct importance in the mode of sensation and appears to give a clue for the determination of the fundamental colors, is the apparent greater color-saturation of the red and violet; a thing which also manifests itself, although indeed less markedly, for green. Since we style colors the more saturated the farther they are removed from white, we must expect that great saturation must belong particularly to those colors of the spectrum which produce most purely the simplest sensations of color. In fact, these colors, if they are very pure, have even with inferior brilliancy, something of an intensively glowing, almost dazzling quality. There are especially red, violet, or blue violet flowers, e.g. of the cameraria, whose colors display this characteristic blending of darkness and brilliancy. Young's hypothesis affords for this a simple explanation. A dark color can cause an intensive excitation of one of the three nerve systems, while the corresponding bright white causes a much weaker excitation of the same. The difference appears analogous to that between the sensation of very hot water upon a small portion of the skin and lukewarm water striking a greater surface.

In particular violet makes upon me this impression of a deeply saturated color. But inasmuch as the strictly violet rays, even when they occur in sunlight, are of slight intensity and are modified by fluorescence, ultramarine blue, which has far the advantage of greater intensity of light, produces an effect approximately equal to it. The strictly pure violet of the spectrum is very little known among the laity, since the violet

Figure 1

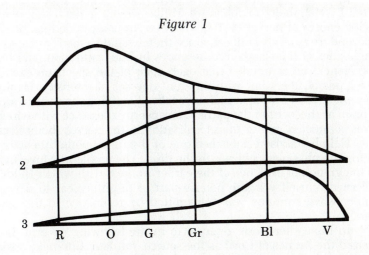

pigments give nearly always the effect of a slight admixture of red, or appear very dark. For that very reason, the shades of the ultramarine blue coming near to the violet excite the general attention much more, are much better known, and are designated by a much older name—that of blue,—than the violet strictly so called. In addition one has in the deep ultramarine blue of the cloudless sky a highly imposing, well-known, and constant example of this color.

In this fact I seek the reason why in former times blue has always been regarded as the one fundamental color. And the more recent observers, like Maxwell and A. Konig, who have sought to determine the composition of color, have also in part returned to it. For both of these had, to be sure, a more definite reason in the above mentioned elevation of the curve of the colors of the spectrum in violet. . . .

The color theory of Thomas Young, above outlined, is, as compared with the general theory of nervous activity as it was worked out by Johannes Müller, a more special application of the law of specific sensations. Corresponding to its hypotheses the sensations of red, green, and violet would be regarded as determined by the specific energy of sensation of the corresponding three nerve systems. Any sort of excitation whatever, which can in any degree excite the nerve system aforesaid, would always be able to produce in it only its specific sensation. As for the cause of the particular quality of these sensations we hardly need look for it in the retina or the constitution of its fibres, but in the activity of the central parts of the brain associated with them.[2]

The Young-Helmholtz color theory, as it came to be called, was related by Helmholtz to Johannes Müller's more general theory of the specific energy of nerves (p. 97). However, in order to do this, he had to go beyond three kinds of fibers, since there would be too few to carry the complexities of thousands of differences in hue, saturation, and brightness. Hence, he contended that each color of the spectrum excites all three kinds of fibers but with different degrees of intensity. Helmholtz also went beyond Müller in unequivocally identifying the cortical areas of the brain as the locus of the particular sensory experience with which the nerves connected, rather than localization in the nerves themselves.

Helmholtz also established one of the fundamental theories concerning the physiological basis for hearing. The problem of investigation and integration of evidence of the earlier workers with which Helmholtz concerned himself was the precise part of the inner ear to which the auditory wave stimulus was transmitted by resonance to the sensory organ.

In his earlier work, referred to in the following excerpt, he emphasized the Arches of Corti as the source, but later findings convinced him that the fibers of the basilar membrane of the cochlea acted through sympathetic vibration. Accordingly, he amended the account to be given, at the same time showing why the Arches of Corti would be inadequate for the task.

We may on the whole assume that the parts of the ear which vibrate sympathetically have an amount of damping power corresponding to the third degree of our table, where the intensity of sympathetic vibration with a Semitone difference of pitch is only $\frac{1}{10}$ of what it is for a complete unison. Of course there can be no question of exact determinations, but is important for us to be able to form at least an approximate conception of the influence of damping on the sympathetic vibration of the ear, as it has great significance in the relations of consonance. Hence when we hereafter speak of individual parts of the ear vibrating sympathetically with a determinate tone, we mean that they are set into strongest motion by that tone, but are also set into vibration less strongly by tones of nearly the same pitch, and that this sympathetic vibration is still sensible for the interval of a Semitone. [Fig. 2] may serve to give a general conception of the law by which the intensity of the sympathetic vibration decreases, as the difference of pitch increases. The horizontal line a b c represents a portion of the musical scale, each of the lengths a b and b c standing for a whole (equally tempered) Tone. Suppose that the body which vibrates sympathetically has been tuned to the tone b and that the vertical line b d represents the maximum of intensity of tone which it can attain when excited by a tone in perfect unison with it. On the base line, intervals of $\frac{1}{10}$ of a whole Tone are set off, and the vertical lines drawn through them shew the corresponding intensity of the tone in the body which vibrates sympathetically, when the exciting tone differs from a unison by the corresponding interval. The following are the numbers from which [Fig. 2] was constructed:—[See top page 120]

Now we cannot precisely ascertain what parts of the ear actually vibrate sympathetically with individual tones. We can only conjecture

Figure 2

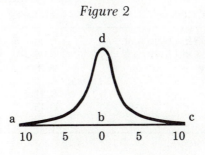

DIFFERENCE OF PITCH	INTENSITY OF SYMPATHETIC VIBRATION	DIFFERENCE OF PITCH	INTENSITY OF SYMPATHETIC VIBRATION
0.0	100	0.6	7.2
0.1	74	0.7	5.4
0.2	41	0.8	4.2
0.3	24	0.9	3.3
0.4	15	Whole Tone	2.7
Semitone	10		

what they are at present in the case of human beings and mammals. The whole construction of the partition of the cochlea, and of Corti's arches which rest upon it, appears most suited for executing independent vibrations. We do not need to require of them the power of continuing their vibrations for a long time without assistance.

But if these formations are to serve for distinguishing tones of different pitch, and if tones of different pitch are to be equally well perceived in all parts of the scale, the elastic formations in the cochlea, which are connected with different nerve fibres, must be differently tuned, and their proper tones must form a regularly progressive series of degrees through the whole extent of the musical scale.

According to the recent anatomical researches of V. Hensen and C. Hasse, it is probably the breadth of the membrana basilaris in the cochlea, which determines the tuning. As its commencement opposite the oval window, it is comparatively narrow, and it continually increases in width as it approaches the apex of the cochlea. The following measurements of the membrane in a newly born child, from the line where

PLACE OF SECTION	BREADTH OF MEMBRANE OR LENGTH OF TRANSVERSE FIBRES	
	Millimetres	*Inches*
0.2625 mm. [=0.010335 in.] from root	0.04125	.00162
0.8626 mm. [=0.033961 in.] from root	0.0825	.00325
Middle of the first spire	0.169	.00665
End of first spire	0.3	.01181
Middle of second spire	0.4125	.01624
End of second spire	0.45	.01772
At the hamulus	0.495	.01949

the nerves pass through on the inner edge, to the attachment to the ligamentum spirale on the outer edge, are given by V. Hensen: [See bottom of previous page]

The breadth therefore increases more than twelvefold from the beginning to the end.

Corti's rods also exhibit an increase of size as they approach the vertex of the cochlea, but in a much less degree than the membrana basilaris. The following are Hensen's measurements:—

| | AT THE ROUND WINDOW | | AT THE HAMULUS | |
	mm.	*inch*	*mm.*	*inch*
Length of inner rod	0.048	0.00189	0.0855	0.00337
Length of outer rod	0.048	0.00189	0.098	0.00386
Span of the arch	0.019	0.00075	0.085	0.00335

Hence it follows, as Henle has also proved, that the greatest increase of breadth falls on the outer zone of the basilar membrane, beyond the line of the attachment of the outer rods. This increases from 0·023 mm. [=·000905 in.] to 0·41 mm. [=·016142 inch] or nearly twentyfold.

In accordance with these measures, the two rows of Corti's rods are almost parallel and upright near to the round window, but they are bent much more strongly towards one another near the vertex of the cochlea.

It has been already mentioned that the membrana basilaris of the cochlea breaks easily in the radial direction, but that its radial fibres have considerable tenacity. This seems to me to furnish a very important mechanical relation, namely that this membrane in its natural connection admits of being tightly stretched in the transverse direction from the modiolus to the outer wall of the cochlea, but can have only little tension in the direction of its length, because it could not resist a strong pull in this direction.

Now the mathematical theory of the vibration of a membrane with different tensions in different directions shews that it behaves very differently from a membrane which has the same tension in all directions. On the latter, vibrations produced in one part, spread uniformly in all directions, and hence if the tension were uniform it would be impossible to set one part of the basilar membrane in vibration, without producing nearly as strong vibrations (disregarding individual nodal lines) in all other parts of the membrane.

But if the tension in direction of its length is infinitesimally small in comparison with the tension in direction of the breadth, then the radial fibres of the basilar membrane may be approximately regarded as forming a system of stretched strings, and the membranous connection as only serving to give a fulcrum to the pressure of the fluid against these strings. In that case the laws of their motion would be the same as if every individual string moved independently of all the others, and obeyed, by itself, the influence of the periodically alternating pressure of the fluid of the labyrinth contained in the vestibule gallery. Consequently any exciting tone would set that part of the membrane into sympathetic vibration, for which the proper tone of one of its radial fibres that are stretched and loaded with the various appendages already described, corresponds most nearly with the exciting tone; and thence the vibrations will extend with rapidly diminishing strength on to the adjacent parts of the membrane. [Fig. 2] . . . might be taken to represent, on an exaggerated scale of height, a longitudinal section of that part of the basilar membrane in which the proper tone of the radial fibres of the membrane are nearest to the exciting tone.

The strongly vibrating parts of the membrane would, as has been explained in respect to all bodies which vibrate sympathetically, be more or less limited, according to the degree of damping power in the adjacent parts, by friction against the fluid in the labyrinth and in the soft gelatinous parts of the nerve fillet.

Under these circumstances the parts of the membrane in unison with higher tones must be looked for near the round window, and those with the deeper, near the vertex of the cochlea, as Hensen also concluded from his measurements. That such short strings should be capable of corresponding with such deep tones, must be explained by their being loaded in the basilar membrane with all kinds of solid formations; the fluid of both galleries in the cochlea must also be considered as weighting the membrane, because it cannot move without a kind of wave motion in that fluid.

The observations of Hasse shew that Corti's arches do not exist in the cochlea of birds and amphibia, although the other essential parts of the cochlea, as the basilar membrane, the ciliated cells in connection with the terminations of the nerves, and Corti's membrane, which stands opposite the ends of these ciliae, are all present. Hence it becomes very probable that Corti's arches play only a secondary part in the function of the cochlea. Perhaps we might look for the effect of Corti's arches in their power, as relatively firm objects, of transmitting the vibrations of the basilar membrane to small limited regions of the upper part of the relatively thick nervous fillet, better than it could be done by the immediate communication of the vibrations of the basilar membrane through the soft mass of this fillet. Close to the outside of the upper end of the arch, connected with it by the stiffer fibriles of the membrana reticulāris, are the ciliated cells of the nervous fillet. . . . In birds, on the other hand, the cilated cells form a thin stratum upon the basilar membrane, and this stratum can readily receive limited vibrations from the membrane, without communicating them too far sideways.

According to this view Corti's arches, in the last resort, will be the means of transmitting the vibrations received from the basilar membrane to the terminal appendages of the conducting nerve. In this sense the reader is requested hereafter to understand references to the vibrations, proper tone, and intonation of Corti's arches; the intonation meant is that which they receive through their connection with the corresponding part of the basilar membrane.

According to Waldeyer there are about 4500 outer arch fibres in the human cochlea. If we deduct 300 for the simple tones which lie beyond musical limits, and cannot have their pitch perfectly apprehended, there remain 4200 for the seven octaves of musical instruments, that is, 600 for every Octave, 50 for every Semitone [that is, 1 for every 2 cents]; certainly quite enough to explain the power of distinguishing small parts of a Semitone. According to Prof. W. Preyer's investigations, practised musicians can distinguish with certainty a difference of pitch arising from half a vibration in a second, in the doubly accented Octave. This would give 1000 distinguishable degrees of pitch in the Octave, from 500 to 1000 vibrations in the second. Towards the limits of the scale the power to distinguish differences diminishes. The 4200 Corti's arches appear then, in this respect, to be enough to apprehend distinctions of this amount of delicacy. But even if it should be found that many more than 4200 degrees of pitch could be distinguished in the Octave, it would not prejudice our assumption. For if a simple tone is struck having a pitch between those of two adjacent Corti's arches, it would set them both in sympathetic vibration, and that arch would vibrate the more strongly which was nearest in pitch to the proper tone. The smallness of the interval between the pitches of two fibres still distinguishable, will therefore finally depend upon the delicacy with which the different forces of the vibrations excited can be compared. And we have thus also an explanation of the fact that as the pitch of an external tone rises continuously, our sensations also alter continuously and not by jumps, as must be the case if only one of Corti's arches were set in sympathetic motion at once.

To draw further conclusions from our hypothesis, when a simple tone is presented to the ear, those Corti's arches which are nearly or exactly in unison with it will be strongly excited, and the rest only slightly or not at all. Hence every simple tone of determinate pitch will be felt only by certain nerve fibres, and simple tones of different pitch will excite different fibres. When a compound musical tone or chord is presented to the ear, all those elastic bodies will be excited, which have a proper pitch corresponding to the various individual simple tones contained in the whole mass of tones, and hence by properly directly attention, all the individual sensations of the individual simple tones can be perceived. The chord must be resolved into its individual compound tones, and the compound tone into its individual harmonic partial tones.

This also explains how it is that the ear resolves a motion of the air into pendular vibrations and no other. Any particle of air can of course execute only one motion at one time. That we considered such a motion mathematically as a sum of pendular vibrations, was in the first instance merely an arbitrary assumption to facilitate theory, and had no meaning in nature. The first meaning in nature that we found for this resolution came from considering sympathetic vibration, when we discovered that a motion which was not pendular, could produce sympathetic vibrations in bodies of those different pitches, which corresponded to the harmonic upper partial tones. And now our hypothesis has also reduced the phenomenon of hearing to that of sympathetic vibration, and thus furnished a reason why an originally simple periodic vibration of the air produces a sum of different sensations, and hence also appears as compound to our perceptions.

The sensation of different pitch would consequently be a sensation in different nerve fibres. The sensation of a quality of tone would depend upon the power of a given compound tone to set in vibration not only those of Corti's arches which correspond to its prime tone, but also a series of other arches, and hence to excite sensation in several different groups of nerve fibres.[3]

The Helmholtz resonance theory gave rise to alternative theories, the most serious competitors being the frequency theories in which it is argued that the basilar membranes vibrate as a whole, not differentially according to the pitch of vibration stimulus as in Helmholtz's theory. To this very day, resolution of the rival claims is not entirely complete.

Helmholtz was sturdily empirical rather than nativistic in his general outlook about psychological problems. This is clearly evident in his discussion of perception that follows.

The general rule determining the ideas of vision that are formed whenever an impression is made on the eye, with or without the aid of optical instruments, is that *such objects are always imagined as being present in the field of vision as would have to be there in order to produce the same impression on the nervous mechanism, the eyes being used under ordinary normal conditions.* To employ an illustration which has been mentioned before, suppose that the eyeball is mechanically stimulated at the outer corner of the eye. Then we imagine that we see an appearance of light in front of us somewhere in the direction of the bridge of the nose. Under ordinary conditions of vision, when our eyes are stimulated by light coming from outside, if the region of the retina in the outer corner of the eye is to be stimulated, the light actually has to enter the eye from the direction of the bridge of the nose. Thus, in accordance with the above rule, in a case of this kind we substitute a luminous object at the place mentioned in the field of view, although as a matter of fact the mechanical stimulus does not act on the eye from in front of the field of view nor from the nasal side of the eye, but, on the contrary, is exerted on the outer surface of the eyeball and more from behind ... when the modes of stimulation of the organs of sense are unusual, incorrect ideas of objects are apt to be formed; which used to be described, therefore, as *illusions of the senses.* Obviously, in these cases there is nothing wrong with the activity of the organ of sense and its corresponding nervous mechanism which produces the illusion. Both of them have to act according to the laws that govern their activity once for all. It is rather simply an illusion in the judgment of the material presented to the senses, resulting in a false idea of it.

The psychic activities that lead us to infer that there in front of us at a certain place there is a certain object of a certain character, are generally not conscious activities, but unconscious ones. In their result they are equivalent to a *conclusion,* to the extent that the observed action on our senses enables us to form an idea as to the possible cause of this action; although, as a matter of fact, it is invariably simply the nervous stimulations that are perceived directly, that is, the actions, but never the external objects themselves. But what seems to differentiate them from a conclusion, in the ordinary sense of that word, is that a conclusion is an act of conscious thought. An astronomer, for example, comes to real conscious conclusions of this sort, when he computes the positions of the stars in space, their distances, etc., from the perspective images he has had of them at various times and as they are seen from different parts of the orbit of the earth. His conclusions are based on a conscious knowledge of the laws of optics. In the ordinary acts of vision this knowledge of optics is lacking. Still it may be permissible to speak of the psychic acts of ordinary perception as *unconscious conclusions,* thereby making a distinction of some sort between them and the common so-called conscious conclusions. And while it is true that there has been, and probably always will be, a measure of doubt as to the similarity of the psychic activity in the two cases, there can be no doubt as to the similarity between the results of such unconscious conclusions and those of conscious conclusions. . . .

Facts like these show the widespread influence that experience, training and habit have on our perceptions. But how far their influence really does extend, it would perhaps be impossible to say precisely at present. Little enough is definitely known about infants and very young animals, and the interpretation of such observations as have been made on them is extremely doubtful. Besides, no one can say that infants are entirely without experience and practice in tactile sensations and bodily movements. Accordingly, the rule given above has been stated in a form which does not anticipate the decision of this question. It merely expresses what the result is. And so it can be accepted even by those who have entirely different opinions as to the way ideas originate concerning objects in the external world. . . .

. . . it may often be rather hard to say how much of our apperceptions (*Anschauungen*) as derived by the sense of sight is due directly to sensation, and how much of them, on the other hand, is due to experience and training. The main point of controversy between various investigators in this territory is connected also with this difficulty. Some are disposed to concede to the influence of experience as much scope as possible, and to derive from it especially all notion of space. This view may be called the *empirical theory (empiristische Theorie).* Others, of course, are obliged to admit the influence of experience in the case of certain classes of perceptions; still with respect to certain elementary apperceptions that occur uniformly in the case of all observers, they believe it is necessary to assume a system of innate apperceptions that are not based on experience, especially with respect to space-relations. In contradistinction to the former view, this may perhaps be called the *intuition theory (nativistische Theorie)* of the sense-perceptions.[4]

The account shows that he considered perception built up by experiences. We infer space from past experiences, he was saying, without awareness that the process is going on (unconscious inference). The evidence he marshalled served as strong support to the empirical position that heretofore had been overshadowed by the nativistic position of Kant (referred to in the excerpt as "intuitionistic"). Of course, as in so many "refutations" past, present, and of the future as well, his answer did not settle the Kantian problem. After all, there is no stimulus "space" which can be summed across experiences, unconscious or otherwise. But for many it did seem to be an answer, so they accepted it uncritically.

All of this work of Helmholtz was to have a strong stimulating influence on Wundt when he formulated psychology as a science (p. 131).

17

WUNDT ON

THE SCIENCE OF PSYCHOLOGY
AS THE EXPERIMENTAL STUDY
OF MENTAL ELEMENTS AND
THEIR CREATIVE SYNTHESIS

WILHELM WUNDT (1832–1920), German psychologist for nearly 35 years at the University of Leipzig, where he founded the first psychological laboratory, is almost certainly the first individual who deserves to be designated a psychologist in the modern sense. The preface to the first edition of *The Principles of Physiological Psychology,* published in part in 1873, begins with the arresting statement, "This work which I here present to the public is an attempt to work out a new domain of science."[1]

He chose to refer to his approach to psychology as "physiological psychology," and it is necessary to make clear what he meant:

Physiological psychology is . . . first of all *psychology.* It has in view the same principal object upon which all other forms of psychological exposition are directed: *the investigation of conscious processes in the modes of connexion peculiar to them.* It is not a province of physiology; nor does it attempt, as has been mistakenly asserted, to derive or explain the phenomena of the psychical from those of the physical life. We may read this meaning into the phrase "physiological psychology," just as we might interpret the title "microscopical anatomy" to mean a discussion, with illustrations from anatomy, of what has been accomplished by the microscope; but the words should be no more misleading in the one case than they are in the other. As employed in the present work, the adjective "physiological" implies simply that our psychology will avail itself to the full of the means that modern physiology puts at its disposal for the analysis of conscious processes. It will do this in two ways.

(1) Psychological inquiries have, up to the most recent times, been undertaken solely in the interest of philosophy; physiology was enabled, by the character of its problems, to advance more quickly towards the application of exact experimental methods. Since, however, the experimental modification of the processes of life, as practised by physiology, oftentimes effects a concomitant change, direct or indirect, in the processes of consciousness,—which, as we have seen, form part of vital processes at large,—it is clear that physiology is, in the very nature of the case, qualified to assist psychology on the side of *method*; thus rendering the same help to psychology that it itself received from physics. In so far as physiological psychology receives assistance from physiology in the elaboration of experimental methods, it may be termed *experimental psychology*. . . .

There are thus two problems which are suggested by the title "physiological psychology": the problem of *method*, which involves the application of experiment, and the problem of a psychophysical *supplement*, which involves a knowledge of the bodily substrates of the mental life. For psychology itself, the former is the more essential; the second is of importance mainly for the philosophical question of the unitariness of vital processes at large. As an experimental science, physiological psychology seeks to accomplish a reform in psychological investigation comparable with the revolution brought about in the natural sciences by the introduction of the experimental method. From one point of view, indeed, the change wrought is still more radical: for while in natural science it is possible, under favorable conditions, to make an accurate observation without recourse to experiment, there is no such possibility in psychology. It is only with grave reservations that what is called "pure self-observation" can properly be termed observation at all, and under no circumstances can it lay claim to accuracy. On the other hand, it is of the essence of experiment that we can vary the conditions of an occurrence at will and, if we are aiming at exact results, in a quantitatively determinable way. Hence, even in the domain of natural science, the aid of the experimental method becomes indispensable whenever the problem set is the analysis of transient and impermanent phenomena, and not merely the observation of persistent and relatively constant objects. But conscious contents are at the opposite pole from permanent objects; they are processes, fleeting occurrences, in continual flux and change. In their case, therefore, the experimental method is of cardinal importance; it and it alone makes a scientific introspection possible. For all accurate observation implies that the object of observation (in this case the psychical process) can be held fast by the attention, and any changes that it undergoes attentively followed. And this fixation by the attention implies, in its turn, that the observed object is independent of the observer. Now it is obvious that the required independence does not obtain in any attempt at a direct self-observation, undertaken without the help of experiment. The endeavour to observe oneself must inevitably introduce changes into the course of mental events,—changes which could not have occurred without it, and whose usual consequence is that the very process which was to have been observed disappears from consciousness. The psychological experiment proceeds very differently. In the first place, it creates external conditions that look towards the production of a determinate mental process at a given moment. In the second place, it makes the observer so far master of the general situation, that the state of consciousness accompanying this process remains approximately unchanged. The great importance of the experimental method, therefore, lies not simply in the fact that, here as in the physical realm, it enables us arbitrarily to vary the conditions of our observations, but also and essentially in the further fact that it makes observation itself possible for us. The results of this observation may then be fruitfully employed in the examination of other mental phenomena, whose nature prevents their own direct experimental modification.

We may add that, fortunately for the science, there are other sources of objective psychological knowledge, which become accessible at the very point where the experimental method fails us. These are certain products of the common mental life, in which we may trace the operation of determinate psychical motives: chief among them are language, myth and custom. In part determined by historical conditions, they are also, in part, dependent upon universal psychological laws; and the phenomena that are referable to these laws form the subject-matter of a special psychological discipline, *ethnic* psychology. The results of ethnic psychology constitute, at the same time, our chief source of information regarding the general psychology of the complex mental processes. In this way, experimental psychology and ethnic psychology form the two principal departments of scientific psychology at large. They are supplemented by *child* and *animal* psychology, which in conjunction with ethnic psychology attempt to resolve the problems of psychogenesis. Workers in both these fields may, of course, avail themselves within certain limits of the advantages of the experimental method. But the results of experiment are here matters of objective observation only, and the experimental method accordingly loses the peculiar significance which it possesses as an instrument of introspection. Finally, child psychology and experimental psychology in the narrower sense may be bracketed together as *individual* psychology, while animal psychology and ethnic psychology form the two halves of a *generic* or *comparative* psychology. These distinctions within psychology are, however, by no means to be put on a level with the analogous divisions of the province of physiology. Child psychology and animal psychology are of relatively slight importance, as compared with the sciences which deal with the corresponding physiological problems of ontogeny and phylogeny. On the other hand, ethnic psychology must always come to the assistance of individual psychology, when the developmental forms of the complex mental processes are in question.[2]

Wundt's position was that, insofar as his psychology drew upon experiment, it could properly be referred to as experimental psychology. Introspection is not sufficient; experiment is necessary for precise quantitative results. In spite of Kant's and Herbart's weighty pronouncements about its impossibility, Wundt made experimentation in psychology the basis for a science of psychology.

His decision to refer to his concept of scientific psychology as "physiological psychology" is sometimes misunderstood. It should be noted that he gives prime importance to the inspiration physiological *methods* were to him. He was very much aware that physiologists such as Müller and Helmholtz worked with methods that could be applied to psychological problems. But it so happens that physiological psychology is currently used to refer to the investigation of the interrelationship of physiological *and* psychological processes and structures. Wundt saw psychology as a separate science in which it was not necessary to refer to physiological processes. A case in point would be Fechner's findings. Wundt interpreted the results as the study of the relation of sensation and judgment, both psychological categories, and not as that between physiological stimulus and psychological sensation. Hence, his psychology was not physiological psychology in the current sense of that term. This does not mean he neglected physiological findings. Despite the lack of interaction, there was a close correspondence between psychological and physiological processes.

Toward the end of the excerpt, Wundt refers to sources of psychological knowledge that are not dependent on experimentation. While mentioned, child and animal psychology, in practice, were either disregarded or denigrated. "Ethnic psychology" or to use a more meaningful term, "cultural psychology" (the study of language, myth, and custom) was pursued vigorously, and he wrote a ten-volume tome on the subject. It indicated that he took the nonexperimental aspects of psychol-

ógy seriously, contrary to the opinion sometimes expressed. His work in
this area became the forerunner of social psychology.

The various editions of the *Principles of Physiological Psychology,*
which followed one another periodically for nearly four decades, was the
vehicle for the integration of the research findings of his students in the
Leipzig laboratory and elsewhere. Rather than report specific research
results, we shall be content to give some conception of the overall nature
of his psychology in terms of his search for the elements of conscious
experience.

In our last chapter we have discussed the general and formal characteristics of consciousness. These have appeared to us in the scope of consciousness, in the different grades of clearness and distinctness of its
content, and lastly, connected with this, in the relations of apprehension
and apperception. The next question that immediately presents itself is:
Of what kind is the specific content that appears to us in these forms?
The answer to this question includes the task of explaining the ultimate
parts of this content, that cannot be further disintegrated. Such ultimate
parts are generally called elements. Now it is one of the first tasks of each
science, that deals with the investigation of empirical facts, to discover
the elements of the phenomena. Its second task is to find out the laws
according to which these elements enter into combinations. The whole
task of psychology can therefore be summed up in these two problems:
(1) What are the elements of consciousness? (2) What combinations do
these elements undergo and what laws govern these combinations?

In contradistinction to the elements of consciousness let us call
any combination of such elements a psychical compound. The relation of
the two to each other can be at once made clear by the examples that lie
at hand. Let us return to our metronome. If we let one single beat work
upon consciousness and then immediately arrest the pendulum, we have
a psychical element. Such a beat cannot in general be further disintegrated if we, as can easily be done in such a case, abstract from the fact
that we hear it from some special direction in space, &c. If, on the other
hand, we let two beats work, they constitute at once a psychical compound. This becomes always more complex, the more such beats we
combine into a row, and the more we increase this complication by dif-
ferent degrees of accentuation, as in the examples of $\frac{2}{8}$ and $\frac{4}{4}$ time described above. Such an element of consciousness as the single beat is
called a sensation, a combination of elements into rhythms of more or less
complicated constitution is called an idea. Even at the present time many
psychologists use the word "idea" only for a complex that does not arise

from direct outward impressions, *i.e.* only for so-called "memory images."
For ideas formed by outward sense impressions they generally use the
word "perception." Now this distinction is psychologically of absolutely
no importance, since there are really no valid differences between memory ideas and so-called sense-perceptions. The memory ideas of our
dreams are in general quite as lively as sense impressions in the waking
state, and it is for this reason that they are often held to be really experienced phenomena. The word "idea" denotes well the essential charac-
teristic of all these complexes. The idea (Greek $\iota\delta\epsilon\alpha$) is the form or appearance of something in the outer world. In the same sense, as belong-
ing to the outer world, we speak of the sensations and their complexes
arising in our own body as organic sensations, because we locate them in
our own body, *e.g.* the sensations of fatigue of our muscles, the pressure
and pain sensations of the inner organs, &c. The relatively uniform elements of touch and organic sensations are distributed among the sensations of pressure, warmth, cold, and pain. In contradistinction to these,
the special senses of hearing, seeing, smelling, and tasting present an
abundance of sensations, each of which, according to its peculiar constitution, is called a quality of sensation. Each such quality is besides
variable in its intensity. We can, for example, produce a certain beat in
very variable intensities, while the quality remains the same.

In all these cases we meet with the same relations between sensations and ideas, as we saw in the metronome beats described above.
Green or red, white or black, &c., are called visual sensations; a green
surface or a black body is called a visual idea. The relation is exactly the
same as between the single beat and the row of beats. Only in this case
the combination of several sensations to an idea of a surface or of a body
forces itself upon us much more directly, and it requires a very careful
abstraction from this combination into an ideational complex, in order to
retain the conception of a sensation. But we can vary our ideas of surfaces
and bodies at will, while the colour remains the same. So at last we are
forced to look upon this element, that remains the same in spite of all
changes in the combinations, as a simple sensatic n. In the same way we
consider a simple tone as a sensation of hearing, and a clang or chord,
composed of several tones, as an auditory idea, and so on. If the tones
follow each other in a melodious and rhythmical combination, then ideas
of increasing complexity arise, and in the same manner several relatively
simple visual ideas may be bound together into more extensive simultaneous or successive unities. The senses of sight and of hearing in
especial form in this way a great variety of sensations and ideas, and they

do this in two ways—firstly, through the qualities of their simple sensations, and secondly, through the complications of ideas, into which these sensations may be combined. The simple scale of tones, from the deepest to the highest tone that can be heard, consists of an infinite gradation of tonal qualities, out of which our musical scale chooses only certain tones, which lie at relatively large distances from each other. Musical clangs are combinations of a number of such simple tonal sensations, and the so-called compound clangs increase this complicated constitution of the clangs by emphasising to a greater degree certain partial tones. The simple light-sensations form a more concise manifoldness, but one that stretches into different directions. Red, for example, on the one hand goes over by constant gradations into orange and then into yellow, and on the other hand we have just as many constant gradations from each of these colour-shades through the lighter colour-tones into white, or through the darker ones into black, and so on. The ideas of this sense are absolutely inexhaustible. If we think of the manifold forms of surfaces and bodies, and of the differences in distance and direction, in which we perceive objects, it is obvious that it is absolutely impossible to find any limit here. Thus the richness in sensations and ideas, which each of the senses conveys, stands in close relation to the spatial distance of the objects which they introduce into consciousness. The narrowest region is that of the touch and organic sense, where the impressions all refer to our own body. Then come the sensations of the two so-called chemical senses of taste and of smell. Even in man they have the important function of organs of help or protection in the choice of food, as is the case in the whole animal kingdom. The sensations and ideas of hearing stretch much further. By means of them the outer world enters into relation with our consciousness in language, song, and music. And last of all, the sense of sight, the sense of distance in the real meaning of the word, gives form and content to the whole picture of the outer world, that we carry in our consciousness.[3]

Immediately after this discussion of sensation as an element of consciousness, he goes on to discuss feelings as the other basic element of consciousness.

The emphasis that Wundt placed on the search for elements has sometimes led to a neglect of the fact that he saw the necessity for a principle of creative synthesis, that complex conscious phenomena could not be reconstituted out of an additive combination of the elements.

...2. The *law of psychical resultants* finds its expression in the fact that every psychical compound shows attributes which may indeed be understood from the attributes of its elements after these elements have once been presented, but which are by no means to be looked upon as the mere sum of the attributes of these elements. A compound clang is more in its ideational and affective attributes than merely a sum of single tones. In spacial and temporal ideas the spacial and temporal arrangement is conditioned, to be sure, in a perfectly regular way by the cooperation of the elements that make up the idea, but still the arrangement itself can by no means be regarded as a property belonging to the sensational elements themselves. The nativistic theories that assume this, implicte themselves in contradictions that cannot be solved; and besides, in so far as they admit subsequent changes in the original space perceptions and time-perceptions, they are ultimately driven to the assumption of the rise, to some extent at least, of new attributes. Finally, in the apperceptive functions and in the activities of imagination and understanding, this law finds expression in a clearly recognized form. Not only do the elements united by apperceptive synthesis gain, in the aggregate idea that results from their combination, a new significance which they did not have in their isolated state, but what is of still greater importance, the aggregate idea itself is a new psychical content that was made possible, to be sure, by these elements, but was by no means contained in them. This appears most strikingly in the more complex productions of apperceptive synthesis, as, for example, in a work of art or a train of logical thought.

3. The law of psychical resultants thus expresses a principle which we may designate, in view of its results, as a *principle of creative synthesis*. This has long been recognized in the case of higher mental creations, but generally not applied to the other psychical processes. In fact, through an unjustifiable confusion with the laws of physical causality, it has even been completely reversed. A similar confusion is responsible for the notion that there is a contradiction between the principle of creative synthesis in the mental world and the general laws of the natural world, especially that of the conservation of energy. Such a contradiction is impossible from the outset because the points of view for judgment, and therefore for measurements wherever such are made, are different in the two cases, and must be different, since natural science and psychology deal, not with different contents of experience, but with one and the same content viewed from different sides ... Physical measurements have to do with *objective masses, forces, and energies*. These are supplementary concepts which we are obliged to use in judging objective experience; and their general laws, derived as they are from experience, must not be contradicted by any single case of experience. Psychical measurements,

which are concerned with the comparison of psychical components and their resultants, have to do with *subjective values and ends*. The subjective value of a whole may increase in comparison with that of its components; its purpose may be different and higher than theirs without any change in the masses, forces, and energies concerned. The muscular movements of an external volitional act, the physical processes that accompany sense-perception, association, and apperception, all follow invariably the principle of the conservation of energy. But the mental values and ends that these energies represent may be very different in quantity even while the quantity of these energies remains the same.[4]

Wundt had marked out "a new domain of science," and before his death in 1920, had seen it meet the claim he had made in 1873, furnishing us with some of the reasons as to why he is often claimed to be the first modern psychologist. He founded the first laboratory, developed its methodological procedures, demarcated some of its area of content, and through his students, investigated many problems in the empirical science of consciousness. The nature of these research problems was not completely and clearly revealed in the excerpts. It will have to suffice to say that, in addition to sensation and perception, reaction-time, attention, feeling, and association, were the other major investigative areas.

18

BRENTANO ON
ACT PSYCHOLOGY

FRANZ BRENTANO (1838–1917), German-Austrian philosopher, published his *Psychology from an Empirical Standpoint* in 1874, the same year that saw the complete publication of Wundt's *The Principles of Physiological Psychology*. Prophetic of the many later clashes between competing systems, he presented an alternative at the very outset of psychology as a science. The intent of his title is reinforced with the opening sentences of the foreword, in which he indicates that his "psychological stand point is empirical; experience alone is my teacher." But an empirical psychology is not necessarily an experimental psychology in the Wundtian sense. Instead, Brentano emphasized analysis of experience. Observation was his primary tool. Having spent part of his life as a Catholic priest, Brentano reached back to Aristotle as a major source for this view. He considered, as did Aristotle, that acts are the proper concern of psychology and that it follows that its task is relating the person, that is, the experiencer, to the environment. We shall return to this issue after presenting an excerpt in which the distinction between the mental and physical is the setting for discussing this task:

Every idea or presentation which we acquire either through sense perception or imagination is an example of a mental phenomenon. By presentation I do not mean that which is presented, but rather the act of presentation. Thus, hearing a sound, seeing a colored object, feeling warmth or cold, as well as similar states of imagination are examples of what I mean by this term. I also mean by it the thinking of a general concept, provided such a thing actually does occur. Furthermore, every judgement, every recollection, every expectation, every inference, every conviction or opinion, every doubt, is a mental phenomenon. Also to be included under this term is every emotion: joy, sorrow, fear, hope, cour-age, despair, anger, love, hate, desire, act of will, intention, astonishment, admiration, contempt, etc. Examples of physical phenomena on the other hand, are a color, a figure, a landscape which I see, a chord which I hear, warmth, cold, odor which I sense; as well as similar images which appear in the imagination.

These examples may suffice to illustrate the differences between the two classes of phenomena.

3. Yet we still want to try to find a different and a more unified way of explaining mental phenomena. For this purpose we make use of a definition we used earlier when we said that the term "mental phenomena" applies to presentations as well as to all the phenomena which are based upon presentations. It is hardly necessary to mention again that by "presentation" we do not mean that which is presented, but rather the presenting of it. This act of presentation forms the foundation not merely of the act of judging, but also of desiring and of every other mental act. Nothing can be judged, desired, hoped or feared, unless one has a presentation of that thing. Thus the definition given includes all the examples of mental phenomena which we listed above, and in general all the phenomena belonging to this domain. . . .

Every mental phenomenon is characterized by what the Scholas-tics of the Middle Ages called the intentional (or mental) inexistence of an object, and what we might call, though not wholly unambiguously, reference to a content, direction toward an object (which is not to be understood here as meaning a thing), or immanent objectivity. Every mental phenomenon includes something as object within itself, although they do not all do so in the same way. In presentation something is presented, in judgment something is affirmed or denied, in love loved, in hate hated, in desire desired and so on. . . .

9. Let us, in conclusion, summarize the results of the discussion about the difference between mental and physical phenomena. First of all, we illustrated the specific nature of the two classes by means of *examples*. We then defined mental phenomena as *presentations* or as phenomena which are based *upon presentation;* all the other phenomena being physical phenomena. Next we spoke of *extension,* which psychologists have asserted to be the specific characteristic of all physical phenomena, while all mental phenomena are supposed to be unextended. This assertion, however, ran into contradictions which can only be clarified by later investigations. All that can be determined now is that all mental phenomena really appear to be unextended. Further we

found that the *intentional in-existence,* the reference to something as an object, is a distinguishing characteristic of all mental phenomena. No physical phenomenon exhibits anything similar. We went on to define mental phenomena as the exclusive *object of inner perception;* they alone, therefore, are perceived with immediate evidence. Indeed, in the strict sense of the word, they alone are perceived. On this basis we proceeded to define them as the only phenomena which possess *actual existence* in addition to intentional existence. Finally, we emphasized as a distinguishing characteristic the fact that the mental phenomena which we perceive, in spite of all their multiplicity, *always* appear to us *as a unity,* while physical phenomena, which we perceive at the same time, do not all appear in the same way as parts of one single phenomenon.

That feature which best characterizes mental phenomena is undoubtedly their intentional in-existence. By means of this and the other characteristics listed above, we may now consider mental phenomena, to have been clearly differentiated from physical phenomena.[1]

When seeing a color, the color itself is not mental, but rather it is the act of seeing that is mental. Psychical phenomena relate to mental content but they are not that content. Here and elsewhere, Brentano was saying that the quality "blue" and the sensing of blue are different, and it is the latter which exemplifies the task of psychology. Blue in the first sense is merely passive mentally and not accessible to psychological inquiry; psychology is concerned with the experience which the mind carries out when it actualizes blue. To see, something must be seen. It "inexists" in the seeing.

For this study of acts of sensing, a method is necessary which brings out clearly its experiential basis:

2. Psychology, like the natural sciences, has its basis in perception and experience. Above all, however, its source is to be found in the *inner perception* of our own mental phenomena. We would never know what a thought is, or a judgement, pleasure or pain, desires or aversions, hopes or fears, courage or despair, decisions and voluntary intentions if we did not learn what they are through inner perception of our own phenomena. Note, however, that we said that inner *perception* [*Wahrnehmung*] and not introspection, i.e. inner *observation* [*Beobachtung*], constitutes this primary and essential source of psychology. These two concepts must be distinguished from one another. One of the characteristics of inner perception is that it can never become inner observation. We can observe objects which, as they say, are perceived externally. In observation, we

direct our full attention to a phenomenon in order to apprehend it accurately. But with objects of inner perception this is absolutely impossible. This is especially clear with regard to certain mental phenomena such as anger. If someone is in a state in which he wants to observe his own anger raging within him, the anger must already be somewhat diminished, and so his original object of observation would have disappeared. The same impossibility is also present in all other cases. It is a universally valid psychological law that we can never focus our *attention* upon the object of inner perception. We will have to discuss this issue in more detail later on. For the moment it will suffice to call attention to the personal experience of any unbiased person. Even those psychologists who believe that inner observation is possible all acknowledge that it involves extraordinary difficulty. This is a clear admission that such observation eludes even their efforts in most cases. But, in those exceptional cases in which they think they have been successful, they are undoubtedly the victims of self-deception. It is only while our attention is turned toward a different object that we are able to perceive, incidentally, the mental processes which are directed toward that object. Thus the observation of physical phenomena in external perception, while offering us a basis for knowledge of nature, can at the same time become a means of attaining knowledge of the mind. Indeed, turning one's attention to physical phenomena in our imagination is, if not the only source of our knowledge of laws governing the mind, at least the immediate and principal source. . . .

Inner perception of our own mental phenomena, then, is the primary source of the experiences essential to psychological investigations. And this inner perception is not to be confused with inner observation of our mental states, since anything of that sort is impossible.

3. It is obvious that in this respect psychology appears to be at a great disadvantage compared with the other general sciences. Although many of these sciences are unable to perform experiments, astronomy in particular, none of them is incapable of making observations.

In truth, psychology would become impossible if there were no way to make up for this deficiency. We can make up for it, however, at least to a certain extent, through the observation of earlier mental states in *memory*. It has often been claimed that this is the best means of attaining knowledge of mental facts, and philosophers of entirely different orientations are in agreement on this point. Herbart has made explicit reference to it; and John Stuart Mill points out in his essay on Comte that it is possible to study a mental phenomenon by means of memory immediately following its manifestation. "And this is," he adds, "really the mode in which our best knowledge of intellectual acts is generally acquired. We reflect on what we have been doing, when the act is past, but when its impression in the memory is still fresh."

If the attempt to observe the anger which stirs us becomes impossible because the phenomenon disappears, it is clear that an earlier state of excitement can no longer be interfered with in this way. And we really can focus our attention on a past mental phenomenon just as we can upon a present physical phenomenon, and in this way we can, so to speak, observe it. Furthermore, we could say that it is even possible to undertake experimentation on our own mental phenomena in this manner. For we can, by various means, arouse certain mental phenomena in ourselves intentionally, in order to find out whether this or that other phenomenon occurs as a result. We can then contemplate the result of the experiment calmly and attentively in our memory.

So at least one of the disadvantages can apparently be remedied. In all the experimental sciences memory makes possible the accumulation of observed facts for the purpose of establishing general truths; in psychology, it makes possible at the same time the observation of the facts themselves. I am certain that the psychologists who believed that they had observed their own mental phenomena in inner perception actually did what Mill described in the passage quoted above. They focused their attention on acts just past, whose impression was still fresh in their memory.[2]

In this excerpt, Brentano has stated his objection to introspection of the Wundtian variety, "inner observations" as he called them. Instead, description of phenomena is the psychological method of choice. "What is characteristic of mental phenomena is their reference to an object," is another way (in his table of contents) he refers to the critical distinction being made.

Brentano stands in contrast to Wundt in offering an alternative way of conceiving psychology. Wundt advanced a psychology of content: Brentano countered with a psychology of act in which contents cannot be investigated without references to processes or acts. A sensory quality, for example, cannot be investigated apart from the person who senses. Psychology is concerned with the experience which the mind carries out in reference to an object other than itself.

His approach to psychology, stressing "phenomena" and "objects," was to have an effect on Edmund Husserl, philosopher of phenomenology, who also conceived experience to be taken at face value, and not analysed into elements. Thus, the phenomenological movement saw its forerunner in Franz Brentano.

19

EBBINGHAUS ON
EXPERIMENTAL RESEARCH ON MEMORY

HERMANN EBBINGHAUS (1850–1909), German psychologist, performed the first experiment on memory and learning. In 1876, after reading a copy of Fechner's *Elements of Psychophysics*, Ebbinghaus decided that, contrary to the pronouncement of Wundt, experimental measurement could be applied to the higher mental processes, specifically to learning and memory. The results of this resolve appeared in 1885 in *Memory: A Contribution to Experimental Psychology*.

Frequency of repetition until the material was learned was seen as the essential condition to be investigated:

Under ordinary circumstances, indeed, frequent repetitions are indispensable in order to make possible the reproduction of a given content. Vocabularies, discourses, and poems of any length cannot be learned by a single repetition even with the greatest concentration of attention on the part of an individual of very great ability. By a sufficient number of repetitions their final mastery is ensured, and by additional later reproductions gain in assurance and ease is secured.

Left to itself every mental content gradually loses its capacity for being revived, or at least suffers loss in this regard under the influence of time. Facts crammed at examination time soon vanish, if they were not sufficiently grounded by other study and later subjected to a sufficient review. But even a thing so early and deeply founded as one's mother tongue is noticeably impaired if not used for several years.[1]

This study was to be done following the method of natural science—through quantitative experiments:

The method of obtaining exact measurements—*i.e.,* numerically exact ones—of the inner structure of causal relations is, by virtue of its nature, of general validity. This method, indeed, has been so exclusively used and so fully worked out by the natural sciences that, as a rule, it is defined as something peculiar to them, as *the* method of natural science. To repeat, however, its logical nature makes it generally applicable to all spheres of existence and phenomena. Moreover, the possibility of defining accurately and exactly the actual behavior of any process whatever, and thereby of giving a reliable basis for the direct comprehension of its connections depends above all upon the possibility of applying this method.

We all know of what this method consists: an attempt is made to keep constant the mass of conditions which have proven themselves causally connected with a certain result; one of these conditions is isolated from the rest and varied in a way that can be numerically described; then the accompanying change on the side of the effect is ascertained by measurement or computation.

Two fundamental and insurmountable difficulties, seem, however, to oppose a transfer of this method to the investigation of the causal relations of mental events in general and of those of memory in particular. In the first place, how are we to keep even approximately constant the bewildering mass of causal conditions which, in so far as they are of mental nature, almost completely elude our control, and which, moreover, are subject to endless and incessant change? In the second place, by what possible means are we to measure numerically the mental processes which flit by so quickly and which on introspection are so hard to analyse?[2]

To control the conditions that seemed to stand in the way of experiment, he devised special material (the nonsense syllable) that would be relatively and equally unfamiliar to subjects learning them.

In order to test practically, although only for a limited field, a way of penetrating more deeply into memory processes—and it is to these that the preceding considerations have been directed—I have hit upon the following method.

Out of the simple consonants of the alphabet and our eleven vowels and diphthongs all possible syllables of a certain sort were constructed, a vowel sound being placed between two consonants.*

These syllables, about 2,300 in number, were mixed together and then drawn out by chance and used to construct series of different lengths, several of which each time formed the material for a test.†

At the beginning a few rules were observed to prevent, in the construction of the syllables, too immediate repetition of similar sounds, but these were not strictly adhered to. Later they were abandoned and the matter left to chance. The syllables used each time were carefully laid aside till the whole number had been used, then they were mixed together and used again.

The aim of the tests carried on with these syllable series was, by means of repeated audible perusal of the separate series, to so impress them that immediately afterwards they could voluntarily just be reproduced. This aim was considered attained when the initial syllable being given, a series could be recited at the first attempt, without hesitation, at a certain rate, and with the consciousness of being correct.

SECTION 12.   ADVANTAGES OF THE MATERIAL

The nonsense material, just described, offers many advantages, in part because of this very lack of meaning. First of all, it is relatively simple and relatively homogeneous. In the case of the material nearest at hand, namely poetry or prose, the content is now narrative in style, now descriptive, or now reflective; it contains now a phrase that is pathetic, now one that is humorous; its metaphors are sometimes beautiful, sometimes harsh; its rhythm is sometimes smooth and sometimes rough. There is thus brought into play a multiplicity of influences which change without regularity and are therefore disturbing. Such are associations which dart here and there, different degrees of interest, lines of verse recalled be-

---

*The vowel sounds employed were a, e, i, o, u, ä, ö, ü, au, ei, eu. For the beginning of the syllables the following consonants were employed: b, d, f, g, h, j, k, l, m, n, p, r, s, (= sz), t, w and in addition ch, sch, soft s, and the French j (19 altogether); for the end of the syllables f, k, l, m, n, p, r, s, (= sz) t, ch, sch (11 altogether). For the final sound fewer consonants were employed than for the initial sound, because a German tongue even after several years practise in foreign languages does not quite accustom itself to the correct pronunciation of the mediae at the end. For the same reason I refrained from the use of other foreign sounds although I tried at first to use them for the sake of enriching the material.

†I shall retain in what follows the designations employed above and call a group of several syllable series or a single series a "test." A number of "tests" I shall speak of as a "test series" or a "group of tests."

cause of their striking quality or their beauty, and the like. All this is avoided with our syllables. Among many thousand combinations there occur scarcely a few dozen that have a meaning and among these there are again only a few whose meaning was realised while they were being memorised.

However, the simplicity and homogeneity of the material must not be overestimated. It is still far from ideal. The learning of the syllables calls into play the three sensory fields, sight, hearing and the muscle sense of the organs of speech. And although the part that each of these senses plays is well limited and always similar in kind, a certain complication of the results must still be anticipated because of their combined action. Again, to particularise, the homogeneity of the series of syllables falls considerably short of what might be expected of it. These series exhibit very important and almost incomprehensible variations as to the ease or difficulty with which they are learned. It even appears from this point of view as if the differences between sense and nonsense material were not nearly so great as one would be inclined *a priori* to imagine. At least I found in the case of learning by heart a few cantos from Byron's "Don Juan" no greater range of distribution of the separate numerical measures than in the case of a series of nonsense syllables in the learning of which an approximately equal time had been spent. In the former case the innumerable disturbing influences mentioned above seem to have compensated each other in producing a certain intermediate effect; whereas in the latter case the predisposition, due to the influence of the mother tongue, for certain combinations of letters and syllables must be a very heterogeneous one.

More indubitable are the advantages of our material in two other respects. In the first place it permits an inexhaustible amount of new combinations of quite homogeneous character, while different poems, different prose pieces always have something incomparable. It also makes possible a quantitative variation which is adequate and certain; whereas to break off before the end or to begin in the middle of the verse or the sentence leads to new complications because of various and unavoidable disturbances of the meaning.[3]

This description of the materials to be used is followed by an account of how he standardized the procedure, including the regulation of his own life pattern, since he was subject as well as experimenter. The studies he conducted with nonsense syllables were spread out over several years.

NO.	I AFTER X HOURS	II SO MUCH OF THE SERIES LEARNED WAS RETAINED THAT IN RELEARNING A SAVING OF Q% OF THE TIME OF ORIGINAL LEARNING WAS MADE	III P.E.$_m$	IV THE AMOUNT FORGOTTEN WAS THUS EQUIVALENT TO v% OF THE ORIGINAL IN TERMS OF TIME OF LEARNING
	X =	Q =		v =
1	0.33	58.2	1	41.8
2	1.	44.2	1	55.8
3	8.8	35.8	1	64.2
4	24.	33.7	1.2	66.3
5	48.	27.8	1.4	72.2
6	6×24	25.4	1.3	74.6
7	31×24	21.1	0.8	78.9

Ebbinghaus' investigations fall into several categories: rapidity of learning series of nonsense syllables as a function of the length of list; retention as a function of the sheer number of repetitions; retention as a function of time; retention as a function of repeated learning; and retention as a function of the order of success in the series. All of these functions became subject to a myriad of later psychological studies, but perhaps the best known of his results concerned retention as a function of time, the topic of the next excerpt:

The investigations in question fell in the year 1879–80 and comprised 163 double tests. Each double test consisted in learning eight series of 13 syllables each (with the exception of 38 double tests taken from 11–12 A.M. which contained only six series each) and then in relearning them after a definite time. The learning was continued until two errorless recitations of the series in question were possible. The relearning was carried to the same point; it occurred at one of the following seven times,—namely, after about one third of an hour, after 1 hour, after 9 hours, one day, two days, six days, or 31 days. . . .

After explaining that the absolute amount of savings fluctuated according to the time of day expressed in a ratio, he presented the results in terms of Q, which he describes as follows:

On the other hand, the values (Q) found for the relation of each saving of work to the time originally spent, are apparently almost independent of this ratio. Their averages are close together for all three times of day, and do not show any character of increase or decrease in the later hours. Accordingly I here tabulate the latter. [See page 146]

SECTION 29.   DISCUSSION OF RESULTS

1. It will probably be claimed that the fact that forgetting would be very rapid at the beginning of the process and very slow at the end should have been foreseen. However, it would be just as reasonable to be surprised at this initial rapidity and later slowness as they come to light here under the definite conditions of our experiment for a certain individual, and for a series of 13 syllables. One hour after the end of the learning, the forgetting had already progressed so far that one half the amount of the original work had to be expended before the series could be reproduced again; after 8 hours the work to be made up amounted to two thirds of the first effort. Gradually, however, the process became slower so that even

for rather long periods the additional loss could be ascertained only with difficulty. After 24 hours about one third was always remembered; after 6 days about one fourth, and after a whole month fully one fifth of the first work persisted in effect. The decrease of this after-effect in the latter intervals of time is evidently so slow that it is easy to predict that a complete vanishing of the effect of the first memorisation of these series would, if they had been left to themselves, have occurred only after an indefinitely long period of time. . . .

3. Considering the special, individual, and uncertain character of our numerical results no one will desire at once to know what "law" is revealed in them. However, it is noteworthy that all the seven values which cover intervals of one third of an hour in length to 31 days in length (thus from singlefold to 2,000fold) may with tolerable approximation be put into a rather simple mathematical formula. I call:

t the time in minutes counting from one minute before the end of the learning,

b the saving of work evident in relearning, the equivalent of the amount remembered from the first learning expressed in percentage of the time necessary for this first learning,

c and k two constants to be defined presently

Then the following formula may be written:

$$b = \frac{100\,k}{(\log t)^c + k}$$

By using common logarithms and with merely approximate estimates, not involving exact calculation by the method of least squares,

$$k = 1.84$$
$$c = 1.25$$

t	b OBSERVED	b CALCULATED	Δ
20	58.2	57.0	+1.2
64	44.2	46.7	−2.5
526	35.8	34.5	+1.3
1440	33.7	30.4	+3.3
2×1440	27.8	28.1	−0.3
6×1440	25.4	24.9	+0.5
31×1440	21.1	21.2	−0.1

The deviations of the calculated values from the observed values surpass the probable limits of error only at the second and fourth values. With regard to the latter I have already expressed the conjecture that the test might have given here too large a value; the second suffers from an uncertainty concerning the correction made. By the determination made for t, the formula has the advantage that it is valid for the moment in which the learning ceases and that it gives correctly $b = 100$. In the moment when the series can just be recited, the relearning, of course, requires no time, so that the saving is equal to the work expended.

Solving the formula for k we have

$$k = \frac{b \, (\log t)^c}{100 - b}$$

This expression, $100 - b$ the complement of the work saved, is nothing other than the work required for relearning, the equivalent of the amount forgotten from the first learning. Calling this, v, the following simple relation results:

$$\frac{b}{v} = \frac{k}{(\log t)^c}$$

To express it in words: when nonsense series of 13 syllables each were memorised and relearned after different intervals, the quotients of the work saved and the work required were about inversely proportional to a small power of the logarithm of those intervals of time. To express it more briefly and less accurately: the quotients of the amounts retained and the amounts forgotten were inversely as the logarithms of the times.

Of course this statement and the formula upon which it rests have here no other value than that of a shorthand statement of the above results which have been found but once and under the circumstances described. Whether they possess a more general significance so that, under other circumstances or with other individuals, they might find expression in other constants I cannot at the present time say.[4]

These findings are epitomized in a well known graph, available to all students of psychology, one in which a logarithmic curve starting high in the left hand corner (representing retention right after the learning process) descends rapidly (representing a rapid loss) at first, then more and more gradually (representing a slower and slower rate of loss).

Ebbinghaus presented a model for others to follow concerning the means of experimental control of factors affecting memory, in order to eliminate sources of error and to quantify his results as precisely as possible. His research was to be the starting point for thousands of studies, extending in influence up to the present day.

20

KÜLPE ON
THE STUDY OF THINKING,
INCLUDING IMAGELESS THOUGHT

OSWALD KÜLPE (1862–1915) German psychologist, was one whose significance arose primarily from the inspiration he provided to students who conducted the research. This work became known as that of the Würzburg, school, because Külpe's major academic affiliation was with that university. Earlier he had served as Wundt's second assistant (after Cattell), but he also studied at other universities and, while originally under the shadow of Wundt, broke away to emphasize that the experimental study of thinking is feasible (contrary to Wundt's pronouncement).

Somewhat late in his career, he presented a short summary of the psychology of thinking:

The study of thinking, which in Germany has been nurtured primarily at the Würzburger Psychological Institute, belongs to [the] developmental phase of experimental psychology.

While earlier psychology in general did not pay adequate attention to thinking, the new experimental direction was so busy bringing order into the more solid institutions of sensations, images, and feelings, that it was quite late before it could devote itself to the airy thoughts. The first mental contents to be noted in consciousness were those of pressures and punctures, tastes and smells, sounds and colors. They were the easiest to perceive, followed by their images and the pleasures and pains. That there was anything else without the palpable constitution of these formations escaped the eye of the scientist who had not been trained to perceive it. The experience of natural science directed the researcher's attention toward sensory stimuli and sensations, after-images, contrast phenomena

and fantastic variations of reality. Whatever did not have such characteristics simply did not seem to exist. And thus when the first experimental psychologists undertook experiments about the meaning of words
they were able to report anything at all only if self-evident representations
or their accompanying phenomena made an appearance. In many other
cases, particularly when the words signified something abstract or general, they found "nothing." The fact that a word could be understood
without eliciting images, that a sentence could be understood and judged
even though only its sounds appeared to be present in consciousness,
never gave these psychologists cause to postulate or to determine imageless as well as imageable contents. . . .

What finally led us in psychology to another theory was the *systematic application of self-observation*. Previously it was the rule not to
obtain reports about all experiences that occurred during an experiment
as soon as it was concluded, but only to obtain occasional reports from
subjects about exceptional or abnormal occurrences. Only at the conclusion of a whole series was a general report requested about the main facts
that were still remembered. In this fashion only the grossest aspects
came to light. Furthermore, the commitment to the traditional concepts
of sensations, feelings, and images prevented the observation or labelling
of that which was neither sensation nor feeling nor image. However, as
soon as persons trained in self-observation were allowed to make complete and unprejudiced reports about their experiences of an experiment
immediately after its completion, the necessity for an extension of the
previous concepts and definitions became obvious. We found in ourselves
processes, states, directions, and acts which did not fit the schema of the
older psychology. Subjects started to speak in the language of everyday
life and to give images only a subordinate importance in their private
world. They knew and thought, judged and understood, apprehended
meaning and interpreted connections, without receiving any real support
from occasionally appearing sensory events [*Versinnlichungen*]. Consider the following example. . . .

The subject is asked: "Do you understand the sentence: Thinking
is so extraordinarily difficult that many prefer to judge?" The protocol
reads: "I knew immediately after the conclusion of the sentence what the
point was. But the thought was still quite unclear. In order to gain clarity.
I slowly repeated the sentence and when I was finished with that the
thought was clear so that I can now repeat it: To judge here implies
thoughtless speech and a dismissal of the subject matter in contrast to
the searching activity of thinking. Apart from the words of the sentence

that I heard and which I then reproduced, there was nothing in the way of images in my consciousness." This is not just a simple process of imageless thought. What is notable is that [subjects] stated that understanding proceeded generally in this fashion with difficult sentences. It is thus not an artificial product of the laboratory, but the blossoming life of reality that has been opened up by these experiments. . . .

Who would experience images here and for whom would such images be the basis, the inescapable condition of comprehension? And who wants to maintain that words alone suffice to represent the meaning? No, these cases provide proof for the existence of imageless conscious contents, especially thoughts.

But if thoughts differ from the images of colors and sounds, of forests and gardens, of men and animals, then this difference will also be found in their behavior, in their forms, and in their course. We know what lawfulness governs images. Everybody speaks of association and reproduction, of the appearance of an image, of its elicitation by others, of its connection with other images. We learn a poem or a new vocabulary, Here knowledge of content, knowledge of meaning is not sufficient; we must learn one word after another so that we can later faithfully reproduce the whole. We develop strong associations between the succeeding or coordinated members of a poem or a list of words, and for this we need a long period of time and a large number of repetitions. If thoughts are nothing but images, then the same tediousness should govern their memorization. Any reflection about the manner in which we assimilate the meaning of a poem shows immediately that the state of affairs is different here. One attentive reading is frequently sufficient to reproduce the thought content. And thus we progress through sheer mental exposure to such comprehensive feats as the reproduction of the thoughts contained in a sermon, a lecture, a dramatic production, a novel, a scientific work, or a long conversation. We not infrequently find to our sorrow how independent we are of the actual words. Sometimes we would like very much to be able to reproduce faithfully a striking expression, the pregnant form of a sentence, or an attractive picture. But even though the sense of what has been said is quite available to us, we cannot reproduce its form. . . .

It is notable that one of the first results of our psychology of thought was negative: The old conceptual notions that experimental psychology had provided for descriptions of sensation, feeling, and imagination, and their relations, did not permit comprehension or definition of intellectual processes. But similarly the new concept of dispositions of consciousness [*Bewusstseinslage*] which was pressed upon us by factual observation, was not sufficient and only made possible circumscription rather than description. Even the study of primitive processes of thinking soon showed that the imageless can be known. Self-observation, in contrast to observations of nature, can perceive the presence and definite characteristics of what is neither color nor sound, of what may be give without image or feeling. The meaning of abstract and general expressions can be shown to exist in consciousness when nothing perceptual may be discovered apart froom the words, and these meanings may be experienced and realized even without words or other signs. The new concept of conscious knowing [*Bewusstheit*] gave expression to these facts. And thus the inflexible schema of the previously accepted elements of mental life was extended in an important direction.

Experimental psychology is thus confronted with new problems which disclose many and varied perspectives. Not only do imageless states include known, meant, and thought objects with all their characteristics and relations, and states of affairs that can be expressed in judgments, but also the many actions whereby we take a position toward a given conscious content, whereby we order, classify, recognize or reject it. Although one once could use sensations and images to construct a mosaic of mental life and an automatic lawfulness of the coming and going of conscious elements, such a simplification and dependence upon chemical analogies has now lost its footing. Perceptual [*anschaulich*] contents could only persist as artificial abstractions, as arbitrarily isolated and separated components. Within a complete consciousness, however, they have become partial phenomena, dependent upon a variety of different conceptions, and it was only when they were placed in a complex of mental processes that they gained meaning and value for the experiencing subject. Just as perception could not be characterized as a mere having of sensation, no less could thinking be conceived as the associative course of images. Association psychology, as it had been founded by Hume, lost its hegemony. . . .

[The psychology of] thinking unlocked the door to the true internal world, and it was no mysticism that led us there, but the abandoning of a prejudice. Bacon already knew that the road to truth is paved with prejudices. In the present instance they happen to derive from the exact natural sciences, for whom in the last decades sensory observation meant everything and for whom concepts were only an expedient used to represent, in the simplest possible fashion, facts based on sensory experience. But now thoughts became not only signs for sensations but independent structures and values that could be ascertained with certainty just as any sensory impression. They were even more faithful, lasting, and freer than the pictures with which our memory and fantasy otherwise operate. But they did not, of course, admit to the same immediate observation as perceptual objects. The discovery was made that the ego could not be divided. To think with a certain devotion and depth and to observe the thoughts at the same time—that could not be done. First one and then the other, that was the watchword of the young psychology of thought. And it succeeded surprisingly well. Once a mental task was solved, the process that had been experienced became in all its phases an object of intensive determination by the retrospective observer. Comparison of several subjects and of several results from the same subject demonstrated that the procedure was unobjectionable. The pronounced agreement of our studies in the psychology of thought, whereby one could be built upon another, was a beautiful confirmation of our results. Once again it became clear why the previously used methods of observation could not find any thinking or other expressions of our conscious activity. Observation itself is a particular act, a committed activity of the ego. No other activity can be executed next to it at the same time. Our mental efficiency is limited, our personality is a unitary whole. But observation can take place after the completion of a function and can make it the object of self-perception. And now many acts were recognized which previously had not existed for psychology: attending and recognizing, willing and rejecting, comparing and differentiating, and many more. All of them were lacking the perceptual [anschaulich] character of sensations, images, and feelings, even though these phenomena could accompany the newly found actions. It is characteristic of the helplessness of the previous psychology that it thought it could define these acts through their symptoms. Attention was considered as a group of tension and muscle sensations, because so-called strained attention gives rise to such sensations. Similarly, willing was dissolved into images of motions because they usually precede an external act of the will. These constructions, whose artificiality immediately becomes apparent, were left without a leg to stand on as soon as the existence of special psychic acts was recognized, thus robbing sensations and images of their sole dominion in consciousness.

With the recognition of these acts another important innovation came to the fore. The center of gravity of mental life had to be moved. Previously one could say: We are attentive because our eyes are fixed on a particular point in the visual field and the muscles that keep the eyes in that position are tensed. It now became clear that this conception inverted the real state of affairs and that what it should rather say is: We direct our eyes toward a certain point and strain our muscles because we want to observe it. *Activity became the central focus,* receptivity and the mechanism of images secondary. . . .

The actions of the ego are always subject to points of view and tasks [*Aufgaben*] and through them are moved to activity. One could also say that they serve a purpose, either self-generated or set by others. The thinking of the theoretician is no more nor less aimless than that of the practitioner. Psychologists are used to taking this into consideration. The subject receives a task, a direction or instruction as to the point of view which he must adopt toward the presented stimulus. He may have to compare two light intensities one with another, to execute a movement upon a pressure or a sound, to reply quickly to a called-out word with the first word that he can think of, to understand a sentence, to draw a conclusion, and so forth. All such tasks, if they are willingly undertaken and remembered, exercise a great determining force upon the behavior of the subject. This force is called the determining tendency. In a sense the ego contains an unlimited variety of response possibilities. If one of these is to come to the fore to the exclusion of all others, then a determination, a selection, is needed.

The independence of the task and the determining tendency that was derived from it was also fateful for association psychology. Such a task is not some ordinary type of reproductive motive. It must be accepted, the subject must support it, and it gives his activity a certain direction. Sensations, feelings, and images are not given tasks; a task is set for a subject, whose mental character does not dissolve into these contents, but whose spontaneity alone can adopt the instructions and execute them. Since in all thinking such determining viewpoints play a role, since abstraction and combination, judgment and conclusion, comparison and differentiation, the finding and construction of relations, all become carriers of determining tendencies, the psychology of the task became an essential part of the modern investigation of thinking. And even the psychology of the task proved to have an importance that significantly transcended the narrower area in which it was developed. No psychological experiments are imaginable without tasks! The tasks must, therefore, be considered just as important an experimental condition as the apparatus and the stimuli that it presents. A variation in the task is at least as important an experimental procedure as a change in external experimental conditions.

This importance of the task and its effects on the structure and course of mental events could not be explained with the tools of association psychology. Rather, Ach was able to show that even associations of considerable strength could be overcome with a counteracting task. The force with which a determining tendency acts is not only greater than the familiar reproductive tendencies, it also derives from a different source and its effectiveness is not tied to associative relations.[1]

It should be noted that Külpe calls for "self-observation" to go beyond that of sensations, feelings, and images. When one does, mental processes, states, and acts are found, which do not fit the "older psychology" (of Wundt). Meanings in thinking, not carried by specific images, were referred to in English as imageless thought. Since the excerpt does not bring out its nature too clearly, brief mention will be made of one of the experiments by Karl Marbe[2], one of Külpe's students. In a psychophysical study of judgment of weights of the already familiar variety (p. 105), Marbe found that while sensations and images were present, their presence told him nothing about how his subjects made their judgments. They said "heavier" or "lighter" and usually were right, but they made these decisions apparently independently of the images that they reported as accompanying the process of judgment.

While disagreeing with the Wundtian position concerning the elements of conscious experience, the members of the Würzburg school were still seeking other elements (thus molecular) in their view of the subject nature of psychology.

In addition to broadening psychology to include the study of thinking, which is the topic of Külpe's excerpt, there is brief mention in it of "willing," "rejecting," "comparing," and the like. Similarly, they refer, here as elsewhere, to "task," "set," and "determining tendencies." All of these terms have a motivational connotation today—they imply direction of behavior. So the Würzburg School consisted of pioneers not only in the study of thinking but also in the study of motivation.

21

DARWIN ON
NATURAL SELECTION AND EMOTIONS
AS SERVICEABLE ASSOCIATED HABITS

CHARLES DARWIN (1809–1882), English biologist, organized old and found much new information to present an overwhelming array of evidence demonstrating that, in the evolution of animals and humans, there was a process of natural selection. In the struggle for survival, the fittest did so, and the biological characteristics that led to this survival were inherited by their progeny. This position was stated in full form in *The Origin of Species by Means of Natural Selection,* first published in 1859. Since it was not thoroughly understood that humans were not an exception to the process of natural selection, he published *The Descent of Man* in 1871 for the express purpose of clearing up this misunderstanding. From the former volume, a portion of the short summary statement from the chapter on natural selection is offered.

If under changing conditions of life organic beings present individual differences in almost every part of their structure, and this cannot be disputed; if there be, owing to their geometrical rate of increase, a severe struggle for life at some age, season, or year, and this certainly cannot be disputed; then, considering the infinite complexity of the relations of all organic beings to each other and to their conditions of life, causing an infinite diversity in structure, constitution, and habits, to be advantageous to them, it would be a most extraordinary fact if no variations had ever occurred useful to each being's own welfare, in the same manner as so many variations have occurred useful to man. But if variations useful to any organic being ever do occur, assuredly individuals thus characterised will have the best chance of being preserved in the struggle for life; and from the strong principle of inheritance, these will tend to produce offspring similarly characterised. This principle of preservation, or the survival of the fittest, I have called Natural Selection. It leads to the improvement of each creature in relation to its organic and inorganic conditions of life, and consequently, in most cases, to what must be regarded as an advance in organisation. Nevertheless, low and simple forms will long endure if well fitted for their simple conditions of life. . . . It is a truly wonderful fact—the wonder of which we are apt to overlook from familiarity—that all animals and all plants throughout all time and space should be related to each other in groups, subordinate to groups, in the manner which we everywhere behold—namely, varieties of the same species most closely related, species of the same genus less closely and unequally related, forming sections and sub-genera, species of distinct genera much less closely related, and genera related in different degrees, forming sub-families, families, orders, sub-classes and classes. The several subordinate groups in any class cannot be ranked in a single file, but seem clustered round points, and these round other points, and so on in almost endless cycles. If species had been independently created, no explanation would have been possible of this kind of classification; but it is explained through inheritance and the complex action of natural selection, entailing extinction and divergence of character, as we have seen illustrated in the diagram.

The affinities of all the beings of the same class have sometimes been represented by a great tree. I believe this simile largely speaks the truth. The green and budding twigs may represent existing species; and those produced during former years may represent the long succession of extinct species. At each period of growth all the growing twigs have tried to branch out on all sides, and to overtop and kill the surrounding twigs and branches, in the same manner as species and groups of species have at all times overmastered other species in the great battle for life. The limbs divided into great branches, and these into lesser and lesser branches, were themselves once, when the tree was young, budding twigs, and this connection of the former and present buds by ramifying branches may well represent the classification of all extinct and living species in groups subordinate to groups. Of the many twigs which flourished when the tree was a mere bush, only two or three, now grown into great branches, yet survive and bear the other branches; so with the species which lived during long-past geological periods very few have left living and modified descendants. From the first growth of the tree, many a limb and branch has decayed and dropped off; and these fallen branches of various sizes may represent those whole orders, families, and genera which have now no living representatives, and which are known to us only in a fossil state. As we here and there see a thin straggling branch springing from a fork low down in a tree, and which by some chance has been favoured and is still alive on its summit, so we occasionally see an animal like the Ornithorhynchus or Lepidosiren, which in some small degree connects by its affinities two large branches of life, and which has apparently been saved from fatal competition by having inhabited a protected station. As buds give rise by growth to fresh buds, and these, if vigorous, branch out and overtop on all sides many a feebler branch, so by generation I believe it has been with the great Tree of Life, which fills with its dead and broken branches the crust of the earth, and covers the surface with its everbranching and beautiful ramifications.[1]

As a part of his efforts to support evolutionary theory, Darwin considered the problem of the expression of emotions, since they, too, could be conceived as originally voluntary movements inherited in the process of evolution.

I have now described, to the best of my ability, the chief expressive actions in man, and in some few of the lower animals. I have also attempted to explain the origin or development of these actions through . . . three principles. . . . The first of these principles is, that movements which are serviceable in gratifying some desire, or in relieving some sensation, if often repeated, become so habitual that they are performed, whether or not of any service, whenever the same desire or sensation is felt, even in a very weak degree.

Our second principle is that of antithesis. The habit of voluntarily performing opposite movements under opposite impulses has become firmly established in us by the practice of our whole lives. Hence, if certain actions have been regularly performed, in accordance with our first principle, under a certain frame of mind, there will be a strong and involuntary tendency to the performance of directly opposite actions, whether or not these are of any use, under the excitement of an opposite frame of mind.

Our third principle is the direct action of the excited nervous system on the body, independently of the will, and independently, in large part, of habit. Experience shows that nerve-force is generated and set free whenever the cerebro-spinal system is excited. The direction which this nerve-force follows is necessarily determined by the lines of connection between the nerve-cells, with each other and with various parts of the body. But the direction is likewise much influenced by habit; inasmuch as nerve-force passes readily along accustomed channels.

The frantic and senseless actions of an enraged man may be attributed in part to the undirected flow of nerve-force, and in part to the effects of habit, for these actions often vaguely represent the act of striking. They thus pass into gestures included under our first principle; as when an indignant man unconsciously throws himself into a fitting attitude for attacking his opponent, though without any intention of making an actual attack. We see also the influence of habit in all the emotions and sensations which are called exciting; for they have assumed this character from having habitually led to energetic action; and action affects, in an indirect manner, the respiratory and circulatory system; and the latter reacts on the brain. Whenever these emotions or sensations are even slightly felt by us, though they may not at the time lead to any exertion, our whole system is nevertheless disturbed through the force of habit and association. Other emotions and sensations are called depressing, because they have not habitually led to energetic action, excepting just at first, as in the case of extreme pain, fear, and grief, and they have ultimately caused complete exhaustion; they are consequently expressed chiefly by negative signs and by prostration. Again, there are other emotions, such as that of affection, which do not commonly lead to action of any kind, and consequently are not exhibited by any strongly marked outward signs. Affection indeed, in as far as it is a pleasurable sensation, excites the ordinary signs of pleasure. . . .

Actions of all kinds, if regularly accompanying any state of the mind, are at once recognized as expressive. These may consist of movements of any part of the body, as the wagging of a dog's tail, the shrugging of a man's shoulders, the erection of the hair, the exudation of perspiration, the state of the capillary circulation, laboured breathing, and the use of the vocal or other sound-producing instruments. Even insects express anger, terror, jealousy, and love by their stridulation. With man the respiratory organs are of especial importance in expression, not only in a direct, but in a still higher degree in an indirect manner. . . .

That the chief expressive actions, exhibited by man and by the lower animals, are now innate or inherited,—that is, have not been learnt by the individual,—is admitted by every one. So little has learning or imitation to do with several of them that they are from the earliest days and throughout life quite beyond our control; for instance, the relaxation of the arteries of the skin in blushing, and the increased action of the heart in anger. We may see children, only two or three years old, and even those born blind, blushing from shame; and the naked scalp of a very young infant reddens from passion. Infants scream from pain directly after birth, and all their features then assume the same form as during subsequent years. These facts alone suffice to show that many of our most important expressions have not been learnt; but it is remarkable that some, which are certainly innate, require practice in the individual, before they are performed in a full and perfect manner; for instance, weeping and laughing. . . .

We are so familiar with the fact of young and old animals displaying their feelings in the same manner, that we hardly perceive how remarkable it is that a young puppy should wag its tail when pleased, depress its ears and uncover its canine teeth when pretending to be savage, just like an old dog; or that a kitten should arch its little back and erect its hair when frightened and angry, like an old cat. When, however, we turn to less common gestures in ourselves, which we are accustomed to look at as artificial or conventional,—such as shrugging the shoulders, as a sign of impotence, or the raising the arms with open hands and extended fingers, as a sign of wonder,—we feel perhaps too much surprise at finding that they are innate. That these and some other gestures are inherited, we may infer from their being performed by very young children, by those born blind, and by the most widely distinct races of man. We should also bear in mind that new and highly peculiar tricks, in association with certain states of the mind, are known to have arisen in certain individuals, and to have been afterwards transmitted to their offspring, in some cases, for more than one generation.

Certain other gestures, which seem to us so natural that we might easily imagine that they were innate, apparently have been learnt like the words of a language. This seems to be the case with the joining of the uplifted hands, and the turning up of the eyes, in prayer. So it is with kissing as a mark of affection; but this is innate, in so far as it depends on the pleasure derived from contact with a beloved person. The evidence with respect to the inheritance of nodding and shaking the head, as signs of affirmation and negation, is doubtful; for they are not universal, yet seem too general to have been independently acquired by all the individuals of so many races. . . .

It is a curious, though perhaps an idle speculation, how early in the long line of our progenitors the various expressive movements, now exhibited by man, were successively acquired. The following remarks will at least serve to recall some of the chief points discussed in this volume. We may confidently believe that laughter, as a sign of pleasure or enjoyment, was practised by our progenitors long before they deserved to be called human; for very many kinds of monkeys, when pleased, utter a reiterated sound, clearly analogous to our laughter, often accompanied by vibratory movements of their jaws or lips, with the corners of the mouth drawn backwards and upwards, by the wrinkling of the cheeks, and even by the brightening of the eyes.

We may likewise infer that fear was expressed from an extremely remote period, in almost the same manner as it now is by man; namely, by trembling, the erection of the hair, cold perspiration, pallor, widely opened eyes, the relaxation of most of the muscles, and by the whole body cowering downwards or held motionless.

Suffering, if great, will from the first have caused screams or groans to be uttered, the body to be contorted, and the teeth to be ground together. But our progenitors will not have exhibited those highly expressive movements of the features which accompany screaming and crying until their circulatory and respiratory organs, and the muscles surrounding the eyes, had acquired their present structure. The shedding of tears appears to have originated through reflex action from the spasmodic contraction of the eyelids, together perhaps with the eyeballs becoming gorged with blood during the act of screaming. Therefore weeping probably came on rather late in the line of our descent; and this conclusion agrees with the fact that our nearest allies, the anthropomorphous apes, do not weep. But we must here exercise some caution, for as certain monkeys, which are not closely related to man, weep, this habit might have been developed long ago in a sub-branch of the group from which man is derived. Our early progenitors, when suffering from grief or anxiety, would not have made their eyebrows oblique, or have drawn down the corners of their mouth, until they had acquired the habit of endeavouring to restrain their screams. The expression, therefore, of grief and anxiety is eminently human.

Rage will have been expressed at a very early period by threatening or frantic gestures, by the reddening of the skin, and by glaring eyes, but not by frowning. For the habit of frowning seems to have been acquired chiefly from the corrugators being the first muscles to contract round the eyes, whenever during infancy pain, anger, or distress is felt, and there consequently is a near approach to screaming; and partly from a frown serving as a shade in difficult and intent vision. It seems probable that this shading action would not have become habitual until man had assumed a completely upright position, for monkeys do not frown when exposed to a glaring light. Our early progenitors, when enraged, would probably have exposed their teeth more freely than does man, even when giving full vent to his rage, as with the insane. We may, also, feel almost certain that they would have protruded their lips, when sulky or disappointed, in a greater degree than is the case with our own children, or even with the children of existing savage races.

Our early progenitors, when indignant or moderately angry, would not have held their heads erect, opened their chests, squared their shoulders, and clenched their fists, until they had acquired the ordinary carriage and upright attitude of man, and had learnt to fight with their fists or clubs. Until this period had arrived the antithetical gesture of shrugging the shoulders, as a sign of impotence or of patience, would not have been developed. From the same reason astonishment would not then have been expressed by raising the arms with open hands and extended fingers. Nor, judging from the actions of monkeys, would astonishment have been exhibited by a widely opened mouth; but the eyes would have been opened and the eyebrows arched. Disgust would have been shown at a very early period by movements round the mouth, like those of vomiting,—that is, if the view which I have suggested respecting the source of the expression is correct, namely, that our progenitors had the power, and used it, of voluntarily and quickly rejecting any food from their stomachs which they disliked. But the more refined manner of showing contempt or disdain, by lowering the eyelids, or turning away the eyes and face, as if the despised person were not worth looking at, would not probably have been acquired until a much later period. . . .

We have seen that the study of the theory of expression confirms to a certain limited extent the conclusion that man is derived from some lower animal form, and supports the belief of the specific or subspecific unity of the several races; but as far as my judgment serves, such confirmation was hardly needed. We have also seen that expression in itself, or the language of the emotions, as it has sometimes been called, is certainly of importance for the welfare of mankind. To understand, as far as possible, the source or origin of the various expressions which may be hourly seen on the faces of the men around us, not to mention our domesticated animals, ought to possess much interest for us. From these several causes, we may conclude that the philosophy of our subject has well deserved the attention which it has already received from several excellent observers, and that it deserves still further attention, especially from any able physiologist.[2]

A word must be said about Darwin's influence on psychology. It had relatively little on the chrologically later, but previously excerpted "new" German psychology, with its absorption in the static human adult mind. They attached little importance to concepts such as development, drive, and emotion which are central to modern biological psychology. But this was not the case for certain British scientists, such as Galton (p. 166), Spencer (p. 173), Romanes (p. 179), and Morgan (p. 184) who, while contemporaries of the German psychologists previously discussed, drew their major inspiration from Darwin. Hence, this deviation from a more strict chronology is justified. In later years, the influence is particularly strong on American psychologists, such as James (p. 186), Hall (p. 207), and the school of functional psychology represented here by Dewey (p. 231) and Angell (p. 241). Darwin's emphasis on individual differences within the same species, drives to action in instincts and emotions which helped or hindered in the struggle for existence, and his varied demonstrations of psychological characteristics of animals made this a potentially fruitful field for later investigation. Humans conceived of as an animal species opened wider vistas for psychological study. It is not too generous to assert that work in animal-comparative psychology grew out of Darwin's work.

22

GALTON ON

INDIVIDUAL DIFFERENCES
EXPRESSED IN EMINENCE
IN FAMILIES
AND IN MENTAL IMAGERY

FRANCIS GALTON, (1822–1911) cousin to Charles Darwin, was a member of the Establishment in Victorian England. Since this fact permeated many of his activities, it is necessary to go into some detail about the evolution and meaning of the term. Originally, it was used to describe the special relation between the state and the established Church, the Church of England, and English citizens. It was further extended to include the landed gentry, Members of Parliament of both houses, military officers, statesmen and civil servants, and the graduates of Oxford and Cambridge Universities who were tacitly marked, not only by special privileges but by special responsibilities, to serve the state. Galton was a member of such a family, which included not only the Darwins but also the Wedgewoods, whose glassware is still prized. He studied medicine, explored Africa, rode to hounds, lived the life of a country gentleman, experimented with electricity, and studied meteorology. But, above all, he was curious about human nature and developed a host of interests centering around individual differences. One of these was very directly stimulated by Darwin's work—his investigation of how ability seemed to run in families, that is, that an eminent person is more apt to have eminent relatives than chance would lead one to expect. He selected eminent individuals in various fields—judges, scientists, university honors men—and then ascertained what relatives of theirs were also eminent. He titled his book, which first appeared in 1869, *Hereditary Genius: An Inquiry into its Laws and Consequences,* and stated his purpose and method in the first paragraphs of the introductory chapter:

I propose to show in this book that a man's natural abilities are derived by inheritance, under exactly the same limitations as are the form and physical features of the whole organic world. Consequently, as it is easy,

notwithstanding those limitations, to obtain by careful selection a permanent breed of dogs or horses gifted with peculiar powers of running, or of
doing anything else, so it would be quite practicable to produce a highly-
gifted race of men by judicious marriages during several consecutive
generations. I shall show that social agencies of an ordinary character,
whose influences are little suspected, are at this moment working towards the degradation of human nature, and that others are working
towards its improvement. I conclude that each generation has enormous
power over the natural gifts of those that follow, and maintain that it is a
duty we owe to humanity to investigate the range of that power, and to
exercise it in a way that, without being unwise towards ourselves, shall be
most advantageous to future inhabitants of the earth. . . .

The general plan of my argument is to show that high reputation is
a pretty accurate test of high ability; next to discuss the relationships of a
large body of fairly eminent men—namely, the Judges of England from
1660 to 1868, the Statesmen of the time of George III, and the Premiers
during the last 100 years—and to obtain from these a general survey of
the laws of heredity in respect to genius. Then I shall examine, in order,
the kindred of the most illustrious Commanders, men of Literature and of
Science, Poets, Painters, and Musicians, of whom history speaks. I shall
also discuss the kindred of a certain selection of Divines and of modern
Scholars. Lastly, I shall collate my results, and draw conclusions.[1]

He then presented the biographical evidence in somewhat disor-
ganized but copious detail. The following constitutes a summary of his
results, in the course of which he refers to several previously presented
tables concerned with each specific group of eminent men. They are not
included in the excerpt itself.

The number of cases of hereditary genius analysed in the several chapters of my book, amounts to a large total. I have dealt with no less than
300 families containing between them nearly 1,000 eminent men, of
whom 415 are illustrious, or, at all events, of such note as to deserve
being printed in small capitals at the head of a paragraph. If there be such
a thing as a decided law of distribution of genius in families, it is sure to
become manifest when we deal statistically with so large a body of examples.

In comparing the results obtained from the different groups of
eminent men, it will be our most convenient course to compare the columns B of the several tables. Column B gives the number of eminent

kinsmen in various degrees on the supposition that the number of
families in the group to which it refers is 100. All the entires under B have
therefore the same common measure, they are all *percentages,* and admit
of direct intercomparison. I hope I have made myself quite clear: lest
there should remain any misapprehension, it is better to give an example.
Thus, the families of Divines are only 25 in number, and in those 25
families there are 7 eminent fathers, 9 brothers, and 10 sons; now in
order to raise these numbers to percentages, 7, 9, and 10 must be multiplied by the number of times that 25 goes into 100, namely by 4. They will
then become 28, 36, and 40, and will be found entered as such, in column
B; the parent numbers 7, 9, 10, appearing in the same table in the
column A.

In the following table, the columns B of all the different groups are
printed side by side; I have, however, thrown Painters and Musicians into
a single group of Artists, because their numbers were too small to make it
worth while to consider them apart. Annexed to these is a column B
calculated from the whole of the families put together, with the intention
of giving a general average; and I have further attached to it its appropriate columns C and D, not so much for particular use in this chapter as
for the convenience of the reader who may wish to make comparisons
with the other tables, from the different point of view which D affords.

The general uniformity in the distribution of ability among the
kinsmen in the different groups, is strikingly manifest. The eminent
sons are almost invariably more numerous than the eminent brothers,
and these are a trifle more numerous than the eminent fathers. On proceeding further down the table, we come to a sudden dropping off of the
numbers at the second grade of kinship, namely, at the grandfathers,
uncles, nephews, and grandsons: this diminution is conspicuous in the
entries in column D. . . .On reaching the third grade of kinship, another
abrupt dropping off in numbers is again met with, but the first cousins
are found to occupy a decidedly better position than other relations within
the third grade.

We further observe, that while the proportionate abundance of
eminent kinsmen in the various grades is closely similar in all the groups,
the proportions deduced from the entire body of illustrious men, 415 in
number, coincide with peculiar general accuracy with those we obtained
from the large subdivision of 109 Judges. There cannot, therefore, remain
a doubt as to the existence of a law of distribution of ability in families, or
that it is pretty accurately expressed by the figures in column B, under

	SEAPARATE GROUPS								ALL GROUPS TOGETHER		
Number of families, each containing more than one eminent man	85	39	27	33	43	20	28	25	300		
Total number of eminent men in all the families	262	130	89	119	148	57	97	75	977		
									Illustrious and Eminent Men of all Classes		
	B	B	B	B	B	B	B	B	B	C	D*
Father	26	33	47	48	26	20	32	28	31	100	31
Brother	35	39	50	42	47	40	50	36	41	150	27
	36	49	31	51	60	45	89	40	48	100	48
Grandfather	15	28	16	24	14	5	7	20	17	200	8
Uncle	18	18	8	24	16	5	14	40	18	400	5
Nephew	19	18	35	24	23	50	18	4	22	400	5
Grandson	19	10	12	9	14	5	18	16	14	200	7
Great-grandfather	2	8	8	3	0	0	0	4	3	400	1
Great-uncle	4	5	8	6	5	5	7	4	5	800	1
First cousin	11	21	20	18	16	0	1	8	13	800	2
Great nephew	17	5	8	6	16	10	0	0	10	800	1
Great grandson	6	0	0	3	7	0	0	0	3	400	1
All more remote	14	37	44	15	23	5	18	16	31	?	...

the heading of "eminent men of all classes.". . . . the general average of all the groups; for, if we say that to every 10 illustrious men, *who have any eminent relations at all,* we find 3 or 4 eminent fathers, 4 or 5 eminent brothers, and 5 or 6 eminent sons, we shall be right in 17 instances out of 24; and in the 7 cases where we are wrong, the error will consist of less than 1 unit in 2 cases (the fathers of the commanders and men of litera- ture), of 1 unit in 4 cases (the fathers of poets, and the sons of judges,

*Editor's footnote: Column D gives percentage of eminent men in each degree of kinship to the most eminent member of distinguished families obtained by dividing B and C and multiplying by 100.

commanders, and divines), and of more than 1 unit in the sole case of the sons of artists.

The deviations from the average are naturally greater in the second and third grades of kinship, because the numbers of instances in the several groups are generally small; but as the proportions in the large subdivision of the 85 Judges correspond with extreme closeness to those of the general average, we are perfectly justified in accepting the latter with confidence.

The final and most important result remains to be worked out; it is this: if we know nothing else about a person than that he is a father, brother, son, grandson, or other relation of an illustrious man, what is the chance that he is or will be eminent? Column E . . .gives the reply for Judges; it remains for us to discover what is it for illustrious men generally. In each of the chapters I have given such data as I possessed, fit for combining with the results in column D, in order to make the required calculation. They consist of the proportion of men whose relations achieved eminence, compared with the total number into whose relationships I inquired. The general result is, that exactly one-half of the illustrious men have one or more eminent relations.[2]

In general, his findings but not his interpretations have been supported by later research. He was so much a member of the Establishment that he almost completely neglected the influence of socioeconomic status, similarity of education, and proximity to other eminent (influential) men in favor of an hereditarian interpretation. He concluded that human beings vary in their genetic mental endowment and these variations are heritable by their offspring. It was this work that served as the impetus for the eugenics movement, whose major tenet of social practice was that in order to improve a race or nation, the productivity of the best stock should be increased and the worst repressed. Eugenics became a social movement with a chequered career that has extended to this very day.

Galton became interested in visual mental imagery, because its presence in varying degrees might help to establish an essential difference in the mental operations of different people. Individuals were asked to describe the imagery of a past scene or object, the famous and most often used situation was one in which the subjects were asked to describe the breakfast table of that morning. A summary of excerpts, first for vividness of imagery and then for color, follows, arrayed from highest to lowest for a sample of 100 men "at least half" of whom were scientists.

Highest.—Brilliant, distinct, never blotchy.

First Suboctile.—The image once seen is perfectly clear and bright.

First Octile.—I can see my breakfast-table or any equally familiar thing with my mind's eye quite as well in all particulars as I can do if the reality is before me.

First Quartile.—Fairly clear; illumination of actual scene is fairly represented. Well defined. Parts do not obtrude themselves, but attention has to be directed to different points in succession to call up the whole.

Middlemost.—Fairly clear. Brightness probably at least from one-half to two-thirds of the original. Definition varies very much, one or two objects being much more distinct than the others, but the latter come out clearly if attention be paid to them.

Last Quartile.—Dim, certainly not comparable to the actual scene. I have to think separately of the several things on the table to bring them clearly before the mind's eye, and when I think of some things the others fade away in confusion.

Last Octile.—Dim and not comparable in brightness to the real scene. Badly defined with blotches of light; very incomplete; very little of one object is seen at one time.

Last Suboctile.—I am very rarely able to recall any object whatever with any sort of distinctness. Very occasionally an object or image will recall itself, but even then it is more like a generalised image than an individual one. I seem to be almost destitute of visualising power as under control.

Lowest.—My powers are zero. To my consciousness there is almost no association of memory with objective visual impressions. I recollect the table, but do not see it.

I next proceed to colour, as specified in the third of my questions, and annex a selection from the returns classified on the same principle as in the preceding paragraph.

COLOUR REPRESENTATION

Highest.—Perfectly distinct, bright, and natural.

First Suboctile.—White cloth, blue china, argand coffee-pot, buff stand with sienna drawing, toast—all clear.

First Octile.—All details seen perfectly.

First Quartile.—Colours distinct and natural till I begin to puzzle over them.

Middlemost.—Fairly distinct, though not certain that they are accurately recalled.

Last Quartile.—Natural, but very indistinct.

Last Octile.—Faint; can only recall colours by a special effort for each.

Last Suboctile.—Power is nil.

Lowest.—Power is nil.[3]

That many scientists seemed to be very deficient in visual imagery especially intrigued him. He accounted for this by arguing for their having developed habits of highly abstract thinking. After collecting a larger, more representative sample in later years, it became evident that this lack of imagery was not true for all scientists, and also that individuals of the general populace lacked imagery.

Many pages could be devoted to Galton's diverse contributions, such as the reaction time taken to produce association, measures of the diversity of associations, results on various sensory and motor tests with which he hoped to measure intelligence, and the first approximation to the formula for the statistical coefficient of correlation. In 1884, he also set up the world's first mental test center in London where, in exchange for taking the tests, a free copy of the results were supplied. Fortunately, one can summarize his contributions by saying that the measurement of individual differences in psychological capacities and the use of psychological tests were launched by Galton.

23

SPENCER ON
EVOLUTION,
ADAPTATION, AND HABIT

HERBERT SPENCER (1820–1903), English philosopher, saw evolution as the master unifying key to understanding of all human knowledge in his so-called *Synthetic Philosophy,* successive volumes of which appeared over more than a thirty-year span. He had espoused evolution before Darwin, depending on philosophical and geological arguments and supporting Lamarck's theory of the inheritance of acquired characters (reported in one of the excerpts).

Psychology, he argued, is related to biology:

54. It is contended by some that Psychology is a part of Biology, and should be merged in it; and those who hold this view will possibly answer the above argument by saying that in many cases the non-psychological part of Biology also takes into account phenomena in the environment, and even definite connections among these phenomena. The life of every organism is a continuous adaptation of its inner actions to outer actions; and a complete interpretation of the inner actions involves recognition of the outer actions. The annual production of leaves, flowers, and seeds by plants, is adjusted to the annual changes of the seasons; and there is in animals an adjustment between external changes in temperature and abundance, and internal production of ova. Moreover, there are many special relations of structure and function in plants and animals, that have reference to special relations of structure and function in surrounding plants and animals: instance those arrangements of the sexual organs that fit particular phaenogams for being fertilized by the particular insects that visit them.

But true as is this conception of Life (and having based the *Principles of Biology* on it I am not likely to question or to undervalue it), I nevertheless hold the distinction above drawn to be substantially valid. For throughout Biology proper, the environment and its correlated phenomena are either but tacitly recognized, or, if overtly and definitely recognized, are so but occasionally; while the organism and its correlated phenomena practically monopolize the attention. But in Psychology, the correlated phenomena of the environment are at every step avowedly and distinctly recognized; and are as essential to every psychological idea as are the correlated phenomena of the organism. Let us observe the contrast as exemplified. We study digestion. Digestion implies food. Food implies neighbouring plants or animals. But this implication scarcely enters into our study of digestion, unless we ask the quite special question—how the digestive organs become fitted to the materials they have to act upon? Again, when we interpret respiration we take for granted a surrounding oxygenated medium. And yet to show how far the two may be separated, we need only remember that the phenomena of respiration may be very well traced out in one who breathes a bladder of gas artificially obtained from peroxide of manganese or chlorate of potash. Once more, if, in following out the life-history of a plant, we have to note the adaptation of its hooked seeds to the woolly fleece of the animal which accidentally carries them off and disperses them, this distinct reference to specially-connected phenomena in the environment occurs either but once in an account of the plant's life, or only at long intervals. In fact, we may say that the great mass of purely biological phenomena may be displayed for some time by an organism detached from its medium, as by a fish out of water. Now observe how different it is with psychological phenomena. We cannot explain a single act of a fish as it moves about in the water, without taking into account its relations to neighbouring objects distinguished by specially-related attributes. The instinctive proceedings of the insect, equally with those which in higher creatures we call intelligent, we are unable even to express without referring to things around.

In brief, then, the propositions of Biology, when they imply the environment at all, imply almost exclusively its few general and constant phenomena, which, because of their generality and constancy, may be left out of consideration; whereas the propositions of Psychology refer to its multitudinous, special, and ever-varying phenomena, which, because of their speciality and changeability, cannot be left out of consideration.[1]

Adaptation of inner actions to outer actions, then, is stressed in both biology and psychology. This adaptation was conceived in a twofold manner, implying consciousness and not implying consciousness.

Moreover, both reason and instinct show a similar adaptive relationship.

203. That the commonly-assumed *hiatus* between Reason and Instinct has no existence, is implied both in the argument of the last few chapters and in that more general argument elaborated in the preceding part. The General Synthesis, by showing that all intelligent action whatever is the effecting of correspondences between internal changes and external co-existences and sequences, and by showing that this continuous adjustment of inner to outer relations progresses in Space, in Time, in Speciality, in Generality, and in Complexity, through insensible gradations; implied that the highest forms of psychical activity arise little by little out of the lowest, and cannot be definitely separated from them. Not only does the recently-enunciated doctrine, that the growth of intelligence is throughout determined by the repetition of experiences, involve the continuity of Reason with Instinct; but this continuity is involved in the previously-enunciated doctrine.

The impossibility of establishing any line of demarkation between the two may be clearly demonstrated. If every instinctive action is an adjustment of inner relations to outer relations, and if every rational action is also an adjustment of inner relations to outer relations; then, any alleged distinction can have no other basis than some difference in the characters of the relations to which the adjustments are made. It must be that while, in Instinct the correspondence is between inner and outer relations that are very simple or general; in Reason, the correspondence is between inner and outer relations that are complex, or special, or abstract, or infrequent. But the complexity, speciality, abstractness, and infrequency of relations, are entirely matters of degree. From a group of two co-existent attributes, up through groups of three, four, five, six, seven co-existent attributes, we may step by step ascend to such involved groups of co-existent attributes as are exhibited in a living body under a particular state of feeling, or under a particular physical disorder. Between relations experienced every moment and relations experienced but once in a life, there are relations that occur with all degrees of commonness. How then can any particular phase of complexity or infrequency be fixed upon as that at which Instinct ends and Reason begins?

From whatever point of view regarded, the facts imply a gradual transition from the lower forms of psychical action to the higher. That progressive complication of the instincts, which, as we have found, involves a progressive diminution of their purely automatic character, likewise involves a simultaneous commencement of Memory and Reason. But this joint evolution must be specifically described.[2]

With his emphasis on adaptation, it is not surprising that the nature and growth of intelligence is given a central place. After arguing that intelligence increases progressively throughout the animal kingdom, Spencer then goes on to consider the growth of intelligence in the individual and asserts that the individual's associations, "his psychical peculiarities," are hereditarily transmitted.

189. In the environment there exist relations of all orders of persistence, from the absolute to the fortuitous. Consequently, in a creature displaying a developed correspondence, there must exist all grades of strength in the connexions between states of consciousness. As a high intelligence is only thus possible, it is manifestly a condition to intelligence in general that the antecedents and consequents of psychical changes shall admit of all degrees of cohesion. And the question to be answered is:—How are their various degrees of cohesion adjusted?

Concerning their adjustments there are two possible hypotheses, of which all other hypotheses can be but modifications. On the one hand, it may be asserted that the strength of the tendency which each state of consciousness has to follow any other, is fixed beforehand by a Creator—that there is a "pre-established harmony" between the inner and outer relations. On the other hand, it may be asserted that the strength of the tendency which each state of consciousness has to follow any other, depends on the frequency with which the two have been connected in experience—that the harmony between the inner and outer relations arises from the fact that the outer relations produce the inner relations. Let us briefly examine these two hypotheses.

For the first the reason given, like the reason given for the special-creation hypothesis at large, is that certain of the phenomena cannot otherwise be explained. This supernatural genesis of the adjustment is alleged because no natural genesis has been assigned. The hypothesis has not a single fact to rest on. The facts that may be cited in its support, such as those of reflex action, are simply facts which have not yet been explained; and this alleged explanation of them as due to a pre-established harmony, is simply a disguised mode of shelving them as inexplicable. . . .

Contrariwise, for the second hypothesis the evidence is over-whelming. The multitudinous facts commonly cited to illustrate the doctrine of association of ideas, support it. It is in harmony with the general truth that from the ignorance of the infant the ascent is by slow steps to the knowledge of the adult. All theories and all methods of education take it for granted—are alike based on the belief that the more frequently states of consciousness are made to follow one another in a certain order, the stronger becomes their tendency to suggest one another in that order. The sayings—"Practice makes perfect," and "Habit is second nature," remind us how long-established and universal is the conviction that such a law exists. Exemplification of it is furnished by the fact that men who, from being differently circumstanced, have had different experiences, reach different generalizations; and by the fact that a wrong conception will become as firmly established as a right one, if the external relation to which it answers has been as often repeated. It is in harmony with these among other familiar truths;—that phenomena wholly unrelated in our experience, we have no tendency to think of together; that where a certain phenomenon has occurred in many relations, we usually imagine it as recurring in the relation in which it has most frequently occurred; that when we have witnessed many recurrences of a certain relation we come to have a strong belief in that relation; that if a relation has been daily experienced throughout life with scarcely an exception, it becomes difficult for us to conceive it as otherwise—to break the connexion between the states of consciousness representing it; and that where a relation has been perpetually repeated in our experience with absolute uniformity, we are entirely disabled from conceiving the negation of it.

The only orders of psychical sequences not obviously included by this general law, are those classed as reflex and instinctive—those which are apparently established before any experience has been had. But it is possible that, rightly interpreted, the law covers these also. Though reflex and instinctive sequences are not determined by the experiences of the *individual* organism manifesting them; yet the experiences of the *race* of organisms forming its ancestry may have determined them. Hereditary transmission applies to psychical peculiarities as well as to physical peculiarities. While the modified bodily structure produced by new habits of life is bequeathed to future generations, the modified nervous tendencies produced by such new habits of life are also bequeathed; and if the new habits of life become permanent the tendencies become permanent. Let us glance at the facts.

Among the families of a civilized society, the changes of occupation and habit from generation to generation and the intermarriage of families having different occupations and habits, greatly confuse the evidence of psychical heredity. But it needs only to contrast national characters to see that mental peculiarities caused by habit become hereditary. We know that there are warlike, peaceful, nomadic, maritime, hunting, commercial, races—races that are independent or slavish, active or slothful; we know that many of these, if not all, have a common origin; and hence it is inferable that these varieities of disposition, which have evident relations to modes of life, have been gradually produced in the course of generations. The tendencies to certain combinations of psychical changes have become organic. In domesticated animals parallel facts are familiar. Not only the forms and constitutions, but the dispositions and instincts of horses, oxen, sheep, pigs, fowls, have become different from those of their wild kindred. The various breeds of dogs exhibit numerous varieties of mental character and faculty permanently established by mode of life; and their several tendencies are spontaneously manifested. A young pointer will point at a covey the first time he is taken afield. A retriever brought up abroad has been remarked to fulfil his duty without instruction. In such cases there is evidently a bequeathed tendency for the psychical changes to take place in a special way.* Even from the conduct of untamed creatures we may gather evidence having like implications. The birds of inhabited countries are far more difficult to approach than those of uninhabited ones. And the manifest inference is, that continued experience of human enmity has wrought organic changes in them—has modified their instincts—has altered the connexions among their psychical states.[3]

The supposition that habits acquired by the individual can be transmitted through heredity depend on the reality of the transmission of acquired characters. Later genetic research has failed to demonstrate this transmission. But Spencer's subtle and extensive treatment of evolution in relation to association along with his emphasis on adaptation was of more general and lasting value and had an impress on the thinking of the functionalists (p. 231, 241) of a later generation.

---

*"Had Mr. Darwin's *Origin of Species* been published before I wrote this paragraph, I should, no doubt, have so qualified my words as to recognize "selection," natural or artificial, as a factor. Being written, however, I prefer to let the passage remain with nothing beyond verbal changes, and to make the needful qualification in a note. I do this partly to avoid an inconvenient complication of the statement. But my chief reason is that, while holding survival of the fittest to be always a cooperating cause, I believe that in cases like these it is not the chief cause. The reasons for this belief are given in the *Principles of Biology, %* 166."

24

ROMANES ON
INSTANCES OF MIND IN ANIMALS

GEORGE JOHN ROMANES (1848–1894), English biologist, was influenced by Darwin and Spencer whom he considered to be his predecessors in investigating the problem of the genesis of mind in animals and humans. His *Animal Intelligence*, published in 1882, concerned the first phase of his project, followed in 1889 by *Mental Evolution in Man*.

He opens the former with consideration of what is meant by mind:

Before we begin to consider the phenomena of mind throughout the animal kingdom it is desirable that we should understand, as far as possible, what it is that we exactly mean by mind. Now, by mind we may mean two very different things, according as we contemplate it in our own individual selves, or in other organisms. For if we contemplate our own mind, we have an immediate cognizance of a certain flow of thoughts or feelings, which are the most ultimate things, and indeed the only things, of which we are cognisant. But if we contemplate mind in other persons or organisms, we have no such immediate cognizance of thoughts or feelings. In such cases we can only *infer* the existence and the nature of thoughts and feelings from the activities of the organisms which appear to exhibit them. Thus it is that we may have a subjective analysis of mind and an objective analysis of mind—the difference between the two consisting in this, that in our subjective analysis we are restricted to the limits of a single isolated mind which we call our own, and within the territory of which we have immediate cognizance of all the processes that are going on, or at any rate of all the processes that fall within the scope of our introspection. But in our objective analysis of other or foreign minds

we have no such immediate cognizance; all our knowledge of their operations is derived, as it were, through the medium of ambassadors—these
ambassadors being the activities of the organism. Hence it is evident that
in our study of animal intelligence we are wholly restricted to the objective method. Starting from what I know subjectively of the operations of
my own individual mind, and the activities which in my own organism
they prompt, I proceed by analogy to infer from the observable activities
of other organisms what are the mental operations that underlie them. . . .

. . . , two conditions require to be satisfied before we even begin to
imagine that observable activities are indicative of mind: first, the activities must be displayed by a living organism; and secondly, they must be of
a kind to suggest the presence of two elements which we recognise as the
distinctive characteristics of mind as such—consciousness and choice.

So far, then, the case seems simple enough. Wherever we see a
living organism apparently exerting intentional choice, we might infer
that it is conscious choice, and therefore that the organism has a mind.
But further reflection shows us that this is just what we cannot do; for
although it is true that there is no mind without the power of conscious
choice, it is not true that all apparent choice is due to mind. In our own
organisms, for instance, we find a great many adaptive movements performed without choice or even consciousness coming into play at all—
such, for instance as in the beating of our hearts. . . .

Objectively considered, the only distinction between adaptive
movements due to reflex action and adaptive movements due to mental
perception, consists in the former depending on inherited mechanisms
within the nervous system being so constructed as to effect *particular*
adaptive movements in response to *particular* stimulations, while the
latter are independent of any such inherited adjustment of special
mechanisms to the exigencies of special circumstances. Reflex actions
under the influence of their appropriate stimuli may be compared to the
actions of a machine under the manipulations of an operator; when certain springs of action are touched by certain stimuli, the whole machine
is thrown into appropriate movement; there is no room for choice, there is
no room for uncertainty; but as surely as any of these inherited
mechanisms are affected by the stimulus with reference to which it has
been constructed to act, so surely will it act in precisely the same way as it
always has acted. But the case with conscious mental adjustment is quite
different. For, without at present going into the question concerning the
relation of body and mind, or waiting to ask whether cases of mental
adjustment are not really quite as *mechanical* in the sense of being the

necessary result of correlative of a chain of physical sequences due to a physical stimulation, it is enough to point to the variable and incalculable character of mental adjustments as distinguished from the constant and foreseeable character of reflex adjustments. All, in fact, that in an objective sense we can mean by a mental adjustment is an adjustment of a kind that has not been definitely fixed by heredity as the only adjustment possible in the given circumstances of stimulation. For were there no alternative of adjustment, the case, in an animal at least, would be indistinguishable from one of reflex action.

It is, then, adaptive action by a living organism in cases where the inherited machinery of the nervous system does not furnish data for our prevision of what the adaptive action must necessarily be—it is only here that we recognise the objective, evidence of mind. The criterion of mind, therefore, which I propose, and to which I shall adhere throughout the present volume, is as follows:—Does the organism learn to make new adjustments, or to modify old ones, in accordance with the results of its own individual experience? If it does so, the fact cannot be due merely to reflex action in the sense above described, for it is impossible that heredity can have provided in advance for innovations upon, or alterations of, its machinery during the lifetime of a particular individual.[1]

The task of psychology, as Romanes saw it, was to infer subjective status from objective data. Romanes then moved chapter by chapter through the various species from protozoa to apes, reporting anecdotes about them gathered from his own observations and accounts of travellers and naturalists. Characteristic is the following excerpt:

I have observed among the sea-gulls at the Zoological Gardens a curious habit, or mode of challenge. This consists in ostentatiously picking up a small twig or piece of wood, and throwing it down before the bird challenged, in the way that a glove used to be thrown down by the old knights. I observed this action performed repeatedly by several individuals of the glaucous and black-back species in the early spring-time of the year, and so it probably has some remote connection with the instinct of nest-building.[2]

Romanes and his sister observed a cebus monkey for about two months, and, as he put it, "not having the facilities for keeping the animal," lodged him at his sister's house. He concludes the account with what happened after he returned the monkey to the zoo with some general observations:

I returned the monkey to the Zoological Gardens at the end of February, and up to the time of his death in October 1881, he remembered me as well as the first day that he was sent back. I visited the monkey-house about once a month, and whenever I approached his cage he saw me with astonishing quickness—indeed, generally before I saw him—and ran to the bars, through which he thrust both hands with every expression of joy. He did not, however, scream aloud; his mind seemed too much occupied by the cares of monkey-society to admit of a vacancy large enough for such very intense emotion as he used to experience in the calmer life that he lived before. Being much struck with the extreme rapidity of his discernment whenever I approached the cage, however many other persons might be standing round, I purposely visited the monkey-house on Easter Monday, in order to see whether he would pick me out of the solid mass of people who fill the place on that day. Although I could only obtain a place three or four rows back from the cage, and although I made no sound wherewith to attract his attention, he saw me almost immediately, and with a sudden intelligent look of recognition ran across the cage to greet me. When I went away he followed me, as he always did, to the extreme end of his cage, and stood there watching my departure as long as I remained in sight.

In conclusion, I should say that much the most striking feature in the psychology of this animal, and the one which is least like anything met with in other animals, was the tireless spirit of investigation. The hours and hours of patient industry which this poor monkey has spent in ascertaining all that his monkey-intelligence could of the sundry unfamiliar objects that fell into his hands, might well read a lesson in carefulness to many a hasty observer. And the keen satisfaction which he displayed when he had succeeded in making any little discovery, such as that of the mechanical principle of the screw, repeating the results of his newly earned knowledge over and over again, till one could not but marvel at the intent abstraction of the 'dumb brute'—this was so different from anything to be met with in any other animal, that I confess I should not have believed what I saw unless I had repeatedly seen it with my own eyes. As my sister once observed, while we were watching him conducting some of his researches, in oblivion to his food and all his other surroundings— "when a monkey behaves like this, it is no wonder that man is a scientific animal!" And in my next work I shall hope to show how, from so high a starting-point, the psychology of the monkey has passed into that of the man.[3]

It is apparent that Romanes' procedure was anecodotal, just as was Darwin's, in that vignettes of animal intelligence were found and reported. The incidents described were the end in themselves, not what had happened to the animals before, nor what happened afterward. Therefore, the given significance was inferential and analogical: the method followed was the inference of the mental processes going on in the animal by analogy with one's own. But he was guided in his fact-collecting by evolutionary theory, of which he was among the earliest, if not the earliest after Darwin, to appreciate the significance of it for psychological matters. Moreover, many of his findings were obtained in naturalistics settings, that, as modern ethologists have shown, have much rich information to offer, lost in the "controlled" laboratory setting.

25

MORGAN ON
THE CANON OF INTERPRETATION
OF ANIMAL ACTIVITY

CONWY LLOYD MORGAN (1852–1936), English philosopher and psychologist, was a pioneer in the field of psychology represented by his best known work, *Introduction to Comparative Psychology,* which first appeared in 1894. It continued in the tradition of Darwin. Like his predecessor, Romanes, he accepted continuity of mind in animals and humans as his proper task. Romanes, however, had argued that since the particular behaviors he had recounted could not be accounted for by instinct, they must necessarily be due to reason. Morgan challenged this contention. The illustration that follows drew upon precisely the sort of anecdote that had been used to proclaim an animal's ability to reason, using a means to an end:

Tony, the fox-terrier pup . . . when he wanted to go out into the road, used to put his head under the latch of the gate, lift it, and wait for the gate to swing open. Now an observer of the dog's intelligent action might well suppose that he clearly perceived how the end in view was to be gained, and the most appropriate means for effecting his purpose. But here much depends on the sense in which this statement is understood. It may be understood in the sense that the situation had acquired what Dr. Stout calls "meaning," so that certain concrete surroundings suggested directly, and without analysis, a given mode of practical behaviour. Or it may be understood in the sense that the dog formed a general conception of means such as could be profitably applied to this particular end. If the former interpretation be correct, I should say that Tony acted intelligently as the result of sense-experience; if the latter, I should regard his conduct as rational. And it may be said that it is quite impossible to decide between the two views, since we cannot ascertain what passed through the dog's mind. Once more, therefore, I must draw attention to the canon of interpretation adopted at the outset of our inquiries concerning other minds than ours, namely, that in no case is an animal activity to be interpreted in terms of higher psychological processes, if it can be fairly interpreted in terms of processes which stand lower in the scale of psychological evolution and development. The question is therefore whether Tony's behaviour can be fairly explained without his forming any conception of the relation of the means employed to the end attained. It appears to me that it can. I watched the development of the habit. The gate is of iron and has iron bars running vertically with interspaces of five or six inches between. On either side is a wall or low parapet, on which are similar vertical rails. The latch of the gate is at a level of about a foot above that of the top of the low wall. When it is lifted, the gate swings open by its own weight. When the dog was put out of the front door he naturally wanted to get out into the road, where there was often much to interest him; cats to be worried, other dogs with whom to establish a sniffing acquaintance, and so forth. I watched the dog at a very early stage of the development of the habit. He then ran up and down the low wall, and put his head out between the iron bars, now here, now there, now elsewhere, keenly gazing into the road. This he did for quite three or four minutes. Although he had gone out of that gate many times, although he had opportunities for seeing me lift the latch (a matter that probably had no interest whatever for him, following me out being a matter of course in his experience), he did not specially look out at or near the gate. He certainly did not seem to have any notion of means to attain an end; nor indeed did he seem to be trying to get out. He appeared only to be looking restlessly and wistfully at the familiar road. At length it so happened that he put out his head beneath the latch, which, as I have said, is at a convenient height for his doing so, being about a foot above the level of the wall. The latch was thus lifted. He withdrew his head and began to look out elsewhere, when he noticed that the gate was swinging open, and out he bolted. After that, whenever I took him out, instead of opening the gate for him, I waited until he lifted the latch. Gradually he went, after less frequent poking of his head in the wrong place, to the one opening from which the latch could be lifted. But it was nearly three weeks, during which I took him out about a dozen times, before he went at once and without hesitation to the right place and put his head without any ineffectual fumbling beneath the latch. Why did he take so long? I think partly because there was so little connection between gazing out into the road and getting out into the road. He did not, at first at any rate, seem to do the former in order to effect the latter. The relation between means and end did not appear to take form in his mind, even subconsciously as means to the end. And I take it that he never had the faintest notion of how or why looking out just there came to mean walking forth into the road.[1]

Interpretation of the dog's behavior as due to reasoning was plausible if the dog was seen only after the habit was fixed. But if you know the dog's varied restless movements, later called trial and error, and their gradual elimination, the cautious interpretation would be to consider it a slowly developed habit.

The interpretative caution that he urged, later to be called Lloyd Morgan's canon, held that in no case should animal activity be interpreted in terms of higher psychological processes, if it could be interpreted in terms of processes standing lower in the scale of psychological evolution. With this canon as a guide, Morgan criticized vigorously the then current anecdotal work on animal mind that was then so fashionable. If there was to be a science of comparative psychology, and he had doubts, it involved the study of mind by inference from activity. A later generation was to reject this view in favor of a study of animal behavior without pretense of making inferences to mind. The research of Pavlov (p. 263), Thorndike (p. 255), and Guthrie (p. 374) is illustrative.

26

JAMES ON

THE STREAM OF CONSCIOUSNESS, ITS FUNCTIONAL AND PERSONAL CHARACTER, AND ON HABIT, INSTINCT, EMOTION, AND MEMORY

WILLIAM JAMES (1842–1910), philosopher and psychologist, was a major intellectual voice in the United States at the turn of the twentieth century. Despite his primary allegiance to philosophy, his *Principles of Psychology* was his most influential work, probably read by more individuals "under no obligation to do so" than any other textbook in psychology. It appeared in 1890 after twelve years in preparation. The excerpts that follow illustrate the colorfulness, grace, and lucidity of his writings.

Although well read in the experimental literature, in most instances the research impetus for what he had to say, if any, receded into the background, to be dominated in his account by a sustained mental effort to wring from the topic all that he believed to be important to say about it—leaving to others the working out of details, including experimental verification. As Perry[1] remarked, James was an explorer, not a mapmaker.

James held that psychology's starting point is whatever is immediately given—the stream of consciousness. This figure of speech was adopted to stress that consciousness is something continuous and unbroken, not a mosaic of bits and pieces.

We now begin our study of the mind from within. Most books start with sensations, as the simplest mental facts, and proceed synthetically, constructing each higher stage from those below it. But this is abandoning the empirical method of investigation. No one ever had a simple sensation by itself. Consciousness, from our natal day, is of a teeming multiplicity of objects and relations, and what we call simple sensations are results of discriminative attention, pushed often to a very high degree. It is astonishing what havoc is wrought in psychology by admitting at the outset apparently innocent suppositions, that nevertheless contain a flaw.

The bad consequences develop themselves later on, and are irremediable, being woven through the whole texture of the work. The notion that sensations, being the simplest things, are the first things to take up in psychology is one of these suppositions. The only thing which psychology has a right to postulate at the outset is the fact of thinking itself, and that must first be taken up and analyzed. If sensations then prove to be amongst the elements of the thinking, we shall be no worse off as respects them than if we had taken them for granted at the start.

The first fact for us, then, as psychologists, is that thinking of some sort goes on.[2]

The method of starting with discrete elements, the sensations, as did Wundt, was rejected in favor of experience.

He goes on to say that every thought is a part of a personal consciousness. While thought is continuous, within personal consciousness, it is always changing and has parts within that stream. To proceed from that point:

I can only define "continuous" as that which is without breach, crack, or division. I have already said that the breach from one mind to another is perhaps the greatest breach in nature. The only breaches that can well be conceived to occur within the limits of a single mind would either be *interruptions, time*-gaps during which the consciousness went out altogether to come into existence again at a later moment; or they would be breaks in the *quality,* or content, of the thought, so abrupt that the segment that followed had no connection whatever with the one that went before. The proposition that within each personal consciousness thought feels continuous, means two things:

1.   That even where there is a time-gap the consciousness after it feels as if it belonged together with the consciousness before it, as another part of the same self;
2.   That the changes from one moment to another in the quality of the consciousness are never absolutely abrupt.

The case of the time-gaps, as the simplest, shall be taken first. And first of all, a word about time-gaps of which the consciousness may not be itself aware.

... we saw that such time-gaps existed, and that they might be more numerous than is usually supposed. If the consciousness is not aware of them, it cannot feel them as interruptions. In the unconsciousness produced by nitrous oxide and other anaesthetics, in that of epilepsy and fainting, the broken edges of the sentient life may meet and merge over the gap, much as the feelings of space of the opposite margins of the "blind spot" meet and merge over that objective interruption to the sensitiveness of the eye. Such consciousness as this, whatever it be for the onlooking psychologist, is for itself unbroken. It *feels* unbroken; a waking day of it is sensibly a unit as long as that day lasts, in the sense in which the hours themselves are units, as having all their parts next each other, with no intrusive alien substance between. To expect the consciousness to feel the interruptions of its objective continuity as gaps, would be like expecting the eye to feel a gap of silence because it does not hear, or the ear to feel a gap of darkness because it does not see. So much for the gaps that are unfelt.

With the felt gaps the case is different. On waking from sleep, we usually know that we have been unconscious, and we often have an accurate judgment of how long. The judgment here is certainly an inference from sensible signs, and its ease is due to long practice in the particular field. The result of it, however, is that the consciousness is, for itself, not what it was in the former case, but interrupted and discontinuous, in the mere sense of the words. But in the other sense of continuity, the sense of the parts being inwardly connected and belonging together because they are parts of a common whole, the consciousness remains sensibly continuous and one. What now is the common whole? The natural name for it is myself, I, or me.

When Paul and Peter wake up in the same bed, and recognize that they have been asleep, each one of them mentally reaches back and makes connection with but *one* of the two streams of thought which were broken by the sleeping hours. As the current of an electrode buried in the ground unerringly finds its way to its own similarly buried mate, across no matter how much intervening earth; so Peter's present instantly finds out Peter's past, and never by mistake knits itself on to that of Paul. Paul's thought in turn is as little liable to go astray. The past thought of Peter is appropriated by the present Peter alone. He may have a *knowledge,* and a correct one too, of what Paul's last drowsy states of mind were as he sank into sleep, but it is an entirely different sort of knowledge from that which he has of his own last states. He *remembers* his own states, whilst he only *conceives* Paul's. Remembrance is like direct feeling; its object is suffused with a warmth and intimacy to which no object of mere conception ever attains. This quality of warmth and intimacy and immediacy is what Peter's *present* thought also possesses for itself. So sure as this present is me, is mine, it says, so sure is anything else that comes with the same warmth and intimacy and immediacy, me and mine. What the qualities called warmth and intimacy may in themselves be will have to be matter for future consideration. But whatever past feelings appear with those qualities must be admitted to receive the greeting of the present mental state, to be owned by it, and accepted as belonging together with it in a common self. This community of self is what the time-gap cannot break in twain, and is why a present thought, although not ignorant of the time-gap, can still regard itself as continuous with certain chosen portions of the past.

Consciousness, then, does not appear to itself chopped up in bits. Such words as "chain" or "train" do not describe it fitly as it presents itself in the first instance. It is nothing jointed; it flows. A "river" or a "stream" is the metaphor by which it is most naturally described. *In talking of it hereafter, let us call it the stream of thought, of consciousness, or of a subjective life....*

As we take, in fact, a general view of the wonderful stream of our consciousness, what strikes us first is this different pace of its parts. Like a bird's life, it seems to be made of an alternation of flights and perchings. The rhythm of language expresses this, where every thought is expressed in a sentence, and every sentence closed by a period. The resting-places are usually occupied by sensorial imaginations of some sort, whose peculiarity is that they can be held before the mind for an indefinite time, and contemplated without changing; the places of flight are filled with thoughts of relations, static or dynamic, that for the most part obtain between the matters contemplated in the periods of comparative rest.

Let us call the resting-places the "substantive parts," and the places of flight the "transitive parts," of the stream of thought. It then appears that the main end of our thinking is at all times the attainment of some other substantive part than the one from which we have just been dislodged. And we may say that the main use of the transitive parts is to lead us from one substantive conclusion to another.

Now it is very difficult, introspectively, to see the transitive parts for what they really are....

The results of this introspective difficulty are baleful. If to hold fast and observe the transitive parts of thought's stream be so hard, then the great blunder to which all schools are liable must be the failure to register them, and the undue emphasizing of the more substantive parts of the stream. Were we not ourselves a moment since in danger of ignoring any feeling transitive between the silence and the thunder, and of treating their boundary as a sort of break in the mind? Now such ignoring as this has historically worked in two ways. One set of thinkers have been led by it to *Sensationalism*. Unable to lay their hands on any coarse feelings corresponding to the innumerable relations and forms of connection between the facts of the world, finding no *named* subjective modifications mirroring such relations, they have for the most part denied that feelings of relation exist, and many of them, like Hume, have gone so far as to deny the reality of most relations *out* of the mind as well as in it. Substantive psychoses, sensations and their copies and derivatives, juxtaposed like dominoes in a game, but really separate, everything else verbal illusion,—such is the upshot of this view. The *Intellectualists,* on the other hand, unable to give up the reality of relations *extra mentem,* but equally unable to point to any distinct substantive feelings in which they were known, have made the same admission that the feelings do not exist. But they have drawn an opposite conclusion. The relations must be known, they say, in something that is no feeling, no mental modification continuous and consubstantial with the subjective tissue out of which sensations and other substantive states are made. They are known, these relations, by something that lies on an entirely different plane, by an *actus purus* of Thought, Intellect, or Reason, all written with capitals and considered to mean something unutterably superior to any fact of sensibility whatever.

But from our point of view both Intellectualists and Sensationalists are wrong. If there be such things as feelings at all, *then so surely as relations between objects exist in rerum natura, so surely, and more surely, do feelings exist to which these relations are known.* There is not a conjunction or a preposition, and hardly an adverbial phrase, syntactic form, or inflection of voice, in human speech, that does not express some shading or other of relation which we at some moment actually feel to exist between the larger objects of our thought. If we speak objectively, it is the real relations that appear revealed; if we speak subjectively, it is the stream of consciousness that matches each of them by an inward coloring of its own. In either case the relations are numberless, and no existing language is capable of doing justice to all their shades.[3]

After arguing for the sensible continuity of consciousness, James discussed the varying pace of its parts with the "resting places," the "substantive," and the "flights," the "transitive," with emphasis on the latter, since they are difficult to observe, but still cannot be disregarded without creating an undue emphasis on the substantive parts.

In view of the central place he gave to consciousness, it is hardly surprising that he reacted strongly against the "unwarrantable impertinence" of the automaton-theory, which held consciousness to be irrelevant to what a person does. He set out to demonstrate the contrary, that consciousness *is* efficacious, by offering a functional interpretation, that is, that consciousness does do things.

It is very generally admitted, though the point would be hard to prove, that consciousness grows the more complex and intense the higher we rise in the animal kingdom. That of a man must exceed that of an oyster. From this point of view it seems an organ, superadded to the other organs which maintain the animal in the struggle for existence; and the presumption of course is that it helps him in some way in the struggle, just as they do. But it cannot help him without being in some way efficacious and influencing the course of his bodily history. If now it could be shown in what way consciousness *might* help him, and if, moreover, the defects of his other organs (where consciousness is most developed) are such as to make them need just the kind of help that consciousness would bring provided it *were* efficacious; why, then the plausible inference would be that it came just *because* of its efficacy—in other words, its efficacy would be inductively proved.

Now the study of the phenomena of consciousness which we shall make throughout the rest of this book will show us that consciousness is at all times primarily *a selecting agency*. Whether we take it in the lowest sphere of sense, or in the highest of intellection, we find it always doing one thing, choosing one out of several of the materials so presented to its notice, emphasizing and accentuating that and suppressing as far as possible all the rest. The item emphasized is always in close connection with some *interest* felt by consciousness to be paramount at the time.

But what are now the defects of the nervous system in those animals whose consciousness seems most highly developed? Chief among them must be *instability*. The cerebral hemispheres are the characteristically "high" nerve-centres, and we saw how indeterminate and unforseeable their performances were in comparison with those of the basal ganglia and the cord. But this very vagueness constitutes their advantage. They allow their possessor to adapt his conduct to the minutest alterations in the environing circumstances, any one of which may be for him a sign, suggesting distant motives more powerful than any present solicitations of sense. It seems as if certain mechanical conclusions should be drawn from this state of things. An organ swayed by slight impressions is an organ whose natural state is one of unstable equilibrium. We may imagine the various lines of discharge in the cerebrum to be almost on a par in point of permeability—what discharge a given small impression will produce may be called *accidental,* in the sense in which we say it is a matter of accident whether a rain-drop falling on a mountain ridge descend the eastern or the western slope. It is in this sense that we may call it a matter of accident whether a child be a boy or a girl. The ovum is so unstable a body that certain causes too minute for our apprehension may at a certain moment tip it one way or the other. The natural law of an organ constituted after this fashion can be nothing but a law of caprice. I do not see how one could reasonably expect from it any certain pursuance of useful lines of reaction, such as the few and fatally determined performances of the lower centres constitute within their narrow sphere. The dilemma in regard to the nervous system seems, in short, to be of the following kind. We may construct one which will react infallibly and certainly, but it will then be capable of reacting to very few changes in the environment—it will fail to be adapted to all the rest. We may, on the other hand, construct a nervous system potentially adapted to respond to an infinite variety of minute features in the situation; but its fallibility will then be as great as its elaboration. We can never be sure that is equilibrium will be upset in the appropriate direction. In short, a high brain may do many things, and may do each of them at a very slight hint. But its hair-trigger organization makes of it a happy-go-lucky, hit-or-miss affair. It is as likely to do the crazy as the same thing at any given moment. A low brain does few things, and in doing them perfectly forfeits all other use. The performances of a high brain are like dice thrown forever on a table. Unless they be loaded, what chance is there that the highest number will turn up oftener than the lowest?

All this is said of the brain as a physical machine pure and simple. *Can consciousness increase its efficiency by loading its dice?* Such is the problem.

Loading its dice would mean bringing a more or less constant pressure to bear in favor of *those* of its performances which make for the most permanent interests of the brain's owner; it would mean a constant inhibition of the tendencies to stray aside.

Well, just such pressure and such inhibition are what consciousness *seems* to be exerting all the while. And the interests in whose favor it seems to exert them are *its* interests and its alone, interests which it *creates,* and which, but for it, would have no status in the realm of being whatever. We talk, it is true, when we are darwinizing, as if the mere *body* that owns the brain had interests; we speak about the utilities of its various organs and how they help or hinder the body's survival; and we treat the survival as if it were an absolute end, existing as such in the physical world, a sort of actual *should-be,* presiding over the animal and judging his reactions, quite apart from the presence of any commenting intelligence outside. We forget that in the absence of some such superadded commenting intelligence (whether it be that of the animal itself, or only ours or Mr. Darwin's), the reactions cannot be properly talked of as "useful" or "hurtful" at all. Considered merely physically, all that can be said of them is that *if* they occur in a certain way survival will as a matter of fact prove to be their incidental consequence. The organs themselves, and all the rest of the physical world, will, however, all the time be quite indifferent to this consequence, and would quite as cheerfully, the circumstances changed, compass the animal's destruction. In a word, survival can enter into a purely physiological discussion only as an *hypothesis made by an onlooker,* about the future. But the moment you bring a consciousness into the midst, survival ceases to be a mere hypothesis. No longer is it, *"if* survival is to occur, then so and so must brain and other organs work." It has now become an imperative decree: "Survival *shall* occur, and therefore organs *must* so work!" *Real* ends appear for the first time now upon the world's stage. The conception of consciousness as a purely cognitive form of being, which is the pet way of regarding it in many idealistic schools, modern as well as ancient, is thoroughly anti-psychological, as the remainder of this book will show. Every actually existing consciousness seems to itself at any rate to be a *fighter for ends,* of which many, but for its presence, would not be ends at all. Its powers of cognition are mainly subservient to these ends, discerning which facts further them and which do not.

Now let consciousness only be what it seems to itself, and it will help an instable brain to compass its proper ends. The movements of the brain *per se* yield the means of attaining these ends mechanically, but only out of a lot of other ends, if so they may be called, which are not the proper ones of the animal, but often quite opposed. The brain is an instrument of possibilities, but of no certainties. But the consciousness, with its own ends present to it, and knowing also well which possibilities lead thereto and which away, will, if endowed with causal efficacy, reinforce the favorable possibilities and repress the unfavorable or indifferent ones. The nerve-currents, coursing through the cells and fibres, must in this case be supposed strengthened by the fact of their awaking one consciousness and dampened by awaking another. *How* such reaction of the consciousness upon the currents may óccur must remain at present unsolved: it is enough for my purpose to have shown that it may not uselessly exist, and that the matter is less simple than the brain-automatists hold.

All the facts of the natural history of consciousness lend color to this view. Consciousness, for example, is only intense when nerve-processes are hesitant. In rapid, automatic, habitual action it sinks to a minimum. Nothing could be more fitting than this, if consciousness have the teleological function we suppose; nothing more meaningless, if not. Habitual actions are certain, and being in no danger of going astray from their end, need no extraneous help. In hesitant action, there seem many alternative possibilities of final nervous discharge. The feeling awakened by the nascent excitement of each alternative nerve-tract seems by its attractive or repulsive quality to determine whether the excitement shall abort or shall become complete. Where indecision is great, as before a dangerous leap, consciousness is agonizingly intense. Feeling, from this point of view, may be likened to a cross-section of the chain of nervous discharge, ascertaining the links already laid down, and groping among the fresh ends presented to it for the one which seems best to fit the case.

The phenomena of "vicarious function" . . . seem to form another bit of circumstantial evidence. A machine in working order acts fatally in one way. Our consciousness calls this the right way. Take out a valve, throw a wheel out of gear or bend a pivot, and it becomes a different machine, acting just as fatally in another way which we call the wrong way. But the machine itself knows nothing of wrong or right: matter has no ideals to pursue. A locomotive will carry its train through an open drawbridge as cheerfully as to any other destination.

A brain with part of it scooped out is virtually a new machine, and during the first days after the operation functions in a thoroughly abnormal manner. As a matter of fact, however, its performances become from day to day more normal, until at last a practised eye may be needed to suspect anything wrong. Some of the restoration is undoubtedly due to "inhibitions" passing away. But if the consciousness which goes with the rest of the brain, be there not only in order to take cognizance of each functional error, but also to exert an efficient pressure to check it if it be a sin of commission, and to lend a strengthening hand if it be a weakness or sin of omission,—nothing seems more natural than that the remaining parts, assisted in this way, should by virtue of the principle of habit grow back to the old teleological modes of exercise for which they were at first incapacitated. Nothing, on the contrary, seems at first sight more unnatural than that they should vicariously take up the duties of a part now lost without those *duties as such* exerting any persuasive or coercive force. . . .

There is yet another set of facts which seem explicable on the supposition that consciousness has causal efficacy. *It is a well-known fact that pleasures are generally associated with beneficial, pains with detrimental, experiences.* All the fundamental vital processes illustrate this law. Starvation, suffocation, privation of food, drink and sleep, work when exhausted, burns, wounds, inflammation, the effects of poison, are as disagreeable as filling the hungry stomach, enjoying rest and sleep after fatigue, exercise after rest, and a sound skin and unbroken bones at all times, are pleasant. Mr. Spencer and others have suggested that these coincidences are due, not to any pre-established harmony, but to the mere action of natural selection which would certainly kill off in the long-run any breed of creatures to whom the fundamentally noxious experience seemed enjoyable. An animal that should take pleasure in a feeling of suffocation would, if that pleasure were efficacious enough to make him immerse his head in water, enjoy a longevity of four or five minutes. But if pleasures and pains have no efficacy, one does not see (without some such *a priori* rational harmony as would be scouted by the "scientific" champions of the automaton-theory) why the most noxious acts, such as burning, might not give thrills of delight, and the most necessary ones, such as breathing, cause agony. The exceptions to the law are, it is true, numerous, but relate to experiences that are either not vital or not universal. Drunkenness, for instance, which though noxious, is to many persons delightful, is a very exceptional experience. But, as the excellent physiologist Fick remarks, if all rivers and springs ran alcohol instead of water, either all men would now be born to hate it or our nerves would have been selected so as to drink it with impunity.[4]

Throughout the discussion of consciousness, James insisted that consciousness tends to appear to be personal—it is not a thought, it is *my* thought. (The qualification in speaking of "tends to appear" is necessary, because James was aware of the phenomena of multiple personality, automatic writing, and post-hypnotic suggestion). It is no wonder, then, that he stressed consciousness of self.

To James, the self had several constituents. Of most interest today are what he called the material self and the social self.

(*a*) The body is the innermost part of *the material Self* in each of us; and certain parts of the body seem more intimately ours than the rest.

The clothes come next. The old saying that the human person is composed of three parts—soul, body and clothes—is more than a joke. We so appropriate our clothes and identify outselves with them that there are few of us who, if asked to choose between having a beautiful body clad in raiment perpetually shabby and unclean, and having an ugly and blemished form always spotlessly attired, would not hesitate a moment before making a decisive reply. Next, our immediate family is a part of ourselves. Our father and mother, our wife and babes, are bone of our bone and flesh of our flesh. When they die, a part of our very selves is gone. If they do anything wrong, it is our shame. If they are insulted, our anger flashes forth as readily as if we stood in their place. Our home comes next. Its scenes are part of our life; its aspects awaken the tenderest feelings of affection; and we do not easily forgive the stranger who, in visiting it, finds fault with its arrangements or treats it with contempt. All these different things are the objects of instinctive preferences coupled with the most important practical interests of life. We all have a blind impulse to watch over our body, to deck it with clothing of an ornamental sort, to cherish parents, wife and babes, and to find for ourselves a home of our own which we may live in and "improve."

An equally instinctive impulse drives us to collect property; and the collections thus made become, with different degrees of intimacy, parts of our empirical selves. The parts of our wealth most intimately ours are those which are saturated with our labor. There are few men who would not feel personally annihilated if a life-long construction of their hands or brains—say an entomological collection or an extensive work in manuscript—were suddenly swept away. The miser feels similarly towards his gold, and although it is true that a part of our depression at the loss of possessions is due to our feeling that we must now go without certain goods that we expected the possessions to bring in their train, yet in every case there remains, over and above this, a sense of the shrinkage of our personality, a partial conversion of ourselves to nothingness, which is a psychological phenomenon by itself. We are all at once assimilated to the tramps and poor devils whom we so despise, and at the same time removed farther than ever away from the happy sons of earth who lord it over land and sea and men in the full-blown lustihood that wealth and power can give, and before whom, stiffen ourselves as we will be appealing to anti-snobbish first principles, we cannot escape an emotion, open or sneaking, of respect and dread.

(b) A man's Social Self is the recognition which he gets from his mates. We are not only gregarious animals, liking to be in sight of our fellows, but we have an innate propensity to get ourselves noticed, and noticed favorably, by our kind. No more fiendish punishment could be devised, were such a thing physically possible, than that one should be turned loose in society and remain absolutely unnoticed by all the members thereof. If no one turned round when we entered, answered when we spoke, or minded what we did, but if every person we met "cut us dead," and acted as if we were non-existing things, a kind of rage and impotent despair would ere long well up in us, from which the cruellest bodily tortures would be a relief; for these would make us feel that, however bad might be our plight, we had not sunk to such a depth as to be unworthy of attention at all.

Properly speaking, *a man has as many social selves as there are individuals who recognize him* and carry an image of him in their mind. To wound any one of these his images is to wound him. But as the individuals who carry the images fall naturally into classes, we may practically say that he has as many different social selves as there are distinct *groups* of persons about whose opinion he cares. He generally shows a different side of himself to each of these different groups. Many a youth who is demure enough before his parents and teachers, swears and swaggers like a pirate among his "tough" young friends. We do not show ourselves to our children as to our club-companions, to our customers as to the laborers we employ, to our own masters and employers as to our intimate friends. From this there results what practically is a division of the man into several selves; and this may be a discordant splitting, as where one is afraid to let one set of his acquaintances know him as he is elsewhere; or it may be a perfectly harmonious division of labor, as where one tender to his children is stern to the soldiers or prisoners under his command.

The most peculiar social self which one is apt to have is in the mind of the person one is in love with. The good or bad fortunes of this self cause the most intense elation and dejection—unreasonable enough as measured by every other standard than that of the organic feeling of the individual. To his own consciousness he *is* not, so long as this particular social self fails to get recognition, and when it is recognized his contentment passes all bounds.

A man's *fame,* good or bad, and his *honor* or dishonor, are names for one of his social selves. The particular social self of a man called his honor is usually the result of one of those splittings of which we have spoken. It is his image in the eyes of his own "set," which exalts or condemns him as he conforms or not to certain requirements that may

not be made of one in another walk of life. Thus a layman may abandon a
city infected with cholera; but a priest or a doctor would think such an act
incompatible with his honor. A soldier's honor requires him to fight or to
die under circumstances where another man can apologize or run away
with no stain upon his social self. A judge, a statesman, are in like manner debarred by the honor of their cloth from entering into pecuniary
relations perfectly honorable to persons in private life. Nothing is commoner than to hear people discriminate between their different selves of
this sort: "As a man I pity you, but as an official I must show you no
mercy; as a politician I regard him as an ally, but as a moralist I loathe
him"; etc., etc. What may be called "club-opinion" is one of the very
strongest forces in life. The thief must not steal from other thieves; the
gambler must pay his gambling-debts, though he pay no other debts in
the world. The code of honor of fashionable society has throughout history been full of permissions as well as of vetoes, the only reason for
following either of which is that so we best serve one of our social selves.
You must not lie in general, but you may lie as much as you please if
asked about your relations with a lady; you must accept a challenge from
an equal, but if challenged by an inferior you may laugh him to scorn:
these are examples of what is meant.[5]

    The preceding excerpts have established some of the fundamen-
tals of the position that James took regarding the nature of psychology as
the science of consciousness. As a textbook writer, he was also obligated
to discuss the major topics of the fledgling science. Attention, conception, discrimination, association, time perception, sensation, imagination,
space perception, perception of reality, reasoning, will, and hypnotism are
among the topics for different chapters not further identified here by
excerpts.
    Still other chapter topics have been selected for excerption. Ne-
glected so far is his rather liberal use of physiological findings, best illustrated by "the aptitude of the brain for acquiring *habits*."
    In Chapter 4 which follows this comment, he went on to relate
habits to the nervous system in their plasticity in taking on ways they are
exercised, their simplification in the ways exercised, the diminishment of
conscious attention necessary to perform perfected habits, the lack of
conscious attention to habits unless something goes wrong, and on to the
social-ethical consequences of habits with which this excerpt is concerned:

Habit is thus the enormous fly-wheel of society, its most precious conservative agent. It alone is what keeps us all within the bounds of ordinance,

and saves the children of fortune from the envious uprisings of the poor. It alone prevents the hardest and most repulsive walks of life from being deserted by those brought up to tread therein. It keeps the fisherman and the deck-hand at sea through the winter; it holds the miner in his darkness, and nails the countryman to his log-cabin and his lonely farm through all the months of snow; it protects us from invasion by the natives of the desert and the frozen zone. It dooms us all to fight out the battle of life upon the lines of our nurture or our early choice, and to make the best of a pursuit that disagrees, because there is no other for which we are fitted, and it is too late to begin again. It keeps different social strata from mixing. Already at the age of twenty-five you see the professional mannerism settling down on the young commercial traveller, on the young doctor, on the young minister, on the young counsellor-at-law. You see the little lines of cleavage running through the character, the tricks of thought, the prejudices, the ways of the "shop," in a word, from which the man can by-and-by no more escape than his coat-sleeve can suddenly fall into a new set of folds. On the whole, it is best he should not escape. It is well for the world that in most of us, by the age of thirty, the character has set like plaster, and will never soften again.

If the period between twenty and thirty is the critical one in the formation of intellectual and professional habits, the period below twenty is more important still for the fixing of *personal* habits, properly so called, such as vocalization and pronunciation, gesture, motion, and address. Hardly ever is a language learned after twenty spoken without a foreign accent; hardly ever can a youth transferred to the society of his betters unlearn the nasality and other vices of speech bred in him by the associations of his growing years. Hardly ever, indeed, no matter how much money there be in his pocket, can he even learn to *dress* like a gentleman-born. The merchants offer their wares as eagerly to him as to the veriest "swell," but he simply *cannot* buy the right things. An invisible law, as strong as gravitation, keeps him within his orbit, arrayed this year as he was the last; and how his better-bred acquaintances contrive to get the things they wear will be for him a mystery till his dying day.

The great thing, then, in all education, is to *make our nervous system our ally instead of our enemy*. It is to fund and capitalize our acquisitions, and live at ease upon the interest of the fund. *For this we must make automatic and habitual, as early as possible, as many useful actions as we can,* and guard against the growing into ways that are likely to be disadvantageous to us, as we should guard against the plague. The more of the details of our daily life we can hand over to the effortless custody of automatism, the more our higher powers of mind will be set free for their own proper work. There is no more miserable human being than one in whom nothing is habitual but indecision, and for whom the lighting of every cigar, the drinking of every cup, the time of rising and going to bed every day, and the beginning of every bit of work, are subjects of express volitional deliberation. Full half the time of such a man goes to the deciding, or regretting, of matters which ought to be so ingrained in him as practically not to exist for his consciousness at all. If there be such daily duties not yet ingrained in any one of my readers, let him begin this very hour to set the matter right. . . .Could the young but realize how soon they will become mere walking bundles of habits, they would give more heed to their conduct while in the plastic state. We are spinning our own fates, good or evil, and never to be undone. Every smallest stroke or virtue or of vice leaves its never so little scar. The drunken Rip Van Winkle, in Jefferson's play, excuses himself for every fresh dereliction by saying, "I won't count this time!" Well! he may not count it, and a kind Heaven may not count it; but it is being counted none the less. Down among his nerve-cells and fibres the molecules are counting it, registering and storing it up to be used against him when the next temptation comes. Nothing we ever do is, in strict scientific literalness, wiped out. Of course, this has its good side as well as its bad one. As we become permanent drunkards by so many separate drinks, so we become saints in the moral, and authorities and experts in the practical and scientific spheres, by so many separate acts and hours of work. Let no youth have any anxiety about the upshot of his education, whatever the line of it may be. If he keep faithfully busy each hour of the working-day, he may safely leave the final result to itself. He can with perfect certainty count on waking up some fine morning, to find himself one of the competent ones of his generation, in whatever pursuit he may have singled out.[7]

As was customary in his time, he devoted a chapter to the problem of instincts, with evolutionary theory serving as background. One facet was his insistence on the flexibility of human instincts.

A very common way of talking about these admirably definite tendencies to act is by naming abstractly the purpose they subserve, such as self-preservation, or defence, or care for eggs and young—and saying the animal has an instinctive fear of death or love of life, or that she has an instinct of self-preservation, or an instinct of maternity and the like. But this represents the animal as obeying abstractions which not once in a million cases is it possible it can have framed. The strict physiological way of interpreting the facts leads to far clearer results. *The actions we call instinctive all conform to the general reflex type;* they are called forth by determinate sensory stimuli in contact with the animal's body, or at a distance in his environment. The cat runs after the mouse, runs or shows fight before the dog, avoids falling from walls and trees, shuns fire and water, etc., not because he has any notion either of life or of death, or of self, or of preservation. He has probably attained to no one of these conceptions in such a way as to react definitely upon it. He acts in each case separately, and simply because he cannot help it, being so framed that when that particular running thing called a mouse appears in his field of vision he *must* pursue; that when that particular barking and obstreperous thing called a dog appears there he *must* retire, if at a distance, and scratch if close by; that he *must* withdraw his feet from water and his face from flame, etc. His nervous system is to a great extent a preorganized bundle of such reactions—they are as fatal as sneezing, and as exactly correlated to their special excitants as it is to its own. Although the naturalist may, for his own convenience, class these reactions under general heads, he must not forget that in the animal it is a particular sensation or perception or image which calls them forth. . . .

Every instinct is an impulse. Whether we shall call such impulses as blushing, sneezing, coughing, smiling, or dodging, or keeping time to music, instincts or not, is a mere matter of terminology. The process is the same throughout. In his delightfully fresh and interesting work, *Der Thierische Wille,* Herr G. H. Schneider subdivides impulses (*Triebe*) into sensation impulses, perception-impulses, and idea-impulses. To crouch from cold is a sensation-impulse; to turn and follow, if we see people running one way, is a perception-impulse; to cast about for cover, if it begins to blow and rain, is an imagination-impulse. A single complex instinctive action may involve successively the awakening of impulses of all three classes. Thus a hungry lion starts to *seek* prey by the awakening in him of imagination coupled with desire; he begins to *stalk* it when, on eye, ear, or nostril, he gets an impression of its presence at a certain distance; he *springs* upon it, either when the booty takes alarm and flees, or when the distance is sufficiently reduced; he proceeds to *tear* and *devour* it the moment he gets a sensation of its contact with his claws and fangs. Seeking, stalking, springing, and devouring are just so many different kinds of muscular contraction, and neither kind is called forth by the stimulus appropriate to the other.

Nothing is commoner than the remark that Man differs from lower creatures by the almost total absence of instincts, and the assumption of their work in him by "reason." A fruitless discussion might be waged on this point by two theorizers who were careful not to define their terms. "Reason" might be used, as it often has been, since Kant, not as the mere power of "inferring," but also as a name for the *tendency to obey impulses* of a certain lofty sort, such as duty, or universal ends. And "instinct" might have its significance so broadened as to cover all impulses whatever, even the impulse to act from the idea of a distant fact, as well as the impulse to act from a present sensation. Were the word instinct used in this broad way, it would of course be impossible to restrict it, as we began by doing, to actions done with no prevision of an end. We must of course avoid a quarrel about words, and the facts of the case are really tolerably plain. Man has a far greater variety of *impulses* than any lower animal; and any one of these impulses, taken in itself, is as "blind" as the lowest instinct can be; but, owing to man's memory, power of reflection, and power of inference, they come each one to be felt by him, after he has once yielded to them and experienced their results, in connection with a *foresight* of those results. In this condition an impulse acted out may be said to be acted out, in part at least, *for the sake* of its results. It is obvious that *every instinctive act, in an animal with memory, must cease to be "blind" after being once repeated,* and must be accompanied with foresight of its "end" just so far as that end may have fallen under the animal's cognizance. An insect that lays her eggs in a place where she never sees them hatched must always do so "blindly"; but a hen who has already hatched a brood can hardly be assumed to sit with perfect "blindness" on her second nest. Some expectation of consequences must in every case like this be aroused; and this expectation, according as it is that of something desired or of something disliked, must necessarily either re-enforce or inhibit the mere impulse. The hen's idea of the chickens would probably encourage her to sit; a rat's memory, on the other hand, of a former escape from a trap would neutralize his impulse to take bait from anything that reminded him of that trap. If a boy sees a fat hopping-toad, he probably has incontinently an impulse (especially if with other boys) to smash the creature with a stone, which impulse we may suppose him blindly to obey. But something in the expression of the dying toad's clasped hands suggests the meanness of the act, or reminds him of sayings he has heard about the sufferings of animals being like his own; so that, when next he is tempted by a toad, an idea arises which, far from spurring him again to the torment, prompts kindly actions, and may even make him the toad's champion against less reflecting boys.

It is plain, then, that, *no matter how well endowed an animal may originally be in the way of instincts, his resultant actions will be much modified if the instincts combine with experience,* if in addition to impulses he have memories, associations, inferences, and expectations, on any considerable scale. An object O, on which he has an instinctive impulse to react in the manner A, would *directly* provoke him to that reaction. But O has meantime become for him a *sign* of the nearness of P, on which he has an equally strong impulse to react in the manner B, quite unlike A. So that when he meets O the immediate impulse A and the remote impulse B struggle in his breast for the mastery. The fatality and uniformity said to be characteristic of instinctive actions will be so little manifest that one might be tempted to deny to him altogether the possession of any instinct about the object O. Yet how false this judgment would be! The instinct about O is there; only by the complication of the associative machinery it has come into conflict with another instinct about P.[8]

In still another chapter, one of the most original and paradoxical theories that James promulgated was that about the emotions.

Our natural way of thinking about these coarser emotions is that the mental perception of some fact excites the mental affection called the emotion, and that this latter state of mind gives rise to the bodily expression. My theory, on the contrary, is that *the bodily changes follow directly the perception of the exciting fact, and that our feeling of the same changes as they occur* IS *the emotion.* Common-sense says, we lose our fortune, are sorry and weep; we meet a bear, are frightened and run; we are insulted by a rival, are angry and strike. The hypothesis here to be defended says that this order of sequence is incorrect, that the one mental state is not immediately induced by the other, that the bodily manifestations must first be interposed between, and that the more rational statement is that we feel sorry because we cry, angry because we strike, afraid because we tremble, and not that we cry, strike, or tremble, because we are sorry, angry, or fearful, as the case may be. Without the bodily states following on the perception, the latter would be purely cognitive in form, pale, colorless, destitute of emotional warmth. We might then see the bear, and judge it best to run, receive the insult and deem it right to strike, but we should not actually *feel* afraid or angry.[9]

He admitted that it was difficult to find experimental support for his view, but proceeded to cite C. G. Lange, a Danish physiologist, who some years earlier, but simultaneously with James in another publication, had advanced essentially the same theory. Since that time, it has been referred to as the James-Lange theory of the emotions. The theory stimulated considerable controversy and many research studies.

In his chapter on memory, James insisted that a human being's native retentiveness is unchangeable and that the common opinion is wrong in holding that memory exercises will increase one's memory not only for these facts but for remembering in general.

It will now appear clear that *all improvement of the memory lies in the line of* ELABORATING THE ASSOCIATES of each of the several things to be remembered. *No amount of culture would seem capable of modifying a man's* GENERAL *retentiveness.* There is a physiological quality, given once for all with his organization, and which he can never hope to change. It differs no doubt in disease and health; and it is a fact of observation that it is better in fresh and vigorous hours than when we are fagged or ill. We may say, then, that a man's native tenacity will fluctuate somewhat with his hygiene, and that whatever is good for his tone of health will also be good for his memory. We may even say that whatever amount of intellectual exercise is bracing to the general tone and nutrition of the brain will also be profitable to the general retentiveness. But more than this we cannot say; and this, it is obvious, is far less than most people believe.

It is, in fact, commonly thought that certain exercises, systematically repeated, will strengthen, not only a man's remembrance of the particular facts used in the exercises, but his faculty for remembering facts at large. And a plausible case is always made out by saying that practice in learning words by heart makes it easier to learn new words in the same say. If this be true, then what I have just said is false, and the whole doctrine of memory as due to "paths" must be revised.[10]

Perhaps because it would interfere with the easy flow of the narrative, he banished his quantitative findings to a footnote, but with James even footnotes are worth quoting:

[1]In order to test the opinion so confidently expressed in the text, I have tried to see whether a certain amount of daily training in learning poetry by heart will shorten the time it takes to learn an entirely different kind of poetry. During eight successive days I learned 158 lines of Victor Hugo's *Satyr*. The total number of minutes required for this was $131\frac{5}{8}$— it should be said that I had learned nothing by heart for many years. I then, working for twenty-odd minutes daily, learned the entire first book

of *Paradise Lost,* occupying 38 days in the process. After this training I went back to Victor Hugo's poem, and found that 158 additional lines (divided exactly as on the former occasion) took me 151 ½ minutes. In other words, I committed my Victor Hugo to memory before the training at the rate of a line in 50 seconds, after the training at the rate of a line in 57 seconds, just the opposite result from that which the popular view would lead one to expect. But as I was perceptibly fagged with other work at the time of the second batch of Victor Hugo, I thought that might explain the retardation; so I persuaded several other persons to repeat the test.[11]

He goes on to cite memorizing experiences that he instigated of several other individuals with the same general result. Practice with one sort of material did not seem to increase retentiveness with other kinds of material. We will return to this issue in our discussion of Thorndike and Woodworth (p. 260).

The receptivity of William James to practically all of the intellectual currents of his time gave his *Principles of Psychology* a tremendous breadth. He was aware of laboratory findings, but he used them to strike out in new directions, in order to trace this implication to the frontiers not yet brought into the range of experimental control.

27

HALL ON
DEVELOPMENT

G. STANLEY HALL (1844–1924), American psychologist, educator, and administrator, served psychology in a variety of capacities. As a voice raised in favor of a new science in a country where the academic community was unfamiliar with it, his personal appeal, flair for the dramatic, talent in attracting faculty and students of superior calibre, and boundless enthusiasm made him the person right for the times. To name but some of his accomplishments, he founded the American Psychological Association, the *American Journal of Psychology* and other journals, served as President of Clark University when it was one of the first authentic graduate schools in the United States, and in that capacity gave Sigmund Freud the first official recognition he received anywhere in the world by inviting him to a celebration of Clark University's twentieth anniversary.

His research and theoretical contributions are noted more for the enthusiasm that he inspired than for their lasting value. It is in the field of development that his major contributions lie. He was a major pioneer in the study of childhood, adolescence, and senescence through his books on these topics.

He also conducted one of the earliest quantitative studies of children's thinking.[1] Under his direction, Boston school teachers administered questionnaires to newly entered school children with questions designed to determine the extent of their knowledge of every day objects and concepts. The questionnaires were administered orally to groups of children and individual follow-up questions were encouraged until the teacher was satisfied that the child did or did not know the answer. The quantitative results were presented in terms of the percentage of children judged unfamiliar with the objects or concepts, such as various trees, animals, fruits, numbers, tools, and colors. A dearth of knowledge was apparent—80 percent were ignorant of a beehive, 50 percent of a frog, and so on.

He also presented a narrative account of the findings as illustrated in the excerpt below:

Many children half believe the doll feels cold or blows, that it pains flowers to tear or burn them, or that in summer when the tree is alive it makes it ache to pound or chop it. Of 48 children questioned 20 believed sun, moon, or stars to live, 15 thought a doll and 16 thought flowers would suffer pain if burned. Children who are accounted dull in school-work are more apt to be imaginative and animistic.

The chief field for such fond and often secret childish fancies is the sky. About three fourths of all questioned thought the world a plain, and many described it as round like a dollar, while the sky is like a flattened bowl turned over it. The sky is often thin, one might easily break through; half the moon may be seen through it, while the other half is this side; it may be made of snow, but is so large that there is much floor-sweeping to be done in heaven. Some thought the sun went down at night into the ground or just behind certain houses, and went across on or under the ground to go up out of or off the water in the morning, but 48 per cent of all thought that at night it goes or rolls or flies, is blown or walks, or God pulls it up higher out of sight. He takes it into heaven, and perhaps put it to bed, and even takes off its clothes and puts them on in the morning, or again it lies under the trees where the angels mind it, or goes through and shines on the upper side of the sky, or goes into or behind the moon, as the moon is behind it in the day. It may stay where it is, only we cannot see it, for it is dark, or the dark rains down so, and it comes out when it gets light so it can see. More than half the children questioned conceived the sun as never more than 40 degrees from the zenith, and, naturally enough, city children knew little of the horizon. So the moon comes around when it is a bright night and people want to walk, or forget to light some lamps; it follows us about and has nose and eyes, while it calls the stars into, under, or behind it at night, and they may be made of bits of it. Sometimes the moon is round a month or two, then it is a rim, or a piece is cut off, or it is half stuck or half buttoned into the sky. The stars may be sparks from fire-engines or houses, or, with higher intelligence, they are silver, or God lights them with matches and blows them out or opens the door and calls them in in the morning.[2]

Public interest became high when he returned to this topic after the lapse of some years through encouraging research from his students. A great enthusiasm for applying and interpreting questionnaires was exhibited by teachers and others and led to the founding of the so-called child-study movement. The poor design of the studies by well-meaning amateurs and the general wooliness of the movement after a few years led to its decline. It did serve, by its very excesses, to bring home the importance of the careful, empirical study of the child.

His theoretical contributions arose in a setting of evolutionary theory, in which he advocated a general genetic stand with a particular enthusiasm for recapitulation theory:

In this process the individual in a general way repeats the history of its species, passing slowly from the protozoan to the metazoan stage, so that we have all traversed in our own bodies ameboid, helminthoid, piscian, amphibian, anthropoid, ethnoid, and we know not how many intercalary stages of ascent. How these lines of heredity and growth along which all the many thousand species, extant and extinct, these viatica of the holy spirit of life, the consummate products of millennia of the slow travail of evolution, have been unfolded, we know scarcely more than we do what has been the impelling force, or will to live, which seems so inexhaustible and insistent. Certain it is that the cellular theory needs to be supplemented by assuming, both in the organism as a whole and in the species, powers that cannot be derived from the cells. Probably, too, the original cause of phylogenetic evolution was no inherent and specific nisus, but, as we know it, was due to a struggle for survival forced upon organisms by their environment.

The early stages of growth are telescoped into each other almost indistinguishably, so that phylogenetically the embryo lives a thousand years in a day, and the higher the species the more rapid relatively is the transit through the lower stages. This law of tachygenesis may perhaps be expressed somewhat as follows: Heredity, which slowly appears as a substitute for the external causes that have produced a given series of characters, tends to produce that succession with increasing economy and speed and also to become in a way more independent of the causes which originally determined it.[3]

From his prefactory summary to his volume on adolescence, his emphasis on developmental considerations is clear.

While inanimate nature and even the lower forms of animal life are relatively stable, some of the latter having persisted from remote geologic ages, man is rapidly changing. His presence on the globe, his dominion over animals, his diffusion, and the historic period, are a series of increasingly recent events. While his bodily form is comparatively stable, his soul is in a transition stage, and all that we call progress is more and more rapid. Old moorings are constantly broken; adaptive plasticity to new environments—somatic, economic, industrial, social, moral and religious— was never so great; and in the changes which we hope are on the whole truly progressive, more and more human traits are too partially acquired to be permanently inherited. All this suggests that man is not a permanent type but an organism in a very active stage of evolution toward a more permanent form. Our consciousness is but a single stage and one type of mind: a late, partial, and perhaps essentially abnormal and remedial outcrop of the great underlying life of man-soul. The animal, savage, and child-soul can never be studied by introspection. Moreover, with missing links and extinct ethnic types, much, perhaps most, soul life has been hopelessly lost. Thus, the adult who seeks self-knowledge by intro- version is banausic, and his system is at its best but one human docu- ment or return to the eternal but ever unanswered question what man can know, what he should do, and how he most truly feels. From this it follows that we must turn to the larger and far more laborious method of observation, description, and induction. We must collect states of mind, sentiments, phenomena long since lapsed, psychic facts that appear faintly and perhaps but once in a lifetime, and that in only few and rare individuals, impulses that, it may be, never anywhere arise above the threshold, but manifest themselves only in automatisms, acts, behavior, things neglected, trivial and incidental, such as Darwin says are often most vital. We must go to school to the folk-soul, learn of criminals and defectives, animals, and in some sense go back to Aristotle in rebasing psychology on biology, and realize that we know the soul best when we can best write its history in the world, and that there are no finalities save formulae of development. The soul is thus still in the making, and we may hope for an indefinite further development. Perhaps other racial stocks than ours will later advance the kingdom of man as far beyond our present standpoint as it now is above that of the lowest savage or even animals. There are powers in the soul that slumber like the sleepers in myth, partially aroused, it may be, in great personal or social crises, but sometime to be awakened to dominance. In a word, the view here repre- sents a nascent tendency and is in striking contrast to all those systems that presume to have attained even an approximate finality. But the twilight is that of dawn and not of evening. It is the morning hours of beginning and not that of completing the day of work, and this can appeal only to those still adolescent in soul.

Holding that the child and the race are each keys to the other, I have constantly suggested phyletic explanations of all degrees of probability. Some of these, I think, have been demonstrated so far as is now possible in this obscure and complicated domain. Realizing the limitations and qualifications of the recapitulation theory in the biologic field, I am now convinced that its psychogenetic applications have a method of their own, and although the time has not yet come when any formulation of these can have much value, I have done the best I could with each instance as it arose. Along with the sense of the immense importance of further coordinating childhood and youth with the development of the race, has grown the conviction that only here can we hope to find true norms against the tendencies to precocity in home, school, church, and civilization generally, and also to establish criteria by which to both diagnose and measure arrest and retardation in the individual and the race. While individuals differ widely in not only the age but the sequence of the stages of repetition of racial history, a knowledge of nascent stages and the aggregate interests of different ages of life is the best safeguard against very many of the prevalent errors of education and of life. . . .

The years from about eight to twelve constitute an unique period of human life. The acute stage of teething is passing, the brain has acquired nearly its adult size and weight, health is almost at its best, activity is greater and more varied than ever before or than it ever will be again, and there is peculiar endurance, vitality, and resistance to fatigue. The child develops a life of its own outside the home circle, and its natural interests are never so independent of adult influence. Perception is very acute, and there is great immunity to exposure, danger, accident, as well as to temptation. Reason, true morality, religion, sympathy, love, and esthetic enjoyment are but very slightly developed. Everything, in short, suggests the culmination of one stage of life as if it thus represented what was once, and for a very protracted and relatively stationary period, the age of maturity in some remote, perhaps pigmoid, stage of human evolution, when in a warm climate the young of our species once shifted for themselves independently of further parental aid. The qualities now developed are phyletically vastly older than all the neo-atavistic traits of body and soul, later to be superposed like a new and higher story built on to our primal nature. Heredity is so far both more stable and more secure. The elements of personality are few, but are well organized and on a simple, effective plan. The momentum of the paleopsychic traits is great, and they are often clearly distinguishable from those to be later added. Thus the boy is father of the man in a new sense in that his qualities are indefinitely older and existed well compacted untold ages before the more distinctly human attributes were developed. Indeed, there are a few faint indications set forth in the text of a yet earlier age nodality or meristic segmentation, as if amid the increased instability of health at the age of about six we could still detect the ripple-marks of an ancient public beach now lifted high above the tides of a receding shore-line as human infancy has been prolonged. I have also given reasons that lead me to the conclusion that, despite its dominance, the function of sexual maturity and procreative power is peculiarly mobile up and down the ageline independently of many of the qualities usually so closely associated with it, so that much that sex created in the phylum now precedes it in the individual.[4]

As a source of stimulation for a later generation of psychologists, Hall had few equals. That he centered his enthusiasm on problems of child development has served to help make this a major field of research in the United States today.

28

CATTELL ON

INDIVIDUAL DIFFERENCES,
THE QUANTITATIVE ASSESSMENT OF
HUMAN CAPACITIES, AND APPLICATIONS
OF PSYCHOLOGY

JAMES MCKEEN CATTELL (1860–1944), American psychologist, although a student of Wundt (p. 128), had a greater feeling of kinship for Francis Galton (p. 166). His characteristic pattern of interests, expressed in the title above, could also have been that for Galton (with whom he was associated for a brief period of time). A consistent tendency in his work is expressed in his resolve to use quantitative assessment of human capacities and to study "individual differences," a phrase he was first to use as early as 1885[1] in a graduate student paper. Five years later, he coined the expression "mental tests" in the paper excerpted below:

Psychology cannot attain the certainty and exactness of the phsysical sciences, unless it rests on a foundation of experiment and measurement. A step in this direction could be made by applying a series of mental tests and measurements to a large number of individuals. The results would be of considerable scientific value in discovering the constancy of mental processes, their interdependence, and their variation under different circumstances. Individuals, besides, would find their tests interesting, and, perhaps, useful in regard to training, mode of life or indication of disease. The scientific and practical value of such tests would be much increased should a uniform system be adopted, so that determinations made at different times and places could be compared and combined. With a view to obtaining agreement among those interested, I venture to suggest the following series of tests and measurements, together with methods of making them.

    The first series of ten tests is made in the Psychological Laboratory of the University of Pennsylvania on all who present themselves, and the complete series on students of Experimental Psychology. The results will be published when sufficient data have been collected. Meanwhile I should be glad to have the tests, and the methods of making them, thoroughly discussed.

The following ten tests are proposed:

1. Dynamometer Pressure.
2. Rate of Movement.
3. Sensation-areas.
4. Pressure causing Pain.
5. Least noticeable differences in Weight.
6. Reaction-time for Sound.
7. Time for naming Colours.
8. Bi-section of a 50 cm. line.
9. Judgment of 10 seconds time.
10. Number of Letters remembered on once Hearing.

It will be noticed that the series begins with determinations rather bodily than mental, and proceeds through psychophysical to more purely mental measurements.

The tests may be readily made on inexperienced persons, the time required for the series being about an hour. The laboratory should be conveniently arranged and quiet, and no spectators should be present while the experiments are being made. The amount of instruction the experimentee should receive, and the number of trials he should be given, are matters which ought to be settled in order to secure uniformity of result. The amount of instruction depends on the experimenter and experimentee, and cannot, unfortunately, be exactly defined. It can only be said that the experimentee must understand clearly what he has to do. A large and uniform number of trials would, of course, be the most satisfactory, the average, average variation, maximum and minimum being recorded. Time is, however, a matter of great importance if many persons are to be tested. The arrangement most economical of time would be to test thoroughly a small number of persons, and a large number in a more rough-and-ready fashion. The number of trials I allow in each test is given below, as also whether I consider the average or "best" trial the most satisfactory for comparison.[2]

Hereafter, he goes into detail about how each test is to be given, the precautions to be taken, and how uniformity of administration is to be achieved. These and other tests suggested in the articles were all measures used in previous research in psychological and physiological laboratories. They were now to be utilized for development of test norms. Very few were concerned with the higher mental processes, for example, time for naming colors, and number of letters remembered. Those dependent on sensory and motor tasks, such as the first six of the ten in the excerpt, predominated. The tests were used for research, relating them to college academic standing; no appreciable degree of correlation was found. The more complex psychological tests, such as those used in current intelligence tests, were to prove more successful for this task.

In 1888, Cattell was appointed professor of psychology at the University of Pennsylvania. He was the first person in the world to receive this title, an event that signified the recognition of the status of psychology as a discipline separate from philosophy. In 1891, he moved on to Columbia University, with which he was associated for the rest of his academic career. During his administration, the psychology department became the dominant one in the United States for training psychologists. He also became a psychological statesman. He was the first psychologist elected to the National Academy of Science, he became the editor and owner of *Science,* the leading general scientific publication, and he organized and published *American Men of Science,* still the leading directory in the field.

His editorship of *American Men of Science* went hand in hand with his use of quantified methods for selection for eminence in each of the various scientific fields, signified by the name of each individual so selected identified by a distinguishing star preceding the entry. His work with psychologists is most pertinent here. One facet of his research was his attempt to find and arrange the then senior contemporary psychologists in order of judged eminence. The order-of-merit method calls for judges to arrange a set of stimuli, whether it be names of individuals, colors, pictures, or whatever, according to some predetermined criteria. It might be the appeal of pictures, pleasingness of the brightness of colors, or, in the case of the task in the excerpt below, the names of psychologists arranged in order of their eminence as judged by fellow psychologists.

I have discussed in various papers the importance to psychology of the study of individual differences and have given some results of a research in which I am taking as the material one thousand students of Columbia College, one thousand eminent men of history, and one thousand American men of science. The thousand men of science have been selected from some 4,000 included in a biographical dictionary that I am compiling, who, in turn, were selected from a list containing some 10,000 names.

On the lists are the names of 131 who appear to me to have contributed to the advancement of psychology. Among them are many whose work is unimportant, and several who have scarcely accomplished anything beyond teaching or the writing of a text-book. There are not included, however, those who have printed a minor study and have not again been heard from, nor most of those working in other sciences whose results may be valuable for psychology, but belong elsewhere. Excluding from the group nearly all those whose work is not primarily in psychology, or in psychology combined with philosophy or education, there remain 270. Omitting those whose work seems to be of the least value, and those whose addresses I have not been able to find or from whom I have no returns, I have taken a group of 200 for consideration. The first 150 or so have been selected objectively in the manner described below, the last fifty are practically those that were left. For certain purposes four groups of fifty each have been used, the first group consisting of those whose work is supposed to have the greatest merit, the second group ranking next, etc.

I have distributed scientific men among twelve principal sciences—mathematics, physics, chemistry, astronomy, geology, botany, zoölogy, physiology, anatomy, pathology, anthropology, and psychology. As there are about 200 psychologists among some 4,000 students of science, the psychologists are about one-twentieth of the scientific workers of the country. They are about equal in number to the astronomers; they are more numerous than the physiologists, anatomists, or anthropologists, and are fewer than the workers in the other principal science.

In each of these sciences I have asked ten leading representatives to arrange the students in that science in the order of merit. I did this (1) to select for special study the thousand regarded as the most meritorious; (2) to be able to discuss distribution in relation to merit, and to correlate merit with various qualities; (3) to learn the meaning and validity of such judgments, and (4) to have on record the order with a view to reference or possible publication ten or twenty years hence.

The memorandum sent to those who were asked to make the arrangement was as follows:

MEMORANDUM

The undersigned is making a study of American men of science. The first problem to be considered is the distribution of scientific men among the sciences and in different regions, institutions, etc., including the relative rank of this country as compared with other countries in the different sciences, the relative strength of different universities, etc. It is intended that the study shall be continued beyond the facts of distribution to what may be called the natural history of scientific men.

For these purposes a list of scientific men in each science, arranged approximately in the order of merit, is needed. This can best be secured if those who are most competent to form an opinion will independently make the arrangement. The average of such arrangements will give the most valid order, and the degree of validity will be indicated by the variation or probable error of position for each individual.

It is obvious that such an order can be only approximate, and for the objects in view an approximation is all that is needed. The judgments are possible, because they are as a matter of fact made in elections to a society of limited membership, in filling chairs at a university, etc. By merit is understood contributions to the advancement of science, primarily by research, but teaching, administration, editing, the compilation of text-books, etc., should be considered. The different factors that make a man efficient in advancing science must be roughly balanced. An effort may be made later to disentangle these factors.

In ranking a man in a given science his contributions to that science only should be considered. Thus, an eminent astronomer may also be a mathematician, but in ranking him as a mathematician only his contributions to mathematics should be regarded. In such a case, however, mathematics should be given its widest interpretation. It is more difficult to arrange the order when the work cannot readily be compared, as, for example, systematic zoölogy and morphology, but, as already stated, it is only expected that the arrangement shall be approximate. The men should be ranked for work actually accomplished,—that is, a man of sixty and a man of forty, having done about the same amount of work, should come near together, though the man of forty has more promise. It may be possible later to calculate a man's value with allowance for age.

In case there is noted the omission of any scientific man from the list who should probably have a place in the first three quarters, a slip may be added in the proper place with his name and address. In case there are names on the list regarding which nothing is known, the slips should be placed together at the end. The slips, as arranged in order, should be tied together and returned to the undersigned.

It is not intended that the lists shall be published, at all events not within ten years. No individual list will be published. They will be destroyed when the averages have been calculated, and the arrangements will be regarded as strictly confidential.[3]

The order, positions, and probable errors assigned to the first ten American psychologists in order of merit turned out to be as follows:

ORDER	POSITIONS	NAME
1	1.0	William James
2	3.7	J. McKeen Cattell
3	4.0	Hugo Münsterberg
4	4.4	G. S. Hall
5	7.5	J. Mark Baldwin
6	7.5	E. B. Titchener
7	7.6	Josiah Royce
8	9.2	G. T. Ladd
9	9.6	John Dewey
10	11.6	Joseph Jastrow

No names were included in the study itself but twenty-six years later they were released.[4] Five are represented by excerpts in this volume, five are not.*

Cattell's support of the professional application of psychology shines clearly through in a paper published in 1937 in which he reviews some aspects of its history and reports on this organization of the Psychological Corporation:

It would be a satisfaction to stand at a place on the bridge of life from which it would be natural to be asked for an article on the future of psychology as a profession rather than for a retrospect. But unfortunately 1937 marks the fiftieth anniversary of my appointment as professor of psychology in the University of Pennsylvania.

Perhaps when a history—modern in point of view as well as in the period covered—comes to be written of these fifty years it will be evident that governments and wars have had less to do with the present condi-

---

*The five individuals not represented by excerpts might be briefly identified in a manner that at least suggests why they do not today hold the degree of eminence they were then accorded. Münsterberg, a German psychologist at Harvard, left experimental psychology for academically unpopular excursions into the psychology of law and of advertising which, before his work, had lacked an empirical base, and was outspoken at his defense of Germany during World War I. Baldwin, essentially "old fashioned" in his approach to developmental psychology even in his day, left the field early in his career. Royce later emphasized almost completely his philosophical interests. Ladd, author of an influential early compendium on physiological psychology, did not do further work of the same stature. Jastrow, early founder of laboratories, turned to writing in psychology that attracted a popular but not a scientific audience, such as his *House that Freud Built*.

tions of the world than the technological developments of science; these have quadrupled the productivity of labor and doubled the length of life. The industrial revolution can be dated from the use of the steam engine of Watts in the coal mines of Cornwall little more than a hundred and fifty years ago. The beginnings of a psychological revolution have occurred in the course of the past fifty years; it is possible that the development of psychology as a science and its application to the control of human conduct—individual and collective—may in the course of the coming century be as significant for civilization as has been the industrial revolution.

In an address given in 1917 on the occasion of the twenty-fifth anniversary of the founding of the American Psychological Association, I noted that of 307 members 272 were engaged in teaching, 16 in the applications of psychology. I then remarked that this latter group "now so small may at our fiftieth anniversary surpass in numbers those engaged in teaching." Then came our entrance into the war and the army service of our psychologists put the applications of psychology on the map and on the front page. We now have clinical, educational and industrial psychologists. There will not, however, be a profession of psychology until we have professional schools and professional standards. . . .

The situation is appalling in its responsibility, for we are a feeble folk. Still our progress in numbers at least has been notable. When the American Psychological Association was founded in 1892 there were 31 members, about half of whom were not primarily psychologists. When I came to New York in the previous year I found only Henry Rutgers Marshall, M. Allen Starr and Nicholas Murray Butler. Now there are 278 members and associates of the American Psychological Association in the city. The Association had 127 members in 1902, 262 in 1912, 422 in 1922; now there are about 2,000 members and associates. This is a geometrical progression which promises numbers commensurate with those in other sciences and other professions. My prediction that at the fiftieth anniversary of the association the numbers engaged in applied work would equal those engaged in teaching will not be fulfilled—as is likely to be the case with predictions—so I shall repeat it for the seventy-fifth anniversary.

The space limit to which this article must be confined makes it impossible to sketch the history of the emergence of psychology as a profession in the course of the last fifty years. Two efforts in which I was interested failed. In the middle of the nineties when we were making the student tests at Columbia I asked President Low to let us establish a psychological clinic which would make tests and examinations of the poor without charge and be supported by fees from those who could afford them. President Low, however, decided that it would not do to charge fees in a university laboratory. I was also concerned with the certification of psychologists by the American Psychological Association which finally was found not to be feasible.

Two undertakings in New York City are now proving themselves useful for psychology as a profession. This new *Journal of Consulting Psychology* represents the work of the Association of Consulting Psychologists. The contributors to the first number include four of the seven members of the executive committee of the Psychological Corporation. This organization was chartered in 1921 with twenty of our leading psychologists as directors. They included G. Stanley Hall, G. T. Ladd and E. B. Titchener, who had not until then cared for applied psychology. The stock was held by about 170 psychologists. Its objects and powers are defined in the charter as the "advancement of psychology and the promotion of the useful applications of psychology." It is planned to pay adequately for services of psychologists and to use the profits from professional and industrial work to support research. The corporation had in its early years a success of esteem and accomplished much to interest a large public in the uses of psychology.

This statement on psychology as a profession may end with a quotation from an address made at the International Congress of Arts and Science held at St. Louis in 1904 and printed in *The Popular Science Monthly* at the time. It reads:

"The present function of a physician, a lawyer, a clergyman, a teacher or a man of business is to a considerable extent that of an amateur psychologist. In the inevitable specialization of modern society, there will become increasing need of those who can be paid for expert psychological advice. We may have experts who will be trained in schools as large and well-equipped as our present schools of medicine, and their profession may become as useful and as honorable. Such a profession clearly offers an opportunity to the charlatan, but it is not the only profession open to him. For the present the psychological expert should doubtless be a member of one of the recognized professions who has the natural endowments, special training and definite knowledge of the conditions that will make his advice ans assistance of value. But in the end there will be not only a science but also a profession of psychology."[5]

Different as Cattell was from G. Stanley Hall (p. 207), there was still an underlying fundamental similarity. Quite apart from research, both did much to give psychology in the United States its characteristic quantitative, pragmatic, and applied qualities.

The contemporary scene stands witness to the essential correctness of Cattell's prediction with perhaps more American psychologists engaged in professional practice than are devoted to scientific pursuit.

29

TITCHENER ON

ELEMENTARISTIC STRUCTURAL PSYCHOLOGY

EDWARD BRADFORD TITCHENER (1867–1927), English student of the German, Wundt, was the most influential of all of his students in promulgating his mentor's version of psychology in the United States. Professor at Cornell University from 1892 to 1927, he built a laboratory and a department that brought him generations of graduate students who were trained in his way of interpreting the nature of psychology. He devoted his most productive years to rendering his mentor's position more systematic, and then went on to develop a more unique view of psychology.

The article, from which excerpts are to be taken, not only presents his earlier systematic position, but it also distinguishes his structural psychology from functional psychology. While he saw his systematic position as that of psychology—all psychology—he agreed, when others more or less forced the designation upon him, that structural psychology was a reasonably appropriate designation, although protesting, as he does in the excerpt, that study of function *after* studying structure was an aspect of his position.

Biology, defined in its widest sense as the science of life and of living things, falls into three parts, or may be approached from any one of three points of view. We may enquire into the structure of an organism, without regard to function,—by analysis determining its component parts, and by synthesis exhibiting the mode of its formation from the parts. Or we may enquire into the function of the various structures which our analysis has revealed, and into the manner of their interrelation as functional organs. Or, again, we may enquire into the changes of form and function that accompany the persistence of the organism in time, the phenomena of growth and of decay. Biology, the science of living things, comprises the three mutually interdependent sciences of morphology, physiology, and ontogeny.

This account is, however, incomplete. The life which forms the subject matter of science is not merely the life of an individual; it is species life, collective life, as well. Corresponding to morphology, we have taxonomy or systematic zoology, the science of classification. The whole world of living things is here the organism, and species and sub-species and races are its parts. Corresponding to physiology, we have that department of biology—it has been termed "oecology"—which deals with questions of geographical distribution, of the function of species in the general economy of nature. Corresponding to ontogeny we have the science of phylogeny (in Cope's sense): the biology of evolution, with its problems of descent and of transmission.

We may accept this scheme as a "working" classification of the biological sciences. It is indifferent, for my present purpose, whether or not the classification is exhaustive, as it is indifferent whether the reader regards psychology as a subdivision of biology or as a separate province of knowledge. The point which I wish now to make is this: that, employing the same principle of division, we can represent modern psychology as the exact counterpart of modern biology. There are three ways of approaching the one, as there are the three ways of approaching the other; and the subject matter in every case may be individual or general. A little consideration will make this clear.

1. We find a parallel to morphology in a very large portion of "experimental" psychology. The primary aim of the experimental psychologist has been to analyze the structure of mind; to ravel out the elemental processes from the tangle of consciousness, or (if we may change the metaphor) to isolate the constituents in the given conscious formation. His task is a vivisection, but a vivisection which shall yield structural, not functional results. He tries to discover, first of all, what is there and in what quantity, not what it is there for. Indeed, this work of analysis bulks so largely in the literature of experimental psychology that a recent writer has questioned the right of the science to its adjective, declaring that an experiment is something more than a measurement made by the help of delicate instruments. And there can be no doubt that much of the criticism passed upon the new psychology depends on the critic's failure to recognize its morphological character. We are often told that our treatment of feeling and emotion, of reasoning, of the self is inadequate; that the experimental method is valuable for the investiga-

tion of sensation and idea, but can carry us no farther. The answer is that the results gained by dissection of the "higher" processes will always be disappointing to those who have not themselves adopted the dissector's standpoint. Protoplasm consists, we are told, of carbon, oxygen, nitrogen, and hydrogen; but this statement would prove exceedingly disappointing to one who had thought to be informed of the phenomena of contractility and metabolism, respiration and reproduction. Taken in its appropriate context, the jejuneness of certain chapters in mental anatomy, implying, as it does, the fewness of the mental elements, is a fact of extreme importance.

2. There is, however, a functional psychology, over and above this psychology of structure. We may regard mind, on the one hand, as a complex of processes, shaped and moulded under the conditions of the physical organism. We may regard it, on the other hand, as the collective name for a system of functions of the psychophysical organism. The two points of view are not seldom confused. The phrase "association of ideas," e.g., may denote either the structural complex, the associated sensation group, or the functional process of recognition and recall, the associating of formation to formation. In the former sense it is morphological material, in the latter it belongs to what I must name (the phrase will not be misunderstood) a physiological psychology.

Just as experimental psychology is to a large extent concerned with problems of structure, so is "descriptive" psychology, ancient and modern, chiefly occupied with problems of function. Memory, recognition, imagination, conception, judgment, attention, apperception, volition, and a host of verbal nouns, wider or narrower in denotation, connote, in the discussions of descriptive psychology, functions of the total organism. That their underlying processes are psychical in character is, so to speak, an accident; for all practical purposes they stand upon the same level as digestion and locomotion, secretion and excretion. The organism remembers, wills, judges, recognizes, etc., and is assisted in its life-struggle by remembering and willing. Such functions are, however, rightly included in mental science, inasmuch as they constitute, in sum, the actual, working mind of the individual man. They are not functions of the body, but functions of the organism, and they may—nay, they must—be examined by the methods and under the regulative principles of a mental "physiology." The adoption of these methods does not at all prejudice the ultimate and extra-psychological problem of the function of mentality at large in the universe of things. Whether consciousness really has a survival-value, as James supposes, or whether it is a mere epiphenomenon, as Ribot teaches, is here an entirely irrelevant question.

It cannot be said that this functional psychology, despite what we may call its greater obviousness to investigation, has been worked out either with as much patient enthusiasm or with as much scientific accuracy as has the psychology of mind structure. It is true, and it is a truth which the experimentalist should be quick to recognize and emphasize, that there is very much of value in "descriptive" psychology. But it is also true that the methods of descriptive psychology cannot, in the nature of the case, lead to results of scientific finality. The same criticism holds, as things stand, of individual psychology, which is doing excellent pioneer work in the sphere of function. Experimental psychology has added much to our knowledge, functional as well as structural, of memory, attention, imagination, etc., and will, in the future, absorb and quantify the results of these other, new coordinate branches. Still, I do not think that anyone who has followed the course of the experimental method, in its application to the higher processes and states of mind, can doubt that the main interest throughout has lain in morphological analysis, rather than in ascertainment of function. Nor are the reasons far to seek. We must remember that experimental psychology arose by way of reaction against the faculty psychology of the last century. This was a metaphysical, not a scientific, psychology. There is, in reality, a great difference between, say, memory regarded as a function of the psychophysical organism, and memory regarded as a faculty of the substantial mind. At the same time, these two memories are nearer together than are the faculty memory and the memories or memory complexes of psychological anatomy. There is, further, the danger that, if function is studied before structure has been fully elucidated, the student may fall into that acceptance of teleological explanation which is fatal to scientific advance; witness, if witness be necessary, the recrudescence of vitalism in physiology. Psychology might thus put herself for the second time, and no less surely though by different means, under the dominion of philosophy. In a word, the historical conditions of psychology rendered it inevitable that, when the time came for the transformation from philosophy to science, problems should be formulated, explicitly or implicitly, as static rather than dynamic, structural rather than functional. We may notice also the fact that elementary morphology is intrinsically an easier study than elementary physiology, and that scientific men are so far subject to the law of inertia, whose effects we see in the conservatism of mankind at large, that they prefer the continued application of a fruitful method to the adoption of a new standpoint for the standpoint's sake.

I may, perhaps, digress here for a moment, to raise and attempt to answer two questions which naturally suggest themselves: the questions whether this conservatism is wise, and whether it is likely to persist. I believe that both should be answered in the affirmative. As has been indicated above, the morphological study of mind serves, as no other method of study can, to enforce and sustain the thesis that psychology is a science, and not a province of metaphysics; and recent writing shows clearly enough that this truth has need of constant reiteration. Moreover, there is still so much to be done in the field of analysis (not simply analysis of the higher processes, though these will of course benefit in the long run, but also analysis of perception and feeling and idea) that a general swing of the laboratories towards functional work would be most regrettable. It seems probable, if one may presume to read the signs of the times, that experimental psychology has before it a long period of analytical research, whose results, direct and indirect, shall ultimately serve as basis for the psychology of function; unless, indeed,—and this is beyond predicting,—the demands laid upon psychology by the educationalist become so insistent as partially to divert the natural channels of investigation. . . .

The object of the present paper is to set forth the state of current opinion upon the question of the structural elements of mind, their number and nature. It may be doubted, at first sight, whether anything like a consensus or opinion can be made out. "Every psychologist of standing," wrote Külpe in 1893, "has its own laws of association." Every psychologist of standing in the year of grace 1898, so the reader may think, has his own favorite "unique" process. Does not Brentano advocate an ultimate "judgment," and James a "fiat of the will," and Stout an ultimate "thought"? Is there not the perennial controversy about the "third conscious element," the process of conation, the "activity experience"? Are not even the clear waters of the psychology of sensation troubled by the possibility of an "efferent" conscious process, a sensation of innervation? The questions are importunate, and cannot be lightly brushed aside. We will begin, therefore, by examining a test case: Brentano's irreducible "judgment." I select this, because Professor Ebbinghaus, in his recent Psychology, seems to put a structural interpretation upon it. He himself classifies the elements of mind (we shall return to this classification later) as sensations, ideas, and feelings; Brentano, he says, ranks alongside of ideas the element of judgment. If this account is correct, we must admit that the morphology of mind is still a battlefield for individual opinions; we shall hardly escape the difficulty by the mere statement that Ebbinghaus is an experimentalist, and Brentano not.

When, however, we turn to Brentano himself, the matter assumes a different complexion. Brentano's principal criterion of psychical, as contraditinguished from physical phenomena, is that of "intentional inexistence" or "immanent objectivity," which we may paraphrase as reference to contents, direction upon something as object. "Every psychical phenomenon contains in it something as object, though not every one in the same way. In ideation something is ideated, in judgment something admitted ot rejected, in love and hate something loved and hated, in desire something desired, etc." This is evidently the language of function, not of structure. Indeed, Brentano uses the phrases *psychisches Phänomen* and *Seelenthatigkeit* interchangeably; his "fundamental" or "principal classes of psychical phenomena" are the "mental activities" of ideation (not "ideal"), judgment and interest (love and hate, the emotive processes). The spirit of his whole psychology is physiological; and when, on occasion, he discusses a point in anatomy, he leaves his reader in no doubt as to the shift of *venue*. Now the mental elements of the experimentalists, the bare sensation and the bare feeling, are abstractions, innocent of any sort of objective reference. We cannot fairly compare Brentano's "judgment" with them. Nay, more, we cannot fairly say that he would have posited an ultimate judgment process *if* he had adopted the anatomical point of view; since he has not adopted it, the speculation is absurd. The "psychology from the empirical standpoint" is a systematization of mental "activities," i.e., of the mental functions of the human organism.

This wave, then, has not overwhelmed us. Escaping it, we may turn now to the positive side of our enquiry. Our appeal will lie, in the first instance, to the experimentalists; but the omission of references to works on descriptive psychology is largely due to considerations of space, and does not by any means necessarily imply that the authors of these works differ from the writers quoted. Some of the "unique" processes still left outstanding will be taken up at the end of this discussion.

We set out from a point of universal agreement. Everyone admits that *sensations* are elementary mental processes. There is, it is true, diversity of opinion as to the range of contents that the term shall cover. Wundt identifies the peripherally excited and the centrally excited processes. "For the psychological attributes of a sensation the circumstance [of external or internal initiation] is entirely irrelevant. . . . It is only the central stimulus that always accompanies sensation." Külpe retains the name "sensation" for both classes, but declares that they "must be treated separately, as they normally present characteristic differences." Ziehen and Ebbinghaus, on the other hand, draw a sharp line of distinction between the "sensation," which is externally aroused, and the "idea" (in Lotze's sense), which is its centrally aroused substitute, and so recognize two elements where Wundt and Külpe see only one. The divergence, however, is not serious. It seems to depend, primarily, upon the admission or exclusion of genetic considerations. If we rule that these are foreign to a strictly morphological examination of mind, the question of one sense element or two becomes a problem set by analysis to analysis, capable of resolution by analytic methods; it is a subject for dispute "inside the ring," and is thus upon a quite different level from the question, e.g., of an elementary will process. . . .

Simple *affective* processes, again, are regarded by a large majority as elemental. Both Wundt and Külpe are at some pains to make clear the essential difference between sensation and affection. Lehmann and Ebbinghaus are equally explicit. Ziehen does not give a place to feeling besides sensation and idea; his chapters are entitled "The Affective Tone of Sensation" and "The Affective Tone of Ideas," and his treatment makes affective tone an attribute coordinate with the intensity and quality of sensation and the clearness and contents (meaning) of idea. Nevertheless, he speaks in one passage of the cortical substrate of this tone as "an entirely new psychophysiological process." Münsterberg, on the other hand, denies the ultimateness of feeling altogether, and seeks to reduce it to the sensations accompanying movements of flexion and extension, reflexly released. There is, further, an "inside" controversy as to the number of affective qualities. But analysis will some day settle the question whether there are two of these (Külpe), or two in the sphere of sensation and many more in that of idea (Ziehen), or an inexhaustible variety under the six heads of pleasantness and unpleasantness, tension and relaxation, excitement and tranquillization (Wundt).

It is natural, in view of the intrinsic difficulty of the subject, that the psychology of feeling should be in a less settled state than the psychology of sensation. All the more striking, when we consider the close relation that obtains between "feeling" and "will," is the unanimity with which experimentalists reject the doctrine of a specific will process. "There is no reason," writes Ebbinghaus, "for looking upon acts of will or appetitions as elementary forms of the mental life." And Wundt, Külpe, Ziehen, and Münsterberg are of the same way of thinking. . . . [What has just been said], implies that we are already familiar with the *attributes* of which sensation and affection are constituted. We must devote a brief space to their consideration.

Once more, we set out from a point of universal agreement. "There are two indispensable determinants of every psychical element, quality and intensity." But discussion is now slow to begin. For these two attributes or determinants are, evidently, of different kinds. Quality is specific and individual; it is quality that makes the elemental process a blue or a sweet, a pleasant or a *c* of the third octave. Intensity, on the contrary, is a general attribute, common to all modalities of sensation and qualities of affection. Hence, while some psychologists rank the two determinations together, as coordinate, others set aside quality for itself, and count intensity along with extent and duration as equipollent characteristics, whether of all the mental elements or of certain great groups of qualities. There is also much difference of opinion as to the precise place to be ascribed to the attributes of extent and duration. For Wundt, who holds a genetic theory, psychological space is the resultant of a two-dimensional system of qualitative local signs multipled into, or fused with, a one-dimensional intensive system of sensations aroused by movement. It is, primarily, tactual or visual. Psychological time, in the same way, is the resultant of qualitatively varied feelings multiplied into, or fused with, the same intensive system of sensations. The affective processes, in abstraction, are timeless; the primary sources of temporal ideas are audition and "internal touch." It follows that space and time, extent and duration, can be predicated only of formations, not of elements. Spatial arrangement (Wundt makes no distinction between "spatial arrangement" and "space" as "absolute contents") cannot "be an original attribute of the elements, analogous to the intensity or quality of sensations;" it "results from the bringing together of these elements," which means the "arising of new psychical conditions;" and the same thing is true of time. Opposed to this genetic theory is the nativistic view, represented for space, e.g., by Stumpf, according to which every sensation has about it something of tridimensionality, a certain bigness or voluminousness, and every elemental process a certain duration. . . .

A similar difficulty confronts us with regard to the attribute of clearness. Variation in degree of clearness of the constituent processes in ideas is the anatomical equivalent of what is functionally termed the "distribution of attention." Wundt places degree of clearness on the same level with spatial and temporal arrangement. "As these attributes [clearness and obscurity, distinctness and indistinctness] arise always and only from the interconnection of the various psychical formations, they cannot be considered as determinants of the psychical elements." Yet, on Wundt's own principle of relativity, the same thing would be true of sensation intensity; we cannot say anything of the intensity of a sensation unless a formation—at least two sensations, side by side—be there for "comparison." Moreover, we must exclude genetic arguments here as before. If we make analytic introspection the test, we cannot but admit that the ultimate sensation may be conceived of as clear or obscure.

I conclude, then, that the affective element is constituted of quality, intensity, and duration; the sense element (sensation or idea) of quality, intensity, duration, clearness, and (in some cases) extent. Quality is
intrinsic and individual; intensity and clearness are "relative" characteristics; duration and extent are, very probably, extrinsic translations
into strructure of the lowest terms of a functional series. And the corollary
is that the "elements" of the experimentalists, as they themselves have
been the first to urge, are artifacts, abstractions, usefully isolated for
scientific ends, but not found in experience save as connected with their
like. . . .

I believe as firmly that the best hope for psychology lies today in a
continuance of structural analysis, and that the study of function will not
yield final fruit until it can be controlled by the genetic and, still more, by
the experimental method—in the form both of laboratory experimenting
and of interpretation of that natural experiment which meets us in certain pathological cases.[1]

While specific points made in this article were modified by his later
work, they are not too unrepresentative of his earlier approach to psychology. He did not change his conviction that structural study in psychology
was both experimentally oriented and prior to functional approaches,
which at time of writing, he considered to be both descriptive and nonexperimental. He goes on to summarize his convictions concerning the
question of the structural elements of mind and their attributes.

Sensation was fundamental, in that "everyone" accepted it as an
element of mind. The various ways in which ideas and feelings, the other
structural elements he considered fundamental, were regarded, was still
a matter of dispute, but these differences of opinion would be solved, he
thought, through research. There was no fourth candidate for fundamental status. On turning to attributes, that is, characteristics capable of
being analyzed into aspects of the elements, he argued that quality and
intensity are indespensible, while duration, (later called protensity), extent (extensity), and attention (attensity) have a somewhat less secure
status so far as indispensibility is concerned.

After about 1915, his views of the nature of psychology changed
considerably. This change has been pieced together by Evans,[2] primarily
from letters, publications of his students, lecture notes, and conversations
too fragmentary or too diffuse for excerpting. The goal of his never completed presentation of systematic psychology would make psychology a
study, not of elements, but of what is conceived as the fundamental
dimensions of mental life—quality, intensity, protensity (duration), extensity (extent), and attensity (clearness). They became the indispensible
and ultimate dimensions of mental life, not further reducible to something else as they had been in the past, when considered attributes.

30

DEWEY ON

THE CIRCULAR
AND FUNCTIONAL CHARACTER
OF THE REFLEX ARC

JOHN DEWEY (1859–1952), versatile American philosopher, educator, and psychologist, in his earlier years was primarily concerned with psychology. He wished to find a unifying concept for mental life and decided to explore the reflex arc as a possibility, even though the upshot was that he rejected it as a unifying concept, while finding that conceiving it as a circuit had value in organizing psychological experiences.

The idea of the reflex arc has upon the whole come nearer to meeting this demand for a general working hypothesis than any other single concept. It being admitted that the sensori-motor apparatus represents both the unit of nerve structure and the type of nerve function, the image of this relationship passed over into psychology, and became an organizing principle to hold together the multiplicity of fact.

In criticising this conception it is not intended to make a plea for the principles of explanation and classification which the reflex arc idea has replaced; but, on the contrary, to urge that they are not sufficiently displaced, and that in the idea of the sensori-motor circuit, conceptions of the nature of sensation and of action derived from the nominally displaced psychology are still in control.

The older dualism between sensation and idea is repeated in the current dualism of peripheral and central structures and functions; the older dualism of body and soul finds a distinct echo in the current dualism of stimulus and response. Instead of interpreting the character of sensation, idea and action from their place and function in the sensori-motor circuit, we still incline to interpret the latter from our preconceived and preformulated ideas of rigid distinctions between sensations, thoughts and acts. The sensory stimulus is one thing, the central activity, standing for the idea, is another thing, and the motor discharge, standing for the act proper, is a third. As a result, the reflex arc is not a comprehensive, or organic unity, but a patchwork of disjointed parts, a mechanical conjunction of unallied processes. What is needed is that the principle underlying the idea of the reflex arc as the fundamental psychical unity shall react into and determine the values of its constitutive factors. More specifically, what is wanted is that sensory stimulus, central connections and motor responses shall be viewed, not as separate and complete entities in themselves, but as divisions of labor, functioning factors, within the single concrete whole, now designated the reflex arc.

What is the reality so designated? What shall we term that which is not sensation-followed-by-idea-followed-by-movement, but which is primary; which is, as it were, the psychical organism of which sensation, idea and movement are the chief organs? Stated on the physiological side, this reality may most conveniently be termed coordination. This is the essence of the facts held together by and subsumed under the reflex arc concept. Let us take, for our example, the familiar child-candle instance. (James, Psychology, Vol. I, p. 25). The ordinary interpretation would say the sensation of light is a stimulus to the grasping as a response, the burn resulting is a stimulus to withdrawing the hand as response and so on. There is, of course, no doubt that is a rough practical way of representing the process. But when we ask for its psychological adequacy, the case is quite different. Upon analysis, we find that we begin not with a sensory stimulus, but with a sensori-motor coordination, the optical-ocular, and that in a certain sense it is the movement which is primary, and the sensation which is secondary, the movement of body, head and eye muscles determining the quality of what is experienced. In other words, the real beginning is with the act of seeing; it is looking, and not a sensation of light. The sensory quale gives the value of the act, just as the movement furnishes its mechanism and control, but both sensation and movement lie inside, not outside the act.

Now if this act, the seeing, stimulates another act, the reaching, it is because both of these acts fall within a larger coordination; because seeing and grasping have been so often bound together to reinforce each other, to help each other out, that each may be considered practically a subordinate member of a bigger coordination. More specifically, the ability of the hand to do its work will depend, either directly or indirectly, upon its control, as well as its stimulation, by the act of vision. If the sight did not inhibit as well as excite the reaching, the latter would be purely indeterminate, it would be for anything or nothing, not for the particular object seen. The reaching, in turn, must both stimulate and control the seeing. The eye must be kept upon the candle if the arm is to do its work; let it wander and the arm takes up another task. In other words, we now have an enlarged and transformed coordination; the act is seeing no less than before, but it is now seeing-for-reaching purposes. There is still a sensori-motor circuit, one with more content or value, not a substitution of a motor response for a sensory stimulus.

Now take the affairs at its next stage, that in which the child gets burned. It is hardly necessary to point out again that this is also a sensori-motor coordination and not a mere sensation. It is worth while, however, to note especially the fact that it is simply the completion, or fulfillment, of the previous eye-arm-hand coordination and not an entirely new occurrence. Only because the heat-pain quale enters into the same circuit of experience with the optical-ocular and muscular quales, does the child learn from the experience and get the ability to avoid the experience in the future.

More technically stated, the so-called response is not merely *to* the stimulus; it is *into* it. The burn is the original seeing, the original optical-ocular experience enlarged and transformed in its value. It is no longer mere seeing; it is seeing-of-a-light-that-means-pain-when-contact-occurs. The ordinary reflex arc theory proceeds upon the more or less tacit assumption that the outcome of the response is a totally new experience; that it is, say, the substitution of a burn sensation for a light sensation through the intervention of motion. The fact is that the sole meaning of the intervening movement is to maintain, reinforce or transform (as the case may be) the original quale; that we do not have the replacing of one sort of experience by another, but the development (or as it seems convenient to term it) the mediation of an experience. The seeing, in a word, remains to control the reaching, and is, in turn, interpreted by the burning.

The discussion up to this point may be summarized by saying that the reflex arc idea, as commonly employed, is defective in that it assumes sensory stimulus and motor response as distinct psychical existences, while in reality they are always inside a coordination and have their significance purely from the part played in maintaining or reconstituting the coordination; and (secondly) in assuming that the quale of experience which precedes the "motor" phase and that which succeeds it are two different states, instead of the last being always the first reconstituted, the motor phase coming in only for the sake of such mediation. The result is that the reflex arc idea leaves us with a disjointed psychology, whether viewed from the standpoint of development in the individual or in the race, or from that of the analysis of the mature consciousness. As to the former, in its failure to see that the arc of which it talks is virtually a circuit, a continual reconstitution, it breaks continuity and leaves us nothing but a series of jerks, the origin of each jerk to be sought outside the process of experience itself, in either an external pressure of "environment," or else in an unaccountable spontaneous variation from within the 'soul' or the 'organism.' As to the latter, failing to see the unity of activity, no matter how much it may prate of unity, it still leaves us with sensation or peripheral stimulus; idea, or central process (the equivalent of attention); and motor response, or act, as three disconnected existences, having to be somehow adjusted to each other, whether through the intervention of an extraexperimental soul, or by mechanical push and pull. . . .

I hope it will not appear that I am introducing needless refinements and distinctions into what, it may be urged, is after all an undoubted fact, that movement as response follows sensation as stimulus. It is not a question of making the account of the process more complicated, though it is always wise to beware of that false simplicity which is reached by leaving out of account a large part of the problem. It is a question of finding out what stimulus or sensation, what movement and response mean; a question of seeing that they mean distinctions of flexible function only, not of fixed existence; that one and the same occurrence plays either or both parts, according to the shift of interest; and that because of this functional distinction and relationship, the supposed problem of the adjustment of one to the other, whether by superior force in the stimulus or an agency *ad hoc* in the center or the soul, is a purely self-created problem.

We may see the disjointed character of the present theory, by calling to mind that it is impossible to apply the phrase "sensori-motor" to the occurrence as a simple phrase of description; it has validity only as a term of interpretation, only, that is, as defining various functions exercised. In terms of description, the whole process may be sensory or it may be motor, but it cannot be sensori-motor. The "stimulus," the excitation of the nerve ending and of the sensory nerve, the central change, are just as much, or just as little, motion as the events taking place in the motor nerve and the muscles. It is one uninterrupted, continuous redistribution of mass in motion. And there is nothing in the process, from the standpoint of description, which entitles us to call this reflex. It is redistribution pure and simple; as much so as the burning of a log, or the falling of a house or the movement of the wind. In the physical process, as physical, there is nothing which can be set off as stimulus, nothing which reacts, nothing which is response. There is just a change in the system of tensions.

The same sort of thing is true when we describe the process purely from the psychical side. It is now all sensation, all sensory quale; the motion, as psychically described, is just as much sensation as is sound or light or burn. Take the withdrawing of the hand from the candle flame as example. What we have is a certain visual-heat-pain-muscular-quale, transformed into another visual-touch-muscular-quale—the flame now being visible only at a distance, or not at all, the touch sensation being altered, etc. If we symbolize the original visual quale by v, the temperature by h, the accompanying muscular sensation by m, the whole experience may be stated as vhm-vhm-vhm'; m being the quale of withdrawing, m' the sense of the status after the withdrawal. The motion is not a certain kind of existence; it is a sort of sensory experience interpreted, just as is candle flame, or burn from candle flame. All are on a par.

But, in spite of all this, it will be urged, there is a distinction between stimulus and response, between sensation and motion. Precisely; but we ought now to be in a condition to ask of what nature is the distinction, instead of taking it for granted as a distinction somehow lying in the existence of the facts themselves. We ought to be able to see that the ordinary conception of the reflex arc theory, instead of being a case of plain science, is a survival of the metaphysical dualism, first formulated by Plato, according to which the sensation is an ambiguous dweller on the border land of soul and body, the idea (or central process) is purely psychical, and the act (or movement) purely physical. Thus the reflex arc formulation is neither physical (or physiological) nor psychological; it is a mixed materialistic-spiritualistic assumption.

If the previous descriptive analysis has made obvious the need of a reconsideration of the reflex arc idea, of the nest of difficulties and assumptions in the apparently simple statement, it is now time to undertake an explanatory analysis. The fact is that stimulus and response are not distinctions of existence, but teleological distinctions, that is, distinctions of function, or part played, with reference to reaching or maintaining an end. With respect to this teleological process, two stages should be discriminated, as their confusion is one cause of the confusion attending the whole matter. In one case, the relation represents an organization of means with reference to a comprehensive end. It represents an accomplished adaptation. Such is the case in all well developed instincts, as when we say that the contact of eggs is a stimulus to the hen to set; or the sight of corn a stimulus to pick; such also is the case with all thoroughly formed habits, as when the contact with the floor stimulates walking. In these instances there is no question of consciousness of stimulus *as* stimulus, of response *as* response. There is simply a continuously ordered sequence of acts, all adapted in themselves and in the order of their sequence, to reach a certain objective end, the reproduction of the species, the preservation of life, locomotion to a certain place. The end has got thoroughly organized into the means. In calling one stimulus, another response we mean nothing more than that such an orderly sequence of acts is taking place. The same sort of statement might be made equally well with reference to the succession of changes in a plant, so far as these are considered with reference to their adaptation to, say, producing seed. It is equally applicable to the series of events in the circulation of the blood, or the sequence of acts occurring in a self-binding reaper.

Regarding such cases of organization viewed as already attained, we may say, positively, that it is only the assumed common reference to an inclusive end which marks each member off as stimulus and response, that apart from such reference we have only antecedent and consequent, in other words, the distinction is one of interpretation. Negatively, it must be pointed out that it is not legitimate to carry over, without change, exactly the same order of considerations to cases where it is a question of *conscious* stimulation and response. We may, in the above case, regard, if we please, stimulus and response each as an entire act, having an individuality of its own, subject even here to the qualification that individuality means not an entirely independent whole, but a division of labor as regards maintaining or reaching an end. But in any case, it is an act, a sensorimotor coordination, which stimulates the response, itself in turn sensori-motor, not a sensation which stimulates a movement. Hence the illegitimacy of identifying, as is so often done, such cases of organized instincts or habits with the so-called reflex arc, or of transferring, without modification, considerations valid of this serial coordination of acts to the sensation-movement case.

The fallacy that arises when this is done is virtually the psychological or historical fallacy. A set of considerations which hold good only because of a completed process, is read into the content of the process which conditions this completed result. A state of things characterizing an outcome is regarded as a true description of the events which led up to this outcome; when, as a matter of fact, if this outcome had already been in existence, there would have been no necessity for the process. Or, to make the application to the case in hand, considerations valid of an attained organization or coordination, the orderly sequence of minor acts in a comprehensive coordination, are used to describe a process, viz., the distinction of mere sensation as stimulus and of mere movement as response, which takes place only because such an attained organization is no longer at hand, but is in process of constitution. Neither mere sensation, nor mere movement, can ever be either stimulus or response; only an act can be that; the *sensation* as stimulus means the lack of and search for such an objective stimulus, or orderly placing of an act; just as mere movement as response means the lack of and search for the right act to complete a given coordination.

A recurrence to our example will make these formulae clearer. As long as the seeing is an unbroken act, which is as experienced no more mere sensation than it is mere motion (though the onlooker or psychological observer can interpret it into sensation and movement), it is in no sense the sensation which stimulates the reaching; we have, as already sufficiently indicated, only the serial steps in a coordination of *acts*. But now take a child who, upon reaching for bright light (that is, exercising the seeing-reaching coordination) has sometimes had a delightful exercise, sometimes found something good to eat and sometimes burned himself. *Now the response is not only uncertain, but the stimulus is equally uncertain; one is uncertain only in so far as the other is.* The real problem may be equally well stated as either to discover the right stimulus, to constitute the stimulus, or to discover, to constitute, the response. The question of whether to reach or to abstain from reaching is the question what sort of a bright light have we here? Is it the one which means playing with one's hands, eating milk, or burning one's fingers? The stimulus must be constituted for the response to occur. Now it is at precisely this juncture and because of it that the distinction of sensation as stimulus and motion as response arises.

The sensation or conscious stimulus is not a thing or existence by itself; it is that phase of a coordination requiring attention because, by reason of the conflict within the coordination, it is uncertain how to complete it. It is to doubt as to the next act, whether to reach or no, which gives the motive to examining the act. The end to follow is, in this sense, the stimulus. It furnishes the motivation to attend to what has just taken place; to define it more carefully. From this point of view the discovery of the stimulus is the "response" to possible movement as "stimulus." We must have an anticipatory sensation, an image, of the movements that may occur, together with their respective values, before attention will go to the seeing to break it up as a sensation of light, and of light of this particular kind. It is the initiated activities of reaching, which, inhibited by the conflict in the coordination, turn round, as it were, upon the seeing, and hold it from passing over into further act until its quality is determined. Just here the act as objective stimulus becomes transformed into sensation as possible, as conscious, stimulus. Just here also, motion as conscious response emerges.

In other words, sensation as stimulus does not mean any particular psychical *existence*. It means simply a function, and will have its value shift according to the special work requiring to be done. At one moment the various activities of reaching and withdrawing will be the sensation, because they are that phase of activity which sets the problem, or creates the demand for, the next act. At the next moment the previous act of seeing will furnish the sensation, being, in turn, that phase of activity which sets the pace upon which depends further action. Generalized, sensation as stimulus, is always that phase of activity requiring to be defined in order that a coordination may be completed. What the sensation will be in particular at a given time, therefore, will depend entirely upon the way in which an activity is being used. It has no fixed quality of its own. The search for the stimulus is the search for exact conditions of action; that is, for the state of things which decides how a beginning coordination should be completed.

Similarly, motion, as response, has only a functional value. It is whatever will serve to complete the disintegrating coordination. Just as the discovery of the sensation marks the establishing of the problem, so the constitution of the response marks the solution of this problem. At one time, fixing attention, holding the eye fixed, upon the seeing and thus bringing out a certain quale of light is the response, because that is the particular act called for just then; at another time, the movement of the arm away from the light is the response. There is nothing in itself which may be labelled response. That one certain set of sensory quales should be marked off by themselves as "motion" and put in antithesis to such sensory quales as those of color, sound and contact, as legitimate claimants to the title of sensation, is wholly inexplicable unless we keep the difference of function in view. It is the eye and ear sensations which fix for us the problem; which report to us the conditions which have to be met if the coordination is to be successfully completed; and just the moment we need to know about our movements to get an adequate report, just that moment, motion miraculously (from the ordinary standpoint) ceases to be motion and become "muscular sensation." On the other hand, take the change in values of experience, the transformation of sensory quales. Whether this change will or will not be interpreted as movement, whether or not any consciousness of movement will arise, will depend upon whether this change is satisfactory, whether or not it is regarded as a harmonious development of a coordination, or whether the change is regarded as simply a means in solving a problem, an instrument in reaching a more satisfactory coordination. So long as our experience runs smoothly we are no more conscious of motion as motion than we are of this or that color or sound by itself.

To sum up: the distinction of sensation and movement as stimulus and response respectively is not a distinction which can be regarded as descriptive of anything which holds of psychical events or existences as such. The only events to which the terms stimulus and response can be descriptively applied are to minor acts serving by their respective positions to the maintenance of some organized coordination. The conscious stimulus or sensation, and the conscious response or motion, have a special genesis or motivation, and a special end or function. The reflex arc theory, by neglecting, by abstracting from, this genesis and this function gives us one disjointed part of a process as if it were the whole. It gives us literally an arc, instead of the circuit; and not giving us the circuit of which it is an arc, does not enable us to place, to center, the arc. This arc, again, falls apart into two separate existences having to be either mechanically or externally adjusted to each other.

The circle is a coordination, some of whose members have come into conflict with each other. It is the temporary disintegration and need of reconstitution which occasions, which affords the genesis of, the conscious distinction into sensory stimulus on one side and motor response on the other. The stimulus is that phase of the forming coordination which represents the conditions which have to be met in bringing it to a successful issue; the response is that phase of one and the same forming coordination which gives the key to meeting these conditions, which serves as instrument in effecting the successful coordination. They are therefore strictly correlative and contemporaneous. The stimulus is something to be discovered; to be made out; if the activity affords its own adequate stimulation, there is no stimulus save in the objective sense already referred to. As soon as it is adequately determined, then and then only is the response also complete. To attain either, means that the coordination has completed itself. Moreover, it is the motor response which assists in discovering and constituting the stimulus. It is the holding of the movement at a certain stage which creates the sensation, which throws it into relief.

It is the coordination which unifies that which the reflex arc concept gives us only in disjointed fragments. It is the circuit within which fall distinctions of stimulus and response as functional phases of its own mediation or completion. The point of this story is in its application; but the application of it to the question of the nature of psychical evolution, to the distinction between sensational and rational consciousness, and the nature of judgment must be deferred to a more favorable opportunity.[1]

Dewey found that one cannot split up a psychological process into arcs. Using the classic example of a child's withdrawing his finger from the flame, he pointed out that, after this experience, the perception of the flame that was previously inviting is now avoided by the child. The situation is now altered; it is another and new situation. The stimulus and response form a unit that does not end with the withdrawal of the finger. The stimulus and response situation now serves as a stimulus for still another situation; every reaction is a circuit, not an arc of stimulus to response.

He found the relation of stimulus to response to be functional and the stimulus and response to be correlative and to form an adaptive whole. The stimulus-response concept is essentially elementaristic, while in reality the psychological experience is situationally global. The significance of the reflex as adaptive aligned Dewey with the functional school of psychology, since it was a specific instance of what Angell (p. 241) and others would formulate as the nature of functional psychology itself.

31

ANGELL ON
THE NATURE
OF FUNCTIONAL PSYCHOLOGY

JAMES ROWLAND ANGELL (1869-1949), psychologist and professor at the University of Chicago, did not set out to found a school of
psychology any more than did the several other leaders of functional
psychology. To some extent, the role was forced on him to formulate a
point of view that would guide psychology in directions different from
those expressed by the structural psychologists (Wundt and Titchener).
The reasons he felt it necessary to do so may be inferred from the excerpt
below.

His most important statement of the nature and justification of
functional psychology was his Presidential Address before the American
Psychological Association, published in 1907. He opened by indicating
that functional psychology at the time was but a program and an ambi-
tion. To clarify the situation, he proposed to identify and discuss three
forms of functional problems.

I.

There is to be mentioned first the notion which derives most immediately
from contrast with the ideals and purposes of structural psychology so-
called. This involves the identification of functional psychology with the
effort to discern and portray the typical *operations* of consciousness
under actual life conditions, as over against the attempt to analyze and
describe its elementary and complex *contents*. The structural psychology
of sensation, *e.g.,* undertakes to determine the number and character of
the various unanalyzable sensory materials, such as the varieties of color,
tone, taste, etc. The functional psychology of sensation would on the
other hand find its appropriate sphere of interest in the determination of

the character of the various sense activities as differing in their *modus operandi* from one another and from other mental processes such as judging, conceiving, willing and the like. . . .

The fact that mental contents are evanescent and fleeting marks them off in an important way from the relatively permanent elements of anatomy. No matter how much we may talk of the preservation of psychical dispositions, nor how many metaphors we may summon to characterize the storage of ideas in some hypothetical deposit chamber of memory, the obstinate fact remains that when we are not experiencing a sensation or an idea it is, strictly speaking, non-existent. Moreover, when we manage by one or another device to secure that which we designate the same sensation or the same idea, we not only have no guarantee that our second edition is really a replica of the first, we have a good bit of presumptive evidence that from the content point of view the original never is and never can be literally duplicated.

Functions, on the other hand, persist as well in mental as in physical life. We may never have twice exactly the same idea viewed from the side of sensuous structure and composition. But there seems nothing whatever to prevent our having as often as we will contents of consciousness which *mean* the same thing. They function in one and the same practical way, however discrepant their momentary texture. The situation is rudely analogous to the biological case where very different structures may under different conditions be called on to perform identical functions; and the matter naturally harks back for its earliest analogy to the instance of protoplasm where functions seem very tentatively and imperfectly differentiated. Not only then are general functions like memory persistent, but special functions such as the memory of particular events are persistent and largely independent of the specific conscious contents called upon from time to time to subserve the functions . . .

Substantially identical with this first conception of functional psychology, but phrasing itself somewhat differently, is the view which regards the functional problem as concerned with discovering how and why conscious processes are what they are, instead of dwelling as the structuralist is supposed to do upon the problem of determining the irreducible elements of consciousness and their characteristic modes of combination. . . .

Stated briefly the ground on which this position rests is as follows: In so far as you attempt to analyze any particular state of consciousness you find that the mental elements presented to your notice are dependent upon the particular exigencies and conditions which call them forth. Not only does the affective coloring of such a psychical moment depend upon

one's temporary condition, mood and aims, but the very sensations themselves are determined in their qualitative texture by the totality of circumstances subjective and objective within which they arise. You cannot
get a fixed and definite color sensation for example, without keeping
perfectly constant the external and internal conditions in which it appears. The particular sense quality is in short functionally determined by
the necessities of the existing situation which it emerges to meet. If you
inquire then deeply enough what particular sensation you have in a given
case, you always find it necessary to take account of the manner in
which, and the reasons why, it was experienced at all. You may of course,
if you will, abstract from these considerations, but in so far as you do so,
your analysis and description is manifestly partial and incomplete. Moreover, even when you do so abstract and attempt to describe certain isolable sense qualities, your descriptions are of necessity couched in terms
not of the experienced quality itself, but in terms of the conditions which
produced it, in terms of some other quality with which it is compared, or
in terms of some more overt act to which the sense stimulation led. That
is to say, the very description itself is functionalistic and must be so. The
truth of this assertion can be illustrated and tested by appeal to any
situation in which one is trying to reduce sensory complexes, *e.g.*, colors
or sounds, to their rudimentary components.

II.

A broader outlook and one more frequently characteristic of contemporary writers meets us in the next conception of the task of functional
psychology. This conception is in part a reflex of the prevailing interest in
the larger formulae of biology and particularly the evolutionary hypotheses within whose majestic sweep is nowadays included the history of the
whole stellar universe. . . .

The functional psychologist then in his modern attire is interested
not alone in the operations of mental process considered merely of and by
and for itself, but also and more vigorously in mental activity as part of a
larger stream of biological forces which are daily and hourly at work
before our eyes and which are constitutive of the most important and
most absorbing part of our world. The psychologist of this stripe is wont to
take his cue from the basal conception of the evolutionary movement,
i.e., that for the most part organic structures and functions possess their
present characteristics by virtue of the efficiency with which they fit into
the extant conditions of life broadly designated the environment. With
this conception in mind he proceeds to attempt some understanding of

the manner in which the psychical contributes to the furtherance of the sum total of organic activities, not alone the psychical in its entirety, but especially the psychical in its particularities—mind as judging, mind as feeling, etc.

This is the point of view which instantly brings the psychologist cheek by jowl with the general biologist. It is the presupposition of every philosophy save that of outright ontological materialism that mind plays the stellar rôle in all the environmental adaptations of animals which possess it. But this persuasion has generally occupied the position of an innocuous truism or at best a jejune postulate, rather than that of a problem requiring, or permitting, serious scientific treatment. At all events, this was formerly true.

This older and more complacent attitude toward the matter is, however, being rapidly displaced by a conviction of the need for light on the exact character of the accommodatory service represented by the various great modes of conscious expression. Such an effort if successful would not only broaden the foundations for biological appreciation of the intimate nature of accommodatory process, it would also immensely enhance the psychologist's interest in the exact portrayal of conscious life. It is of course the latter consideration which lends importance to the matter from our point of view. Moreover, not a few practical consequences of value may be expected to flow from this attempt, if it achieves even a measurable degree of success. Pedagogy and mental hygiene both await the quickening and guiding counsel which can only come from a psychology of this stripe. For their purposes a strictly structural psychology is as sterile in theory as teachers and psychiatrists have found it in practice.

As a concrete example of the transfer of attention from the more general phases of consciousness as accommodatory activity to the particularistic features of the case may be mentioned the rejuvenation of interest in the quasi-biological field which we designate animal psychology. This movement is surely among the most pregnant with which we meet in our own generation. Its problems are in no sense of the merely theoretical and speculative kind, although, like all scientific endeavor, it possesses an intellectual and methodological background on which such problems loom large. But the frontier upon which it is pushing forward its explorations is a region of definite, concrete fact, tangled and confused and often most difficult of access, but nevertheless a region of fact, accessible like all other facts to persistent and intelligent interrogation.

That many of the most fruitful researches in this field have been achievements of men nominally biologists rather than psychologists in no wise affects the merits of the case. A similar situation exists in the experimental psychology of sensation where not a little of the best work has been accomplished by scientists not primarily known as psychologists. . . .

This broad biological ideal of functional psychology of which we have been speaking may be phrased with a slight shift of emphasis by connecting it with the problem of discovering the fundamental utilities of consciousness. If mental process is of real value to its possessor in the life and world which we know, it must perforce be by virtue of something which it does that otherwise is not accomplished. Now life and world are complex and it seems altogether improbable that consciousness should express its utility in one and only one way. As a matter of fact, every surface indication points in the other direction. It may be possible merely as a matter of expression to speak of mind as in general contributing to organic adjustment to environment. But the actual contributions will take place in many ways and by multitudinous varieties of conscious process. The functionalist's problem then is to determine if possible the great types of these processes in so far as the utilities which they present lend themselves to classification.

The search after the various utilitarian aspects of mental process is at once suggestive and disappointing. It is on the one hand illuminating by virtue of the strong relief into which it throws the fundamental resemblances of processes often unduly severed in psychological analysis. Memory and imagination, for example, are often treated in a way designed to emphasize their divergences almost to the exclusion of their functional similarities. They are of course functionally but variants on a single and basal type of control. An austere structuralism in particular is inevitably disposed to magnify differences and in consequence under its hands mental life tends to fall apart; and when put together again it generally seems to have lost something of its verve and vivacity. It appears stiff and rigid and corpse-like. It lacks the vital spark. Functionalism tends just as inevitably to bring mental phenomena together, to show them focalized in actual vital service. The professional psychologist, calloused by long apprenticeship, may not feel this distinction to be scientifically important. But to the young student the functionalistic stress upon community of service is of immense value in clarifying the intricacies of mental organization. On the other hand the search of which we were speaking is disappointing perhaps in the paucity of the basic modes in which these conscious utilities are realized. . . .

The ultimate value of a psychological classification based on functions, if interpreted in the light of these considerations, would apparently hinge on one's conception of the analogy between consciousness and undifferentiated protoplasm. In the measure in which consciousness is immanently unstable and variable, one might anticipate that a functional classification would be more significant and penetrating than one based upon any supposedly structural foundation. But the analogy on which this inference rests is perhaps too insecure to permit a serious conclusion to be drawn from it. In any event it is to be said that functions as such seem to be the most stable characters in the biological field. They extend in a practically unbroken front from the lowest to the highest levels of life—allowing for a possible protest in certain quarters against including consciousness in this list. That they are not everywhere so useful as structures for classificatory purposes reflects on the aims of classification, not on the fundamental and relatively fixed character of functions.

A survey of current usage discloses two general types of functional categories. of these, the one is in spirit and purpose dominantly physiological. It groups all the forms of life functions, whether animal or vegetable in manifestation, under the four headings of assimilation, reproduction, motion and sensibility. In such a schema assimilation is made to include digestion, circulation, respiration, secretion, and excretion, while motion in the sense here intended applies primarily to those forms of movement which enable the organism to migrate from place to place and thus accommodate itself to the exigencies of local conditions.

Another group of categories which concerns a deeper and more general level of biological interpretations is given by such terms as selection, adaptation, variation, accommodation, heredity, etc. These are categories of a primarily functional sort for they apply in a large sense to modes of behavior. Indeed, behavior may be said to be itself the most inclusive of these categories. But as compared with the members of the first group they have to do with the general trend of organic development and not with the specific physiological processes which may be concerned in any special case. This does not mean that a specific physiological setting cannot sometime be given these problems; but it does mean that at present the gaps in our knowledge of these matters are generally too large to be spanned with certainty. . . .

III.

The third conception which I distinguish is often in practice merged with the second, but it involves stress upon a problem logically prior perhaps to the problem raised there and so warrants separate mention. Functional psychology, it is often alleged, is in reality a form of psychophysics. To be sure, its aims and ideals are not explicitly quantitative in the manner characteristic of that science as commonly understood. But it finds its major interest in determining the relations to one another of the physical and mental portions of the organism.

It is undoubtedly true that many of those who write under functional prepossessions are wont to introduce frequent references to the physiological processes which accompany or condition mental life. Moreover, certain followers of this faith are prone to declare forthwith that psychology is simply a branch of biology and that we are in consequence entitled, if not indeed obliged, to make use where possible of biological materials. But without committing ourselves to so extreme a position as this, a mere glance at one familiar region of psychological procedure will disclose the leanings of psychology in this direction.

The psychology of volition affords an excellent illustration of the necessity with which descriptions of mental process eventuate in physiological or biological considerations. If one takes the conventional analysis of a voluntary act drawn from some one or other of the experiences of adult life, the descriptions offered generally portray ideational activities of an anticipatory and deliberative character which serve to initiate immediately or remotely certain relevant expressive movements. Without the execution of the movements the ideational performances would be as futile as the tinkling cymbals of Scripture. To be sure, many of our psychologists protest themselves wholly unable to suggest why or how such muscular movements are brought to pass. But the fact of their occurrence or of their fundamental import for any theory of mental life in which consciousness is other than an epiphenomenon, is not questioned.

Moreover, if one considers the usual accounts of the ontogenesis of human volitional acts one is again confronted with intrinsically physiological data in which reflexes, automatic and instinctive acts are much in evidence. Whatever the possibilities, then, of an expurgated edition of the psychology of volition from which should be blotted out all reference to contaminating physiological factors, the actual practice of our representative psychologists is quite otherwise, and upon their showing volition cannot be understood either as regards its origin or its outcome without constant and overt reference to these factors. It would be a labor of supererrogation to go on and make clear the same doctrine as it applies to the psychology of the more recondite of the cognitive processes; so intimate is the relation between cognition and volition in modern psychological theory that we may well stand excused from carrying out in detail the obvious inferences from the situation we have just described.

Now if someone could but devise a method for handling the mind-body relationships which would not when published immediately create cyclonic disturbances in the philosophical atmosphere, it seems improbable that this disposition of the functional psychologist to inject physiology into his cosmos would cause comment and much less criticism. But even parallelism, that most insipid, pale and passionless of all the inventions begotten by the mind of man to accomplish this end, has largely failed of its pacific purpose. It is no wonder, therefore, that the more rugged creeds with positive programs to offer and a stock of red corpuscles to invest in their propagation should also have failed of universal favor.

This disposition to go over into the physiological for certain portions of psychological doctrine is represented in an interesting way by the frequent tendency of structural psychologists to find explanation in psychology substantially equivalent to physiological explanation. Professor Titchener's recent work on *Quantitative Psychology* represents this position very frankly. It is cited here with no intent to comment disparagingly upon the consistency of the structuralist position, but simply to indicate the wide-spread feeling of necessity at certain stages of psychological development for resort to physiological considerations. . . .

IV.

If we now bring together the several conceptions of which mention has been made it will be easy to show them converging upon a common point. We have to consider (1) functionalism conceived as the psychology of mental operations in contrast to the psychology of mental elements. . . . We have (2) the functionalism which deals with the problem of mind conceived as primarily engaged in mediating between the environment and the needs of the organism. This is the psychology of the fundamental utilities of consciousness; (3) and lastly we have functionalism described as psychophysical psychology, that is the psychology which constantly recognizes and insists upon the essential significance of the mind-body relationship for any just and comprehensive appreciation of mental life itself.

The second and third delineations of functional psychology are rather obviously correlated with each other. No description of the actual circumstances attending the participation of mind in the accommodatory activities of the organism could be other than a mere empty schematism without making reference to the manner in which mental processes eventuate in motor phenomena of the physiological organism. The overt accommodatory act is, I take it, always sooner or later a muscular movement. But this fact being admitted, there is nothing for it, if one will describe accommodatory processes, but to recognize the mind-body relations and in some way give expression to their practical significance. It is only in this regard, as was indicated a few lines above, that the functionalist departs a trifle in his practice and a trifle more in his theory from the rank and file of his colleagues. . . .

It remains then to point out in what manner the conception of functionalism as concerned with the basal operations of mind is to be correlated with the other two conceptions just under discussion. The simplest view to take of the relations involved would apparently be such as would regard the first as an essential propaedeutic to the other two. Certainly if we are intent upon discerning the exact manner in which mental process contributes to accommodatory efficiency, it is natural to begin our undertaking by determining what are the primordial forms of expression peculiar to mind. However plausible in theory this conception of the intrinsic logical relations of these several forms of functional psychology, in practice it is extremely difficult wholly to sever them from one another.

Again like the biological accommodatory view the psychophysical view of functional psychology involves as a rational presupposition some acquaintance with mental processes as these appear to reflective consciousness. The intelligent correlation in a practical way of physiological and mental operations evidently involves a preliminary knowledge of the conspicuous differentiations both on the side of conscious function and on the side of physiological function.

In view of the considerations of the last few paragraphs it does not seem fanciful nor forced to urge that these various theories of the problem of functional psychology really converge upon one another, however divergent may be the introductory investigations peculiar to each of the several ideals. Possibly the conception that the fundamental problem of the functionalist is one of determining just how mind participates in accommodatory reactions, is more nearly inclusive than either of the others, and so may be chosen to stand for the group. But if this vicarious duty is assigned to it, it must be on clear terms of remembrance that the other phases of the problem are equally real and equally necessary. Indeed the three things hang together as integral parts of a common program.[1]

This paper was prophetic of what was to happen in psychology in the two or three decades to follow. Hardly more than it was when he wrote it, functional psychology was to have the relatively clear-cut allegiance of the sort that characterized other schools of psychology. A functional point of view and not school adherence, characterizes psychology to this very day. Activities rather than structures are now the more important in psychological study, despite a shift of major emphasis from the study of mind that characterized the thinking of the original adherents to the study of behavioral activities that are emphasized by contemporary psychologists.

32

MCDOUGALL ON
THE DEFINITION OF PSYCHOLOGY,
THE NATURE OF SOCIAL PSYCHOLOGY,
AND THE SIGNIFICANCE OF INSTINCTS

WILLIAM McDOUGALL (1871–1938), British-American psychologist, after medical training and anthropological and physiological research, then led a somewhat tenuous academic existence at Oxford University as "Reader in Mental Philosophy," that is, a researcher and writer without a professorial chair. He was extremely productive, pouring forth books in great profusion on physiological, abnormal, social, and general psychology. He came to the United States in 1920, where he first taught at Harvard and then at Duke University.

As early as 1905, he defined psychology as the study of conduct (for which, in a few years, without changing the meaning, he substituted the word "behavior").

Psychology may be best and most comprehensively defined as the positive science of the conduct of living creatures. That is to say, it is the science which attempts to describe and explain the conduct of men and of other living creatures, and is not concerned with questions as to what their conduct ought to be. These questions it leaves to Ethics, the normative science of conduct. In adopting this definition we must understand the word conduct in the widest possible sense as denoting the sum of the activities by which any creature maintains its relations with other creatures and with the world of physical things. Psychology is more commonly defined as the science of mind, or as the science of mental or psychical processes, or of consciousness, or of individual experience. Such definitions are ambiguous, and without further elaboration are not sufficiently comprehensive. They express the aims of a psychologist who relies solely upon introspection, the observation and analysis of his own experience, and who unduly neglects the manifestations of mental life afforded by the conduct of his fellow-creatures. They do not adequately define the task that modern physiological psychology sets before itself. For physiological psychology aims at describing and explaining, as far as possible, all the factors that take part in determining the conduct of all living creatures, and though conduct seems to be in great part determined by our sensations, feelings, desires, emotions and all those other varieties of states or processes of consciousness which introspection discovers and distinguishes, psychology finds itself compelled in an ever-increasing degree to recognize the co-operation in all mental process of factors that are unconscious and so cannot be introspectively observed; and though some of these may be inferred from the nature of the processes revealed by introspection, others can only be inferred from the study of movements and other bodily changes. To define psychology as the science of experience or of consciousness is therefore to exclude the study of these unconscious factors, whereas the definition stated above brings all these within the scope of psychology without excluding the study of any part of experience or element of consciousness, for all experience affects conduct.[1]

It is apparent that he was insisting that conduct included conscious experiences, unconscious processes, *and* bodily movements, not to the exclusion of any one of these. In broad outline, his definition might even be seen as possibly appropriate as a definition to be used today. But between its formulation in 1905 and today, there was to be a most bitter controversy concerning acceptance or rejection of each of these aspects.

The concept of instinct was a guiding theme. The excerpt that follows is in the setting of social psychology, so that it illustrates not only his approach to motivation, but also that to social factors.

The department of psychology that is of primary importance for the social sciences is that which deals with the springs of human action, the impulses and motives that sustain mental and bodily activity and regulate conduct; and this, of all the departments of psychology, is the one that has remained in the most backward state, in which the greatest obscurity, vagueness, and confusion still reign. The answers to such problems as the proper classification of conscious states, the analysis of them into their elements, the nature of these elements and the laws of the compounding of them, have but little bearing upon the social sciences; the same may be said of the range of problems connected with the relations of soul and body, of psychical and physical process, of consciousness and brain processes; and also of the discussion of the more purely intellectual processes, of the way we arrive at the perception of relations of time and place or of likeness and difference, of the classification and description of the intellectual process of ideation, conception, comparison, and abstraction, and of their relations to one another. Not these processes themselves, but only the results or products of these processes—the knowledge or system of ideas and beliefs achieved by them, and the way in which these ideas and beliefs regulate conduct and determine social institutions and the relations of men to one another in society are of immediate importance for the social sciences. It is the mental forces, the sources of energy, which set the ends and sustain the course of all human activity—of which forces the intellectual processes are but the servants, instruments, or means—that must be clearly defined, and whose history in the race and in the individual must be made clear, before the social sciences can build upon a firm psychological foundation. Now, it is with the questions of the former classes that psychologists have chiefly concerned themselves and in regard to which they have made the most progress towards a consistent and generally acceptable body of doctrine: and they have unduly neglected these more socially important problems.[2]

He follows this by a discussion on the nature of instincts.

The human mind has certain innate or inherited tendencies which are the essential springs or motive powers of all thought and action, whether individual or collective, and are the bases from which the character and will of individuals and of nations are gradually developed under the guidance of the intellectual faculties. These primary innate tendencies have different relative strengths in the native constitutions of the individuals of different races, and they are favoured or checked in very different degrees by the very different social circumstances of men in different stages of culture; but they are probably common to the men of every race and of every age. If this view, that human nature has everywhere and at all times this common native foundation, can be established, it will afford a much-needed basis for speculation on the history of the development of human societies and human institutions. For so long as it is possible to assume, as has often been done, that these innate tendencies of the human mind have varied greatly from age to age and from race to race, all such speculation is founded on quicksand and we cannot hope to reach views of a reasonable degree of certainty.

The evidence that the native basis of the human mind, constituted by the sum of these innate tendencies, has this stable unchanging character is afforded by comparative psychology. For we find, not only that these tendencies, in stronger or weaker degree, are present in men of all races now living on the earth, but that we may find all of them, or at least the germs of them, in most of the higher animals. Hence there can be little doubt that they played the same essential part in the minds of the primitive human stock, or stocks, and in the pre-human ancestors that bridged the great gap in the evolutionary series between man and the animal world.

These all-important and relatively unchanging tendencies, which form the basis of human character and will, are of two main classes—

(1)   The specific tendencies or instincts;
(2)   The general or non-specific tendencies arising out of the constitution of mind and the nature of mental process in general, when mind and mental process attain a certain degree of complexity in the course of evolution.[3]

As McDougall saw it, the principal instincts of humans are each related to a particular kind of emotional excitement. Hence, the instict of flight and the emotion of fear, the instict of curiosity and the emotion of wonder, the instinct of pugnacity and the emotion of anger, the instincts of self abasement and self-assertion and the emotions of subjection and elation, the parental instinct and the tender emotion, are interrelated.

McDougall's conception of social psychology as based on instincts has been very influential, especially in England. His book on social psychology went through thirty-three editions between 1908 and 1950. Now that instinct as a conceptual framework is no longer fashionable, the more nonspecific tendencies mentioned in the preceding excerpt have become major problems for social psychology.

33

THORNDIKE ON

ANIMAL AND HUMAN LEARNING
BY TRIAL AND ERROR AND
THE INFLUENCE OF EXERCISE AND EFFECT

EDWARD LEE THORNDIKE (1874–1949), American psychologist
and educator, had been a student of William James at Harvard, but he
had finished his degree in 1898 under Cattell at Columbia. After a year at
Western Reserve University, he returned to Columbia where he taught
for over 40 years, and where he made its Teachers College a major center
for psychological research.

One facet of this research concerned animal learning under controlled conditions, which stands in contrast to the earlier anecdotal obser-
vational techniques of Romanes (p. 179) and Morgan (p. 184). One line
of research had been started on learning at Harvard with the so-called
puzzle box. It involved animals learning to escape from an open-slatted
box to secure food outside the box. If the animal clawed the loop or button
that held up the front of the box, the animal would cause it to fall. The
time required to open the box was the measure of learning. Cats, dogs,
and chicks were the animals used in the studies. The following excerpt
on the behavior of cats is representative:

When put into the box the cat would show evident signs of discomfort
and of an impulse to escape from confinement. It tries to squeeze through
any opening; it claws and bites at the bars or wire; it thrusts its paws out
through any opening and claws at everything it reaches; it continues its
efforts when it strikes anything loose and shaky; it may claw at things
within the box. It does not pay very much attention to the food outside,
but seems imply to strive instinctively to escape from confinement. The
vigor with which it struggles is extraordinary. For eight or ten minutes it
will claw and bite and squeeze incessantly.[1]

There was little in his results to suggest solution by inference or reasoning. Specifically, he tested this by allowing animals to watch other animals and by guiding the paw of the animal to the escape device. Neither helped. He summarized his results as follows:

The cat does not look over the situation, much less *think* it over, and then decide what to do. It bursts out at once into the activities which instinct and experience have settled on as suitable reactions to the situation "confinement when hungry with food outside." The one impulse, out of many accidental ones, which leads to pleasure, becomes strengthened and stamped in thereby, and more and more firmly associated with the sense-impression of that box's interior.... Futile impulses are gradually stamped out. The gradual slope of the timecurve, then, shows the absence of reasoning. They represent the wearing smooth of a path in the brain, not the decision of a rational consciousness.[2]

A similarity is apparent in the results obtained by Morgan and the dog who lifted the latch to escape down the road (p. 184). By verbal argument, Morgan had been content to show that it was not due to reasoning. Thorndike went further and developed from this and other research procedures a theory of trial and error learning. Excessive random activity was first shown in the clawing and squeezing his animals exhibited. On repeated trials, the erroneous acts began to drop out. After repeated trials, when the animal was placed in the puzzle box, it would immediately claw the escape device and release the door. Although there was considerable variability from animal to animal and from task to task, the decrease in time after the initial rapid decline was gradual.

The previous excerpt referred to pleasure as strengthening certain reactions which are "stamped in" while "futile" impulses are "stamped out." In 1913, Thorndike, on the basis of these and other experiments, referred to these processes as "rewards" and "punishments."

When a modifiable connection between a situation and a response is made and is accompanied or followed by a satisfying state of affairs, that connection's strength is increased: When made and accompanied or followed by an annoying state of affairs, its strength is decreased.[3]

Later work convinced him about the efficacy of reward in promoting learning. Typical of his results are those contained in a paper entitled, "A proof of the law of effect," given below:

Psychologists and physiologists all agree that the behavior of man and of many other animals is modifiable by the experiences of life. He learns, so that the situation, S, which at first evokes, say, responses 1, 2, 3, 4 and 5 equally often, comes to evoke one response, say 4, always or ninety-nine times out of a hundred. The connection S → 4 has become enormously strengthened relatively to S → 1 or S → 2 or S → 3 or S → 5.

Concerning the forces producing learning there has been great disagreement. The writer (1898, 1914 and 1931) has maintained that the after-effects of a modifiable connection work back upon it, and that, in particular, a satisfying state of affairs accompanying or directly following a connection strengthens it. Troland maintained a similar doctrine.

The great majority of psychologists have maintained, on the contrary, that the strengthening of any connection is due to forces operating within the connection itself or prior to it. Repetition or frequency of occurrence, recency, intensity, finality or consummatoriness, tendency to attain equilibrium, and other features of the process have been alleged to be adequate to explain the strengthening of connections.

I have presented recently evidence from a variety of experiments to show that a satisfying after-effect of a connection does in fact strengthen it under conditions equalized in respect of all other forces than the satisfying after-effect. It is the purpose of this report to present an entirely independent experimental proof of the strengthening influence of a satisfying state of affairs upon the connection of which it is the after-effect and important new facts concerning the method of action of that influence.

We provide in an experiment a long series of situations to each of which several responses are possible, one of which is arbitrarily followed by a reward, any other being followed by a punishment. For example, a series of words is said by the experimenter, to each of which the subject may respond by any number from 1 to 10. If he says the number that has been chosen to be "right" he is rewarded; if he says any other, he is punished. So we have a long sequence of connections and after-effects, in the form Word 1 → number, reward or punishment, Word 2 → number, reward or punishment, Word 3 → number, reward or punishment, Word 4 → number, reward or punishment, etc.

This series is repeated again and again. We quote the results for the first ten words in trials 1 to 4,* from a sample record.

The time-intervals were as follows: One unit of the series from word to word or number to number took about 2.2 sec. The time from the

---

*"In this experiment the series of words, each with its "right" number, was read to the subject first, so that correct choices even in the first round would be a matter of ability plus chance rather than of chance alone."

	TRIAL OR ROUND 1	TRIAL OR ROUND 2	TRIAL OR ROUND 3	TRIAL OR ROUND 4
catnip	2	4	10	2
cedar	3	3	6	2
chamber	1	2	9	8
chorus	8	10	7	6
dally	4	8	5	4
dazzle	C2	6	9	1
debate	9	7	2	5
deduce	5	2	2	2
early	4	C5	C5	C5
effort	3	6	C7	C7

announcement of "Right" or "Wrong" to the approximate mid-point of the word-number connection to which it belonged was about 0.5½ sec. The time to the mid-point of the next preceding connection was about 2.8 sec., to the next, 5.0 sec., to the next, 7.2 sec., and so on. The time to the mid-point of the word-number connection following the annnouncement of "Right" or "Wrong" was 1.7 sec. The time to the next following was 3.9 sec.; to the next, 61.; and so on.

In such a series the rewarded connections are strengthened, but that fact is not our present concern. The fact to which I invite attention now is that the punished connections do not behave alike, but that the ones that are nearest to a reward are strengthened most. The strengthening influence of a reward spreads to influence positively not only the connection which it directly follows and to which it may be said to belong, but also any connections which are near enough to it. We may measure nearness in terms of time or in terms of number of connections or steps. Thus the punished connection *catnip* → 2 in Trial 1 preceded the reward for *dazzle* → 2 by about 11.6 seconds and by 5 connections or steps. The punished connection *cedar* → 3 in Trial 1 preceded the reward of *dazzle* → 2 by about 9.4 seconds and by 4 connections or steps. The punished connection *daily* → 4 in Trial 1 preceded the reward of *dazzle* → 2 by about 2.8 seconds and by one connection or step.

The amount of strengthening is measured by the percentage of repetitions in the following trial. For example, for the ten subjects of the experiment chosen as an illustration we find the following for punished connections alike in all respects save their proximity to a reward:

	N	PERCENTAGE OF REPETITIONS IN THE FOLLOWING TRIAL
One step removed	4136	26.4
Two steps removed	2250	23.6
Three or four steps removed	1933	21.0
Five or more steps removed	1228	20.8
Three or more steps removed	3161	20.7

For 905 connections like these in all respects, save that a reward directly followed and belonged to them, the percentage of repetitions was about 50.

In such experiments the fact that a person responds to a word by a certain number makes him more likely to respond to that word at the next trial by that same number, even though the response was punished. The connection is strengthened more by being made than it is weakened by being punished. This has been indicated by Thorndike ('32, p. 112, and p. 280ff), and demonstrated by Lorge in articles to appear shortly in the *Journal of Experimental Psychology* and by the present series of experiments. The best measure of strengthening due to one occurrence of a punished connection at some specified proximity to a reward is then the excess strengthening over that due to one occurrence of a punished connection so remote from a reward as to receive zero influence from it. In the illustrative experiment those excesses are 5½ for one occurrence of a punished connection one step away from a reward, and 2½ for one two steps away.

We have made fifteen experiments, using various sorts of learning. The results show that a satisfying after-effect strengthens greatly the connection which it follows directly and to which it belongs, and also strengthens by a smaller amount the connections preceding and following that, and by a still smaller amount the preceding and succeeding connections two steps removed.

One occurrence of a rewarded connection produces an average excess strengthening of 22 (per hundred) with a probable error of 3. One occurrence of a punished connection next to and preceding a rewarded connection produces an average excess strengthening of 4 (per hundred) with a probable error of 0.4. A punished connection occurring after a rewarded connection receives an excess strengthening of about 5 (per hundred). A punished connection between two rewarded connections receives an excess strengthening of 7½ per hundred. Punished connections two steps and 5 or more seconds away from a rewarded connection are influenced favorably by it.

The proof that a satisfying after-effect strengthens directly the connection producing it, and also other connections in close proximity to it, is important, because it explains selective modifiability. It solves many problems for which the forces of frequency, recency and intensity are inadequate. It accounts for the true contentions of purposivism without recourse to mystical agencies.

The physiological explanation of the influence of a satisfying after-effect is as yet unknown, just as the physiological explanation of the influence of mere repetition of a connection is unknown. But we can now proceed to find out facts about the former which may lead us to a physiological explanation of it, and which are valuable in any case.[4]

Thorndike did, however, encounter numerous instances in which punishment did not weaken response strength. Accordingly, in 1932, he wrote:

Rewarding a connection always strengthens it substantially; punishing it weakened it little or not at all.[5]

Later research seemed to make this conclusion too sweeping. There are exceptions, even some in which punishment had a strengthening effect on the response.

Considerations of space permit description of only one other area of learning research, first published in 1901, by Thorndike and Robert S. Woodworth entitled, "The Influence of Inprovement in One Mental Function upon the Efficiency of other Functions."[6] This article resists excerpting because of its diffuse style and because it did not place in clear perspective its central implication, although this was to be appreciated only shortly after publication. This had to do with the demonstration of the fundamental falsity of the earlier faculty psychology upon which the prevailing educational system was based. It had been held that faculties, when exercised, were strengthened, that is, memorizing strengthened memory, irrespective of the material being used. William James had already cast doubt on this conviction in some impromptu studies (p. 000). Thorndike and Woodworth demonstrated conclusively that the faculty doctrine was false. Forty years later, Thorndike published an account that serves as an admirable summary of this and other studies and their major implication.

At first psychology accepted the popular view that attention, memory, imagination, reasoning and the like were fundamental and unitary faculties or powers of the mind. If you had a notably superior memory it would be equally superior for words, numbers, faces, localities, and so forth. If your faculty of attention was weak, you would be unable to concentrate well on lessons, stories, games and all else. Consequently, it was expected that a dozen or score of rather simple tests would reveal the fundamental abilities of a person and measure them, at least, roughly.

Two lines of experimentation, begun about forty years ago, caused the abandonment of this expectation. The first studied the training of abilities and found such facts as the following: If a person practices finding and checking A's, he gains notably in speed and accuracy, but his ability to find and check B's shows much less improvement, and his ability to find and check words containing two given letters, such as e and s, or n and o, or i and p, shows little or none. If a person is trained at memorizing series of digits or series of nonsense syllables, he may improve notably in the amount that he remembers from, say, ten minutes of study, but when he transfers his efforts to memorizing shapes, or poems, or passages of music, he shows very little improvement over the ability he had before the training. What has been improved by the training is not a general power of attention, or a general faculty of memory that operates regardless of what is to be memorized.

The second line of experimentation studied the correlations or covariances of different manifestations of an ability and found such facts as the following: If a thousand twelve-year-old boys are tested in respect of the ability to add integers, the ability to add fractions, the ability to divide fractions by fractions, the correlations or covariances of these sub-abilities are far from perfect. The boy who is ablest in adding integers will not be the ablest in the other three sub-abilities. A boy's rank among the thousand will not be the same in all four, but will vary rather widely. Mathematical ability is not one thing, but a complex of many.

If the thousand boys take a number of tests chosen to measure intelligence, their scores on the tests that concern words will not correlate perfectly with their scores in the tests that concern pictures, or space relations, or numbers. Intelligence is not a unitary ability that operates regardless of the data on which it operates.

Mental abilities are not an orderly retinue of a few easily defined and unitary faculties or powers, somewhat like the chemical elements, for each of which a mental meter or test can be found by sufficient labor and ingenuity. A mental ability is a probability that certain situations will evoke certain responses, that certain tasks can be achieved, that certain mental products can be produced by the possessor of the ability. It is defined by the situations, responses, products, and tasks, not by some inner essence.[7]

After the negative results of the experiment in 1901, there began a continued discussion among psychologists of the question of how much, if anything, of what is learned is transferred from one situation to another. The research that eventuated in the next several decades showed that planning the curriculum of the basis of the presumed disciplinary value of the subjects studied was sterile, and that transfer of learning takes place only if the same general principles or identical elements are involved in the learning and transfer situation.

Although this account has stressed Thorndike's research on learning, he also made significance contributions to the theory and measurement of intelligence and achievement, to statistics and individual differences, and to educational theory itself.

34

PAVLOV ON

CONDITIONING AND
THE FIRST AND SECOND
SIGNAL SYSTEMS

IVAN PETROVITCH PAVLOV (1849–1936), Russian physiologist, had two major careers. For his investigation of the processes of digestion, he received the Nobel prize for medicine in 1904. The specific emphasis for a second career, his work on conditioning, arose from a phase of digestive study. A surgical procedure had been developed to allow flow of saliva to the outside of the body for collection and measurement, using dogs as experimental animals. While studying digestion, he noted that dogs secrete saliva not only before meat powder was given, but even to the sound of the footsteps of the attendant bringing the meat. From these leads, there eventuated nearly forty years of research on the topic.

Both under the Czar and after the 1917 October Revolution in Russia, his research received generous government support and he attracted numerous collaborators; literally thousands of research reports were published. One might despair of even beginning to summarize his work in a few pages. Fortunately, in 1934, two years before his death, the *Great Russian Encyclopedia* appeared with a summarizing article on conditioning by Pavlov, which has since been translated and published in English.

The conditioned reflex is now used as a separate physiological term to denote a certain nervous phenomenon, the detailed study of which has led to the creation of a new branch in the physiology of animals—the physiology of the higher nervous activity, as the first chapter in the physiology of the higher parts of the central nervous system. For many years empirical and scientific observations have been accumulated which show that a mechanical lesion or a disease of the brain, and especially of the cerebral hemispheres, causes a disturbance in the higher, most complex behaviour of the animal and man, usually referred to as psychical activity. At present hardly anyone with a medical education would doubt that our neuroses and psychoses are connected with the weakening or disappearance of the normal physiological properties of the brain, or with its greater or lesser destruction. But the following persistent, fundamental questions arise: what is the connection between the brain and the higher activity of the animal and man? With what and how must we begin the study of this activity? It would seem that psychical activity is the result of the physiological activity of a certain mass of the brain and that physiology should investigate it in exactly the same way as the activity of all other parts of the organism is now being successfully investigated. However, this has not been done for a long time. Psychical activity has long (for thousands of years) been the object of study by a special branch of science—psychology. But physiology, strange as it may seem, only recently—in 1870—obtained with the help of its usual method of artificial stimulation the first precise facts relating to a certai (motor) physiological function of the cerebral hemispheres; with the help of its other usual method of partial destruction it acquired additional facts relating to the establishment of connections between other parts of the cerebral hemispheres and the most important receptors of the organism—the eye, the ear, etc. This raised hopes among physiologists, as well as psychologists, that close connection would be established between physiology and psychology. On the one hand, the psychologists used to begin text-books on psychology with a preliminary exposition of the theory of the central nervous system, and especially of the cerebral hemispheres (sense organs). On the other hand, the physiologists when experimenting with the destruction of various parts of the hemispheres in animals viewed the results obtained by them psychologically, by analogy with the human internal world (for example, Munk's assertion that the animal "sees," but "does not understand"). However, both camps soon became disappointed. The physiology of the cerebral hemispheres perceptibly stopped at these first experiments and made no further substantial advance. In the meantime many resolute psychologists again took up the cudgels saying that psychological research should be fully independent of physiological. At the same time there were other attempts to link the triumphant natural science with psychology through the method of numerical measurement of psychical phenomena. At one time an attempt was made to create in physiology a special branch of psychophysics on the basis of the fortunate discovery by Weber and Fechner of the law

(named after them) which establishes a certain numerical relation between the intensity of an external stimulus and the strength of a sensation. But the new branch failed to go beyond this single law. More successful was the attempt made by Wundt, a physiologist who became a
psychologist and philosopher, experimentally to apply the method of numerical measurement to psychical phenomena in the form of the so-
called experimental psychology; thus, considerable material has been
collected already and more is being accumulated. Mathematical analysis
of the numerical material obtained by experimental psychology is called
by some people, as Fechner did it, psychophysics. But now even among
psychologists and especially psychiatrists, there are many who are bitterly disappointed in the practical application of experimental psychology.

So what is to be done? However, a new method of solving the
fundamental question was already on the way. Was it possible to discover
an elementary psychical phenomenon which at the same time could be
fully and rightly regarded as a purely physiological phenomenon? Was it
possible to begin with it, and by a strictly objective study (as generally
done in physiology) of the conditions of its emergence, its various complexities and its disappearance, to obtain first of all an objective physiological picture of the entire higher nervous activity in animals, i.e., the
normal functioning of the higher part of the brain, instead of the previous
experiments involving its artificial irritation and destruction? Fortunately, such a phenomenon had long been observed by a number of
researchers; many of them paid attention to it and some even began to
study it (special mention should be made of Thorndike), but for some
reason or other they stopped the study at the very beginning and did not
utilize the knowledge of this phenomenon for the purpose of elaborating a
fundamental method of systematic physiological study of the higher activity in the animal organism. This was the phenomenon now termed the
"conditioned reflex," thorough study of which has fully justified the previous expressed hope. I shall mention two simple experiments that can be
successfully performed by all. We introduce into the mouth of a dog a
moderate solution of some acid; the acid produces a usual defensive
reaction in the animal: by vigorous movements of the mouth it ejects the
solution, and at the same time an abundant quantity of saliva begins to
flow first into the mouth and then overflows, diluting the acid and cleans-
ing the mucous membrane of the oral cavity. Now let us turn to the
second experiment. Just prior to introducing the same solution into the
dog's mouth we repeatedly act on the animal by a certain external agent,

say, a definite sound. What happens then? It suffices simply to repeat the sound, and the same reaction is fully reproduced—the same movements of the mouth and the same secretion of saliva.

Both of the above-mentioned facts are equally exact and constant. And both must be designated by one and the same physiological term—"reflex.". . .

In the light of these facts even the strictest judgement cannot raise any objection to such a physiological conclusion; at the same time, however, there is a manifest difference between the two reflexes. In the first place, their centres, as already mentioned, are different. In the second place, as is clear from the procedure of our experiments, the first reflex was reproduced without any preparation or special condition, while the second was obtained by means of a special method. This means that in the first case there took place a direct passage of the nervous current from one kind of drives to the other, without any special procedure. In the second case the passage demanded a certain preliminary procedure. The next natural assumption is that in the first reflex there was a direct conduction of the nervous current, while in the second it was necessary preliminarily to prepare the way for it; this concept had long been known to physiology and had been termed "Bahnung." Thus, in the central nervous system there are two different central mechanisms—one directly conducting the nervous current and the second—closing and opening it. There is nothing surprising in this conclusion. The nervous system is the most complex and delicate instrument on our planet, by means of which relations, connections are established between the numerous parts of the organism, as well as between the organism, as a highly complex system, and the innumerable, external influences. If the closing and opening of electric current is now regarded as an ordinary technical device, why should there be any objection to the idea that the same principle acts in this wonderful instrument? On this basis the *constant connection between the external agent and the response of the organism, which it evokes, can be rightly called an unconditioned reflex, and the temporary connection—a conditioned reflex.* . . .

The basic condition for the formation of a conditioned reflex is, generally speaking, a single or repeated coincidence of the indifferent stimulus with the unconditioned one. The formation of the reflex is quickest and meets with least difficulties when the first stimulus directly precedes the second, as shown in the above-mentioned auditory acid reflex.

The conditioned reflex is formed on the basis of all unconditioned reflexes and from various agents of the internal medium and external environment both in their simplest and most complex forms, but with one limitation: it is formed only from those agents for the reception of which there are receptor elements in the cerebral hemispheres. Thus we have before us a very extensive synthesizing activity effected by this part of the brain.

But this is not enough. The conditioned temporary connection is at the same time highly specialized, reaching the heights of complexity and extending to the most minute fragmentation of the conditioned stimuli as well as of some activities of the organism, particularly such as the skeletal movements and the speech movements. Thus we have before us a highly delicate analysing activity of the same cerebral hemispheres! Hence the enormous breadth and depth of the organism's adaptability, of its equilibration with the surrounding world. The synthesis is, apparently, a phenomenon of nervous coupling. . . .

This is how the process develops. First we elaborate a conditioned generalized reflex to a definite tone. Then we continue our experiment with this reflex, constantly accompanying and reinforcing it with the unconditioned reflex; but along with it we apply other, so to speak, spontaneously acting tones, but without any reinforcement. The latter gradually lose their effect, and, finally, the same thing takes place with the closest tone; for example, a tone of 500 oscillations per second will produce an effect, whereas the tone of 498 oscillations will not, i.e., it will be differentiated. These tones, which have now lost their effect, are inhibited. This is proved in the following way:

If immediately after the application of the inhibited tone we apply the constantly reinforced conditioned tone, the latter will either produce no effect at all or a considerably lesser effect than usual. This signifies that the inhibition which has eliminated the effect of all accessory tones, has acted on this tone as well. But this is a fleeting phenomenon—it is no longer observed if some time passes after the application of the inhibited tones. From this it can be deduced that the inhibitory process irradiates in the same way as the excitatory process. But the more frequently the non-reinforced tones are repeated, the more concentrated becomes the inhibitory process both in space and in time. Consequently the analysis begins with the special activity of the peripheral mechanisms of the afferent conductors and is terminated in the cerebral hemispheres by means of the inhibitory process. The case of inhibition described above is known as differential inhibition. I shall mention other cases. In order to obtain a definite, more or less constant strength of the conditioned effect, usually, after a certain period of action of the conditioned stimulus, the latter is supplemented by an unconditioned stimulus, that is, it is reinforced. Then, depending on the duration of the isolated application of the conditioned stimulus, no effect is observed during the first seconds or minutes of the stimulation, since being premature as a signal of the unconditioned stimulus, it is inhibited. This is the analysis of the different moments of the acting stimulus. Inhibition of this kind is called the inhibition of a delayed reflex. But the conditioned stimulus, as a signalling one, is itself corrected by the inhibition, gradually being reduced to zero, if it is not reinforced during a certain period of time.

This is the extinguishing inhibition. It persists for some time and then disappears of itself. The restoration of the extinguished conditioned effect of the stimulus is accelerated by reinforcement. Thus, there are positive conditioned stimuli, i.e., provoking an excitatory process in the cerebral cortex, and negative ones, provoking an inhibitory process. In the above cases we have a special inhibition of the cerebral hemispheres, the cortical inhibition. It arises under certain conditions at points where previously it was absent, it varies in size and disappears under other conditions; this distinguishes it from a more or less constant and stable inhibition of the lower parts of the central nervous system, and this is why, in contrast to the latter, (i.e., to external inhibition), it is called internal inhibition. It would be more correct to call it elaborated, conditioned inhibition. The participation of inhibition in the work of the cerebral hemispheres is as continuous, complex and delicate as that of the excitatory process.

Just as in some cases the stimulations coming into the hemispheres from without enter into connection with definite cerebral points which are in a state of excitation, in other cases similar stimulations can, also on the basis of simultaneity, enter into temporary connection with the inhibitory state of the cortex, if there is any. This follows from the fact that such stimuli have an inhibitory effect, evoke by themselves an inhibitory process in the cortex and are conditioned negative stimuli. In this case, as in the foregoing cases, we have a conversion, under certain conditions, of the excitatory process into the inhibitory. And this can to a degree be explained if we recall that in the peripheral apparatus of the afferent conductors there takes place a constant transformation of various kinds of energy into an excitatory process. Why, then, should there not take place in certain conditions a similar transformation of the energy of the excitatory process into the energy of the inhibitory process, and vice versa?

As we have just seen, both the excitatory and inhibitory processes, arising in the cerebral hemispheres, first spread over them or irradiate, and then concentrate in the point of origin. This is one of the fundamental laws of the entire central nervous system, but here, in the cerebral hemispheres, it manifests itself with the mobility and complexity which are inherent only in them. Among the conditions which determine the onset and course of irradiation and concentration of the processes, the strength of these processes must be considered of prime importance. The facts which have been accumulated up to date entitle us to draw the conclusion that given a weak excitatory process irradiation takes place, given a medium one—concentration, and under a very strong one—again irradiation. Exactly the same thing occurs in the inhibitory process. All that has been said above, obviously, represents indubitable physiological material, i.e., the objectively reproduced normal physiological activity of the higher part of the central nervous system; and it is precisely with this activity that the study of every part of the animal organism must begin and actually does begin. However, this does not prevent certain physiologists from regarding the above facts as having no relation to physiology. A case of conservatism not infrequent in science!

It is not difficult to bring this physiological activity of the higher part of the animal brain into natural and direct connection with numerous manifestations of our subjective world.

As already mentioned, a conditioned connection is, apparently, what we call association by simultaneity. The generalization of a conditioned connection corresponds to what is called association by likeness. The synthesis and analysis of conditioned reflexes (associations) are, in essence, the same as the basic processes of our mental activity. When we are absorbed in our thoughts or carried away by certain work, we do not see and hear what is going on around us; this is obvious negative induction. Who would separate in the unconditioned highly complex reflexes (instincts) the physiological, the somatic from the psychical, i.e., from the powerful emotions of hunger, sexual attraction, anger, etc.? Our sense of pleasure, displeasure, composure, difficulty, joy, pain, triumph, despair, etc., is connected now with the conversion of very strong instincts and of their stimuli into corresponding effector acts, now with their inhibition; they are connected with all the variations of an easy or difficult course of development of the nervous processes in the cerebral hemispheres, as is observed in dogs which are able or unable to cope with nervous tasks of varying degrees of difficulty. Our contrasting emotions are, of course, phenomena of reciprocal induction. The irradiation of excitation makes us speak and act in a manner that would not be admitted by us in a state of calm. Obviously, the wave of excitation transforms the inhibition of certain points into a positive process. A drastic weakening of the memory for the near past—a normal phenomenon in old age—signifies a senile decrease of the mobility of the excitatory process, its inertness, and so on.

When the developing animal world reached the stage of man, an extremely important addition was made to the mechanisms of the nervous activity. In the animal, reality is signalized almost exclusively by stimulations and by the traces they leave in the cerebral hemispheres, which come directly to the special cells of the visual, auditory or other receptors of the organism. This is what we, too, possess as impressions, sensations and notions of the world around us, both the natural and the social—with the exception of the words heard or seen. This is the first system of signals of reality common to man and animals. But speech constitutes a second signalling system of reality which is peculiarly ours, being the signal of the first signals. On the one hand, numerous speech stimulations have removed us from reality, and we must always remember this in order not to distort our attitude to reality. On the other hand, it is precisely speech which has made us human, a subject on which I need not dwell in detail here. However, it cannot be doubted that the fundamental laws governing the activity of the first signalling system must also govern that of the second, because it, too, is activity of the same nervous tissue.

The most convincing proof that the study of the conditioned reflexes has brought the investigation of the higher part of the brain on to the right trail and that the functions of this part of the brain and the phenomena of our subjective world have finally become united and identical, is provided by the further experiments with conditioned reflexes on animals reproducing pathological states of the human nervous system—neuroses and certain psychotic symptoms; in many cases it is also possible to attain a rational deliberate return to the normal—recovery—i.e., a truly scientific mastery of the subject.[1]

It is apparent from his comments in the early part of the excerpt about psychology as a science that Pavlov did not hold the field in high esteem. He considered his research to be physiology. Partly as a consequence of his influence, Russian psychology floundered for some decades, although various relatively unsuccessful attempts were made to relate psychology to the ideological scene.

However, there is a section of his report, published you may re-member just before his death, that shows a mellowing of his previously implacable stand that gives a possible place for psychology among the sciences. It will be noted that in the last two pages of the excerpt, without using the term psychology, Pavlov is relating conditioning through the so-called second signal system to traditional psychological concepts—"higher part of the brain," "association," "instincts," "emotions," "mem-ory." Moreover, in sections omitted for the sake of brevity, he discusses hypnosis and temperament as related to his approach. Both of these are areas of investigation more closely identified with psychology than with physiology.

Reconciliation of psychology with physiology and a restoration for psychology to governmental favor came in 1950 at a Moscow conference. The crux of the matter was the second signal system just mentioned. The second signal system involves conditioned reflexes to verbal stimuli, which are specific to man and distinguishable from the first signal sys-tem, which involves nonverbal stimuli and with which most of the ex-cerpt was concerned. The laws of the interaction of the second signal system are considered as different from those to the first, the nonverbal stimuli. It was decreed at this conference that thereafter, psychology be reorganized with this second signal system as its basic concept and as the bridge between it and physiology. Soviet psychologists lost no time, how-ever, in moving out beyond the now secure ideological base in the second signal system and, contrary to opinion often expressed, are not bound to relate their research to a rigid system of Pavlovian conditioning. Pres-ently, Soviet psychology is much more diverse than this simplistic stereotype would have it.

35

WATSON ON
BEHAVIORISM AS PSYCHOLOGY,
ITS APPROPRIATE METHODS,
AND HIS APPROACHES TO EMOTION
AND CONDITIONING

JOHN B. WATSON (1878–1958), American psychologist, took his degree through a study of animal behavior at the University of Chicago under J.R. Angell, the functionalist (p. 241). His most important work was conducted after 1908 while he was professor of psychology at Johns Hopkins University. It included a second declaration of independence for psychology. In 1873, the ringing words by Wilhelm Wundt that he was marking "out a new domain of science" (p. 128) had been psychology's declaration of independence. Forty years later, in 1913, a rebellion was announced against his psychology by John B. Watson in his manifesto, "Psychology as the Behaviorist Views It." The rebellion, however, was directed not only against Wundtian and Titchenarian introspectionism but also against the functional view represented here by excerpts from Dewey (p. 231) and Angell (p. 241). This rebellion was stated as follows:

Psychology as the behaviorist views it is a purely objective experimental branch of natural science. Its theoretical goal is the prediction and control of behavior. Introspection forms no essential part of its methods, nor is the scientific value of its data dependent upon the readiness with which they lend themselves to interpretation in terms of consciousness. The behaviorist, in his efforts to get a unitary scheme of animal response, recognizes no dividing line between man and brute. The behavior of man, with all of its refinement and complexity, forms only a part of the behaviorist's total scheme of investigation.

It has been maintained by its followers generally that psychology is a study of the science of the phenomena of consciousness. It has taken as its problem, on the one hand, the analysis of complex mental states (or processes) into simple elementary constituents, and on the other the construction of complex states when the elementary constituents are given. The world of physical objects (stimuli, including here anything which may excite activity in a receptor), which forms the total phenomena of the natural scientist, is looked upon merely as means to an end. That end is the production of mental states that may be "inspected" or "observed." The psychological object of observation in the case of an emotion, for example, is the mental state itself. The problem in emotion is the determination of the number and kind of elementary constituents present, their loci, intensity, order of appearance, etc. It is agreed that introspection is the method *par excellence* by means of which mental states may be manipulated for purposes of psychology. On this assumption, behavior data (including under this term everything which goes under the name of comparative psychology) have no value *per se*. They possess significance only in so far as they may throw light upon conscious states. Such data must have at least an analogical or indirect reference to belong to the realm of psychology. . . .

The time seems to have come when psychology must discard all reference to consciousness; when it need no longer delude itself into thinking that it is making mental states the object of observation. We have become so enmeshed in speculative questions concerning the elements of mind, the nature of conscious content (for example, imageless thought, attitudes, and Bewusseinslage, etc.) that I, as an experimental student, feel that something is wrong with our premises and the types of problems which develop from them. There is no longer any guarantee that we all mean the same thing when we use the terms now current in psychology. Take the case of sensation. A sensation is defined in terms of its attributes. One psychologist will state with readiness that the attributes of a visual sensation are *quality, extension, duration,* and *intensity*. Another will add *clearness*. Still another that of *order*. I doubt if any one psychologist can draw up a set of statements describing what he means by sensation which will be agreed to by three other psychologists of different training. Turn for a moment to the question of the number of isolable sensations. Is there an extremely large number of color sensations—or only four, red, green, yellow and blue? Again, yellow, while psychologically simple, can be obtained by superimposing red and green spectral rays upon the same diffusing surface! If, on the other hand, we say that every just noticeable difference in the spectrum is a simple sensation, and that every just noticeable increase in the white value of a given color gives simple sensations, we are forced to admit that the number is so large and the conditions for obtaining them so complex that the concept of sensation is unusable, either for the purpose of analysis or that of synthesis. Titchener, who has fought the most valiant fight in this country for a psychology based upon introspection, feels that these differences of opinion as to the number of sensations and their attributes; as to whether there are relations (in the sense of elements) and on the many others which seem to be fundamental in every attempt at analysis, are perfectly natural in the present undeveloped state of psychology. While it is admitted that every growing science is full of unanswered questions, surely only those who are wedded to the system as we now have it, who have fought and suffered for it, can confidently believe that there will ever be any greater uniformity than there is now in the answers we have to such questions. I firmly believe that two hundred years from now, unless the introspective method is discarded, psychology will still be divided on the question as to whether auditory sensations have the quality of "extension," whether intensity is an attribute which can be applied to color, whether there is a difference in 'texture' between image and sensation and upon many hundreds of others of like character. . . .

My psychological quarrel is not with the systematic and structural psychologist alone. The last fifteen years have seen the growth of what is called functional psychology. This type of psychology decries the use of elements in the static sense of the structuralists. It throws emphasis upon the biological significance of conscious processes instead of upon the analysis of conscious states into introspectively isolable elements. I have done my best to understand the difference between functional psychology and structural psychology. Instead of clarity, confusion grows upon me. The terms sensation, perception, affection, emotion, volition are used as much by the functionalist as by the structuralist. The addition of the word "process" ("mental act as a whole," and like terms are frequently met) after each serves in some way to remove the corpse of 'content' and to leave "function" in its stead. Surely if these concepts are elusive when looked at from a content standpoint, they are still more deceptive when viewed from the angle of function, and especially so when function is obtained by the introspection method. It is rather interesting that no functional psychologist has carefully distinguished between "perception" (and this is true of the other psychological terms as well) as employed by the systematist, and "perceptual process" as used in functional psychology. It seems illogical and hardly fair to criticize the psychology which the systematist gives us, and then to utilize his terms without carefully showing the changes in meaning which are to be attached to them. I was greatly surprised some time ago when I opened Pillsbury's book and saw psychology defined as the "science of behavior." A still more recent text states that psychology is the "science of mental behavior." When I saw these promising statements I thought, now surely we will have texts based upon different lines. After a few pages the science of behavior is dropped and one finds the conventional treatment of sensation, perception, imagery, etc., along with certain shifts in emphasis and additional facts which serve to give the author's personal imprint....

This leads me to the point where I should like to make the argument constructive. I believe we can write a psychology, define it as Pillsbury, and never go back upon our definition: never use the terms consciousness, mental states, mind, content, introspectively verifiable, imagery, and the like.... It can be done in terms of stimulus and response, in terms of habit formation, habit integrations and the like. Furthermore, I believe that it is really worth while to make this attempt now.

The psychology which I should attempt to build up would take as a starting point, first, the observable fact that organisms, man and animal alike, do adjust themselves to their environment by means of hereditary and habit equipments. These adjustments may be very adequate or they may be so inadequate that the organism barely maintains its existence; secondly, that certain stimuli lead the organisms to make the responses. In a system of psychology completely worked out, given the response the stimuli can be predicted; given the stimuli the response can be predicted.[1]

The brave new psychology of Wundt was to be banished to the outer darkness to dwell in the shadowy world of ghosts and goblins. In psychology, as Watson envisioned it, behavior was not merely to be at a level of coexistence with the study of consciousness, but it was to occupy the entire field.

As always in historical matters, there had been earlier contentions relating to the point of view that is now being stressed as novel. Psychologists had already insisted that behavior was proper subject matter for psychological study, as had McDougall in 1905 (p. 251). Already, many research problems had been studied by purely behavioral means. The Ebbinghaus approach to learning of nonsense syllables did not depend on inquiries into his subjects' experiences. Research work on animals and human infants could do nothing but study their behavior except by inference. Psychological tests, such as that of putting puzzle pictures together, demanded only kinds of muscular responses. What was novel was Watson's claim that all references to mind, consciousness, or experience be ignored as irrelevant to psychology. The pallid, half-way measures of McDougall by no means satisfied him.

The pronouncement of 1913, just excerpted, closed with a hope that refined methods of the study of behavior would be found that would bring all aspects of psychology under study by objective methods. What are these methods? In *Psychology from the Standpoint of a Behaviorist,* first published six years later, he lists them as follows:

I. Observation, with and without instrumental control.
II. The conditioned reflex methods.
   (*a*) Methods employed in obtaining conditioned secretion reflexes.
   (*b*) Methods employed in obtaining conditioned motor re flexes.
III. The verbal report method.
IV. Methods of testing.[2]

Observation as a general method presumably is familiar; conditioning has been examined earlier through the work of Pavlov (p. 262) and will be again in later excerpts from the writings of Watson; psychological tests have been illustrated through the work of Cattell (p. 213). This leaves to be excerpted the crucial and most controversial of all proposed methods, that of verbal report:

III. VERBAL REPORT METHODS.

Introduction.—The methods so far discussed have dealt with the integrated motor and glandular behavior of individuals other than ourselves. The methods have been largely developed by and have come into prominence through the study of animal behavior and infant human subjects. Indeed, in these fields we must depend largely upon such methods, since the observation of the happenings in their own bodies and the verbal reports of the same are impossible in the case of animals, or very imperfect in the case of abnormal individuals. Man is above all an animal which reacts most often and most complexly with speech reactions. The notion has somehow gained ground that objective psychology does not deal with speech reactions. This, of course, is a mistake. It would be foolish and one-sided to an absurd degree to neglect man's verbal behavior. Often the sole observable reaction in man is speech. In other words, his adjustments to situations are made more frequently by speech than through action of the remaining motor mechanisms. We shall in a later chapter develop our notion of the implicit and explicit language adjustments. We wish here mainly to show the use of speech reactions as a part of general psychological methods. As an illustration of the use of the verbal report method in an actual experiment we may glance for a moment at the tests on sensitivity to warmth and cold on a given area of the skin. We first mark off a small area and go over it with a warm and a cold cylinder: we say to the subject, "Tell us each time the cold cylinder is applied and each time the warm cylinder is applied." If the area touched is sensitive to cold he *responds with the word "cold,"* and similarly when the warm cylinder is applied with the word *"warm."* The verbal report or response is put down in our records of the results of the experiment and is used exactly as the conditioned reflex responses would be used had we adopted that form of experimentation in our test.

Is There a Verbal Report Method Distinct from Other Observable Methods?—Up to the present time psychologists have employed the verbal report method in a somewhat different sense from that used here. Without entering into this bitterly contested and controversial field, we can briefly outline the position of this text in regard to it. The question: Can I make the same observations upon myself that I make on other individuals? brings home the difficulties. The answer is, of course, "yes," but ... we stated that all we can observe in another individual is his behavior, and we defined behavior as the integrated responses of muscles and glands. The question now becomes simpler: Can I observe the movements of my own muscles and glands and their integration? For example, that I am writing, that my face is flushed, etc.? Who would deny it?

At this point we diverge for a moment to correct a misconception which has arisen with reference to objective psychology. The misconception lies in the fact that a good many psychologists have misunderstood the behaviorist's position. They insist that he is only observing the individual movements of the muscles and glands; that he is interested in the muscles and glands in exactly the same way the physiologist is interested in them. This is not the whole statement. *The behaviorist is interested in integrations and total activities of the individual.* At one moment we ask the question: What is the individual doing? We observe that he is typewriting, searching for a lost pocket-book or "reacting" to an emotional stimulus. If the latter happens to be true and we are interested in the way his emotional life as a whole hangs together, we may go on to show why the individual reacts in an emotional way to this particular stimulus. We may show how his fear reactions to certain situations arose in his infancy and how they have affected his whole personality and more highly organized habit activities.[3]

His rejection of reports of sensory experience while accepting verbal report smacked of quibbling—and verbal quibbling at that! A hot debate developed over whether or not Watson had banished introspection by the front door to have it return by the back. His failure to say precisely what he meant, his failing to qualify carefully enough, added to the difficulty.

An experimental finding that excited considerable interest in the 1920s was his sweeping claim about the limited nature of the stimuli that produced emotional responses in infants:

After observing a large number of infants, especially during the first months of life, we suggest the following group of emotional reactions as belonging to the original and fundamental nature of man: *fear, rage,* and *love,* (using love in approximately the same sense that Freud uses sex). We use these terms which are current in psychology with a good deal of hesitation. The reader is asked to find nothing in them which is not fully statable in terms of situation and response. Indeed we should be willing to call them original reaction states, X, Y, and Z. They are far more easily observable in animals than in infants. While we do not claim that this list is complete, we do claim that our own observation of the first few months of infancy has not yielded any larger number.

Fear. What stimulus apart from all training will call out fear responses; what are these responses; and how early may they be called out? The principal situations which call out fear responses are as follows: (1) To suddenly remove from the infant all means of support, as when one drops it from the hands to be caught by an assistant. (In the experiment the child is held over a bed upon which has been placed a soft feather pillow.) (2) By loud sounds. (3) Occasionally when an infant is just falling to sleep the sudden pulling of the blanket upon which it is lying will produce the fear responses. (4) Finally, again when the child has just fallen to sleep or is just ready to awaken, a sudden push or a slight shake is an adequate stimulus. (2) and (4) above may be looked upon as belonging under (1). The responses are a sudden catching of the breath, clutching randomly with the hands (the grasping reflex invariably appearing when the child is dropped), blinking of the eye lids, puckering of the lips, then crying; in older children possibly flight and hiding (not yet observed by us as 'original' reactions). In regard to the age at which fear responses first appear we can state with some sureness that with few exceptions the above mentioned group of reactions appear at birth. . . .

Rage. In a similar way the question arises as to what is the original situation which brings out the activities seen in rage. Observations seem to show that the *hampering of the infant's movements* is the factor which apart from all training brings out the movements characterized as rage. If the face or head is held crying results, quickly followed by screaming. The body stiffens and fairly well coordinated slashing or striking movements of the hands and arms result; the feet and legs are drawn up and down; the breath is held until the child's face is flushed. In older children the slashing movements of the arms and legs are better coordinated and appear as kicking, slapping, biting, pushing etc. These reactions continue until the irritating situation is removed, and sometimes do not cease then. Almost any child from birth can be thrown into a rage if its arms are held tightly to its sides: oftentimes even if the elbow joint is clamped tightly between the fingers the responses appear: at times just the placing of the head between cotton pads will produce them. Even the best natured child will show rage if its nose is held for a few seconds.

Love. The original situation which calls out the observable love responses seems to be the stroking or manipulation of some erogenous zone, tickling, shaking, gentle rocking, patting, turning upon the stomach across the attendant's knee, etc. The response varies—if the infant is crying, crying ceases, a smile may begin, attempts at gurgling, cooing, and finally, in slightly older children, the extension of the arms which we should class as the forerunner of clasping in the narrowed sex act in coitus.[4]

To summarize, fear was produced by loud sounds and loss of support, rage by hampering of movement and love by stroking. This was the entire repertoire of the infants' emotional responses. Moreover, he had specified what stimuli produced these particular reactions.

Considerable research was stimulated, including many studies in refutation. The overall evidence demonstrated that Watson's evidence was too simplistic. Particularly telling in this regard was the evidence produced by Mandel Sherman,[5] who took motion pictures of infants using Watsonian conditions of stimulation. When dropping or restraint were used, judgments of the motion pictures fit rather well with his results—fear was identified when loss of support was the source of stimulation. But when observers saw only the response (by cutting out the stimulus portion of the film), there was little correspondence. And when they viewed the motion pictures so spliced that the stimulus they saw did not correspond to the responses shown, they then made judgments based on the stimulus. If, for example, a baby was stimulated by striking an iron bar while the response was actually that for restraint, they judged it to be a fear response. Current opinion would have it that infants do not show as clear-cut emotional responses as Watson claimed, and that what they do show is a mass of random movements to severe stimuli of any sort.

The conditioning of fear in infants was also studied by Watson and Rosalie Raynor. Their subject, Albert B., is one of the most famous in literature and thus deserves to be mentioned by name. Normal and healthy at birth, they claim "he was on the whole, solid and unemotional." To proceed, in their words:

At approximately nine months of age we ran him through the emotional tests that have become a part of our regular routine in determining whether fear reactions can be called out by other stimuli than sharp noises and the sudden removal of support.... In brief, the infant was confronted suddenly and for the first time successively with a white rat, a rabbit, a dog, a monkey, with masks with and without hair, cotton wool, burning newspapers, etc. A permanent record of Albert's reactions to these objects and situations has been preserved in a motion picture study. Manipulation was the most usual reaction called out. *At no time did this infant ever show fear in any situation.* These experimental records were confirmed by the casual observations of the mother and hospital attendants. No one had ever seen him in a state of fear and rage. The infant practically never cried.

Up to approximately nine months of age we had not tested him with loud sounds. The test to determine whether a fear reaction could be called out by a loud sound was made when he was eight months, twenty-six days of age. The sound was that made by striking a hammer upon a suspended steel bar four feet in length and three-fourths of an inch in diameter. The laboratory notes are as follows:

One of the two experimenters caused the child to turn its head and fixate her moving hand; the other, stationed back of the child, struck the steel bar a sharp blow. The child started violently, his breathing was checked and the arms were raised in a characteristic manner. On the second stimulation the same thing occurred, and in addition the lips began to pucker and tremble. On the third stimulation the child broke into a sudden crying fit. This is the first time an emotional situation in the laboratory has produced any fear or even crying in Albert.

We had expected just these results on account of our work with other infants brought up under similar conditions. It is worth while to call attention to the fact that removal of support (dropping and jerking the blanket upon which the infant was lying) was tried exhaustively upon this infant on the same occasion. It was not effective in producing the fear response....

The steps taken to condition emotional responses are shown in our laboratory notes.

11 MONTHS 3 DAYS

1. White rat suddenly taken from the basket and presented to Albert. He began to reach for rat with left hand. Just as his hand touched the animal the bar was struck immediately behind his head. The infant jumped violently and fell forward, burying his face in the mattress. He did not cry, however.

2. Just as the right hand touched the rat the bar was again struck. Again the infant jumped violently, fell forward and began to whimper.

In order not to disturb the child too seriously no further tests were given for one week.

11 MONTHS 10 DAYS

1. Rat presented suddenly without sound. There was steady fixation but no tendency at first to reach for it. The rat was then placed nearer, whereupon tentative reaching movements began with the right hand. When the rat nosed the infant's left hand, the hand was immediately withdrawn. He started to reach for the head of the animal with the forefinger of the left hand, but withdrew it suddenly before contact. It is thus seen that the two joint stimulations given the previous week were not without effect. . . .He was tested with his blocks.

2. Joint stimulation with rat and sound. Started, then fell over immediately to right side. No crying.

3. Joint stimulation. Fell to right side and rested upon hands, with head turned away from rat. No crying.

4. Joint stimulation. Same reaction.

5. Rat suddenly presented alone. Puckered face, whimpered and withdrew body sharply to the left.

6. Joint stimulation. Fell over immediately to right side and began to whimper.

7. Joint stimulation. Started violently and cried, but did not fall over.

8. Rat alone. *The instant the rat was shown the baby began to cry. Almost instantly he turned sharply to the left, fell over on left side, raised himself on all fours and began to crawl away so rapidly that he was caught with difficulty before reaching the edge of the table.*

This was as convincing a case of a completely conditioned fear response as could have been theoretically pictured. In all seven joint stimulations were given to bring about the complete reaction. . . .

11 MONTHS 15 DAYS

1. Tested first with blocks. He reached readily for them, playing with them as usual. This shows that there has been no general transfer to the room, table, blocks, etc.
2. Rat alone. Whimpered immediately, withdrew right hand and turned head and trunk away.
3. Blocks again offered. Played readily with them, smiling and gurgling.
4. Rat alone. Leaned over to the left side as far away from the rat as possible, then fell over, getting up on all fours and scurrying away as rapidly as possible.
5. Blocks again offered. Reached immediately for them, smiling and laughing as before.

The above preliminary test shows that the conditioned response to the rat had carried over completely for the five days in which no tests were given. The question as to whether or not there is a transfer was next taken up.

6. Rabbit alone. The rabbit was suddenly placed on the mattress in front of him. The reaction was pronounced. Negative responses began at once. He leaned as far away from the animal as possible, whimpered, then burst into tears. When the rabbit was placed in contact with him he buried his face in the mattress, then got up on all fours and crawled awy, crying as he went. This was a most convincing test. . . .

11 MONTHS 20 DAYS

1. Blocks alone. Played with them as usual.
2. Rat alone. Withdrawal of the whole body, bending over to left side, no crying. Fixation and following with eyes. The response was much less marked than on first presentation the previous week. It was thought best to freshen up the reaction by another joint stimulation.
3. Just as the rat was placed on his hand the rod was struck. Reaction violent.

4. Rat alone. Fell over at once to left side. Reaction practically as strong as on former occasion but no crying.

5. Rat alone. Fell over to left side, got up on all fours and started to crawl away. On this occasion there was no crying, but strange to say, as he started away he began to gurgle and coo, even while leaning far over to the left side to avoid the rat.

6. Rabbit alone. Leaned over to left side as far as possible. Did not fall over. Began to whimper but reaction not so violent as on former occasions.

7. Blocks again offered. He reached for them immediately and began to play.[6]

Tested again at the age of one year and twenty-one days, fear reactions were elicited when Albert was shown the Santa Claus mask, the fur coat, the rat, the rabbit, and the dog, although sometimes there was a preliminary tentative reaching out. Fear, however, was not always as quickly elicited as before.

Watson's academic career at Johns Hopkins came to an abrupt end in 1920 due to a divorce scandle. Thereafter, he worked in advertising in New York City, lectured, and wrote books and articles on psychology for the popular market.

More than one of his books became a best seller. His *Behaviorism,* first published in 1924, is marked by an aggressive appeal to the openness of human nature to the effects of environment, with the virtual elimination of any effects of heredity. One of the most striking and often-quoted sentences is as follows:

Give me a dozen healthy infants, well-formed, and my own specified world to bring them up in and I'll guarantee to take any one at random and train him to become any type of specialist I might select—doctor, lawyer, artist, merchant-chief and, yes, even beggar-man and thief, regardless of his talents, penchants, tendencies, abilities, vocations, and race of his ancestors.[7]

In this quotation, we have a clue to his popularity—Watson mirrored his time and place. Psychologically speaking, all men were equal, and no one person was better than another. Environment made the person whatever that person turned out to be—and behaviorism guides that direction. His was an optimistic doctrine: obstacles could be overcome.

When Watson issued his manifesto in 1913, he used the singular voice both for the sake of forcefulness and also because, since he stood alone, it was more appropriate than it would have been to use the plural "we." While his career in psychology lasted hardly more than two decades, it was sufficient to make the psychology of the 1920s and 1930s in many respects a new field with behaviorism the school of psychology that was clearly dominant, since by then it was adhered to by the majority of psychologists.

36

VON EHRENFELS ON
FORM QUALITIES

CHRISTIAN VON EHRENFELS (1859–1932), Austrian philosopher, did much to originate the school of Form Qualities, while associated with the University of Graz during the last decade of the nineteenth century and the first decades of the twentieth century. The major contention of the school was that Wundtian psychology failed to appreciate an important element of the perceptual situation—the form quality.

Von Ehrenfel's major paper[1] on form qualities was published in 1890. Some weeks before his death in 1932, he dictated a summary of his position to his wife. It is this paper that is presented below:

The theory of Gestalt-qualities began with the attempt to answer a question: What is melody? First and most obvious answer: the sum of the individual notes which make up the melody. But opposed to this is the fact that the same melody may be made up of quite different groups of notes, as happens when the self-same melody is transposed into different keys. If the melody were nothing else than the sum of the notes, different melodies would have to be produced, because different groups of notes are here involved. Mach, who was struck by this fact, drew from it the conclusion that the essence of melody must reside in a sum of special sensations which as note-sensations (*Tonempfindungen*) accompany the notes. But he did not know how to give any account of these sensations; and in fact we are unable to discover any sign of them in inner experience. The decisive step in the founding of a theory of Gestalt-quality was my own assertion: when the memory-images of successive notes are present as a simultaneous complex in consciousness, then an idea (*Vorstellung*), belonging to a new category, can arise in consciousness, a unitary idea, which is connected in a manner peculiar to itself with the ideas (*Vorstellungen*) of the complex of notes involved. The idea of this whole belongs to a new category, for which the name 'founded contents' (*fundierte Inhalte*) came into use. Not all founded contents are perceptual in character and allied to the idea of melody. There are also founded contents which are not perceptual, as for example relations. The essence of the connection between the founded content and its base (*Fundament*) is the irreversible conditioning of the former by the latter. Every founded content necessarily requires a base. A certain complex of basic ideas can support only a certain founded content. But not every base need be crowned, so to speak, and held together, by a founded content. At least that was my view when I formed the concept of Gestalt-quality. Others held a different view, which was, that the Gestalt-quality is necessarily given along with the base, and that the effort which we contribute—for instance, in apprehending a melody—is not located in production of the founded content, but merely in its observation. Meinong and his pupil Benussi adhered to the first view, while the second is represented by Wertheimer and Köhler.

Gestalt-qualities may be divided into apprehension (*Auffassung*) of processes and apprehension of momentary states. I have distinguished these groups as temporal and nontemporal Gestalt-qualities. Examples of processes are melody and motion; of momentary states, harmony, and what in everyday life is designated spatial structure (*Raumgestalt*). But there are not only melody and harmony of sound, but also, for example, color-melodies and color-harmonies as well. Indeed, in the realm of all sense-qualities it is possible to find analogues of melody and harmony. But the field of Gestalten extends far more widely than is shown by these examples. In the first place there is Gestalt not only in the realm of musical notes, but also in that of the sound-sensations which we call "noises" (*Geräusche*) in order to distinguish between musical notes and mere sounds. Language is composed of such noises, even if in the individual vowels, as elements, tones are distinguishable. Every word of a language is a Gestalt-quality. As to the extension of Gestalt-qualities into psychical life, one can form an idea from the fact that the so-called laws of association operate much more frequently when Gestalten and not elements are concerned. Thus, for instance, with the image of an individual person is associated (certainly physically and in all probability psychically) a Gestalt-quality, which, according to the law of similarity, is numerous images of other persons; while with the idea of a simple element, for example of a musical note or a color, the idea of other elements is never associated. Our memory for simple elements in the realm of musical notes, the so-called absolute pitch, is incomparably less developed than the memory for melodies and harmonies. The so-called mnemonic aids are based on Gestalt-qualities. The essence of the aids consists in this, that a Gestalt-quality is discovered which for some reason or other is easily imprinted on the memory and whose parts have a certain mechanical relation to the ideational objects which are to be retained in memory: as for example the often-cited phrase, readily accepted by the ear: "Kilometertal, Euer Urpokal," in which the first two syllables are readily associated with the name Klio, and every following syllable is identical with the first syllable of the name of one of the nine muses.[2]

Form qualities stand over and above the elements but are constructed out of the elements which are its sensory data base. Von Ehrenfels thus continued an old tradition—he did not start a new one. This new tradition was to appear in the work of Wertheimer (p. 287) and the other Gestalt psychologists.

37

WERTHEIMER ON

PERCEPTUAL ORGANIZATION
INTO WHOLES AND GESTALT PSYCHOLOGY

MAX WERTHEIMER (1880–1943), German-American psychologist, published in 1912 the paper that launched Gestalt psychology.[1] It was a study of the perception of movement, when no movement had actually taken place. Two lines were exposed, each for a very short time, on two different places on the face of a tachistoscope (gravity or electrical device exposing material for a brief interval of time). If the time between exposures was too short, they were seen simultaneously; if too long, they were seen successively; if optimal, then movement from one place to the other was experienced.

What Wertheimer called phi phenomena was known before this experiment, but in the past, it had been labeled an illusion and thus explained away. The interpretation he offered and supported by crucial tests was the original inpetus for Gestalt psychology. This is a point of view that psychological phenomena are experienced as unified wholes, each whole possessing properties that cannot be derived by summing up its parts and the part processes, themselves, seem to be determined by the nature of the whole phenomenal experience. The summation point of view called for unchanged elements to be combined. Von Ehrenfels (p. 284) had recognized the omission of whole psychological properties and tried to meet their neglect by arguing that *form qualities* stand over and above the otherwise unchanged elements. But where are the unchanged elements in phi phenomenon? His answer did not solve the problem as Wertheimer saw it.

In the course of a career which took him from the universities of Frankfurt and Berlin and, on Hitler's rise to power, to the New School for Social Research in New York, Wertheimer continued actively demonstrating and writing on Gestalt psychology.

By the early 1920s, Wertheimer had amassed considerable information about perceptual organization from a Gestalt point of view and published two important articles. The first of the two following excerpts concerns the general theoretical situation, beginning with a statement of his objections to the prevailing elementarism.

The fundamental attitude towards mind prevailing in most scientific psychology, when its real implications are appreciated, appears to the naïve man alien, wooden, monstrous. Yet its advantages in scientific precision over mere opinion have led to its acceptance as obvious—especially since an attitude of this sort seems essential for clean-cut scientific work. The hypothesis has appeared obviously sound that scientific comprehension of a mental phenomenon required the discovery of its "elements" and then, by laws applicable to those elements, a reconstruction of the phenomenon.

But it is good in science to subject our principles themselves to investigation, and not merely in some general, discursive fashion but by a concrete and positive inquiry. Although the attitude and hypothesis we have mentioned were supported by certain findings, there were others where this point of view *should* have been submitted to suspicious scrutiny. Instead, they were either somehow forced into line or simply carried along. Let us formulate some of these underlying principles. In doing so we shall express the positions more bluntly than is customary in order to bring out the maximum force of their concrete meaning.

I. *The mosaic or "bundle" hypothesis.*—Every "complex" consists of a sum of elementary contents or pieces (e.g. sensations). Example: If I have $a_1\ b_1\ c_1$ and $b_2\ c_2$ are substituted for $b_1\ c_1$, I then have $a_1\ b_2\ c_2$. We are dealing essentially with a summative multiplicity of variously constituted components (a "bundle") and all else is erected somehow upon this and-summation. Thus to sensations are added "residues" of earlier perceptions, feelings, attention, comprehension, will. Also memory attaches itself to the sum of contents.

II. *The association hypothesis.*—If a certain content A has frequently occurred with B ("in spatio-temporal contiguity"), then there is a tendency for A to call up B. (*Typical* case: nonsense syllables.) This is the ground plan of associationism. The principle here is one of merely *existential connection,* a union only as regards the appearance of these or those contents, a concatenation essentially extraneous in character. The concatenated contents are arbitrary; the question of their intrinsic relations to one another is *on principle* never raised.

In both hypotheses we find the *identical principle*: and-summation, i.e. a construction from pieces—a first, a second, a third, and so on—which, as primarily given fundaments, underlie all else. Their contents are adventitious with respect to one another. Now from this assemblage of pieces there may emerge higher structures, unifications, complexes—erected, as secondary, upon the *and*-summation of pieces. It is on principle quite arbitrary *what* is coupled in simultaneity and succession. For the togetherness itself the "content" or the relation of contents is really irrelevant. No intrinsic moments determine the aggregation; there are instead such foreign, extrinsic factors as frequency or simultaneity of presentation (of the constituents), and so on. . . .

In contrast to the foregoing hypothesis: Only rarely, only under certain characteristic conditions, only within very narrow limits and perhaps never more than approximately do we find purely summative relationships. It is inappropriate to treat so special a case as typical of all mental events.

In saying "only rarely," the point is that only in exceptional cases is an "and-summation" in experience possible. These may arise under conditions of extreme fatigue; they may occur when one encounters a kind of stone wall in thinking; or, again, when a situation is artificially so arranged as to present a succession of irrelevant and unrelated objects; or, when, as part of a certain experimental procedure, the instructions specifically require an attitude favouring "piecewise" reception of the presented material.

The expression "within very narrow limits" reminds us that the "span of consciousness" for unrelated elements is exceedingly small, varying directly with degrees of structuration; the same may also be said of immediate and extended memory.

"Never more than approximately" is intended to suggest that closer scrutiny frequently discloses how an apparently unrelated aggregate of elements may really be a united, organized whole. Even the impression of a chaos is not a case of and-summation. Indeed the realization of an and-group is possible only in approximation and then at the risk of artificiality or of having altered, flattened, and emptied the pieces themselves.

The given is itself in varying degrees "structured" ("gestaltet"), it consists of more or less definitely structural wholes and whole-processes with their whole-properties and laws, characteristic whole-tendencies and whole-determinations of parts. "Pieces" almost always appear "as parts" in whole processes.

Empirical inquiry discloses not a construction of primary pieces, but gradations of givenness "in broad strokes" (relative to more inclusive whole-properties), and varying articulation. The upper limit is complete internal organization of the entire given; the lower limit is that of additive adjacency between two or more relatively independent wholes. To sever a "part" from the organized whole in which it occurs—whether it itself be a subsidiary whole or an "element"—is a very real process usually involving alterations in that "part." Modifications of a part frequently involve changes elsewhere in the whole itself. Nor is the nature of these alterations arbitrary, for they *too* are determined by whole-conditions and the events initiated by their occurrence run a course defined by the laws of functional dependence in wholes. The role played here by the parts is one *of* "parts" genuinely "participating"—not of extraneous, independent and-units.

Combination, integration, completion, far from being the adventitious results of blind extrinsic factors (such as mechanized habit) are determined by concrete Gestalt laws. "Elements" are therefore *not* to be placed together as fundaments in and-summation and under conditions involving extrinsic combinations. Instead they are determined as parts by the intrinsic conditions of these wholes and are to be understood "as parts" relative to such wholes. Nor are "Gestalten" the sums of aggregated contents erected subjectively upon primarily given pieces: contingent subjectively determined, adventitious structures. They are not simply blind, additional "*Qualitäten*," essentially as pieceable and intractable as "elements"; nor are they merely something added to already given material, merely "formal". Instead we are dealing here with wholes and whole-processes possessed of specific inner, intrinsic laws; we are considering structures with their concrete structural principles.

Expressed in tersm of the foregoing hypothesis we may assert that the scientific study of perception will not be grounded in a "purely summative" point of view; a total array of stimulus points over against a total of sensations plus the secondary factors necessary to bind these into an additive total. Instead, perception must be treated from the point of view of stimulus-constellations on the one side and actually given mental Gestalt phenomena on the other. And this leads in physiological theory to the assumption of whole processes. The cells of an organism are *parts* of the whole and excitations occurring in them are thus to be viewed as part-processes functionally related to whole-processes of the entire organism. This does not mean, however, a rejection of the psychological approach—as if, in emphasizing physiology, the psychological treatment were being excluded. What *is* repudiated is the piecewise handling of psychological data. Indeed psychological penetration of this problem is not only *de-*

manded but really now for the first time *permitted* by an hypothesis such as ours.

But quite apart from the problems of stimulus configuration and physiology it is clear that in psychology itself the possibility of advance requires a procedure "from above," *not* "from below upward." Thus the comprehension of whole-properties and whole-conditions *must* precede consideration of the real significance of "parts." Observe, for instance, the different implications of the following: (1) I have *a* and *b* and *c* and . . . ; these are the self-subsistent constituents of a total reached by coupling together a series of "ands." (Each is, say, a sensation determined only by its own corresponding stimulus.) Or, conversely, (2) here is a whole, determined by concrete properties and laws, from which parts may be derived *not* by mere changes of attention, bare subtractive abstraction or the like, but by a genuine dismemberment. Such derivation yields a group of subsidiary wholes any alterations in which (as a consequence of dismemberment) may be clearly ascertained.

In "completion" phenomena we may again see the operation of these principles. Thus the *completion* of an incomplete experience is effected not by the bare addition of just any, arbitrary datum, but through the operation of whole-factors and concrete Gestalt laws.

Memory, too, is concerned primarily with the whole-properties and structural unity of the thing remembered. Memory processes and "experience" do not consist in a bare sequence of events each essentially alien to all the rest. Contextual indifference in association or habit ("mechanical" memory in general) is simply a limiting case. In this connection consider the nature of a genuine thought process: the solution of a problem, the act of comprehending and grasping what one hears or sees, the process of discovering what a problem is, in seeing the point, the act of passing in thought from *in*comprehension to comprehension of a given situation. Here is no "sequence of images," nor could anyone confuse such mental activities with and-like additions and subtractions of knowledge. Instead the essential property of these processes is that they are Gestalt processes. (Analogies may be seen also in the processes of perception, feeling, and will.)

The whole-conditions to which we have referred are proposed as objects of scientific investigation, not as topics for generalization and speculation. Of fundamental importance is the difference between processes whose factors are externality and adventitiousness *and* those exemplifying genuine meaningfulness. The processes of whole-phenomena are not blind, arbitrary, and devoid of meaning—as this term is understood in everyday life. To comprehend an inner coherence is meaningful; it is meaningful to sense an inner necessity. A prediction may be meaningful in this sense as may also a completion of something incomplete; behaviour is meaningful or not, and so on. In all such cases meaningfulness obtains when the happening is determined not by blindly external factors but by concrete "inner stipulation." Hence we may say in general that a whole is meaningful when concrete mutual dependency obtains among its parts. The mosaic or associationistic hypothesis is therefore on principle unable to supply *any* direct approach to the problem of meaning. Whether there is such a thing as meaningfulness or not is simply a question of fact.[2]

In this account, Wertheimer first considered the positions with which he disagreed, the so-called bundle-and-association hypothesis, and then presented the view that what is given in perception is structured wholes.

In a second article, he presented evidence in defense of that position, a portion of which is excerpted below:

I stand at the window and see a house, trees, sky. Now on theoretical grounds I could ry to count and say: "here there are . . . 327 brightnesses and hues." Do I *have* "327"? No, I see sky, house, trees; and no one can really have these "327" as such. Furthermore, if in this strange calculation the house should have, say, 120 and the trees 90 and the sky 117, I have in any event *this* combination, this segregation, and not, say, 127 and 100 and 100; or 150 and 177. I *see* it in this particular combination, this particular segregation; and the sort of combination or segregation in which I see it is not simply up to my choice: it is almost impossible for me to see it in any desired combination that I may happen to choose. When I succeed in seeing some unusual combination, what a strange process it is. What surprise results, when, after looking at it a long time, after many attempts, I *discover*—under the influence of a very unrealistic set—that over there parts of the window frame make an *N* with a smooth branch . . .

As another example, take two faces, cheek to cheek. I see the one (with, if you like, "57" brightnesses) and the other (with its "49"), but not in the division 66 plus 40 or 6 plus 100. Again, I hear a melody (17 notes) with its accompaniment (32 notes). I hear melody and accompaniment, not just "49"; or at least not 20 or 29.

This is true even when there is no question at all of stimulus continua; for instance if the melody and its accompaniment is played by an old music box, in short, separate little tones; or in the visual area, when figures composed of discontinuous parts (e.g., dots) become segregated on an otherwise quite homogeneous ground. Even though alternative organizations may be easier here than in the preceding cases, it is still true that a spontaneous, natural, normally expected combination and segregation occurs; and other organizations can be achieved only rarely, under particular conditions and usually with special effort and some difficulty.

In general, if a number of stimuli are presented together, a correspondingly large number of separate "givens" do not generally occur for the human; rather there are more comprehensive givens, in a particular segregation, combination, separation.

Are there principles for this resulting organization? What are they? One can try to determine and isolate the factors operating here experimentally, but a simpler procedure can be used in the presentation of the most critical factors: demonstration with a few simple, characteristic cases. The following is limited to the exposition of some essentials.

1. Given, in an otherwise homogeneous field, a row of dots with alternating distances, e.g., $d_1 = 3$ mm, $d_2 = 12$ mm.

• •　　• •　　• •　　• •　　• •　　• •　　• •

Normally such a row of dots is spontaneously seen as a row of small groups of points, in the arrangement ab/cd, and not, say, in the arrangement a/bc/de.... Really to see this arrangement (a/bc/de...) simultaneously in the entire series is quite impossible for most people. (If the constellation is composed of *few* dots, the opposing organization is easier to achieve and the result is more ambiguous. The situation is in general more labile. For instance, if the series above is decreased to
• •　　• •　　• •, the grouping a/bc/de/f is readily achieved.)

Of course a real *seeing* is meant here, not just conceiving some arbitrary combination; perhaps this will be clearer in dot series like the following:

You see a row of slanted groups (•ᐧ•), slanting from lower left to upper right, with the arrangement ab/cd/ef... ; the opposite arrangement, a/bc/de... , with long slanted groups (•　　ᐧ•) is much more difficult to achieve. For most people it is impossible to achieve *simultaneously throughout the entire series* in such a constellation. It is difficult to achieve and when it does occur, it is much less certain—much more labile than the first, in relation to eye movements and changes in attention. . . .

In all of these cases, a first simple principle emerges. The naturally resulting organization is the grouping together of the dots with small separation. The organization of the dots with greater separation into groups either does not occur at all or occurs only with difficulty and artificially, and is more labile. As a tentative formulation: other things being equal, *grouping occurs on the basis of small distance* (the factor of nearness). . . .

This principle has wider applications. It holds not only in vision and in spatial relations. Tapping continuously in the rhythm of our first example (● ●   ● ●   ● ●   ● ●   ● ● etc.) or the next to the last one (● ● ●   ● ● ●   ● ● ●   ● ● ●   ● ● ●) demonstrates this effect in a very convincing way.

2. Given a constellation of dots with equal distances, with successive pairs different colors, in a homogeneous field—e.g., white and black in a gray field, in the following schema:

a. ○ ○ ● ● ○ ○ ● ● ○ ○ ● ● ○ ○ ● ● ○ ○ ● ●

Or better, a surface filled as follows:

b. ○ ● ○ ● ○ ● ○ ● ○ ●   *c.* ○ ○ ○ ○ ○ ○ ○ ○ ○ ○
     ○ ● ○ ● ○ ● ○ ● ○ ●   ● ● ● ● ● ● ● ● ● ●
     ○ ● ○ ● ○ ● ○ ● ○ ●   ○ ○ ○ ○ ○ ○ ○ ○ ○ ○
     ○ ● ○ ● ○ ● ○ ● ○ ●   ● ● ● ● ● ● ● ● ● ●
     ○ ● ○ ● ○ ● ○ ● ○ ●   ○ ○ ○ ○ ○ ○ ○ ○ ○ ○
     ○ ● ○ ● ○ ● ○ ● ○ ●   ● ● ● ● ● ● ● ● ● ●
     ○ ● ○ ● ○ ● ○ ● ○ ●   ○ ○ ○ ○ ○ ○ ○ ○ ○ ○
     ○ ● ○ ● ○ ● ○ ● ○ ●   ● ● ● ● ● ● ● ● ● ●
     ○ ● ○ ● ○ ● ○ ● ○ ●   ○ ○ ○ ○ ○ ○ ○ ○ ○ ○
     ○ ● ○ ● ○ ● ○ ● ○ ●   ● ● ● ● ● ● ● ● ● ●

Or:

d. ○ ○ ○ ● ● ● ○ ○ ○ ● ● ● ○ ○ ○ ● ● ● ○ ○ ○ ● ● ●

One sees the groups that are determined by similarity. In *a*, ab/cd/ . . . ; in *b*, verticals; in *c*, horizontals; in *d*, abc/def/ . . . ; to see the opposite organization clearly and simultaneously in the entire figure is usually impossible: *a*, a/bc/de/ . . . ; *b*, the horizontals; *c*, the verticals; *d*, any of the arrangements, like cde/fgh/ . . . etc. . . .

Analogous to corresponding simultaneous brightness and color series are the schemas:

If one confronts this principle of the size of the stepwise differences with that of nearness, there seems to arise the possibility of a more general principle which encompasses both of these and which would, in a certain sense, include spatial, temporal, *and* qualitative characteristics. If it should turn out that intensive and qualitative distance can be coordinated to a general spatio-temporal lawfulness, the instances discussed above could be considered instances of the principle of nearness. This must be carefully tested, but it *can* be experimentally studied.

Fields which were, previously, psychologically separate and heterogeneous could then be compared quantitatively in respect to the applicability of the same laws. . . .

9. To summarize, all of these factors and principles point in a single direction: perceptual organization occurs from above to below; the way in which parts are seen, in which subwholes emerge, in which grouping occurs, is not an arbitrary, piecemeal and-summation of elements, but is a process in which characteristics of the whole play a major determining role.[3]

He devoted a good share of his later years to the study of thinking from the Gestalt point of view, which culminated in the posthumously published book, *Productive Thinking*.[4] It is replete with examples of how the crux of creative thinking is to grasp the whole structure of a situation.

Wertheimer, the senior Gestalt psychologist, left to his younger colleagues two major tasks—the defense of Gestalt psychology as a school and the preparation of more systematic statements of the overall system.

38

KÖHLER ON
LEARNING, ISOMORPHISM,
AND PERCEPTION

Wolfgang Köhler (1882–1967), German-American psychologist, had been a subject in the epoch-making phi phenomenon study of Wertheimer (p. 000), after having taken his degree at the University of Berlin. He became convinced of the significance of the study and decided to pursue independent research along these lines.

In 1913, Köhler went to Tenerife in the Canary Islands where an animal research colony had been organized. Forced by internment during the World War I years to remain there longer than he intended, he performed the studies that eventuated in the book, *The Mentality of Apes*,[1] first published in 1917. From a later summary, some of the typical procedures and subsequent results are excerpted:

The ape was sitting behind the bars of his cage. On the other side of these bars I made a hole in the ground, put some fruit in it, and covered the hole and the surroundings with sand. The ape, who with great interest had observed what I did, could not reach the place of the food because it was too far away for his arm; but when I was careless enough to come too near his cage he immediately seized my arm and tried to push it in the direction of the hidden food, as he would do whenever he could not find a method of approach towards his food himself. Of course this was already a delayed reaction. But as I wanted a larger delay I did not do him the favor, and the ape began soon to play in his room apparently not giving any attention to the place of the food. After three quarters of an hour a stick was thrown into his cage from the side farthest from the fruit. The ape accustomed to the use of sticks as instruments, instantly took it, went to the bars nearest the place of the food, began to scratch away the sand exactly in the right spot, and pulled the fruit toward him. Repetitions of the experiment with other positions of the food had the same result.

Since the reaction was always surprisingly correct I made the interval of delay much greater. I let the apes see how I buried the food somewhere in the earth of the very large playground and brought them, immediately afterwards, into their sleeping room so that they went on the playground not before the following day when more than seventeen hours had elapsed, more than half of them spent sleeping. One of the apes, when leaving the sleeping room, did not hesitate a moment but went straight to the place of the food and found it there after some searching.

In another experiment a stick was hidden in the wooden framework of the roof, where the apes could not see it from the ground. Again they observed with great interest our unusual action. But we at once brought them into their dormitory. The next morning, when one of them came back into the same room, he discovered some bananas on the ground outside the cage and too far away for his arm. As apes, accustomed to the use of sticks, do under these circumstances, he looked around in exactly the way of a man seeking something, but could not find such a tool. After some seconds, however, his eyes went up to the place where the stick was hidden the evening before. He could not see it, but he climbed at once in the shortest possible way up to that part of the ceiling where the stick was hidden, came down with it, and scratched the food towards him. I repeated the experiment with all the chimpanzees who had seen how we put the stick in its place in the roof. They all independently solved the problem in the same manner. . . .

One of the chimpanzees at Tenerife was almost stupid; at least when compared with the other apes. He had been present a great many times when other chimpanzees had used the box as a tool for reaching objects in high places. So, eventually, I expected this animal to be able to do the same thing when left alone in such a situation, *i.e.,* with a banana somewhere in the ceiling, a box some yards apart on the ground. The ape went to the box; but instead of moving it in the direction of the food, he either climbed up on the box and jumped from there vertically in the air, though the food was elsewhere, or he tried to jump from the ground and to reach the banana. The others showed him the simple performance a number of times, but he could not imitate them and only copied parts of their behavior which, without the right connection in the whole act, did not help him at all. He climbed up on the box, ran from there under the banana, and jumped again from the ground. Decidedly the right connection of box and food in this situation was not yet apparent to our chimpanzee. Sometimes he moved the box a little from its place, but as often as not away from the food. Only after many more demonstrations of the simple act did he finally learn to do it in a manner which I cannot describe briefly. One sees there is a serious task in learning by imitation even for a less intelligent *ape*. An *intelligent* chimpanzee, observing another in this little performance will, for instance, soon become aware that moving the box means from the first moment moving it to a place underneath the food, the movement will be grasped as one with this essential orientation, whereas a stupid animal sees first the movement of the box, not relating it instantly to the place of the food. He will observe single phases of the whole performance, but he will not perceive them as parts related to the essential structure of the situation, in which alone they are parts of the solution.[2]

Later in the same article, he compares the results he had obtained with the behavior of a man in similar circumstances, "who, after a while in a certain individual experiment, would grasp the principle of the problem and say to himself "Oh, that's the point!..." of course with the consequence that, he, too, would never make a mistake again."[3] He was presenting some of the characteristics of what he called "insight," the grasping of the significance of the learning situation so that, thereafter, when faced with the same situation, the solution was immediate once it was understood to be same (or related) situation.

In keeping with the Gestalt emphasis, the tasks Köhler had investigated with chimpanzees were such that all aspects of the problem needed for solution were open to them. This procedure was in considerable contrast with, say, that of Thorndike's cats (p. 255) who were limited to a situation only parts of which were capable of their observation, a condition which caused them to use trial-and-error procedures.

In 1920, Köhler, who had been a student of Max Planck, the physicist, published a book for which the title may be translated as *The Physical Gestalten at Rest and in a Stationary State*.[4] It was an ambitious, technically very abstruse, attempt to demonstrate that the Gestalt wholes are present in the physical phenomena of physics, astronomy, and chemistry, exemplified by "field theory" in physics. He argued that Gestalt psychology can be conceived to be an application of field physics. Since he marshalled evidence that satisfied him that this was the case, he concluded that it follows that biological psychological facts, too, can be understood in terms of the laws which hold for the inanimate world, since the physical world has a point of relationship with them; physiological-psychological phenomena possess a principle of relationship to one another and to the physical world. The crux of that relationship was isomorphism.

Physiological and psychological Gestalts show a principle of relationship—isomorphism:

Under normal conditions, objective experience depends upon physical events which stimulate sense organs. But it also depends upon physiological events of the kind which we now wish to explore. The physicist is interested in the former fact: the dependence of objective experience upon physical events outside the organism enables him to infer from experience what those physical events are. We are interested in the latter fact: since experience depends upon physiological events in the brain, such experience ought to contain hints as to the nature of these processes. In other words, we argue that if objective experience allows us to draw a picture of the physical world, it must also allow us to draw a picture of the physiological world to which it is much more closely related.

Obviously, however, if the characteristics of concomitant physiological processes are to be inferred from given characteristics of experience, we need a leading principle which governs the transition. Many years ago, a certain principle of this kind was introduced by E. Hering. Its content is as follows. Experiences can be systematically ordered, if their various kinds and nuances are put together according to their similarities. The procedure is comparable to the one by which animals are ordered in zoology and plants in botany. The processes upon which experiences depend are not directly known. But if they were known, they could also be ordered according to their similarities. Between the two systematic orders, that of experiences and that of concomitant phsyiological processes, various relationships may be assumed to obtain. But the relation between the two orderly systems will be simple and clear only if we postulate that both have the same form of structure *qua* systems. Sometimes this principle is more explicitly formulated in a number of "psychophysical axioms." In our connection, it will suffice if we give some examples of its application.

A sound of given pitch can be produced in many degrees of experienced loudness. In geometrical terms, the natural systematic order of all these loudnesses is a straight line, because in proceeding from the softest to the loudest sounds we have the impression of moving continuously in the same direction. Now, what characteristic of accompanying brain events corresponds to experienced loudness? The principle does not give a direct answer. Rather, it postulates that whatever the characteristic in question may be, its various nuances or degrees must show exactly the same order as the loudnesses do, i.e., that of a straight line. Also, if in the system of experiences a particular loudness is situated between two other loudnesses, then in the order of related brain events the physiological factor corresponding to the first loudness must also have its place between the processes corresponding to the two others. This gives the equality of structure of the two systems to which the principle refers.

It seems that the all-or-none law does not allow us to choose "intensity of nervous activity" as the physiological correlate of experienced degrees of loudness. But the principle can be equally well applied if the frequency or density of nerve impulses is taken as the correlate of loudness.

As another example, colors may be discussed in their relation to accompanying brain processes. This relation has been considered most thoroughly by G. E. Müller. To be sure, his assumptions go beyond the principle now under discussion in that he makes hypotheses about *retinal* processes. The principle as such applies only to the brain processes which underlie visual experience directly. His theory is also more specific, since it includes a statement about the nature of the retinal processes as such. They are assumed to be chemical reactions. This transgression of the principle is perfectly sound for the following reason. If the system of color experiences and that of related physiological processes are to have the same structure, these physiological events must be variable in just as many directions or "dimensions" as the colors are. It is quite possible that chemical reactions constitute the only type of process which satisfies this condition. Thus the principle of identity of system structure serves to restrict the number of facts which may be considered when more specific hypotheses are desired.

Gestalt Psychology works with a principle which is both more general and more concretely applicable than that of Hering and Müller. These authors refer to the merely *logical* order of experiences which, for this purpose, are abstracted from their context and judged as to their similarities. The thesis is that when related physiological events are also taken from their context, and also compared as to their similarities, the resulting logical order must be the same as that of the experiences. In both cases, it will be seen, the order in question is the order of dead specimens as given the right places in a museum. But experience as such exhibits an order *which is itself experienced*. For instance, at this moment I have before me three white dots on a black surface, one in the middle of the field and the others in symmetrical positions on both sides of the former. This is also an order; but, instead of being of the merely logical kind, it is concrete and belongs to the very facts of experience. This order, too, we assume to depend upon physiological events in the brain. And our principle refers to the relation between concrete experienced order and the underlying physiological processes. When applied to the present example, the principle claims, first, that these processes are distributed in a certain order, and secondly, that this distribution is just as symmetrical in functional terms as the group of dots is in visual terms. In the same example, one dot is seen between the two others; and this relation is just as much a part of the experience as the white of the dots is. Our principle says that something in the underlying processes must correspond to what we call "between" in vision. More particularly, it is maintained that the experience "between" goes with a functional "between" in the dynamic interrelations of accompanying brain events. When applied to all cases of experienced spatial order, the principle may be formulated as follows: *Experienced order in space is always structurally identical with a functional order in the distribution of underlying brain processes.*

This is the principle of *psychophysical isomorphism* in the particular form which it assumes in the case of spatial order. Its full significance will become clearer in the following chapters. For the present I will mention another application of the same principle. It is a frequent experience that one event lies temporarily between two others. But experienced time must have a functional counterpart in brain events just as experienced space has. Our principle says that the temporal "between" in experience goes with a functional "between" in the sequence of underlying physiological events. If in this manner the principle is again generally applied we arrive at the proposition that *experienced order in time is always structurally identical with a functional order in the sequence of correlated brain processes.*

The field of application of the principle is not restricted to temporal and spatial orders. We experience more order than merely that of spatial and temporal relations. Certain experiences belong together in a specific fashion, whereas others do not, or belong together less intimately. Such facts are again matters of experience. The very moment I am writing this sentence, a disagreeable voice begins to sing in a neighbor's house. My sentence is something which, though extended in time, is experienced as a certain unit to which those sharp notes do not belong. This is true even though both are experienced at the same time. In this case our principle assumes this form: *units in experience go with functional units in the underlying physiological processes.* In this respect also, the experienced order is supposed to be a true representation of a corresponding order in the processes upon which experience depends. This last application of the principle has perhaps the greatest importance for Gestalt Psychology. As a physiological hypothesis about sensory experiences as well as about more subtle processes, it covers practically the whole field of psychology.

I have just taken an example from outside the realm of objective experience in the strict sense of this term. A sentence which I am formulating is not a part of objective experience in the way in which a chair before me is such an experience. And yet my statement about the sentence is no less simple and obvious than were the others, which referred to order in experienced space and time. This is not always so, however. The observation of subjective experiences cannot be recommended without limitation. In the present connection, only very simple statements in this field can be regarded as sufficiently reliable. Nor need we at present transcend the realm of objective experience. We have just seen that it provides an adequate basis of operations for our immediate purpose.

In the preceding paragraphs my own experience has served as a material which suggests assumptions about the nature of otherwise unobservable constituents of behavior. Now, the only way in which I can bring my observations in this field before the scientific public is through spoken or written language which, as I understand it, refers to this experience. But we have decided that language as a sequence of physiological facts is the peripheral outcome of antecedent physiological processes, among others of those upon which my experience depends. According to our general hypothesis, the concrete order of this experience pictures the dynamic order of such processes. Thus, if to me my words represent a description of my experiences, they are at the same time objective representations of the processes which underlie these experiences. Consequently, it does not matter very much whether my words are taken as messages about experience or about these physiological facts. For, so far as the order of events is concerned, the message is the same in both cases.[5]

The principle of the relationship between physical and psychological wholes is called isomophism, that is, the brain and the experienced contents of consciousness have a similar functional *form*. In 1935, Köhler emigrated to the United States, where he taught at Swarthmore College. A considerable amount of Köhler's subsequent research was directed to further specifying this relationship experimentally, particularly with regard to visual phenomena.

One other formulation must be excerpted here, concerning his attempt to state the basic Gestalt conception of perception. A bewildering variety of Gestalt principles of perception have been determined—closure, symmetry, "pragnanz," and goodness. Is there any salient overarching way of considering the matter? There is, and Köhler has provided, a general statement:

A visual field contains as a rule circumscribed specific entities which are to some degree detached from other such entities, and from a less differentiated environment. In the formation of these particular units, figures for instance, certain rules seem to be followed. We seldom experience much of the actual genesis of visual percepts, but we can observe what things or figures appear under different conditions of stimulation; and then we can find the rules which connect the first with the second. These I call the rules which the formation of thing-percepts obeys. The first to formulate them with a full realization of their fundamental importance was Wertheimer. He has also given a more general principle of which these rules seem to be more particular expressions. The principle contends that organization of a field tends to be as simple and clear as is compatible with the conditions given in each case. It is not always easy to prove that a particular given organization is actually clearer and simpler than any other organization that would be possible under the same conditions. But sometimes we have a natural standard of reference which gives those terms a definite meaning. A circle is simpler than are other closed figures; a straight line is simpler than are curves or broken contours which extend mainly in one direction; a regular pattern is simpler and clearer than are others in which such regularity does not altogether prevail. These and similar instances may be profitably used for testing the validity of the principle. If the principle is right, a figure which comes sufficiently near one of those natural standards should, or at least might, appear in perception as though it were the standard itself; organization should, in this sense, be "too good." Confirming observations have been reported from several sides. The following example seems to me particularly instructive.

The faces of other human beings appear to us as a rule bilaterally symmetrical. Occasionally, it is true, we see at once that a nose is strikingly askew or that the outline of one cheek is quite different from that of the other. On the other hand, few of us are aware of the fact that fairly considerable degrees of objective facial asymmetry are the rule rather than an exception. There are two ways of making people realize this asymmetry. The first consists in "psychological analysis." Normally faces are perceived as visual units. For the present purpose, however, we should, for instance, concentrate on the eyes to such a degree that the rest of the face in question becomes almost an indifferent background. Under these circumstances we shall often discover that the two eyes have different sizes, or different shapes, or slightly different heights. A similar result may be found if the same procedure is applied to the ears. Again, when concentrating on the contours of the two cheeks, we may realize with surprise that they do not actually correspond with each other as they ought to in the case of perfect symmetry. Thus, when perceived quite naturally, faces as wholes have for the most part a symmetrical appearance. And yet a more analytical scrutiny—which interferes of course with natural organization—will often reveal that details of the same faces deviate considerably from such symmetry.

A second method which serves the same purpose uses front-view photographs of faces. If such a photograph is copied twice, once correctly and then a second time from the wrong side of the film, so that a mirror-image results, we can cut both copies vertically along the median axis of the face and then combine the halves of the first picture with those halves of the second which are their mirror images. In this manner perfectly symmetrical pictures are obtained. In the case of most persons these pictures look surprisingly different from the original or from a normal photograph of the same person. Generally the objectively symmetrical pictures have a less "interesting," an "emptier," appearance than have normal photographs of the same person.

Why is the fact that most faces lack perfect objective symmetry so seldom observed under normal conditions? Wertheimer's principle applies here: So long as a face is at least approximately symmetrical and, thus, sufficiently near a standard condition of clearness and simple regularity, organization of this face as a percept will tend to overcome such minor irregularities as exist objectively. With regard to symmetry it will have "too good" an appearance.[6]

It is significant that this last excerpt was taken from a volume bearing the title, *The Place of Value in a World of Facts*. In it, Köhler had moved again, as he did in work on physical *Gestalten*, beyond the confines of psychology, in this case to grapple with problems of philosophy, particularly that of values. We live in a world of facts, Köhler argues, and what ought to be expressed in values, are, in truth, facts.

Köhler was primarily a psychologist, but he also had the courage to work on intersecting problems from biology, physics, and philosophy. The legacy of a systematic breadth to the phenomenal world of the psychologist was a consequence.

39

KOFFKA ON

CONVERGENCE IN DEVELOPMENT,
PHENOMENOLOGY, AND THE PSYCHOPHYSICAL
FIELD AS THE BASIS FOR
GESTALT PSYCHOLOGY

KURT KOFFKA (1886–1941) German-American psychologist, was also a subject in Wertheimer's historic phi phenomenon study, along with Köhler. He, too, had taken his degree previously. After his participation, he taught for some years at Giessen in Germany and, from 1927 on, at Smith College in Massachusetts.

In 1921, while still in Germany, his first major effort was the application of Gestalt thinking to developmental psychology, as expressed in his book, *The Growth of the Mind*. His was an attempt to show that Gestalt principles apply to all aspects of developmental psychology. Categories such as psychophysical methods, maturation, heredity and environment, reflexes, instincts, motor, sensory, and ideational development are the chapter headings with each topic interpreted from a Gestalt point of view. The choice of topics afforded him the opportunity to be sharply critical of the behaviorist position, since he contrasted it with a Gestalt point of view.

Gestalt psychologists had become sensitive to what they believed to be the mistaken charge by American behaviorists that they were nativistic rather than empirical in outlook, so they tried to be explicit about the matter. Koffka's formulation was in terms of convergence.

We have had occasion to refer repeatedly to conditions other than those of inherited disposition but affecting development—namely, the conditions set by the outer world, or environment. The question now arises: How are these two sets of conditions related to each other? This question, since it involves philosophical, ethical, sociological, and pedagogical consequences, can not be answered off-hand; yet neither can we overlook the fundamental opposition of these two tendencies as they are embodied in the well-known theories of Heredity and Environment. According to the former theory, development is determined in all its important issues by an inherited predisposition; whereas, according to the latter theory, this determination comes chiefly from environment. The same opposition is found in psychology between the rival positions of Nativism and Empiricism, according to which the quality of our perceptions—and especially those of space—is taken to be either an inborn function or a product of experience.

In contrast to both these theories, Stern advances a point of view which he calls the "convergence-theory," and which plays an essential part in his philosophy of personality. 'Mental development," he writes, "is not simply the gradual appearance of inborn qualities, nor a simple acceptance of and a response to outside influences, but the result of a 'convergence' between inner qualities and outer conditions of development. . . . It is never permissible to ask of any function or quality: 'Does this come from within or without?' but rather: 'How much of this comes from within, how much from without?'—for both of these influences always share in its making, only varying in degree at different times."

It is at once apparent that we can not side with either of the extreme theories of heredity or environment; for we have already agreed that learning is essentially a type of development, and learning involves the reaction of the individual to a definite situation wherein the reaction is certainly not unequivocally tied up with inherited dispositions. But before we can proceed we must inquire into the nature of learning, and it seems to me that we can not arrive even at a clear statement of the question—much less at a final decision between psychological empiricism and nativism—so long as the problems of experience itself, and of learning, have neither been solved, nor, indeed, for the most part, recognized as definite problems.

Our aim, therefore, may be characterized by the statement that we are trying to investigate the facts which underlie the formation of all theories, and for this reason we must not allow ourselves to be hindered by the acceptance of any special theory. The concept of convergence advanced by Stern merely indicates a problem which, before it is solved must first be more clearly defined; for at present we do not even know what is meant by saying that "a certain behaviour comes from within or from without."[1]

This principle was extended to psychological events; a convergence between inner and outer factors occurred in all psychological events.

Koffka moved on to the even more ambitious undertaking, the systematizing of Gestalt psychology in general, in his *Principles of Gestalt Psychology,* written after he had arrived in the United States. We begin with his statement of the distinction between a geographical and a behavioral environment based on an old German legend:

... On a winter evening amidst a driving snowstorm a man on horseback arrived at an inn, happy to have reached a shelter after hours of riding over the wind-swept plain on which the blanket of snow had covered all paths and landmarks. The landlord who came to the door viewed the stranger with surprise and asked him whence he came. The man pointed in the direction straight away from the inn, whereupon the landlord, in a tone of awe and wonder, said: "Do you know that you have ridden across the Lake of Constance?" At which the rider dropped stone dead at his feet.

In what environment, then, did the behaviour of the stranger take place? The Lake of Constance. Certainly, because it is a true proposition that he rode across it. And yet, this is not the whole truth, for the fact that there was a frozen lake and not ordinary solid ground did not affect his behaviour in the slightest. It is interesting for the geographer that this behaviour took place in this particular locality, but not for the psychologist as the student of behaviour; because the behaviour would have been just the same had the man ridden across a barren plain. But the psychologist knows something more: since the man died from sheer fright after having learned what he had "really" done, the psychologist must conclude that had the stranger known before, his riding behaviour would have been very different from what it actually was. Therefore the psychologist will have to say: There is a second sense to the word environment according to which our horseman did not ride across the lake at all, but across an ordinary snow-swept plain. His behaviour was a riding-over-a-plain, but not a riding-over-a-lake.[2]

This behavioral environment alone, important though it may be, he contended, is inadequate as the psychological field which Gestalt psychology wishes to study. The argument he offered is complex and manifold, but, suffice it to say, that the solution lies in depending on isomorphism as the bridge between the behavioral and psychological field. This can be noted in the next excerpt by reference to a "psychophysical field" in his statement of the "task of our psychology" instead of to a behavioral or psychological field alone:

And now we can formulate the task of our psychology: it is *the study of behaviour in its causal connection with the psychophysical field.* This general programme must be made more concrete. Anticipating, we can say that the psychophysical field is organized. First of all it shows the polarity of the Ego and the environment, and secondly each of these two polar parts has its own structure. Thus the environment is neither a mosaic of sensations nor a "blooming, buzzing confusion," nor a blurred and vague total unit; rather does it consist of a definite number of separate objects and events, which, as separate objects and events, are products of organization. Likewise, the Ego is neither a point nor a sum or mosaic of drives or instincts. To describe it adequately we shall have to introduce the concept of personality with all its enormous complexity. Therefore if we want to study behaviour as an event in the psychophysical field, we must take the following steps:

(1) We must study the organization of the environmental field, and that means (a) we must find out the forces which organize it into separate objects and events, (b) the forces which exist between these different objects and events; and (c) how these forces produce the environmental field as we know it in our behavioural environment.

(2) We must investigate how such forces can influence movements of the body.

(3) We must study the Ego as one of the main field parts.

(4) We must show that the forces which connect the Ego with the other field parts are of the same nature as those between different parts of the environmental field, and how they produce behaviour in all its forms.

(5) We must not forget that our psychophysical field exists within a real organism which in its turn exists in a geographical environment. In this way the questions of true cognition and adequate or adapted behaviour will also enter our programme.

Points (3) and (4) are the nucleus of a theory of behaviour; (1) and (2) are necessary for their solution. And therefore one cannot wonder that the two problems (3) and (4) have been much less studied than others; moreover, experimentation was started within the province of our first point, both in psychology in general and in gestalt psychology in particular. Therefore the reader must not be surprised when we devote more space to our first point than seems proportionate in consideration of its importance in the whole scheme. The value of theoretical concepts is tested by their application in actual research. The concepts which we have so far developed cannot be understood without a good knowledge of the concrete experimental research work in which they have played the leading rôle. But there is another point to remember. In our fifth item we have touched upon a fundamental philosophical problem. The studies in perception to which my last remarks referred will give us valuable clues for the solution of this philosophical problem. This must be kept in mind if perspective is not to be lost. There will be many experiments, which, though they appear neat and ingenious enough, will seem trivial when seen by themselves. Why such experiments? What can they contribute to a real knowledge of behaviour? The answer is that they serve as demonstrations of general principles; they are not meant to be of great significance in their own right.[3]

It is on the basis of this outline that Koffka gave a systematic statement of Gestalt psychology. One must be struck by the number of conceptions utilized by Gestalt psychologists that have not been caught in our earlier excerpts, for example, the ego "as one of the main field parts," and the references to philosophy. The excerpt brings home that Gestalt psychology has ramifications for many problems and that perception, a central theme stressed in our account of Wertheimer, Köhler, and Koffka, is but part of a larger whole.

In discussing methodology, Koffka dealt squarely with the issue of how the application of phenomenology was different from introspection:

On the Phenomenological Method. Before we continue, a methodological remark may be in place. One can read many American books and articles on psychology without finding any such or similar description, whereas in German works one will meet with them quite frequently. This difference is not superficial, but reveals a thoroughgoing difference in the character of American and German work. Americans will call the German psychology speculative and hairsplitting; Germans will call the American branch superficial. The Americans are justified, when they find an author introducing such descriptions, refining them, playing with them, without really doing anything to them. The Germans are right, because American psychology all too often makes no attempt to look naïvely, without bias, at the facts of direct experience, with the result that American experiments quite often are futile. In reality experimenting *and* observing must go hand in hand. A good description of a phenomenon may by itself rule out a number of theories and indicate definite features which a true theory must possess. We call this kind of observation "phenomenology," a word which has several other meanings which must not be confused with ours. For us phenomenology means as naïve and full a description of direct experience as possible. In America the word "introspection" is the only one used for what we mean, but this word has also a very different meaning in that it refers to a special kind of such description, namely, the one which analyzes direct experience into sensations or attributes, or some other systematic, but not experimental, ultimates.[4]

What was said by Koffka about his own approach to phenomenology applies to those of Wertheimer and Köhler as well. Phenomenological inquiry is a preliminary to research of an empirical nature, not a substitute for it.

Of the three cofounders of Gestalt psychology, Koffka was the most prolific and perhaps the most effective as the spokesperson for Gestalt psychology in America.

40

LEWIN ON
FIELD THEORY
AND ACTION RESEARCH

KURT LEWIN (1890–1947), German-American psychologist, early in his career worked in the Psychological Institute of the University of Berlin where Köhler and Wertheimer had appointments. Although never an orthodox Gestalt psychologist, he was stimulated by Gestalt holism, especially by its concern with the relation of the individual to the psychological environment. In fact, Koffka's preceding excerpt on geographical, behavioral, and psychophysical fields, serves as an introduction to Lewin's work on the life space—that a person lives in a psychological field.

Lewin systematized the psychological characteristics of the field by an analogy with fields of force in physics. These characteristics are derived from or dependent on the total, of which for a time they are parts. People's behavior and experience expend energy and may be defined by the field forces thus exhibited. A summary of some of the properties of field theory follows:

. . . to understand or predict the psychological behavior (B) one has to determine for every kind of psychological event (actions, emotions, expressions, etc.) the momentary whole situation, that is, the momentary structure and the state of the person (P) and of the psychological environment (E). $B = f(PE)$. Every fact that exists psychobiologically must have a position in this field and only facts that have such position have dynamic effects (are causes of events). The environment is for all of its properties (directions, distances, etc.) to be defined not physically but *psychobiologically,* that is, according to its quasi-physical, quasi-social, and quasi-mental structure.

It is possible to represent the dynamic structure of the person and of the environment by means of mathematical concepts. The coordination between the mathematical representation and its psychodynamic meaning has to be strict and without exception.

We shall first describe the psychological field forces and their mode of operation, without consideration of the question whether the object in any particular case has acquired its valence through some previous experience or in some other way .

The first presupposition for the understanding of the child is the determination of the psychological place at which the child concerned is and of his region of freedom of movement, that is, of the regions that are accessible to him and of those regions that psychologically exist for the child but are inaccessible to him by reason of the social situation (prohibition by the adult, limitation by other children, etc.) or because of the limitations of his own social, physical, and intellectual abilities. Whether his region of freedom of movement is large or small is of decisive significance for the whole behavior of the child.

One can characterize these possible and not possible psychodynamic locomotions (quasi-bodily, quasi-social, and quasi-mental locomotions) at every point of the environment with the help of the concept of topology, which is a nonquantitative discipline about the possible kinds of connections between "spaces" and their parts.

The basis for the coordination between mathematical and psychodynamic concepts so far as environmental questions are concerned is the coordination of topological path and psychodynamic locomotion. The topological description determines which points the different paths lead to and which regions these paths cross. The region which a child cannot reach one can characterize by means of barriers between these regions and their neighboring regions. The barrier corresponds as a dynamic concept to the mathematical concept of boundary. One must distinguish between different strengths of barriers. . . .

A force is defined through three properties: (1) direction, (2) strength, and (3) point of application. The first and second properties are to be represented through the mathematical concept *vector*. The point of application is indicated in the figures (as is the custom in physics) by the point of the arrow.

Dynamically the force is correlated with psychobiological locomotions in a one-to-one correspondence. "The real locomotion must occur in every case according to the direction and the strength of the resultant of the momentary forces" and "In any case of locomotion there exists a resultant of forces in its direction."

The direction which the valence imparts to the child's behavior varies extremely, according to the content of the wants and needs. Nevertheless, one may distinguish two large groups of valences according to the sort of initial behavior they elicit: the positive valences (+), those effecting approach; and the negative (−), or those producing withdrawal or retreat.

The *actions* in the direction of the valence may have the form of uncontrolled impulsive behavior or of directed voluntary activity; they may be "appropriate" or "inappropriate."

Those processes which make an especially goal-striving impression are usually characterized dynamically by a reference to a positive valence.

One has to distinguish between *driving* forces, which correspond to positive or negative valences, and *restraining* forces, which correspond to barriers.

Direction of the Field Force. That the valence is not associated merely with a subjective experience of direction, but that a directed force, determinative of the behavior, must be ascribed to it, may be seen in the fact that a change in the position of the attractive object brings about (other things being equal) a change in the direction of the child's movements.

An especially simple example of an action in the direction of a positive valence is illustrated in Fig.... 2. A six-months-old infant stretches arms, legs, and head toward a rattle or a spoonful of porridge in accordance with the direction of the vector (V).

The direction of the field forces plays an important part in such intelligent behavior as has to do with detour [*Umweg*] problems. The child perhaps wants to get a piece of chocolate on the other side of a

Figure 2

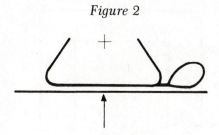

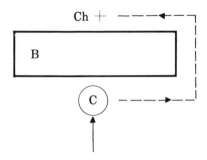

Figure 3.   C, child; Ch, chocolate; B, bench.

bench (see Fig. 3). The difficulty of such a problem consists primarily not in the length of the detour (*D*) but in the fact that the initial direction of the appropriate route does not agree with that of the vector from the valence. The detour is the more difficult, other things being equal, the more the barrier makes it necessary for the child in making the detour to start off in a direction opposed to the direction of the valence (Fig. 4).

The situation is similar when the child wants to take a ring off a stick, while the stick stands so that the ring cannot be pulled directly toward the child, but must first be moved upward or away from himself. Similar forces are operative when a child at a certain age may have difficulties in sitting down on a chair or a stone. The child approaches with his face toward the stone (*S*). In order to sit down he must turn around, that is, execute a movement opposed to the direction of the field force (Fig. 5).

When the child finds the solution of such a detour problem, it happens by reason of a restructuring of the field. There occurs a percep-

Figure 4

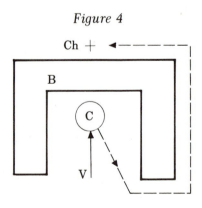

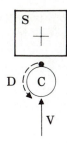

Figure 5

tion of the total situation of such a kind that the path to the goal becomes a unitary whole. The initial part of the route, which objectively is still a moment away from the goal (see Fig. 4), thereby loses psychologically that character and becomes the first phase of a general movement toward the goal.

How critically important the question of *direction* is in this case is indicated by the fact that one cannot force a solution of the detour by increasing the *strength* of the valence. If the attraction is much too weak, it is, to be sure, unfavorable, because the child does not concern himself sufficiently with the affair. But if we continue to strengthen the valence, the solution of the task ceases to be facilitated and instead becomes more difficult. The strength of the attraction then makes it doubly difficult for the child to start in a direction opposed to the field force. Instead, the child will execute, with all its energy, affective meaningless actions in the direction of the valence. . . . Above all, that relative detachment and inward retirement from the valence which are so favorable to perception of the whole situation and hence to the transformation [*Umstrukturierung*] of the total field, which occurs in the act of insight, are made much more difficult. . . . For the same reason, the prospect of an especially intense reward or punishment may impede the solution of intellectual tasks.

To older children of normal intelligence the preceding examples of detour problems offer no difficulty, because they already have a sufficient survey of such situations or corresponding experiences. For them, it no longer requires a special act of intelligence in order that, instead of the spatial directions, the *functional* directions become decisive for the movement.

We may at this point remark a circumstance of general importance: direction in the psychobiological field is not necessarily to be identified with physical direction, but must be defined primarily in psychological terms. The difference between psychological and physical direction appears more prominently in older children. When the child fetches a tool or applies to the experimenter for help, the action does not mean, even when it involves a physical movement in a direction opposite to the goal, a turning away from the goal but an approach to it. Such indirect approaches are more rare among babies. This is due to the slighter functional differentiation of their environment and to the fact that *social* structure has not yet the overwhelming significance for them that it has for older children.[1]

   The field with which Lewin was concerned was not the brain field isomorphic with the experience of the individual as it was for the Gestalt psychologists, for example, (p. 301) but rather the environment of the person, including other individuals. Hence, his was a social psychological approach to the motivational forces working on the individual and expressed by him through relating need, valence, and vector which had been adapted from mathematical topological theory and vector analysis, the former supplying the life space, the latter, the motives of the individual.

   Lewin remained at the University of Berlin until the early 1930s; thereafter, he held appointments at Stanford, Cornell, Iowa, and the Massachusetts Institute of Technology, where he was director of the Research Center for Group Dynamics. As the name implies, he had now come to stress motivational factors in groups. This research occurred both in laboratory and social settings. Lewin became interested in "action research," that is, the investigation of a contemporary social problem while it is taking place.

   A characteristic expression of this interest is to be found in his discussion of an attempt to produce change in intergroup minority relations.

One example may illustrate the potentialities of co-operation between practitioners and social scientists. In the beginning of this year the Chairman of the Advisory Committee on Race Relations for the State of Connecticut, who is at the same time a leading member of the Interracial Commission of the State of Connecticut, approached us with a request to conduct a workshop for fifty community workers in the field of intergroup relations from all over the state of Connecticut.

   A project emerged in which three agencies co-operated, the Advisory Committee on Intergroup Relations of the State of Connecticut, The Commission on Community Interrelations of the American Jewish Congress, and the Research Center for Group Dynamics at the Massachusetts Institute of Technology. The State Advisory Committee is composed of members of the Interracial Commission of the State of Connecticut, a member of the State Department of Education of the State of Connecticut, and the person in charge of the Connecticut Valley Region of the Conference of Christians and Jews. The state of Connecticut seems to be unique in having an interracial commission as a part of its regular government. It was apparent that any improvement of techniques which could be linked with this strategic central body would have a much better chance of a wide-spread and lasting effect. After a thorough discussion of various possibilities the following change-experiment was designed cooperatively.

Recent research findings have indicated that the ideologies and stereotypes which govern inter-group relations should not be viewed as individual character traits but that they are anchored in cultural standards, that their stability and their change depend largely on happenings in groups as groups. Experience with leadership training had convinced us that the workshop setting is among the most powerful tools for bringing about improvement of skill in handling inter-group relations.

Even a good and successful workshop, however, seems seldom to have the chance to lead to long-range improvements in the field of inter-group relations. The individual who comes home from the workshop full of enthusiasm and new insights will again have to face the community, one against perhaps 100,000. Obviously, the chances are high that his success will not be up to his new level of aspiration, and that soon disappointments will set him back again. We are facing here a question which is of prime importance for any social change, namely the problem of its permanence.

To test certain hypotheses in regard to the effect of individual as against group settings, the following variations were introduced into the experimental workshop. Part of the delegates came as usual, one individual from a town. For a number of communities, however, it was decided the attempt would be made to secure a number of delegates and if possible to develop in the workshop teams who would keep up their team relationship after the workshop. This should give a greater chance for permanency of the enthusiasm and group productivity and should also multiply the power of the participants to bring about the desired change. A third group of delegates to the workshop would receive a certain amount of expert help even after they returned to the community.

The first step in carrying out such a design calls for broad factfinding about the different types of inter-group problems which the various communities have to face. Communities and teams of group workers in the communities would have to be selected so that the results of the three variations would be possible to compare. In other words, this project had to face the same problems which we mention as typical for the planning process in general.

The experiences of the members of the State Advisory Board of the Interracial Commission of the State of Connecticut were able quickly to provide sufficient data to determine the towns which should be studied more accurately. To evaluate the effect of the workshop a diagnosis before the workshop would have to be carried out to determine, among other things, the line of thinking of the community workers, their main line of action and the main barriers they have to face. A similar rediagnosis would have to be carried out some months after the workshop.

To understand why the workshop produced whatever change or lack of change would be found, it is obviously necessary to record scientifically the essential happenings during the workshop. Here, I feel, research faces its most difficult task. To record the content of the lecture or the program would by no means suffice. Description of the form of leadership has to take into account the amount of initiative shown by individuals and subgroups, the division of the trainees into subgroups, the frictions within and between these subgroups, the crises and their outcome, and, above all, the total management pattern as it changes from day to day. These large-scale aspects, more than anything else, seem to determine what a workshop will accomplish. The task which social scientists have to face in objectively recording these data is not too different from that of the historian. We will have to learn to handle these relatively large units of periods and social bodies without lowering the standards of validity and reliability to which we are accustomed to in the psychological recording of the more microscopic units of action and periods of minutes or seconds of activity.

The methods of recording the essential events of the workshop included an evaluation session at the end of every day. Observers who had attended the various subgroup sessions reported (into a recording machine) the leadership pattern they had observed, the progress or lack of progress in the development of the groups from a conglomeration of individuals to an integrated "we" and so on. The group leaders gave their view of the same sessions and a number of trainees added their comments.

I have been deeply impressed with the tremendous pedagogical effect which these evaluation meetings, designed for the purpose of scientific recording, had on the training process. The atmosphere of objectivity, the readiness by the faculty to discuss openly their mistakes, far from endangering their position, seemed to lead to an enhancement of appreciation and to bring about that mood of relaxed objectivity which is nowhere more difficult to achieve than in the field of inter-group relations which is loaded with emotionality and attitude rigidity even among the so-called liberals and those whose job it is to promote inter-group relations.

This and similar experiences have convinced me that we should consider action, research, and training as a triangle that should be kept to improve the action pattern without training personnel. In fact today the lack of competent training personnel is one of the greatest hindrances to progress in setting up more experimentation. The training of large numbers of social scientists who can handle scientific problems but are also equipped for the delicate task of building productive, hard-hitting teams with practitioners is a prerequisite for progress in social science as well as in social management for intergroup relations.

As I watched, during the workshop, the delegates from different towns all over Connecticut transform from a multitude of unrelated individuals, frequently opposed in their outlook and their interests, into cooperative teams not on the basis of sweetness but on the basis of readiness to face difficulties realistically, to apply honest fact-finding, and to work together to overcome them; when I saw the pattern of role-playing emerge, saw the major responsibilities move slowly according to plan from the faculty to the trainees; when I saw, in the final session, the State Advisory Committee receive the backing of the delegates for a plan of linking the teachers colleges throughout the state with certain aspects of group relations within the communities; when I heard the delegates and teams of delegates from various towns present their plans for city workshops and a number of other projects to go into realization immediately, I could not help feeling that the close integration of action, training, and research holds tremendous possibilities for the field of inter-group relations. I would like to pass on this feeling to you.

Inter-group relations are doubtless one of the most crucial aspects on the national and international scene. We know today better than ever before that they are potentially dynamite. The strategy of social research must take into account the dangers involved.

We might distinguish outside adversities and barriers to social science and the inner dangers of research procedures. Among the first we find a group of people who seem to subscribe to the idea that we do not need more social science. Among these admirers of common sense we find practitioners of all types, politicians and college presidents. Unfortunately there are a good number of physical scientists among those who are against a vigorous promotion of the social sciences. They seem to feel that the social sciences have not produced something of real value for the practice of social management and therefore will never do so. I guess there is no other way to convince these people than by producing better social science.

A second threat to social science comes from "groups in power." These people can be found in management on any level, among labor leaders, among politicians, some branches of the government, and among members of Congress. Somehow or other they all seem to be possessed by the fear that they could not do what they want to do if they, and others, really knew the facts. I think social scientists should be careful to distinguish between the legitimate and not legitimate elements behind this fear. For instance, it would be most unhealthy if the findings of the Gallup Poll were automatically to determine policy for what should and should not become law in the United States. We will have to recognize the difference between fact-finding and policy setting and to study carefully the procedures by which fact-finding should be fed into the social machinery of legislation to produce a democratic effect.

Doubtless, however, a good deal of unwillingness to face reality lies behind the enmity to social research of some of the people in power positions.

A third type of very real anxiety on the part of practitioners can be illustrated by the following example. Members of community councils to whom I have had the occasion to report results of research on group interrelations reacted with the feeling that the social scientists at the university or in the research arm of some national organization would sooner or later be in the position to tell the local community workers all over the states exactly what to do and what not to do.

They obviously envisaged a social science "technocracy." This fear seems to be a very common misunderstanding based on the term "law." The community workers failed to realize that lawfulness in social as in physical science means an "if so" relation, a linkage between hypothetical conditions and hypothetical effects. These laws do *not* tell *what* conditions exist locally, at a given place at a given time. In other words, the laws don't do the job of diagnosis which has to be done locally. Neither do laws prescribe the strategy for change. In social management, as in medicine, the practitioner will usually have the choice between various methods of treatment and he will require as much skill and ingenuity as the physician in regard to both diagnosis and treatment.

It seems to be crucial for the progress of social science that the practitioner understand that through social sciences and only through them he can hope to gain the power necessary to do a good job. Unfortunately there is nothing in social laws and social research which will force the practitioner toward the good. Science gives more freedom and power to both the doctor and the murderer, to democracy and Fascism. The social scientist should recognize his responsibility also in respect to this.[2]

Lewin's adroitness in transforming a life problem into a controlled research study, that is action research, was to broaden and invigorate social psychology in a unique and important way, and still is very much part of contemporary social psychology.

41

FREUD ON

PSYCHOANALYSIS AS
A METHOD OF INVESTIGATION,
A MEANS OF TREATMENT,
AND A SYSTEM OF PSYCHOLOGY

SIGMUND FREUD (1856–1939), Austrian psychoanalyst, introduced and developed psychoanalysis. At first he worked alone, but at
about the turn of the century, he attracted fellow workers, some of whom
stayed within the field while others, including Alfred Adler (p. 342) and
Carl Jung (p. 351), developed independent approaches. Until the advent
of Hitler's occupation of Austria, Freud lived and practiced in Vienna.

He conceived psychoanalysis to be a method of psychological investigation, a means of treatment, and a theoretical psychological system.
All aspects had their origin in the clinical relation of therapist to patient.
Since this setting is so different from that heretofore found in psychology's earlier basic writings, a considerable portion of the account will be
given over to its description.

Early in his medical career, Freud had used a variety of methods to
treat his neurotic patients, including face-to-face questioning, elec-
trotherapy, and hypnosis, but found these methods disappointingly ineffective. From suggestions of patients, from reading, and from the professional assistance of Josef Breuer, an older Viennese physician, he created
the method of free association—to allow one's thoughts to flow without
critical selection of any sort in reporting. This process of letting one's
mind go, saying whatever occurred to one, holding back nothing, although akin to that very facile process of day-dreaming, turned out to be
very difficult for the patient to express to the therapist. On the patient's
part there was a strong tendency to avoid what turned out to be the
crucial factors to understanding and cure of his problems by rearranging,
by "making sense," by making comments socially acceptable.

An illustration of the workings of free association is provided below. It is atypical only in that, rather than being in the clinical setting, it
occurred in the course of a conversation with an acquaintance who was
familiar with his work. This young man stumbled over a word in a quota-

tion from Virgil, during which he omitted the word "aliquis." To continue:

'How stupid to forget a word like that! By the way, you claim that one never forgets a thing without some reason. I should be very curious to learn how I came to forget the indefinite pronoun "*aliquis*" in this case.'

I took up this challenge most readily, for I was hoping for a contribution to my collection. So I said: 'That should not take us long. I must only ask you to tell me, *candidly* and *uncritically*, whatever comes into your mind if you direct your attention to the forgotten word without any definite aim.'*

'Good. There springs to my mind, then, the ridiculous notion of dividing up the word like this: *a* and *liquis*.'

'What does that mean?' 'I don't know.' 'And what occurs to you next?' 'What comes next is *Reliquien* [relics], *liquefying, fluidity, fluid.* Have you discovered anything so far?'

'No. Not by any means yet. But go on.'

'I am thinking', he went on with a scornful laugh, 'of *Simon of Trent,* whose relics I saw two years ago in a church at Trent. I am thinking of the accusation of ritual blood-sacrifice which is being brought against the Jews again just now, and of *Kleinpaul's* book [1892] in which he regards all these supposed victims as incarnations, one might say new editions, of the Saviour.'

'The notion is not entirely unrelated to the subject we were discussing before the Latin word slipped your memory.'

'True. My next thoughts are about an article that I read lately in an Italian newspaper. Its title, I think, was "What St. *Augustine* says about Women." What do you make of that?'

'I am waiting.'

'And now comes something that is quite clearly unconnected with our subject.'

'Please refrain from any criticism and————'

'Yes, I understand. I am thinking of a fine old gentleman I met on my travels last week. He was a real *original,* with all the appearance of a huge bird of prey. His name was *Benedict,* if it's of interest to you.'

'Anyhow, here are a row of saints and Fathers of the Church: St. *Simon,* St. *Augustine,* St. *Benedict.* There was, I think, a Church Father

---

*"This is the general method of introducing concealed ideational elements to consciousness. Cf. my *Interpretation of Dreams, Standard Ed.*, 4, 101."

called *Origen*. Moreover, three of these names are also first names, like *Paul* in *Kleinpual.*'

'Now it's St. *Januarius* and the miracle of his blood that comes into my mind—my thoughts seem to me to be running on mechanically.'

'Just a moment: St. *Januarius* and St. *Augustine* both have to do with the calendar. But won't you remind me about the miracle of his blood?'

'Surely you must have heard of that? They keep the blood of St. Januarius in a phial inside a church at Naples, and on a particular holy day it miraculously *liquefies*. The people attach great importance to this miracle and get very excited if it's delayed, as happened once at a time when the French were occupying the town. So the general in command—or have I got it wrong? was it Garibaldi?—took the reverend gentleman aside and gave him to understand, with an unmistakable gesture towards the soldiers posted outside, that he *hoped* the miracle would take place very soon. And in fact it did take place . . .'

'Well, go on. Why do you pause?'

'Well, something *has* come into my mind . . . but it's too intimate to pass on. . . . Besides, I don't see any connection, or any necessity for saying it.'

'You can leave the connections to me. Of course I can't force you to talk about something that you find distasteful; but then you mustn't insist on learning from me how you came to forget your *aliquis*.'

'Really? Is that what you think? Well then, I've suddenly thought of a lady from whom I might easily hear a piece of news that would be very awkward for both of us.'

'That her periods have stopped?'

'How could you guess that?'

'That's not difficult any longer; you've prepared the way sufficiently. Think of *the calendar saints, the blood that starts to flow on a particular day, the disturbance when the event fails to take place, the open threats that the miracle must be vouchsafed, or else* . . . In fact you've made use of the miracle of St. Januarius to manufacture a brilliant allusion to women's periods.'

'Without being aware of it. And you really mean to say that it was this anxious expectation that made me unable to produce an unimportant word like *aliquis*?'

'It seems to me undeniable. You need only recall the division you made into *a-liquis*, and your associations: *relics, liquefying, fluid*. St. Simon was *sacrificed as a child*—shall I go on and show how he comes in? You were led on to him by the subject of relics.

'No, I'd much rather you didn't. I hope you don't take these thoughts of mine too seriously, if indeed I really had them. In return I will confess to you that the lady is Italian and that I went to Naples with her. But mayn't all this just be a matter of chance?'

'I must leave it to your own judgement to decide whether you can explain all these connections by the assumption that they are matters of chance. I can however tell you that every case like this that you care to analyse will lead you to "matters of chance" that are just as striking.'[1]

The use of the expression, "my collection" in the excerpt refers to the fact that he was in the process of preparing the book from which the excerpt is derived, concerned with the unconscious significance of *The Psychopathology of Every Day Life,* as expressed in the forgetting of names and words, in mistakes in speech, in "chance" actions, and the like. Essentially, it is a volume devoted to showing that what these many reported incidents have in common is that they reveal unconscious desires of which the individuals were unaware and were reluctant to impart.

The same paragraph just referred to contains a version of what Freud considered the fundamental mandate of free association, an unembellished frankness demanded of the patient in presenting thoughts.

The determination of the psychological significance of dreams was another facet of his approach. To Freud, dreams have meaning; unconscious desires can be identified by the psychoanalyst and the patient by mutual analysis through the method of free association, expressed by asking the patient of what each fragment of the dream makes him think. What is sought in the dream is its significance, the so-called latent content, in the midst of the actual incidents, the manifest content.

A major source of his first experiences with dreams came from Freud's analysis of his own dreams. What follows is a dream in which the central figure is Irma, a patient who was also a friend of the family. Freud believed her treatment had been a partial success and she had been cured of some, but not all, of her symptoms. Treatment had been discontinued for the summer holidays, and when Otto, a younger colleague, called on Freud, in the course of the conversation, Freud asked him how Irma was. Freud received an annoying reply, since it seemed to imply that Otto did not approve of the treatment Freud had given her. That night, Freud had the following dream, followed by his interpretations of it.

A large hall—numerous guests, whom we were receiving.—Among them was Irma. I at once took her on one side, as though to answer her letter and to reproach her for not having accepted my 'solution' yet. I said to her: 'If you still get pains, it's really only your fault.' She replied: 'If you only knew what pains I've got now in my throat and stomach and abdomen—it's choking me'—I was alarmed and looked at her. She looked pale and puffy. I thought to myself that after all I must be missing some organic trouble. I took her to the window and looked down her throat, and she showed signs of recalcitrance, like women with artificial dentures. I thought to myself that there was really no need for her to do that.—She then opened her mouth properly and on the right I found a big white patch; at another place I saw extensive whitish grey scabs upon some remarkable curly structures which were evidently modelled on the turbinal bones of the nose.—I at once called in Dr. M., and he repeated the examination and confirmed it. . . . Dr. M. looked quite different from usual; he was very pale, he walked with a limp and his chin was clean-shaven. . . . My friend Otto was now standing beside her as well, and my friend Leopold was percussing her through her bodice and saying: 'She has a dull area low down on the left.' He also indicated that a portion of the skin on the left shoulder was infiltrated. (I noticed this, just as he did, in spite of her dress.) . . . M. said: 'There's no doubt it's an infection, but no matter; dysentery will supervene and the toxin will be eliminated.' . . . We were directly aware, too, of the origin of the infection. Not long before, when she was feeling unwell, my friend Otto had given her an injection of a preparation of propyl, propyls . . . propionic acid . . . trimethylamin (and I saw before me the formula for this printed in heavy type). . . .Injections of that sort ought not to be made so thoughtlessly. . . . And probably the syringe had not been clean.

This dream has one advantage over many others. It was immediately clear what events of the previous day provided its starting-point. My preamble makes that plain. The news which Otto had given me of Irma's condition and the case history which I had been engaged in writing till far into the night continued to occupy my mental activity even after I was asleep. Nevertheless, no one who had only read the preamble and the content of the dream itself could have the slightest notion of what the dream meant. I myself had no notion. I was astonished at the symptoms of which Irma complained to me in the dream, since they were not the same as those for which I had treated her. I smiled at the senseless idea of an injection of propionic acid and at Dr. M.'s consoling reflections. Towards its end the dream seemed to me to be more obscure and compressed than it was at the beginning. In order to discover the meaning of all this it was necessary to undertake a detailed analysis.

ANALYSIS

The hall—numerous guests, whom we were receiving. We were spending that summer at Bellevue, a house standing by itself on one of the hills adjoining the Kahlenberg. The house had formerly been designed as a place of entertainment and its reception-rooms were in consequence unusually lofty and hall-like. It was at Bellevue that I had the dream, a few days before my wife's birthday. On the previous day my wife had told me that she expected that a number of friends, including Irma, would be coming out to visit us on her birthday. My dream was thus anticipating this occasion: it was my wife's birthday and a number of guests, including Irma, were being received by us in the large hall at Bellevue.

I reproached Irma for not having accepted my solution; I said: 'If you still get pains, it's your own fault.' I might have said this to her in waking life, and I may actually have done so. It was my view at that time (though I have since recognized it as a wrong one) that my task was fulfilled when I had informed a patient of the hidden meaning of his symptoms: I considered that I was not responsible for whether he accepted the solution or not—though this was what success depended on. I owe it to this mistake, which I have now fortunately corrected, that my life was made easier at a time when, in spite of all my inevitable ignorance, I was expected to produce therapeutic successes.—I noticed, however, that the words which I spoke to Irma in the dream showed that I was specially anxious not to be responsible for the pains which she still had. If they were her fault they could not be mine. Could it be that the purpose of the dream lay in this direction?

Irma's complaint: pains in her throat and abdomen and stomach; it was choking her. Pains in the stomach were among my patient's symptoms but were not very prominent; she complained more of feelings of nausea and disgust. Pains in the throat and abdomen and constriction of the throat played scarcely any part in her illness. I wondered why I decided upon this choice of symptoms in the dream but could not think of an explanation at the moment.

She looked pale and puffy. My patient always had a rosy complexion. I began to suspect that someone else was being substituted for her.

I was alarmed at the idea that I had missed an organic illness. This, as may well be believed, is a perpetual source of anxiety to a specialist whose practice is almost limited to neurotic patients and who is in the habit of attributing to hysteria a great number of symptoms which other physicians treat as organic. On the other hand, a faint doubt crept into my mind—from where, I could not tell—that my alarm was not entirely genuine. If Irma's pains had an organic basis, once again I could not to be held responsible for curing them; my treatment only set out to get rid of *hysterical* pains. It occurred to me, in fact, that I was actually *wishing* that there had been a wrong diagnosis; for, if so, the blame for my lack of success would also have been got rid of.

I took her to the window to look down her throat. She showed some recalcitrance, like women with false teeth. I thought to myself that really there was no need for her to do that. I had never had any occasion to examine Irma's oral cavity. What happened in the dream reminded me of an examination I had carried out some time before of a governess: at a first glance she had seemed a picture of youthful beauty, but when it came to opening her mouth she had taken measures to conceal her plates. This led to recollections of other medical examinations and of little secrets revealed in the course of them—to the satisfaction of neither party. *'There was really no need for her to do that'* was no doubt intended in the first place as a compliment to Irma; but I suspected that it had another meaning besides. (If one carries out an analysis attentively, one gets a feeling of whether or not one has exhausted all the background thoughts that are to be expected.) The way in which Irma stood by the window suddenly reminded me of another experience. Irma had an intimate woman friend of whom I had a very high opinion. When I visited this lady one evening I had found her by a window in the situation reproduced in the dream, and her physician, the same Dr. M., had pronounced that she had a diphtheritic membrane. The figure of Dr. M. and the membrane reappear later in the dream. It now occurred to me that for the last few months I had had every reason to suppose that this other lady was also a hysteric. Indeed, Irma herself had betrayed the fact to me. What did I know of her condition? One thing precisely: that, like my Irma of the dream, she suffered from hysterical choking. So in the dream I had replaced my patient by her friend. I now recollected that I had often played with the idea that she too might ask me to relieve her of her symptoms. I myself, however, had thought this unlikely, since she was of a very reserved nature. She was *recalcitrant,* as was shown in the dream. Another reason was that *there was no need for her to do it*: she had so far shown herself strong enough to master her condition without outside help. There still remained a few features that I could not attach either to Irma or to her friend: *pale; puffy; false teeth.* The false teeth took me to the governess whom I have already mentioned; I now felt inclined to be satisfied with *bad* teeth. I then thought of someone else to whom these features might be alluding. She again was not one of my patients, nor should I have liked to have her as a patient, since I had noticed that she was bashful in my presence and I could not think she would make an amenable patient. She was usually pale, and once, while she had been in specially good health, she had looked puffy. † Thus I had been comparing my patient Irma with two other people who would also have been recalcitrant to treatment. What could the reason have been for my having exchanged her in the dream for her friend? Perhaps it was that I should have *liked* to exchange her: either I felt more sympathetic towards her friend or had a higher opinion of her intelligence. For Irma seemed to me foolish because she had not accepted my solution. Her friend would have been wiser, that is to say she would have yielded sooner. She would then have *opened her mouth properly,* and have told me more than Irma. ‡

What I saw in her throat: a white patch and turbinal bones with scabs on them. The white patch reminded me of diphtheritis and so of Irma's friend, but also of a serious illness of my eldest daughter's almost two years earlier and of the fright I had had in those anxious days. The scabs on the turbinal bones recalled a worry about my own state of health. I was making frequent use of cocaine at that time to reduce some troublesome nasal swellings, and I had heard a few days earlier that one of my women patients who had followed my example had developed an extensive necrosis of the nasal mucous membrane. I had been the first to recommend the use of cocain, in 1885, § and this recommendation had brought serious reproaches down on me. The misuse of that drug had hastened the death of a dear friend of mine. This had been before 1895 [the date of the dream].

I at once called in Dr. M., and he repeated the examination. This simply corresponded to the position occupied by M. in our circle. But the *'at once'* was sufficiently striking to require a special explanation. It reminded me of a tragic event in my practice. I had on one occasion produced a severe toxic state in a woman patient by repeatedly prescrib-

---

† "The still unexplained complaint about *pains in the abdomen* could also be traced back to this third figure. The person in question was, of course, my own wife; the pains in the abdomen reminded me of one of the occasions on which I had noticed her bashfulness. I was forced to admit to myself that I was not treating either Irma or my wife very kindly in this dream; but it should be observed by way of excuse that I was measuring them both by the standard of the good and amenable patient."

‡ "I had a feeling that the interpretation of this part of the dream was not carried far enough to make it possible to follow the whole of its concealed meaning. If I had pursued my comparison between the three women, it would have taken me far afield.—There is at lest one spot in every dream at which it is unplumbable—a navel, as it were, that is its point of contact with the unknown. . . ."

§ "[This is a misprint (which occurs in every German edition) for '1884,' the date of Freud's first paper on cocaine. A full account of Freud's work in connection with cocaine will be found in Chapter VI of the first volume of Ernest Jones's life of Freud. From this it appears that the 'dear friend' was Fleischl von Marxow. . . .]"

ing what was at that time regarded as a harmless remedy (sulphonal), and had hurriedly turned for assistance and support to my experienced senior colleague. There was a subsidiary detail which confirmed the idea that I had this incident in mind. My patient—who succumbed to the poison—had the same name as my eldest daughter. It had never occurred to me before, but it struck me now almost like an act of retribution on the part of destiny. It was as though the replacement of one person by another was to be continued in another sense: this Mathilde for that Mathilde, an eye for an eye and a tooth for a tooth. It seemed as if I had been collecting all the occasions which I could bring up against myself as evidence of lack of medical conscientiousness.

Dr. M. was pale, had a clean-shaven chin and walked with a limp. This was true to the extent that his unhealthy appearance often caused his friends anxiety. The two other features could only apply to someone else. I thought of my elder brother, who lives abroad, who is clean-shaven and whom, if I remembered right, the M. of the dream closely resembled. We had had news a few days earlier that he was walking with a limp owing to an arthritic affection of his hip. There must, I reflected, have been some reason for my fusing into one the two figures in the dream. I then remembered that I had a similar reason for being in an ill-humour with each of them: they had both rejected a certain suggestion I had recently laid before them.

My friend Otto was now standing beside the patient and my friend Leopold was examining her and indicated that there was a dull area low down on the left. My friend Leopold was also a physician and a relative of Otto's. Since they both specialized in the same branch of medicine, it was their fate to be in competition with each other, and comparisons were constantly being drawn between them. Both of them acted as my assistants for years while I was still in charge of the neurological out-patients' department of a children's hospital.' Scenes such as the one represented in the dream used often to occur there. While I was discussing the diagnosis of a case with Otto, Leopold would be examining the child once more and would make an unexpected contribution to our decision. The difference between their characters was like that between the bailiff Bräsig and his friend Karl.r: one was distinguished for his

---

' "[For details of this hospital see Section II of Kris's introduction to the Fliess correspondence. . . .]"

r"[The two chief figures in the once popular novel, *Ut mine Stromtid*, written in Mecklenburg dialect, by Fritz Reuter (1862-4). There is an English translation, *An Old Story of my Farming Days* (London, 1878).]"

quickness, while the other was slow but sure. If in the dream I was contrasting Otto with the prudent Leopold, I was evidently doing so to the advantage of the latter. The comparison was similar to the one between my disobedient patient Irma and the friend whom I regarded as wiser than she was. I now perceived another of the lines along which the chain of thought in the dream branched off: from the sick child to the children's hospital.—*The dull area low down on the left* seemed to me to agree in every detail with one particular case in which Leopold had struck me by his thoroughness. I also had a vague notion of something in the nature of a metastatic affection; but this may also have been a reference to the patient whom I should have liked to have in the place of Irma. So far as I had been able to judge, she had produced an imitation of a tuberculosis.

A portion of the skin on the left shoulder was infiltrated. I saw at once that this was the rheumatism in my own shoulder, which I invariably notice if I sit up late into the night. Moreover the wording in the dream was most ambiguous: '*I noticed this, just as he did. . . .*' I noticed it in my own body, that is. I was struck, too, by the unusual phrasing: 'a portion of the skin was infiltrated'. We are in the habit of speaking of 'a left upper posterior infiltration,' and this would refer to the lung and so once more to tuberculosis.

In spite of her dress. This was in any case only an interpolation. We naturally used to examine the children in the hospital undressed: and this would be a contrast to the manner in which adult female patients have to be examined. I remembered that it was said of a celebrated clinician that he never made a physical examination of his patients except through their clothes. Further than this I could not see. Frankly, I had no desire to penetrate more deeply at this point.

Dr. M. said: 'It's an infection, but no matter. Dysentery will supervene and the toxin will be eliminated.' At first this struck me as ridiculous. But nevertheless, like all the rest, it had to be carefully analysed. When I came to look at it more closely it seemed to have some sort of meaning all the same. What I discovered in the patient was a local diphtheritis. I remembered from the time of my daughter's illness a discussion on diphtheritis and diphtheria, the latter being the general infection that arises from the local diphtheritis. Leopold indicated the presence of a general infection of this kind from the existence of a dull area, which might thus be regarded as a metastatic focus. I seemed to think, it is true, that metastases like this do not in fact occur with diphtheria: it made me think rather of pyaemia.

No matter. This was intended as a consolation. It seemed to fit into the context as follows. The content of the preceding part of the dream had been that my patient's pains were due to a severe organic affection. I had a feeling that I was only trying in that way to shift the blame from myself. Psychological treatment could not be held responsible for the persistence of diphtheritic pains. Nevertheless I had a sense of awkwardness at having invented such a severe illness for Irma simply in order to clear myself. It looked so cruel. Thus I was in need of an assurance that all would be well in the end, and it seemed to me that to have put the consolation into the mouth precisely of Dr. M. had not been a bad choice. But here I was taking up a superior attitude towards the dream, and this itself required explanation.

And why was the consolation so nonsensical?

Dysentery. There seemed to be some remote theoretical notion that morbid matter can be eliminated through the bowels. Could it be that I was trying to make fun of Dr. M.'s fertility in producing far-fetched explanations and making unexpected pathological connections? Something else now occurred to me in relation to dysentery. A few months earlier I had taken on the case of a young man with remarkable difficulties associated with defaecating, who had been treated by other physicians as a case of 'anaemia accompanied by malnutrition.' I had recognized it as a hysteria, but had been unwilling to try him with my psychotherapeutic treatment and had sent him on a sea voyage. Some days before, I had had a despairing letter from him from Egypt, saying that he had had a fresh attack there which a doctor had declared was dysentery. I suspected that the diagnosis was an error on the part of an ignorant practitioner who had allowed himself to be taken in by the hysteria. But I could not help reproaching myself for having put my patient in a situation in which he might have contracted some organic trouble on top of his hysterical intestinal disorder. Moreover 'dysentery' sounds not unlike 'diphtheria'—a word of ill omen which did not occur in the dream.** Yes, I thought to myself, I must have been making fun of Dr. M. with the consoling prognosis 'Dysentery will supervene, etc.': for it came back to me that, years before, he himself had told an amusing story of a similar kind about another doctor. Dr. M. had been called in by him for consultation over a patient who was seriously ill, and had felt obliged to point out, in view of the very optimistic view taken by his colleague, that he had found albumen in the patient's urine. The other, however, was not in the least put out: '*No matter*', he had said, 'the albumen will soon be eliminated!'—I could no longer feel any doubt, therefore, that this

***"[The German words '*Dysenterie*' and '*Diphtherie*' are more alike than the English ones.]"

part of the dream was expressing derision at physicians who are ignorant of hysteria. And, as though to confirm this, a further idea crossed my mind: 'Does Dr. M. realize that the symptoms in his patient (Irma's friend) which give grounds for fearing tuberculosis also have a hysterical basis? Has he spotted this hysteria? or has he been taken in by it?'

But what could be my motive for treating this friend of mine so badly? That was a very simple matter. Dr. M. was just as little in agreement with my 'solution' as Irma herself. So I had already revenged myself in this dream on two people: on Irma with the words 'If you still get pains, it's your own fault', and on Dr. M. by the wording of the nonsensical consolation that I put into his mouth.

We were directly aware of the origin of the infection. This direct knowledge in the dream was remarkable. Only just before we had had no knowledge of it, for the infection was only revealed by Leopold.

When she was feeling unwell, my friend Otto had given her an injection. Otto had in fact told me that during his short stay with Irma's family he had been called in to a neighbouring hotel to give an injection to someone who had suddenly felt unwell. These injections reminded me once more of my unfortunate friend who had poisoned himself with cocaine. . . . I had advised him to use the drug internally [i.e. orally] only, while morphia was being withdrawn; but he had at once given himself cocaine *injections*.

A preparation of propyl . . . propyls . . . propionic acid. How could I have come to think of this? During the previous evening, before I wrote out the case history and had the dream, my wife had opened a bottle of liqueur, on which the word 'Ananas'†† appeared and which was a gift from our friend Otto: for he has a habit of making presents on every possible occasion. It was to be hoped, I thought to myself, that some day he would find a wife to cure him of the habit.‡‡ This liqueur gave off such a strong smell of fusel oil that I refused to touch it. My wife suggested our giving the bottle to the servants, but I—with even greater prudence—vetoed the suggestion, adding in a philanthropic spirit that there was no need for *them* to be poisoned either. The smell of fusel oil (amyl . . .) evidently stirred up in my mind a recollection of the whole series—propyl, methyl,

††"I must add that the sound of the word 'Ananas' bears a remarkable resemblance to that of my patient Irma's family name."

‡‡"[*Footnote added* 1909, but omitted again from 1925 onwards:]In this respect the dream did not turn out to be prophetic. But in another respect it *was*. For my patient's 'unsolved' gastric pains, for which I was so anxious not to be blamed, turned out to be the forerunners of a serious disorder caused by gall-stones."

and so on—and this accounted for the propyl preparation in the dream. It is true that I carried out a substitution in the process: I dreamt of propyl after having smelt amyl. But substitutions of this kind are perhaps legitimate in organic chemistry.

Trimethylamin. I saw the chemical formula of this substance in my dream, which bears witness to a great effort on the part of my memory. Moreover the formula was printed in heavy type, as though there had been a desire to lay emphasis on some part of the context as being of quite special importance. What was it, then, to which my attention was to be directed in this way by trimethylamin? It was to a conversation with another friend who had for many years been familiar with all my writings during the period of their gestation, just as I had been with his. §§ He had at that time confided some ideas to me on the subject of the chemistry of the sexual processes, and had mentioned among other things that he believed that one of the products of sexual metabolism was trimethylamin. Thus this substance led me to sexuality, the factor to which I attributed the greatest importance in the origin of the nervous disorders which it was my aim to cure. My patient Irma was a young widow; if I wanted to find an excuse for the failure of my treatment in her case, what I could best appeal to would no doubt be this fact of her widowhood, which her friends would be so glad to see changed. And how strangely, I thought to myself, a dream like this is put together! The other woman, whom I had as a patient in the dream instead of Irma, was also a young widow.

I began to guess why the formula for trimethylamin had been so prominent in the dream. So many important subjects converged upon that one word. Trimethylamin was an allusion not only to the immensely powerful factor of sexuality, but also to a person whose agreement I recalled with satisfaction whenever I felt isolated in my opinions. Surely this friend who played so large a part in my life must appear again elsewhere in these trains of thought. Yes. For he had a special knowledge of the consequences of affections of the nose and its accessory cavities; and he had drawn scientific attention to some very remarkable connections between the turbinal bones and the female organs of sex. (Cf. the three curly structures in Irma's throat.) I had had Irma examined by him to see whether her gastric pains might be of nasal origin. But he suffered himself from suppurative rhinitis, which caused me anxiety; and no doubt

---

§§ "[This was Wilhelm Fliess the Berlin biologist and nose and throat specialist, who exercised a great influence on Freud during the years immediately preceding the publication of this book, and who figures frequently, though as a rule anonymously, in its pages. . . .]"

there was an allusion to this in the pyaemia which vaguely came into my mind in connection with the metastases in the dream.

Injections of that sort ought not to be made so thoughtlessly. Here an accusation of thoughtlessness was being made directly against my friend Otto. I seemed to remember thinking something of the same kind that afternoon when his words and looks had appeared to show that he was siding against me. It had been some such notion as: 'How easily his thoughts are influenced! How thoughtlessly he jumps to conclusions!'— Apart from this, this sentence in the dream reminded me once more of my dead friend who had so hastily resorted to cocaine injections. As I have said, I had never contemplated the drug being given by injection. I noticed too that in accusing Otto of thoughtlessness in handling chemical substances I was once more touching upon the story of the unfortunate Mathilde, which gave grounds for the same accusation against myself. Here I was evidently collecting instances of my conscientiousness, but also of the reverse.

And probably the syringe had not been clean. This was yet another accusation against Otto, but derived from a different source. I had happened the day before to meet the son of an old lady of eighty-two, to whom I had to give an injection of morphia twice a day. At the moment she was in the country and he told me that she was suffering from phlebitis. I had at once thought it must be an infiltration caused by a dirty syringe. I was proud of the fact that in two years I had not caused a single infiltration; I took constant pains to be sure that the syringe was clean. In short, I was conscientious. The phlebitis brought me back once more to my wife, who had suffered from thrombosis during one of her pregnancies; and now three similar situations came to my recollection involving my wife, Irma and the dead Mathilde. The identity of these situations had evidently enabled me to substitute the three figures for one another in the dream.[2]

Freud concluded that the content of the dream is the fulfillment of a wish, which analysis had revealed. Not he, but Otto, was responsible for the persistence of Irma's pain. Freud got his revenge by throwing back on Otto the reproach he had received from him the day before.

Present as a guiding threat in what has gone before is the question of why did not his patients just tell Freud the sources of their difficulties directly that he had to find by the round-about methods of free association and dream analysis? The first answer might be that these crucial facts were unconscious. But why, in turn, were they unconscious? Freud said this was due to repression and resistance.

Repression, psychoanalytically speaking, means that something is rejected from consciousness—a form of fleeing from something painful.

Resistance is the unwillingness to disclose that which is painful, although the individual is unconscious of his reluctance.

The task of the psychoanalyst then becomes that of making the patient conscious of that which heretofore had been unconscious. Time and again, Freud found that his patient's repressions centered on sexual matters, as it did, for example very clearly, in the illustration of free association just excerpted.

It is now possible to use this background from investigation and treatment and turn to his view of psychology, more specifically, the nature of personality, that emerged, particularly in his later writings. In the interest of greater dynamic precision, while still considering the consciousness and the unconscious as essential, he preferred to develop his own terminology to describe the nature of personality.

We have arrived at our knowledge of this psychical apparatus by studying the individual development of human beings. To the oldest of these psychical provinces or agencies we give the name of *id*. It contains everything that is inherited, that is present at birth, that is laid down in the constitution—above all, therefore, the instincts, which originate from the somatic organization and which find a first psychical expression here [in the id] in forms unknown to us.''

Under the influence of the real external world around us, one portion of the id has undergone a special development. From what was originally a cortical layer, equipped with the organs for receiving stimuli and with arrangements for acting as a protective shield against stimuli, a special organization has arisen which henceforward acts as an intermediary between the id and the external world. To this region of our mind we have given the name of *ego*.

Here are the principal characteristics of the ego. In consequence of the pre-established connection between sense perception and muscular action, the ego has voluntary movement at its command. It has the task of self-preservation. As regards *external* events, it performs that task by becoming aware of stimuli, by storing up experiences about them (in the memory), by avoiding excessively strong stimuli (through flight), by dealing with moderate stimuli (through adaptation) and finally by learning to bring about expedient changes in the external world to its own advantage (through activity). As regards *internal* events, in relation to the id, it performs that task by gaining control over the demands of the

''This oldest portion of the psychical apparatus remains the most important throughout life; moreover, the investigations of psychoanalysis started with it."

instincts, by deciding whether they are to be allowed satisfaction, by postponing that satisfaction to times and circumstances favourable in the external world or by suppressing their excitations entirely. It is guided in its activity by consideration of the tensions produced by stimuli, whether these tensions are present in it or introduced into it. The raising of these tensions is in general felt as *unpleasure* and their lowering as *pleasure*. It is probable, however, that what is felt as pleasure or unpleasure is not the *absolute* height of this tension but something in the rhythm of the changes in them. The ego strives after pleasure and seeks to avoid unpleasure. An increase in unpleasure that is expected and foreseen is met by a *signal of anxiety*; the occasion of such an increase, whether it threatens from without or within, is known as a *danger*. From time to time the ego gives up its connection with the external world and withdraws into the state of sleep, in which it makes far-reaching changes in its organization. It is to be inferred from the state of sleep that this organization consists in a particular distribution of mental energy.

The long period of childhood, during which the growing human being lives in dependence on his parents, leaves behind it as a precipitate the formation in his ego of a special agency in which this parental influence is prolonged. It has received the name of *super-ego*. In so far as this super-ego is differentiated from the ego or is opposed to it, it constitutes a third power which the ego must take into account.

An action by the ego is as it should be if it satisfies simultaneously the demands of the id, of the super-ego and of reality—that is to say, if it is able to reconcile their demands with one another. The details of the relation between the ego and the super-ego become completely intelligible when they are traced back to the child's attitude to its parents. This parental influence of course includes in its operation not only the personalities of the actual parents but also the family, racial and national traditions handed on through them, as well as the demands of the immediate social *milieu* which they represent. In the same way, the super-ego, in the course of an individual's development, receives contributions from later successors and substitutes of his parents, such as teachers and models in public life of admired social ideals. It will be observed that, for all their fundamental difference, the id and the super-ego have one thing in common: they both represent the influences of the past—the id the influence of heredity, the super-ego the influence, essentially, of what is taken over from other people—whereas the ego is principally determined by the individual's own experience, that is by accidental and contemporary events.

This general schematic picture of a psychical apparatus may be supposed to apply as well to the higher animals which resemble man mentally. A super-ego must be presumed to be present wherever, as is the case with man, there is a long period of dependence in childhood. A distinction between ego and id is an unavoidable assumption. Animal psychology has not yet taken in hand the interesting problem which is here presented.... The power of the id expresses the true purpose of the individual organism's life. This consists in the satisfaction of its innate needs. No such purpose as that of keeping itself alive or of protecting itself from dangers by means of anxiety can be attributed to the id. That is the task of the ego, whose business it also is to discover the most favourable and least perilous method of obtaining satisfaction, taking the external world into account. The super-ego may bring fresh needs to the fore, but its main function remains the limitation of satisfactions.

The forces which we assume to exist behind the tensions caused by the needs of the id are called *instincts*. They represent the somatic demands upon the mind. Though they are the ultimate cause of all activity, they are of a conservative nature; the state, whatever it may be, which an organism has reached gives rise to a tendency to re-establish that state so soon as it has been abandoned. It is thus possible to distinguish an indeterminate number of instincts, and in common practice this is in fact done. For us, however, the important question arises whether it may not be possible to trace all these numerous instincts back to a few basic ones. We have found that instincts can change their aim (by displacement) and also that they can replace one another—the energy of one instinct passing over to another. This latter process is still insufficiently understood. After long hesitancies and vacillations we have decided to assume the existence of only two basic instincts, *Eros* and *the destructive instinct*. (The contrast between the instincts of self-preservation and the preservation of the species, as well as the contrast between ego-love and object-love, fall within Eros.) The aim of the first of these basic instincts is to establish ever greater unities and to preserve them thus—in short, to bind together; the aim of the second is, on the contrary, to undo connections and so to destroy things. In the case of the destructive instinct we may suppose that its final aim is to lead what is living into an inorganic state. For this reason we also call it the *death instinct*. If we assume that living things came later than inanimate ones and arose from them, then the death instinct fits in with the formula we have proposed to the effect that instincts tend towards a return to an earlier state. In the case of Eros (or the love instinct) we cannot apply this formula. To do so would presuppose that living substance was once a unity which had later been torn apart and was now striving towards re-union.

In biological functions the two basic instincts operate against each other or combine with each other. Thus, the act of eating is a destruction of the object with the final aim of incorporating it, and the sexual act is an act of aggression with the purpose of the most intimate union. This concurrent and mutually opposing action of the two basic instincts gives rise to the whole variegation of the phenomena of life. The analogy of our two basic instincts extends from the sphere of living things to the pair of opposing forces—attraction and repulsion—which rule in the inorganic world.

Modifications in the proportions of the fusion between the instincts have the most tangible results. A surplus of sexual aggressiveness will turn a lover into a sex-murderer, while a sharp diminution in the aggressive factor will make him bashful or impotent.

There can be no question of restricting óne or the other of the basic instincts to one of the provinces of the mind. They must necessarily be met with everywhere. We may picture an initial state as one in which the total available energy of Eros, which henceforward we shall speak of as 'libido,' is present in the still undifferentiated ego-id and serves to neutralize the destructive tendencies which are simultaneously present. (We are without a term analogous to 'libido' for describing the energy of the destructive instinct.) At a later stage it becomes relatively easy for us to follow the vicissitudes of the libido, but this is more difficult with the destructive instinct.

So long as that instinct operates internally, as a death instinct, it remains silent; it only comes to our notice when it is diverted outwards as an instinct of destruction. It seems to be essential for the preservation of the individual that this diversion should occur; the muscular apparatus serves this purpose. When the super-ego is established, considerable amounts of the aggressive instinct are fixated in the interior of the ego and operate there self-destructively. This is one of the dangers to health by which human beings are faced on their path to cultural development. Holding back aggressiveness is in general unhealthy and leads to illness (to mortification). A person in a fit of rage will often demonstrate how the transition from aggressiveness that has been prevented to self-destructiveness is brought about by diverting the aggressiveness against himself: he tears his hair or beats his face with his fists, though he would evidently have preferred to apply this treatment to someone else. Some portion of self-destructiveness remains within, whatever the circumstances; till at last it succeeds in killing the individual, not, perhaps, until his libido has been used up or fixated in a disadvantageous way. Thus it may in general be suspected that the *individual* dies of his internal conflicts but that the *species* dies of its unsuccessful struggle against the external world if the latter changes in a fashion which cannot be adequately dealt with by the adaptations which the species has acquired.

It is hard to say anything of the behaviour of the libido in the id and in the super-ego. All that we know about it relates to the ego, in which at first the whole available quota of libido is stored up. We call this state absolute, primary *narcissism*. It lasts till the ego begins to cathect the ideas of objects with libido, to transform narcissistic libido into object-libido. Throughout the whole of life the ego remains the great reservoir from which libidinal cathexes are sent out to objects and into which they are also once more withdrawn, just as an amoeba behaves with its pseudopodia. It is only when a person is completely in love that the main quota of libido is transferred on to the object and the object to some extent takes the place of the ego. A characteristic of the libido which is important in life is its *mobility*, the facility with which it passes from one object to another. This must be contrasted with the *fixation* of the libido to particular objects, which often persists throughout life.

There can be no question but that the libido has somatic sources, that it streams to the ego from various organs and parts of the body. This is most clearly seen in the case of that portion of the libido which, from its instinctual aim, is described as sexual excitation. The most prominent of the parts of the body from which this libido arises are known by the name of '*erotogenic zones*', though in fact the whole body is an erotogenic zone of this kind. The greater part of what we know about Eros—that is to say, about its exponent, the libido—has been gained from a study of the sexual function, which, indeed, on the prevailing view, even if not according to our theory, coincides with Eros. We have been able to form a picture of the way in which the sexual urge, which is destined to exercise a decisive influence on our life, gradually develops out of successive contributions from a number of component instincts, which represent particular erotogenic zones.[3]

This excerpt is perhaps the most condensed statement of a particular point of view in the entire collection of Freud's many writings. Yet certain major points came through clearly. The primordial, innate id has a transformation which acts as its intermediary with the world, the so-called ego, aware of reality and yet seeking pleasure, which develops anxiety when this is unsuccessful. Parental influence produces the "third power" with which the ego must contend, the super-ego which is the heir of the social ideals of admired older models, including the parents.

The tensions caused by the id are basically two kinds of instincts—Eros, the life and sexual urges, and the destructive instincts. The energy of the former is referred to as libido. Such, in the barest of outline, is Freud's view of personality.

It would be hard to overestimate the influence that Freud has had on psychology. By no means was this influence confined to fellow psychoanalysts. Psychologists, even though ostensibly opposed to his views or unaware of his influence on their thinking, were affected. This came about because of the new emphasis that Freud introduced into psychological thinking. The emphasis on the individual as the focus of interest, although not completely absent heretofore, began to permeate work in nonanalytic psychology. Emphasis on dynamic developmental and irrational factors received greater impetus. But above all, the importance of unconscious forces on the psychological processes could no longer be ignored.

42

ADLER ON
COMPENSATION,
INFERIORITY FEELINGS,
STRIVING FOR SUPERIORITY,
AND STYLE OF LIFE

ALFRED ADLER (1870–1937), Austrian-American psychiatrist, had been associated with Freud from 1902 until 1911 when, as explained later, they parted company. Thereafter, he went on to develop his own approach, referred to as individual psychology.

In the middle of his period of association with Freud, his interest centered on medical questions concerning organ inferiority and superiority. He wrote about this matter in 1907:

The inferiority to which I refer applies to an organ which is developmentally retarded, which has been inhibited in its growth or altered, in whole or in part. These inferior organs may include the sense organs, the digestive apparatus, the respiratory tracts, the genito-urinary apparatus, the circulatory organs, and the nervous system. Such inferiority can usually be proved only at birth or often only at the embryonic stage. The innate anomalies of organs range from malformation to slow maturation of otherwise normal organs. Since there is a strong relationship between inferiority and disease, we may expect that an inherited inferiority corresponds to an inherited disease.

The fate of the inferior organs is extremely varied. Development and the external stimuli of life press toward overcoming the expressions of such inferiority. Thus we may find approximately the following outcomes with innumerable intermediate stages: inability to survive, anomaly of form, anomaly of function, lack of resistance and disposition to disease, compensation within the organ, compensation through a second organ, compensation through the psychological superstructure, and organic or psychological overcompensation. We find pure, compensated, and overcompensated inferiorities.[1]

It was not until three years later that he considered compensation and inferiority feelings at the psychological level. When he did so, it should be noted, it was in a setting of working with children.

Children who have an organ inferiority, who are weak, clumsy, sickly, retarded in growth, ugly or deformed, or who have retained infantile forms of behavior are very prone to acquire through their relations to the environmenta a feeling of inferiority [later revision: *increased* feeling of inferiority]. This feeling rests heavily upon them, and they aim to overcome it by all means.

The character traits which are grouped around this inferiority feeling, and those usually more clearly grouped around the resulting increased aggression against the environment, may be called abnormal attitudes. Such traits as timidity, indecision, insecurity, shyness, cowardliness, increased need for support, submissive obedience, . . . as well as phantasies and even wishes, which one can summarize as ideas of 'smallness' or masochistic tendencies, correspond to the inferiority feeling. Above this network of personality traits there appear, with defensive and compensatory intent, impudence, courage, impertinence, inclination toward rebellion, stubbornness, and defiance, accompanied by phantasies and wishes of the role of a hero, warrior, robber, in short, ideas of grandeur and sadistic impulses.

The inferiority feeling finally culminates in a never-ceasing, always exaggerated feeling of being slighted, so that the Cinderella fantasy becomes complete with its longing expectation of redemption and triumph. The frequent fantasies of children regarding their princely origin and temporary banishment from their "real" home are of this kind.

But reality defies the harmlessness of the fairy tale. The entire drive life of the child is intensified and gains the upper hand. At the slightest injury, thoughts of revenge and death become expressed against the self and the environment, childhood disorders and bad habits are defiantly retained, and sexual precocity and desire burst forth in order to be like the grown-ups, those who really count. The father is the one who is big, knows everything, and has everything, or it is his substitute, the mother, older brother, or the teacher. He becomes the opponent who must be fought. The child becomes blind and deaf to his guidance, misunderstands all good intentions, becomes suspicious and extremely keen to all injuries coming from him. In short, the child has an attitude of defiance, but precisely on account of it has rendered himself completely dependent upon the opinion or attitude of others.

In other cases the child may lose his aggression tendency through his disposition and his experiences and, learning from the latter, may seek to gain drive satisfaction and his final triumph through passive behavior, submission, and honest and dishonest obedience. Hate breaks out at times, although often only in dreams and neurotic symptoms. These are signs, however, to those who understand, that the ground has been undermined and is suited for neurosis and prohibited behavior, unless the child proves himself capable of triumphant achievements or complete indifference. If the attitude of obedience and submission predominates, the next of kin frequently congratulate themselves on the model child without suspecting that in unfavorable cases life, love, or vocation may easily bring about decay and submersion into neurosis.

Thus in both main groups of character traits we see the effect of erroneous attitudes, the compensatory significance of which consists in the annihilation of the inferiority feeling through a compensatory protest and through phantasies of greatness. For the most part, we find mixed cases in which traits of obedience and defiance run parallel.[2]

He had now made the transition from considering compensation in physical terms, to viewing it as a psychological problem.

In 1911, Adler broke with Freud, as the latter saw it, because of Adler's underemphasis on sexual factors and overemphasis on social factors. In the same year, Adler became acquainted with the work of Hans Vaihinger who had just published a work with the intriguing title, *The Philosophy of "As If."* Man, says Vaihinger, lives by fictions that have no counterpart in reality. That the universe is an orderly determined affair may be a fiction. But by acting as if it were so, the individual, in a sense, makes it orderly even though in reality it may be chaos. Moreover, as Vaihinger saw it, we create the fiction of a God when we act as if He existed. These fictions may be falsifications, but when we act as if they are real, they are real in the sense that they affect our thinking and behavior.

From this, Adler drew the inference that a person is more motivated by future expectations than by past experiences (the latter is the deterministic position of Freud). While fictions are created by the individual, they are unconscious and subjective. An individual sets up fictional final goal (self-ideal), which is the unifying principle of personality.

The human mind shows an urge to capture into fixed forms through unreal assumptions, that is, fictions, that which is chaotic, always in flux, and incomprehensible. Serving this urge, the child quite generally uses a schema in order to act and to find his way. We proceed much the same when we divide the earth by meridians and parallels, for only thus do we obtain fixed points which we can bring into a relationship with one another. In all similar attempts with which the human psyche is filled, it is always a matter of entering an unreal, abstract schema into real life. I consider it the main task of this work [*The Neurotic Character*] to advance this knowledge which I have gained from the psychological consideration of the neurosis and psychosis and which is found, according to the evidence of Vaihinger, in all scientific views. No matter at which point one investigates the psychological development of the healthy or the neurotic person, one always finds him enmeshed in his schema, the neurotic believing in his fiction and not finding his way back to reality, the healthy person using it to attain a goal in reality. . . .

This artifice of thinking would have the stamp of paranoia and of dementia praecox—which conditions create for themselves hostile forces out of life's difficulties for the purpose of safeguarding their self-esteem—were not the child able at all times to free himself from the bonds of his fiction, to eliminate his projections (Kant) from his calculations, and to use only the impetus which springs from this guiding line. His insecurity is great enough to make him set up a fantastic goal for the purpose of orientation in the world, but not so great as to devalue reality and to dogmatize the guiding image, as occurs in the psychoses. One must point out, however, that insecurity and the artifice of the fiction have a similar significance in normal persons, neurotics, and the insane.[3]

It became evident to him that the personality of the individual reflects a striving toward a goal of superiority, perhaps best expressed in a chapter published in 1930, a few years before Adler settled permanently in New York City.

I began to see clearly in every psychological phenomenon the striving for superiority. It runs parallel to physical growth and is an intrinsic necessity of life itself. It lies at the root of all solutions of life's problems and is manifested in the way in which we meet these problems. All our functions follow its direction. They strive for conquest, security, increase, either in the right or in the wrong direction. The impetus from minus to plus never ends. The urge from below to above never ceases. Whatever premises of all our philosophers and psychologists dream of—self-preservation, pleasure principle, equalization—all these are but vague representations, attempts to express the great upward drive.

The history of the human race points in the same direction. Will-ing, thinking, talking, seeking after rest and pleasure, learning, under-standing, working and loving, all betoken the essence of this eternal melody. From this network, which in the last analysis is simply given with the man-cosmos relationship, no one may hope to escape. Even if anyone wanted to escape, even if he could escape, he would still find himself in the general system, striving upward from below. This not only states a fundamental category of thought, a thought construct, but, what is more, represents the fundamental fact of our life.

The origin of humanity and the ever-repeated beginning of infant life impresses with every psychological act: "Achieve! Arise! Conquer!" This feeling, this longing for the abrogations of every imperfection, is never absent. In the search for relief, in Faustian wrestling against the forces of nature, rings always the basic chord: "I relinquish thee not, thou bless me withal." The unreluctant search for truth, the ever-unsatisfied seeking for solution of the problems of life, belongs to this longing for perfection of some sort.[4]

Here, Adler was stressing superiority in terms of perfection, as shown throughout humankind, normal as well as neurotic.
He also considered as indispensible, a striving toward self-advancement and power placed in a setting of neurotic strivings.

Much of our view of the enhancement of the self-esteem as the guiding fiction is included in Nietzsche's "will to power" and "will to seem." Our view touches in many points also on those of Féré and older authors, according to whom the feeling of pleasure is founded in a feeling of power, that of displeasure in a feeling of powerlessness.

So far we have considered the guiding force and final purpose of the neurosis to be a desire for enhancement of the self-esteem which always asserts itself with special strength. This is merely the expression of a striving which is deeply founded in human nature in general. The expression and the deepening of this guiding thought, which could also be described as will to power, teaches us that a particular compensatory force is involved which attempts to put an end to the general human inner insecurity.

Every neurotic character trait reveals through its direction that it is permeated by the striving for power which tries to make the trait an infallible means for excluding permanent humiliation from the patient's experiences.

The constitutional inferiority and similarly effective childhood situations give rise to a feeling of inferiority which demands a compensation in the sense of an enhancement of the self-esteem. Here the fictional, final purpose of the striving for power gains enormous influence and draws all psychological forces into its direction. This fictional final purpose, itself originating in the safeguarding tendency, organizes psychological readinesses for the purpose of [further] safeguarding. Among these the neurotic character and the functional neurosis stand out as prominent devices.

We wish to point out the absolute primacy of the will to power, a guiding fiction which asserts itself the more forcibly and is developed the earlier, often precipitously, the stronger the inferiority feeling of the organically inferior child comes to the foreground.

In the functioning of constitutionally inferior organs, the impression of insecurity increases due to the greater tension towards the demands of the external environment, and the low self-estimation of the child brings about a permanent inferiority feeling. Already in early childhood mastery of the situation according to a model, and usually beyond this model, is taken as the guiding motif. A permanent volitional impulse is fixed and automatized to ascribe the permanent leadership to a guiding idea, the will to power. This is also the goal setting in the neurotic psyche which consciously or unconsciously corresponds to the formula: "I must act so that in the end I will be master of the situation."

With great avidity, directly or by detours, consciously or unconsciously, through appropriate thinking and action or through the arrangement of symptoms, the neurotic strives for increased possession, power, and influence, and for the disparagement and cheating of other persons.[5]

While it would not be inappropriate to infer from this excerpt that Adler viewed both neurotics and normals as being driven by a lust for power and the need to dominate, it is also known that he modified his position in later years to stress the motivative effect of social interest, rather than the drive for power as operative in normal individuals.

The normal person strives for self-advancement but does so in a setting in which reality, cooperation, and interest in others are operative. The individual responds to his social situation by "social interest," an urge to adapt positively to the experienced social environment. This will be expressed through the following excerpt, concerned with ways with which individuals handle the three major forms of social ties:

The three ties in which human beings are bound set the three problems of life, but none of these problems can be solved separately. Each of them demands a successful approach to the other two.

a. *Occupation*. The first tie sets the problem of occupation. We are living on the surface of this planet, with only the resources of this planet, with the fertility of its soil, with its mineral wealth, and with its climate and atmosphere. It has always been the task of mankind to find the right answer to the problem these conditions set us, and even today we cannot think that we have found a sufficient answer. In every age, mankind has arrived at a certain level of solution, but it has always been necessary to strive for improvement and further accomplishments. . . .

b. *Society*. The second tie by which men are bound is their membership in the human race and their association with others of their kind. The attitude and behavior of a human being would be altogether different if he were the only one of his kind alive on earth. We have always to reckon with others, to adapt ourselves to others, and to interest ourselves in them. This problem is best solved by friendship, social feeling, and cooperation. With the solution of this problem, we have made an incalculable advance towards the solution of the first. It was only because men learned to cooperate that the great discovery of the division of labor was made, a discovery which is the chief security for the welfare of mankind. Through the division of labor we can use the results of many different kinds of training and organize many different abilities, so that all of them contribute to the common welfare and guarantee relief from insecurity and increased opportunity for all the members of society.

Some people attempt to evade the problem of occupation, to do no work, or to occupy themselves outside of common human interests. We shall always find, however, that if they dodge this problem, they will in fact be claiming support from their fellows. In one way or another, they will be living on the labor of others without making a contribution of their own.

c. *Love*. The third tie of a human being is that he is a member of one of the two sexes and not of the other. On his approach to the other sex and on the fulfillment of his sexual role depends his part in the continuance of mankind. This relationship between the two sexes also sets a problem. It, too, is a problem which cannot be solved apart from the other two problems. For a successful solution of the problem of love and marriage, an occupation contributing to the division of labor is necessary, as well as a good and friendly contact with other human beings. In our own day, the highest solution for this problem, the solution most coherent with the demands of society and of the division of labor, is monogamy. In the way in which an individual answers this problem the degree of his cooperation can always be seen.

These three problems are never found apart, for they all throw crosslights on one another. A solution of one helps towards the solution of the others, and indeed we can say that they are all aspects of the same situation and the same problem—the necessity for a human being to preserve life and to further life in the environment in which he finds himself.[6]

We shall close with consideration of how the individual implements these various aspects in personal and idiographic unique form. He does so by what Adler calls the development of a style of life.

If we look at a pine tree growing in the valley we will notice that it grows differently from one on top of a mountain. It is the same kind of a tree, a pine, but there are two distinct styles of life. Its style on top of the mountain is different from its style when growing in the valley. The style of life of a tree is the individuality of a tree expressing itself and moulding itself in an environment. We recognize a style when we see it against a background of an environment different from what we expect, for then we realize that every tree has a life pattern and is not merely a mechanical reaction to the environment.

It is much the same way with human beings. We see the style of life under certain conditions of environment and it is our task to analyze its exact relation to the existing circumstances, inasmuch as mind changes with alteration of the environment. As long as a person is in a favorable situation we cannot see his style of life clearly. In new situations, however, where he is confronted with difficulties, the style of life appears clearly and distinctly. A trained psychologist could perhaps understand a style of life of a human being even in a favorable situation, but it becomes apparent to everybody when the human subject is put into unfavorable or difficult situations. . . .

How does the notion of the style of life tie up with what we have discussed in previous chapters? We have seen how human beings with weak organs, because they face difficulties and feel insecure, suffer from a feeling or complex of inferiority. But as human beings cannot endure this for long, the inferiority feeling stimulates them, as we have seen, to movement and action. This results in a person having a goal. Now Individual Psychology has long called the consistent movement toward this goal a plan of life. But because this name has sometimes led to mistakes among students, it is now called a style of life.[7]

It is now possible to summarize Adler's intellectual journey. He first became interested in the problem of compensation at the physical level. Next, the importance of inferiority feelings related to compensation, real or imagined, impressed him. In this setting, the creation of fictional goals as a way of coping with reality and its consequent compensations became important to Adler. Disregarding chronology hereafter, all individuals strive toward superiority and self-enhancement. Individuals respond to their social situations by social interest which they express in the various ways that they handle social ties. These various facets culminate in a style of life unique to each individual.

Practically from the beginning of this journey, Adler had been interested in reaching a wider audience than his fellow-professionals in the conventional sense of the term. He did this in his writings, speeches, and workshops by appealing to teachers and laymen as fellow-workers in the task of understanding human nature. His was a characteristically "open" way of regarding life and its problems. He saw problems of the individual as existing in a social matrix in which the unique individual makes choices based on his individuality and the social setting. In all of this, Adler was prophetic of the current scene among all psychodynamic approaches to psychology, including the neo-Freudian approach.

43

JUNG ON

SYMBOLS, THE COLLECTIVE UNCONSCIOUSNESS, COMPLEXES, AND TYPES OF PERSONALITY

CARL GUSTAVE JUNG (1875–1961), Swiss psychiatrist, met Freud in 1907 and, despite the lack of geographical proximity, for several years was probably closest to him of all his followers, so much so that he was chosen by Freud as the first president of the International Psychoanalytic Society. Early in their relationship, he harbored doubts about the overwhelming importance Freud attached to sexual conflict situations, but wholeheartedly accepted conflict itself, the analysis of dreams and, above all, unconscious motivation. He also went on to stress other factors to be mentioned in the following material. The complete break with Freud came in 1914.

Only in his very last years did Jung turn to writing about what he had come to call analytic psychology for the general public. He chose to begin with the importance of dreams as symbols. We can do no better than follow his lead.

Man uses the spoken or written word to express the meaning of what he wants to convey. His language is full of symbols, but he also often employs signs or images that are not strictly descriptive. Some are mere abbreviations or strings of initials, such as UN, UNICEF, or UNESCO; others are familiar trade marks, the names of patent medicines, badges, or insignia. Although these are meaningless in themselves, they have acquired a recognizable meaning through common usage or deliberate intent. Such things are not symbols. They are signs, and they do no more than denote the objects to which they are attached.

What we call a symbol is a term, a name, or even a picture that may be familiar in daily life, yet that possesses specific connotations in addition to its conventional and obvious meaning. It implies something vague, unknown, or hidden from us. Many Cretan monuments, for instance, are marked with the design of the double adze. This is an object that we know, but we do not know its symbolic implications. For another example, take the case of the Indian who, after a visit to England, told his friends at home that the English worship animals, because he had found eagles, lions, and oxen in old churches. He was not aware (nor are many Christians) that these animals are symbols of the Evangelists and are derived from the vision of Ezekiel, and that this in turn has an analogy to the Egyptian sun god Horus and his four sons. There are, moreover, such objects as the wheel and the cross that are known all over the world, yet that have a symbolic significance under certain conditions. Precisely what they symbolize is still a matter for controversial speculation.

Thus a word or an image is symbolic when it implies something more than its obvious and immediate meaning. It has a wider "unconscious" aspect that is never precisely defined or fully explained. Nor can one hope to define or explain it. As the mind explores the symbol, it is led to ideas that lie beyond the grasp of reason. The wheel may lead our thoughts toward the concept of a "divine" sun, but at this point reason must admit its incompetence; man is unable to define a "divine" being. When, with all our intellectual limitations, we call something "divine," we have merely given it a name, which may be based on a creed, but never on factual evidence.

Because there are innumerable things beyond the range of human understanding, we constantly use symbolic terms to represent concepts that we cannot define or fully comprehend. This is one reason why all religions employ symbolic language or images. But this conscious use of symbols is only one aspect of a psychological fact of great importance: Man also produces symbols unconsciously and spontaneously, in the form of dreams.

It is not easy to grasp this point. But the point must be grasped if we are to know more about the ways in which the human mind works. Man, as we realize if we reflect for a moment, never perceives anything fully or comprehends anything completely. He can see, hear, touch, and taste; but how far he sees, how well he hears, what his touch tells him, and what he tastes depend upon the number and quality of his senses. These limit his perception of the world around him. By using scientific instruments he can partly compensate for the deficiencies of his senses. For example, he can extend the range of his vision by binoculars or of his hearing by electrical amplification. But the most elaborate apparatus cannot do more than bring distant or small objects within range of his eyes, or make faint sounds more audible. No matter what instruments he uses, at some point he reaches the edge of certainty beyond which conscious knowledge cannot pass.

There are, moreover, unconscious aspects of our perception of reality. The first is the fact that even when our senses react to real phenomena, sights, and sounds, they are somehow translated from the realm of reality into that of the mind. Within the mind they become psychic events, whose ultimate nature is unknowable (for the psyche cannot know its own psychical substance). Thus every experience contains an indefinite number of unknown factors, not to speak of the fact that every concrete object is always unknown in certain respects, because we cannot know the ultimate nature of matter itself.

Then there are certain events of which we have not consciously taken note; they have remained, so to speak, below the threshold of consciousness. They have happened, but they have been absorbed subliminally, without our conscious knowledge. We can become aware of such happenings only in a moment of intuition or by a process of profound thought that leads to a later realization that they must have happened; and though we may have originally ignored their emotional and vital importance, it later wells up from the unconscious as a sort of afterthought.

It may appear, for instance, in the form of a dream. As a general rule, the unconscious aspect of any event is revealed to us in dreams, where it appears not as a rational thought but as a symbolic image. As a matter of history, it was the study of dreams that first enabled psychologists to investigate the unconscious aspect of conscious psychic events.[1]

Jung then credits Freud with discovering that if the dreamer is encouraged to free associate to his dream images, then the unconscious background of the dream will be revealed. Symbols are devised unconsciously, not consciously. He goes on:

Freud attached particular importance to dreams as the point of departure for a process of "free association." But after a time I began to feel that this was a misleading and inadequate use of the rich fantasies that the unconscious produces in sleep. My doubts really began when a colleague told me of an experience he had during the course of a long train journey in Russia. Though he did not know the language and could not even decipher the Cyrillic script, he found himself musing over the strange letters in which the railway notices were written, and he fell into a reverie in which he imagined all sorts of meanings for them.

One idea led to another, and in his relaxed mood he found that this "free association" had stirred up many old memories. Among them he was annoyed to find some long-buried disagreeable topics—things he had wished to forget and had forgotten *consciously*. He had in fact arrived at what psychologists would call his "complexes"—that is, repressed emotional themes that can cause constant psychological disturbances or even, in many cases, the symptoms of a neurosis.

This episode opened my eyes to the fact that it was not necessary to use a dream as the point of departure for the process of "free association" if one wished to discover the complexes of a patient. It showed me that one can reach the center directly from any point of the compass. One could begin from Cyrillic letters, from meditations upon a crystal ball, a prayer wheel, or a modern painting, or even from casual conversation about some quite trivial event. The dream was no more and no less useful in this respect than any other possible starting point. Nevertheless, dreams have a particular significance, even though they often arise from an emotional upset in which the habitual complexes are also involved. (The habitual complexes are the tender spots of the psyche, which react most quickly to an external stimulus or disturbance.) That is why free association can lead one from any dream to the critical secret thoughts.

At this point, however, it occurred to me that (if I was right so far) it might reasonably follow that dreams have some special and more significant function of their own. Very often dreams have a definite, evidently purposeful structure, indicating an underlying idea or intention—though, as a rule, the latter is not immediately comprehensible. I therefore began to consider whether one should pay more attention to the actual form and content of a dream, rather than allowing "free" association to lead one off through a train of ideas to complexes that could as easily be reached by other means.

This new thought was a turning-point in the development of my psychology. It meant that I gradually gave up following associations that led far away from the text of a dream. I chose to concentrate rather on the associations to the dream itself, believing that the latter expressed something specific that the unconscious was trying to say.[2]

Much of what he writes in this account thereafter has to do with the salient importance of symbolism.

Elsewhere, he indicates that there are both individual, personal symbols and collective symbols. The archetypal nature of symbols in relation to the collective unconscious is central:

The collective unconscious is a part of the psyche which can be negatively distinguished from a personal unconscious by the fact that it does not, like the latter, owe its existence to personal experience and consequently is not a personal acquisition. While the personal unconscious is made up essentially of contents which have at one time been conscious but which have disappeared from consciousness through having been forgotten or repressed, the contents of the collective unconscious have never been in consciousness, and therefore have never been individually acquired, but owe their existence exclusively to heredity. Whereas the personal unconscious consists for the most part of *complexes,* the content of the collective unconscious is made up essentially of *archetypes.*

The concept of the archetype, which is an indispensable correlate of the idea of the collective unconscious, indicates the existence of definite forms in the psyche which seem to be present always and everywhere. Mythological research calls them "motifs"; in the psychology of primitives they correspond to Lévy-Bruhl's concept of "représentations collectives," and in the field of comparative religion they have been defined by Hubert and Mauss as "categories of the imagination." Adolf Bastian long ago called them "elementary" or "primordial thoughts." From these references it should be clear enough that my idea of the archetype—literally a pre-existent form—does not stand alone but is something that is recognized and named in other fields of knowledge.

My thesis, then, is as follows: In addition to our immediate consciousness, which is of a thoroughly personal nature and which we believe to be the only empirical psyche (even if we tack on the personal unconscious as an appendix), there exists a second psychic system of a collective, universal, and impersonal nature which is identical in all individuals. This collective unconscious does not develop individually but is inherited. It consists of pre-existent forms, the archetypes, which can only become conscious secondarily and which give definite form to certain psychic contents.[3]

Myths and legends as sources for the meanings of unconscious symbols occupied much of his time after his break with Freud. Field expeditions to visit primitive peoples, readings in mythology, alchemy (whose practioners were interested in psychic as well as physical trans-

formation), fairy tales, oriental philosophy, poetry, and religion interpreted as the external dynamic forces which control human beings absorbed much of his attention. In his collected works, this is reflected in
titles such as *Psychology and Religion; West and East; Psychology and
Alchemy; The Spirit in Man, Art and Literature.*

He also carried on a private practice in psychotherapy, in which, as
to be expected, the symbolism unique to the individual was sought while
he, the therapist, aimed at understanding the complexes being exhibited
in their situational (environmental) patterns.

It was in his very early work in the empirical tradition that he
obtained a major clue to his eventual approach—the presence of complexes through the association method. The excerpt to follow shortly is
drawn from his presentation at the 1909 anniversary celebration at Clark
University which Freud and he attended several years before their
schism. It first appeared in an American psychological journal, making it
all the more fitting to include here. Earlier in the article, he had explained
that it was his practice to present, one word at a time, 100 words, to which
the individual was to respond with the first word that occurred to him.
"Disturbing effects" of the words, in his opinion, were shown when "incorrect" reproductions were offered, and when there was repetition of the
stimulus word, slips of the tongue, laughter, or the use of several words
instead of one.

These disturbing effects were the indicators of the complex or
complexes, that is, constellations or systems of psychological elements
grouped around feeling toned contents that have been repressed. The
aforementioned excerpt that follows is a brief case history:

The patient was an educated woman of thirty years of age, who had been
married for three years. Since her marriage she had suffered periodically
from states of agitation in which she was violently jealous of her husband.
The marriage was in every other respect a happy one and in fact the
husband gave no grounds for jealousy. The patient was sure that she
loved him and that her agitated states were absolutely groundless. She
could not imagine how this situation had come about and felt quite at a
loss. It should be noted that she was a Roman Catholic and had been
brought up to practise her religion, whereas her husband was a Protestant. This difference of religion was stated to be of no consequence. A
more thorough anamnesis revealed an astounding prudishness: for instance, no one was allowed to talk in the patient's presence about her
sister's confinement, because the sexual implication caused her the
greatest agitation. She never undressed in her husband's presence but
always in another room, and so on. At the age of twenty-seven she was
supposed to have had no idea how children were born. (Her association
test gave [pertinent] . . .results. . . .)

The stimulus-words that stood out because of their strong disturbing effect were these: *yellow, to pray, to part, to marry, to quarrel, old, family, happiness, unfaithful, anxiety, to kiss, bride, to choose, contented.* The following stimulus-words produced the strongest disturbances: *to pray, to marry, happiness, unfaithful, anxiety,* and *contented.* These then are the words that clearly pointed towards the complex. The conclusion that can be drawn from this is: that she was not indifferent to the fact that her husband was a Protestant, that she was again thinking about prayer and felt there was something wrong with the married state; that she was unhappy; she was false—that is, she was having fantasies about being unfaithful; she suffered from anxiety (about her husband? about the future?); she was dissatisfied with her choice (*to choose*) and was thinking about *parting.* The patient therefore had a divorce-complex, for she was very dissatisfied with her married life. When I told her this result she was very shaken and at first tried to deny it, then to gloss it over, but finally she gave in and admitted it. Moreover, she produced a great deal of material, consisting of fantasies about being unfaithful, reproaches against her husband, and so on. Her prudishness and jealousy were merely a projection of her own sexual wishes onto her husband. She was jealous of her husband because she herself was unfaithful in fantasy and could not admit it to herself.[4]

It is work in this tradition that has been most appealing to and best known among psychologists in general. For Jung's systematic approach, however, it is of less importance. Only one volume out of seventeen in his *Collected Works* is devoted to similar themes, and the publications that it contains were invariably prepared early in his career. The concept of a complex was retained although investigated in the other ways he obtained his interpretive material.

From his work in all of these various sources, Jung went on to weave an intricate tapestry of a view of human nature. Space permits only a discussion of personality types. Immediately preceding the portion excerpted, he had discussed extraversion in some detail. The extravert is directed outside of self to objects.

In this short essay I have to content myself with an allusive sketch. It is intended merely to give the reader some idea of what extraversion is like, something he can bring into relationship with his own knowledge of human nature. I have purposely started with a description of extraversion because this attitude is familiar to everyone; the extravert not only lives in this attitude, but parades it before his fellows on principle. Moreover it accords with certain popular ideals and moral requirements.

Introversion, on the other hand, being directed not to the object but to the subject, and not being oriented by the object, is not so easy to put into perspective. The introvert is not forthcoming, he is as though in continual retreat before the object. He holds aloof from external happenings, does not join in, has a distinct dislike of society as soon as he finds himself among too many people. In a large gathering he feels lonely and lost. The more crowded it is, the greater becomes his resistance. He is not in the least "with it," and has no love of enthusiastic get-togethers. He is not a good mixer. What he does, he does in his own way, barricading himself against influences from outside. He is apt to appear awkward, often seeming inhibited, and it frequently happens that, by a certain brusqueness of manner, or by his glum unapproachability, or some kind of malapropism, he causes unwitting offence to people. His better qualities he keeps to himself, and generally does everything he can to dissemble them. He is easily mistrustful, self-willed, often suffers from inferiority feelings and for this reason is also envious. His apprehensiveness of the object is not due to fear, but to the fact that it seems to him negative, demanding, overpowering or even menacing He therefore suspects all kinds of bad motives, has an everlasting fear of making a fool of himself, is usually very touchy and surrounds himself with a barbed wire entanglement so dense and impenetrable that finally he himself would rather do anything than sit behind it. He confronts the world with an elaborate defensive system compounded of scrupulosity, pedantry, frugality, cautiousness, painful conscientiousness, stiff-lipped rectitude, politeness, and open-eyed distrust. His picture of the world lacks rosy hues, as he is over-critical and finds a hair in every soup. Under normal conditions he is pessimistic and worried, because the world and human beings are not in the least good but crush him, so he never feels accepted and taken to their bosom. Yet he himself does not accept the world either, at any rate not outright, for everything has first to be judged by his own critical standards. Finally only those things are accepted which, for various subjective reasons, he can turn to his own account.

For him self-communings are a pleasure. His own world is a safe harbour, a carefully tended and walled-in garden, closed to the public and hidden from prying eyes. His own company is the best. He feels at home in his world, where the only changes are made by himself. His best work is done with his own resources, on his own initiative, and in his own way. If ever he succeeds, after long and often wearisome struggles, in assimilating something alien to himself, he is capable of turning it to excellent account. Crowds, majority views, public opinion, popular enthusiasm never convince him of anything, but merely make him creep still deeper into his shell.

His relations with other people become warm only when safety is guaranteed, and when he can lay aside his defensive distrust. All too often he cannot, and consequently the number of friends and acquaintances is very restricted. Thus the psychic life of this type is played out wholly within. Should any difficulties and conflicts arise in this inner world, all doors and windows are shut tight. The introvert shuts himself up with his complexes until he ends in complete isolation.

In spite of these peculiarities the introvert is by no means a social loss. His retreat into himself is not a final renunciation of the world, but a search for quietude, where alone it is possible for him to make his contribution to the life of the community. This type of person is the victim of numerous misunderstandings—not unjustly, for he actually invites them. Nor can he be acquitted of the charge of taking a secret delight in mystification, and that being misunderstood gives him a certain satisfaction, since it reaffirms his pessimistic outlook. That being so, it is easy to see why he is accused of being cold, proud, obstinate, selfish, conceited, cranky, and what not, and why he is constantly admonished that devotion to the goals of society, clubbableness, imperturbable urbanity, and selfless trust in the powers-that-be are true virtues and the marks of a sound and vigorous life.

The introvert is well enough aware that such virtues exist, and that somewhere, perhaps—only not in his circle of acquaintances—there are divinely inspired people who enjoy undiluted possession of these ideal qualities. But his self-criticism and his awareness of his own motives have long since disabused him of the illusion that he himself would be capable of such virtues; and his mistrustful gaze, sharpened by anxiety, constantly enables him to detect on his fellow men the ass's ear sticking up from under the lion's mane. The world and men are for him a disturbance and a danger, affording no valid standard by which he could ultimately orient himself. What alone is valid for him is his subjective world, which he sometimes believes, in moments of delusion, to be the objective one. We could easily charge these people with the worst kind of subjectivism, indeed with morbid individualism, if it were certain beyond a doubt that only one objective world existed. But this truth, if such it be, is not axiomatic; it is merely a half truth, the other half of which is the fact that the world *also* is as it is seen by human beings, and in the last resort by the individual. There is simply no world at all without the knowing subject. This, be it never so small and inconspicuous, is always the other pier supporting the bridge of the phenomenal world. The appeal to the subject therefore has the same validity as the appeal to the so-called objective world, for it is grounded on psychic reality itself. But this is a reality with its own peculiar laws which are not of a secondary nature.

The two attitudes, extraversion and introversion, are opposing modes that make themselves felt not least in the history of human thought. The problems to which they give rise were very largely anticipated by Friedrich Schiller, and they underlie his *Letters on the Aesthetic Education of Man*. But since the concept of the unconscious was still unknown to him, he was unable to reach a satisfactory solution. Moreover philosophers,who would be the best equipped to go more closely into this question, do not like having to submit their thinking function to a thorough psychological criticism, and therefore hold aloof from such discussions. It should, however, be obvious that the intrinsic polarity of such an attitude exerts a very great influence on the philosopher's own point of view.

For the extravert the object is interesting and attractive *a priori,* as is the subject, or psychic reality, for the introvert. We could therefore use the expression "numinal accent" for this fact, by which I mean that for the extravert the quality of positive significance and value attaches primarily to the object, so that it plays the predominant, determining, and decisive role in all psychic processes from the start, just as the subject does for the introvert.

But the numinal accent does not decide only between subject and object; it also selects the conscious function of which the individual makes the principal use. I distinguish four functions: *thinking, feeling, sensation,* and *intuition.* The essential function of sensation is to establish that something exists, thinking tells us what it means, feeling what its value is, and intuition surmises whence it comes and whither it goes. Sensation and intuition I call irrational functions, because they are both concerned simply with what happens and with actual or potential realities. Thinking and feeling, being discriminative functions, are rational. Sensation, the *fonction du réel,* rules out any simultaneous intrinsic activity, since the latter is not concerned with the present but is rather a sixth sense for hidden possibilities, and therefore should not allow itself to be unduly influenced by existing reality. In the same way, thinking is opposed to feeling, because thinking should not be influenced or deflected from its purpose by feeling values, just as feeling is usually vitiated by too much reflection. The four functions therefore form, when arranged diagrammatically, a cross with a rational axis at right angles to an irrational axis.

The four orienting functions naturally do not contain everything that is in the conscious psyche. Will and memory, for instance, are not included. The reason for this is that the differentiation of the four orienting functions is, essentially, an empirical consequence of typical differences in the functional attitude. There are people for whom the numinal accent falls on sensation, on the perception of actualities, and elevates it into the sole determining and all-overriding principle. These are the fact-minded men, in whom intellectual judgment, feeling, and intuition are driven into the background by the paramount importance of actual facts. When the accent falls on thinking, judgment is reserved as to what significance should be attached to the facts in question. And on this significance will depend the way in which the individual deals with the facts. If feeling is numinal, then his adaptation will depend entirely on the feeling value he attributes to them. Finally, if the numinal accent falls on intuition, actual reality counts only in so far as it seems to harbour possibilities which then become the supreme motivating force, regardless of the way things actually are in the present.

The localization of the numinal accent thus gives rise to four function-types, which I encountered first of all in my relations with people and formulated systematically only very much later. In practice these four types are always combined with the attitude-type, that is, with extraversion or introversion, so that the functions appear in an extraverted or introverted variation. This produces a set of eight demonstrable function-types. It is naturally impossible to present the specific psychology of these types within the confines of an essay, and to go into its conscious and unconscious manifestations, I must therefore refer the interested reader to the aforementioned study.

It is not the purpose of a psychological typology to classify human beings into categories—this in itself would be pretty pointless. Its purpose is rather to provide a critical psychology which will make a methodical investigation and presentation of the empirical material possible. First and foremost, it is a critical tool for the research worker, who needs definite points of view and guidelines if he is to reduce the chaotic profusion of individual experiences to any kind of order. In this respect we could compare typology to a trigonometric net or, better still, to a crystallographic axial system. Secondly, a typology is a great help in understanding the wide variations that occur among individuals, and it also furnishes a clue to the fundamental differences in the psychological theories now current. Last but not least, it is an essential means for determining the "personal equation" of the practising psychologist, who, armed with an exact knowledge of his differentiated and inferior functions, can avoid many serious blunders in dealing with his patients.

The typological system I have proposed is an attempt, grounded on practical experience, to provide an explanatory basis and theoretical framework for the boundless diversity that has hitherto prevailed in the formation of psychological concepts. In a science as young as psychology, limiting definitions will sooner or later become an unavoidable necessity. Some day psychologists will have to agree upon certain basic principles secure from arbitrary interpretation if psychology is not to remain un unscientific and fortuitous conglomeration of individual opinions.[5]

The dynamic unconscious influence of symbols, their influence through the collective unconscious, the presence of complexes, and the psychological significance of types and functions by no means exhaust the intricate pattern that Jung presented about the nature of personality. They are, nevertheless, crucial salient aspects of that view.

Jung's doctrines about personality have had a considerable impact on novelists, theologians, anthropologists, linguists, and archeologists. Psychologists and psychiatrists have been proportionally less affected, because many Jungian sources, such as mythology and religion, are foreign to their training. If they have not attended Jungian training institutes, they are not equipped to utilize to the full his point of view. Moreover, the reservations held about the relative absence of empirical research, especially among psychologists, has made them less receptive. Word association and introversion-extraversion are the only areas that have seemed capable of research penetration by psychologists.

Jung's theory of psychological types was appealing to many individuals, both psychotherapists and laymen. Indeed, the words "introvert" and "extrovert" are household terms for many who do not know Jung by name. But it was not a crude typology, both because of his relating extraversion and introversion to the four function types—thinking, feeling, sensation, and intuition—and because of his repeated insistence that individuals are unique examples of ideal types.

The breadth of Jung's views cannot be captured in a few excerpts. However, enough has been cited here to show that humans are guided by symbols and that these arise from the past experiences in terms of causal factors expressed in one's individual and collective history, but perhaps not enough to indicate that they arise from aims and aspirations as well. Jung's view is functionally oriented toward the present and the future, another characteristic that puts him in sharp contrast to Freud.

44

LASHLEY ON

CEREBRAL LOCALIZATION OF FUNCTION, EQUIPOTENTIALITY AND MASS ACTION

KARL LASHLEY (1890–1958), American psychologist, had been a student of John B. Watson at Johns Hopkins and a junior coworker of Shepard Ivory Franz, then at St. Elizabeth's Hospital in Washington, D.C.. From the former, he had accepted a behavioral stance concerning psychological research, and from the latter, he had learned the fundamentals of his major method, the surgical removal of parts of the brain and the study of its effect on learning. From his 1917 collaborative study with Franz,[1] he concluded that removal of large portions of the frontal lobes of the rat brain did not interfere with maze learning, confirming results obtained earlier by Franz alone.

Lashley was now launched on his life's work involving many expansions and refinements of concepts and methods of study, apparatus used, and procedures followed. He published a summary of his methodological approach.[2]

An overall design was maintained in many of his experiments on rats, monkey, and chimpanzees. The behavioral approach followed the customary pattern of having the animals learn reactions to particular forms of sensory stimulation. Either before or after the learning trials, there was surgical destruction of parts of their brains. The effects of these operations, either on initial learning or post-operative retention, was then measured. After completion of the experiment, the brains were sectioned, and the precise extent of the damage ascertained.

In 1929, he published his major work, *Brain Mechanisms and Intelligence*. The excerpts that follow first concern the implication of his research for theories of learning ability (intelligence), followed by his general conclusions.

The doctrine of isolated reflex conduction has been widely influential in shaping current psychological theories. Its assumptions that reactions are determined by local conditions in limited groups of neurons, that learning consists of the modification of resistance in isolated synapses, that retention is the persistence of such modified conditions, all make for a conception of behavior as rigidly departmentalized. Efficiency in any activity must depend upon the specific efficiency of the systems involved; and, since the condition of one synapse cannot influence that of others, there must be as many diverse capacities as there are independent reflex systems.

The effects of such a theory can be traced in many present-day beliefs. If learning is restricted to particular synapses, there can be no influence of training upon other activities than those actually practiced; any improvement in unpracticed functions must be the result of nervous connections which they have in common with the practiced activities. The rejection of doctrines of formal discipline seems to have been based far more upon such reasoning than upon any convincing experimental evidence.

The doctrine of identical elements has been applied also to the problem of insight. When similarities between two situations are recognized, it is because both call out a basic set of reactions involving identical reflex paths. Thus the application of past habits to new situations is limited to those in which an identity of elements can exist; all other adaptive behavior must be explained by the selection of random activities.

There is no evidence to support this belief in identity of nervous elements. On the contrary, it is very doubtful if the same neurons or synapses are involved even in two similar reactions to the same stimulus. Our data seem to prove that the structural elements are relatively unimportant for integration and that the common elements must be some sort of dynamic patterns, determined by the relations or ratios among the parts of the system and not by the specific neurons activated. If this be true, we cannot, on the basis of our present knowledge of the nervous system, set any limit to the kinds or amount of transfer possible or to the sort of relations which may be directly recognized. . . .

The influence of the extent of cerebral destruction in the rat was tested for a variety of functions, including retention of maze habits formed before cerebral insult, and learning and retention of several habits after the insult. The results may be summarized as follows:

1.   The capacity to form maze habits is reduced by destruction of cerebral tissue.

2. The reduction is roughly proportional to the amount of destruction.

3. The same retardation in learning is produced by equal amountsof destruction in any of the cyto-architectural fields. Hence the capacity to learn the maze is dependent upon the amount of functional cortical tissue and not upon its anatomical specialization.

4. Additional evidence is presented to show that the interruption of association or projection paths produces little disturbance of behavior, so long as cortical areas supplied by them remain in some functional connection with the rest of the nervous system.

5. The more complex the problem to be learned, the greater the retardation produced by an given extent of lesion.

6. The capacity to form simple habits of sensory discrimination is not significantly reduced by cerebral lesions, even when the entire sensory field is destroyed.

7. This immunity is probably due to the relative simplicity of such habits.

8. The capacity to retain is reduced, as is the capacity to learn.

9. The maze habit, formed before cerebral insult, is disturbed by lesions in any part of the cortex. The amount of reduction in efficiency of performance is proportional to the extent of injury and is independent of locus.

10. Reduction in ability to learn the maze is accompanied by many other disturbances of behavior, which cannot be stated quantitatively but which give a picture of general inadequacy in adaptive behavior.

11. No difference in behavior in maze situations could be detected after lesions in different cerebral areas, and the retardation in learning is not referable to any sensory defects.

12. A review of the literature on cerebral function in other mammals, including man, indicates that, in spite of the greater speicalization of cerebral areas in the higher forms, the prob lems of cerebral function are not greatly different from those raised by experiments with the rat.

From these facts the following inferences are drawn:

1. The learning process and the retention of habits are not dependent upon any finely localized structural changes within

the cerebral cortex. The results are incompatible with theories of learning by changes in synaptic structure, or with any theories which assume that particular neural integrations are dependent upon definite anatomical paths specialized for them. Integration cannot be expressed in terms of connections between specific neurons.

2. The contribution of the different parts of a specialized area or of the whole cortex, in the case of non-localized functions, is qualitatively the same. There is not a summation of diverse functions, but a non-specialized dynamic function of the tissue as a whole.

3. Analysis of the maze habit indicates that its formation involves processes which are characteristic of intelligent behavior. Hence the results for the rat are generalized for cerebral function in intelligence. Data on dementia in man are suggestive of conditions similar to those found after cerebral injury in the rat.

4. The mechanisms of integration are to be sought in the dynamic relations among the parts of the nervous system rather than in details of structural differentiation. Suggestions toward a theory of the nature of these forces are presented.[3]

The principles of equipotentiality and mass action had emerged from this research. Equipotentiality is the principle that an area of the cortex is qualitatively the same, while that for mass action calls for large areas of the brain to function as a whole in learned actions.[4] The rate and accuracy of learning, he was saying is, in some measure, proportionate to the amount of brain tissue, (mass action) but is independent of the available particular tissue involved (equipotentiality). On the basis of these principles, the brain seems to function as a whole, and different parts of the brain can take over similar functions. But this is subject to exceptions and qualification that must be minimized in a summarization. Unfortunately, he was too often interpreted as though accepting these principles denied localization of any sort. There was the further, even more farfetched inference that physiological research was irrelevant to psychological interests, and, therefore, brain research could be bypassed by the psychologists. Scepticism concerning the relevance of brain study for psychology became the result. Lashley was neither denying localization completely nor saying there was no relevance for psychology in the functioning of the brain. He was saying that localization is both less precise, more complex, and different from what had been held previously, and that it does have global functions. In some cases, equipotentiality held; in others, it did not; sometimes, but not always, mass action was a factor. In his view, physiological findings were still very much relevant to psychology.

It should be remembered that Lashley was a follower of Watson, and Watson had depended on the conditioned reflexes. In fact, Lashley started his research with the expectations that the reflex arc would be the principle conceptual tool with which to trace learning mechanisms as related to the cortex. He concluded in *Brain Mechanisms and Intelligence* that the experimental findings never did fit the reflex arc scheme. Mass action and equipotentiality, as a matter of fact, make Lashley's thinking compatible to a Gestalt position. At any rate he had delivered a telling blow against associationistic connectionism of the nineteenth century variety. He was, however, true to behaviorism in his insistence on contentual objectivity in his behavioral approach to his research problems; thus, on this salient issue, he remained faithful. Just as behaviorism does not require an environmentalistic approach, so it does not demand a molecular one.

45

TOLMAN ON

MOLAR, PURPOSIVE, AND COGNITIVE BEHAVIORISM

EDWARD CHACE TOLMAN (1886–1959), American psychologist, shortly after completing graduate work at Harvard (and a short period with Koffka), arrived at the University of California, Berkeley, where he remained. In 1914, a visiting professor at Harvard, Robert M. Yerkes, a student of animal behavior, had directed Tolman's attention to the work of Watson. Tolman was, then and there, convinced that psychology was to be contentually objective but rebelled at accepting Watson's particular formulation. He contended, as did his mentor at Harvard, E.B. Holt, that mentalistic psychology could be written in behavioral terms. Above all, he objected to the molecularism of muscle twitches and glandular secretions, a finding which he believed marred much of Watson's work. In his major work, *Purposive Behavior in Animals and Man*, he went on to indicate that it was his opinion that Watson really had two different notions about behavior—the molecular and the molar.

It is this second, or molar, conception of behavior that is to be defended in the present treatise. It will be contended by us (if not by Watson) that "behavior-acts," though no doubt in complete one-to-one correspondence with the underlying molecular facts of physics and physiology, have, as "molar" wholes, certain emergent properties of their own. And it is these, the molar properties of behavior-acts, which are of prime interest to us as psychologists. Further, these molar properties of behavior-acts cannot in the present state of our knowledge, i.e., prior to the working-out of many empirical correlations between behavior and its physiological correlates, be known even inferentially from a mere knowledge of the underlying, molecular, facts of physics and physiology. For, just as the properties of a beaker of water are not, prior to experience, in any way envisageable from the properties of individual water molecules, so neither are the properties of a "behavior-act" deducible directly from the properties of the underlying physical and physiological processes which make it up. Behavior as such cannot, at any rate at present, be deduced from a mere enumeration of the muscle twitches, the mere motions *qua* motions, which make it up. It must as yet be studied first hand and for its own sake.

An act *qua* "behavior" has distinctive properties all its own. These are to be identified and described irrespective of whatever muscular, glandular, or neural processes underlie them. These new properties, thus distinctive of molar behavior, are presumably strictly correlated with, and, if you will, dependent upon, physiological motions. But descriptively and per se they are other than those motions.

A rat running a maze; a cat getting out of a puzzle box; a man driving home to dinner; a child hiding from a stranger; a woman doing her washing or gossiping over the telephone; a pupil marking a mental-test sheet; a psychologist reciting a list of nonsense syllables; my friend and I telling one another our thoughts and feelings—*these are behaviors (qua molar)*. And it must be noted that in mentioning no one of them have we referred to, or, we blush to confess it, for the most part even known, what were the exact muscles and glands, sensory nerves, and motor nerves involved. For these responses somehow had other sufficiently identifying properties of their own. . . .

Granting, then, that behavior *qua* behavior has descriptive properties of its own, we must next ask just what, in more detail, these identifying properties are.

The first item in answer to this question is to be found in the fact that behavior, which is behavior in our sense, always seems to have the character of getting-to or getting-from a specific goal-object, or goal-situation. The complete identification of any single behavior-act requires, that is, a reference first to some particular goal-object or objects which that act is getting to, or, it may be, getting from, or both. Thus, for example, the rat's behavior of "running the maze" has as its first and perhaps most important identifying feature the fact that it is a getting to food. Similarly, the behavior of Thorndike's kitten in opening the puzzle box would have as its first identifying feture the fact that it is a getting away from the confinement of the box, or, if you will, getting to the freedom outside. Or, again, the behavior of the psychologist reciting nonsense syllables in the laboratory has as its first descriptive feature the fact that it is a getting to (shall we say) "an offer from another university." Or, finally, the gossiping remarks of my friend and myself have as their first identifying feature a set of gettings to such and such mutual readinesses for further behaviors.

As the second descriptive feature of a behavior-act we note the further fact that such a getting to or from is characterized not only by the character of the goal-object and this persistence to or from it, but also by the fact that it always involves a specific pattern of commerce-, intercourse-, engagement-, communion-with such and such intervening means-objects, as the way to get thus to or from.

For example, the rat's running is a getting to food which expresses itself in terms of a specific pattern of running, and of running in some alleys rather than in others. Similarly the behavior of Thorndike's kitten is not merely a getting from the confinement of the box but it is also the exhibition of a specific pattern of biting, chewing, and clawing such and such features of the box. Or, again, the man's behavior is not merely that of getting from his office to his be-wife-ed and be-pantry-ed home; it is also the doing so by means of such and such a specific pattern of commerce with the means-objects—automobile, roads, etc. Or, finally, the psychologist's behavior is not merely that of getting to an offer from another university; but also it is characterized in that it expresses itself as a specific pattern of means-activities or means-object commerces, viz., those of reading aloud and reciting nonsense syllables; of recording the results of these, and a lot of other bosh besides, in a *Protokoll,* and later in a typed manuscript, etc.

As the third descriptive feature of behavior-acts we find that, in the service of such gettings to and from specific goal-objects by means of commerces with such and such means-objects, behavior-acts are to be characterized, also, in terms of a *selectively greater readiness* for *short* (i.e., easy) means activities as against *long* ones. Thus, for example, if a rat is presented with two alternative spatial means-object routes to a given goal-object, one longer and one shorter, he will within limits select the shorter. And so in similar fashion for temporally and gravitationally shorter means-object routes. And what thus holds for rats will hold, no doubt, in similar and even more distinctive fashion for still higher animals and for man. But this is equivalent to saying that this selectiveness towards means-objects and means-routes is relative to the means-end "direction" and "distance" of the goal-object. The animal when presented with alternatives always comes sooner or later to select those only which finally get him to, or from, the given demanded, or to-be-avoided, goal-object or situation and which get him there by the shorter commerce-with routes.

To sum up, the complete descriptive identification of any behavior-act per se requires descriptive statements relative to (a) the goal-object or objects, being got to or from; (b) the specific pattern of commerces with means-objects involved in this getting to or from; and (c) the facts exhibited relative to the selective identification of routes and means-objects as involving short (easy) commerces with means-objects for thus getting to or from.[1]

He then goes on to discuss the purposive and cognitive determinants of behavior.

But surely any "tough-minded" reader will by now be up in arms. For it is clear that thus to identify behaviors in terms of goal-objects, and patterns of commerces with means-objects as selected short ways to get to or from the goal-objects, is to imply something perilously like purposes and cognitions. And this surely will be offensive to any hard-headed, well-brought-up psychologist of the present day.

And yet, there seems to be no other way out. Behavior as behavior, that is, as molar, *is* purposive and *is* cognitive. These purposes and cognitions are of its immediate descriptive warp and woof. It, no doubt, is strictly and completely dependent upon an underlying manifold of physics and chemistry, but initially and as a matter of first identification, behavior as behavior reeks of purpose and of cognition. And such purposes and such cognitions are just as evident, as we shall see later, if this behavior be that of a rat as if it be that of a human being.

Finally, however, it must nonetheless be emphasized that purposes and cognitions which are thus immediately, immanently, in behavior are wholly objective as to definition. They are defined by characters and relationships which we observe out there in the behavior. We, the observers, watch the behavior of the rat, the cat, or the man, and note its character as a getting to such and such by means of such and such a selected pattern of commerces-with. It is we, the independent neutral observers, who note these perfectly objective characters as immanent in the behavior and have happened to choose the terms *purpose* and *cognition* as generic names for such characters.[2]

To illustrate, the elimination of blind alleys in the maze, and the eventual adoption of the shortest route, shows that what the rat is learning is a route to a goal, a means to an end. If a goal is not reached by one route, another is taken.

That for Tolman behavior is molar calls for consideration of the relation of his view to that of the Gestalt psychologists. This need is reinforced by the fact that he made considerable conceptual use of what he called sign-gestalt expectations (and other related so-called sign-gestalt behavior). Baldly put, a sign-gestalt expectation is a sign for an object or means to relate to it. Tolman's sign-gestalts differ from the Gestalt of Köhler and the others in that while, "the whole in some degree governs its parts, these wholes, I felt, were acquired by learning . . . and not . . . innately ready pure perceptual gestalten."[3] Indeed, much of his earlier research was devoted to showing how the Gestalt laws of learning must be supplemented by research on the learning of the parts of the perceptual wholes. This "getting to" by means of "commerces with" is descriptive in nature. He shows that the animal exhibits persistence in moving toward or away from a goal, selects the shortest, or, if the condition arises, finds another route to that goal. Tolman argues that "persistent selection" and "choice" just used in this summary are imminently inferred by us as abstractions from the behavior. Research support for these and the other contentions to follow are always presented by Tolman but must be omitted here for the sake of brevity.

In 1959, in his last formal presentation of his system, these imminent inferences were identified as intervening variables. He chose to cast the structure of his system in terms of independent variables from past and present, intervening variables (divided into (1) mean-end-readiness and (2) expectations, perceptions, representations and valences) and dependent variables (response, or better, the performance.)

Indeed, years before, Tolman had written the first clear formulation of what is meant by an intervening variable.[4] The factor that is varied, the independent variable, and the resulting behavioral variable, the dependent variable, were already commonplace when discussing experimental research. Intervening variables are those functionally connected with a preceding independent and following dependent variables. Means-end-readiness and expectation purposes, and so on, are those, Tolman held, that can be tied by some experimental variables as those mentioned in the excerpt below. In the 1959 formulation, each of the categories of variables is carefully defined. He does this for several settings, such as a simple approach situation to the eating of food, and a simple case of escape from electric shock.

The means-end-readiness variable is illustrative:

Let me sum up. A means-end readiness, as I conceive it, is a condition in the organism which is equivalent to what in ordinary parlance we call a "belief" (a readiness or disposition) to the effect that an instance of this *sort* of stimulus situation, if reacted to by an instance of this *sort* of response, will lead to an instance of that *sort* of further stimulus situation, or else, that an instance of this *sort* of stimulus situation will simply by itself be accompanied, or followed, by an instance of that *sort* of stimulus situation. Further, I assume that the different readinesses or beliefs (dispositions) are stored up together (in the nervous system). When they are concretely activated in the form of expectancies they tend to interact and/or consolidate with one another. And I would also assert that "thinking," as we know it in human beings, is in essence no more than an activated interplay among expectancies resulting from such previously acquired readinesses which result in new expectancies and resultant new means-end readinesses.[5]

Tolman proposed and defended a cognitive theory of learning and a cognitive approach to psychology, currently of major importance, was mapped in a manner forcefully suggestive to those psychologists who followed. The organism, animal or human, learns to *know* his environment through learning its parts and their interrelation with the goal to be obtained. In so doing, behavioristic and Gestalt approaches were to some extent rendered compatible, one with the other.

46

GUTHRIE ON
CONTIGUITY IN LEARNING

EDWIN RAY GUTHRIE (1886–1959), American psychologist, was trained as a philosopher but, early in his career, adopted a strong behavioral position which led him to adopt psychology as a career. True to both his philosophical training and to his psychological position, he combined the associationistic tradition with that of conditioning. One of his earlier publications (in 1921) was a general textbook written in collaboration with a University of Washington colleague, Stevenson Smith. In an earlier chapter, they describe conditioning in a way not too dissimilar from that of Pavlov (p. 263). Later in the book, they discuss the laws of association, calling them the means of stating for ideas what conditioned responses describe for behavior.

Before the science of behavior was developed, certain laws of association were formulated to describe the origin of the sequence of ideas. These laws state that in any train of thought one idea follows another only when the experiences from which these ideas result have occurred in certain relationships. It was shown that if two experiences occur in immediate succession, the first, being repeated either as a sensory experience or as a memory, was capable of calling up the other. When we smell or think of the odor of roses, we are reminded of their visual appearance because roses have been smelled and then seen many times. When we see lightning or even think about it, the idea of thunder is apt to come to mind. The law describing this sequence is that of *association by temporal contiguity*. The law that describes associations as due to *spatial contiguity* is reducible to the first law. Objects experienced together in space are also experienced adjacent in time. Even where two experiences, though separated in time, occur in the same place and are later associated, such as becoming acquainted with two individuals on separate occasions at the house of a friend, the matter may be described as a double temporal association. *Cause and effect* become associated ideas, but only when these ideas or the experiences that underlie them have been known to us in immediate succession. Ideas that are *similar* tend to arouse each other because they are partially identical. Thus rats may make us think of mice on account of their similar shape and odor, though the two have never been seen together; cigars may remind us of cigarettes because both are made of tobacco; red flowers may call to mind blood. Some consecutive ideas that seem to be associated on the basis of their similarity show a likeness that is not so evidently an identity of elements. There is, for example, a similarity between any musical note and its octave, or between the colors red and violet. Though in these cases the physical stimuli are far from similar, the neural mechanisms they stimulate are probably in part identical.

These laws of association state for ideas what the conditioned response describes in behavior.[1]

In 1930, he mapped out his theoretical position under the title, "Conditioning as a Principle of Learning," signifying that the crucial form of learning is contiguity, which he conceived to be basic to conditioning and, therefore, to other forms of learning. He made his position clear when he stated that not all learning is to be described in terms of *conditioned reflexes*, despite his insistence that learning may be described in terms of *conditioning*. In the paper, after considering several more specific kinds of conditioning, he moved on to show that what others had considered to be other forms of learning, are actually forms of conditioning.

4. *The Effects of Practice.* Improvement as the result of practice is a familiar fact. The increased certainty of successful performance which results on repeated practice has led numerous psychologists to the notion that the attachment of a conditioning stimulus to its response is somehow increased by repetition of the sequence, which is a very different matter. Improvement demands more *detachment* of stimuli *from* responses than *attachment* of stimuli *to* responses. In order to improve in a performance the awkward, embarrassing, misdirected movements must be eliminated and replaced by movements which lead to a successful outcome. At the end of training the individual must be doing something quite different from what he was doing at the beginning of training.

The assumption that a stimulus-response sequence is made more certain by repetition has been embodied in a number of "laws of exercise" or "laws of frequency." It is quite possible, however, that the assumption is a mistaken one.

Pavlov's results in experiments in conditioning seem at first glance to indicate unambiguously that a conditioning stimulus is "established" by its repetition with a stimulus combination which elicits salivary flow, and to indicate that the "strength" or certainty and lasting quality of its establishment is a function of the number of occasions on which the two stimuli have been paired.

These experiments may be given a quite different interpretation. Conditioning, so far as elementary conditioning stimuli are concerned, may be an all-or-nothing affair, analogous to the setting of a switch, and not analogous to the wearing of a path, which has been a favorite simile. The increased certainty of response following on a given stimulus situation may involve an increase in the number of conditioners, rather than an increased "strength" of individual conditioners. In Pavlov's experiment, for instance, the bell signal results in extensive movements of orientation and postural adjustment, each movement causing appropriate stimulation to proprioceptors and exteroceptors. These movements are not identical each time the bell is struck because they depend in part on initial posture as well as on the bell. Repetition of the bell may enlist an increasing number of postural and other reflexes as conditioners of saliva flow, and hence gradually increase the certainty that salivary secretion will follow the bell.

It is entirely possible that if Pavlov could have controlled all stimuli instead of a very few, conditioning would be definitely established with one trial instead of fifty or more. The writer suggests that it is quite plausible that the more nearly such a complete control is established, the more nearly certain will be the result of the bell as a conditioner. Pavlov's whole method and experience suggest this.

The "strengthening" of a stimulus-response connection with repetition may very possibly be the result of the enlistment of increasing numbers of stimuli as conditioners, and not the result of the "strengthening" of individual connections.

5. *Forgetting.* The conception of forgetting presented in the textbooks has been that the effects of learning tend to be dissipated by some sort of physiological change at synapses which is a function of time. The form of the forgetting curve, though it differs for different sorts of material, indicates that forgetting is comparatively rapid when practice is discontinued and that the rate regularly diminishes.

There are some signs of a shift of opinion toward an explanation of forgetting in terms of conditioning. Hunter, in his article on learning in the recent volume of "The fundamentals of experimental psychology," quotes with approval the statement of Jenkins and Dallenbach in an article on "Obliviscence during sleep and waking" that "the results of our study as a whole indicate that forgetting is not so much a matter of decay of old impressions and associations as it is a matter of interference, inhibition, or obliteration of the old by the new."

The evidence that forgetting is to be explained in terms of new conditioning is of several kinds. Forgetting is radically affected by intervening activities. If the intervening situations are materially different from the practice situations forgetting is less evident than when a certain amount of similarity holds of the situations. Probably the stimuli which are repeated while new responses prevail lose their conditioning effect on their previous responses and become conditioners of the new responses, and consequently inhibitors of the original ones. Furthermore, forgetting during a period of sleep is less than forgetting during a period of waking activity. This seems to be readily explained in the same terms. The stimuli which had become conditioners of certain responses are not repeated during sleep, and have no chance to be alienated from their attachment to these responses. During a period of waking, multitudes of stimuli from postural adjustments, movements, or from exteroceptive sources, which had been made conditioners of the activities in question, are components of new situations and become conditioners of new responses. If we accept evidence from outside the laboratory we may quote those instances of vivid and detailed memories conserved for many years, which would, incidentally, have depended on one conditioning occasion rather than a practice series. The occasion for the restoration of such memories is probably an unusually complete restoration of situation, usually aided by such an absence of present distraction and inhibition as is found when we are on the border of sleep. Marcel Proust has described a common experience in which a memory evoked while lying in bed with closed eyes has persisted until a change in posture dissipated it completely. Association *may* occur after one connection, and *may* last indefinitely.

If forgetting is to be explained as new conditioning which replaces the old, how is the form of the curve of forgetting to be explained? Is it not entirely possible that the increased uncertainty of a conditioned response to a stimulus situation is due to the progressive alienation of conditioners from their response, an alienation explained by their acquisition of new allegiances? The curves of forgetting may owe their shapes to the cumulative effect of this alienation. Since the bulk of the conditioners are probably proprioceptive, the result of the organism's own movements, the activities following on a given case of conditioning would alienate whole regiments of conditioners at the start and a decreasing number as time elapsed, because there would be a decreasing number to eliminate.

This statistical decrease in conditioners with time which is described by the forgetting curve would resemble, to use a frivolous illustration, the decreased expenditures of a certain artist whose method of protecting himself from starvation was to change the proceeds of his rare sales into dimes and broadcast these about his large and disordered studio. The following day dimes were retrieved easily in numbers. As time went on more and more search was required, though he seldom reached such a pass that an afternoon's search would not yield a dime.

These last faithful dimes resemble the last faithful conditioners which are indicated by the failure of forgetting curves to reach the zero point. The fact that some forgetting occurs during sleep may be due to the fact that some activity occurs during sleep, and hence some chance for the alienation of stimuli.

This conception of forgetting explains forgetting entirely in terms of new conditioning. It is, of course, not denied that there may be physiological changes like those in senility which do result in the deterioration of memory, but the normal occasion of forgetting is the alienation of cues following the occurrence of these cues at times when their conditioned responses are excluded by the general situation....

7. *Emotional Reinforcement and Dynamogenesis.* Explanation of the facilitating effect of exciting emotion on learning cannot be complete until a satisfactory physiology of the emotions has appeared. In the meantime attention may be called to the fact that exciting emotion involves general muscular tonus, and may possibly consist very largely in such increase in general tension. The physiologists have described many types of muscle-to-muscle reflexes which are excited by muscular contraction, the stretching of a muscle, or resistance to the contraction of a muscle. Intense stimulation of one receptor field resulting in the contraction of a limited number of muscles results in the contraction of other muscle groups through such muscle-to-muscle reflexes. States of general tension may be built up by the "reverberation" of impulses in this fashion.

The origin of such states of general tension probably lies in intense stimulation of some receptor field, or in obstacles to free movement. In such states of general tension the acts which "go through" are more energetic and complete. They involve the stimulation of many proprioceptor systems which would be undisturbed by action not so energetic.

The increased stimulation would give opportunity for increased conditioners, especially since the excitement itself is subject to conditioned revival.

In what has been called "dynamogenesis" we have possibly two ways in which the irrelevant stimuli may facilitate learning. The new stimuli may serve to increase general tonus through the "reverberation" which has been described above and so serve to make action more vigorous and complete; and they may also, through the tendency to deflection which constitutes conditioning, serve to reinforce directly the prevailing responses. . . .

9. *Patterns.* That we do respond to patterns as such is not open to question. And this would seem to involve the complete breakdown of any theory of conditioning such as is being presented, for at varying distances the actual receptors and afferent paths activated by a visual pattern must be quite distinct. The fact, indeed, cannot be questioned, though it should be noted that it is not a general or uniform occurrence. The child who has learned to read the raised letters on his blocks will not ordinarily recognize the letters when he sits on them. The effectiveness of patterns applies only within very limited fields.

Is it not entirely possible that the method by which we come to recognize a face at different distances as that of one and the same person is essentially the same method by which we come to recognize the rear aspect of this same person as his own back? In this case of recognition there is no question of similar patterns, for the back of his head resembles his face less than his face resembles the faces of others. If we maintain an attitude, or repeat a response to an object while that object is the occasion of shifting stimulation and of new stimulus patterns the maintained response may be conditioned on the new stimuli. Our response to a person at different distances is the same, with differences appropriate to the distance. Why may we not attribute this sameness and this difference to the sameness and the differences originally present in the stimuli furnished by our original behavior in his presence?

If we accept conditioning as an explanation for responding appropriately to a person on hearing his footstep, which offers a stimulation pattern quite different from the visual pattern to which we previously responded, why should we consider it mysterious that the appropriate response could be called out by the stimulation of a quite different group of visual receptors? The fact that they have the same pattern is irrelevant.

The Gestalt psychologists assert not only that we respond in similar ways to similar patterns, which we undoubtedly do, but also that we do this *without any opportunity for conditioning,* which the writer does not at all believe. In the case of the hen which performed its trick using the eye which had been blindfolded during learning it is entirely possible that the cues for the proper movement were not primarily visual, but were furnished by movements connected with vision before the experiment was begun. Animals and man both have movements of skeletal muscles congenitally associated with vision. These movements may be in part identical for stimulation of either retina. If the act is conditioned on these movements, it might be elicited from either eye, without regard to which eye entered into practice.

10. *Insight*. Concerning insight as described by the Gestalt psychologists the writer has much the same opinion as concerning response to patterns. The facts which are reported are not to be questioned and are typical of the behavior of the higher animals. An important part of the report has, however, been omitted. If the behavior described as insight is asserted to occur without previous learning, the essential part of the experiment would be the control of previous learning, and in the experiments the histories of insight are conspicuously lacking. No new category of facts concerning learning has been shown to be offered by the behavior described as insight.

In the writer's experience, insight in animals and in man is the result of accumulated habit. It was not a strange coincidence that the most ingenious person ever at work in the local laboratory has been a practical engineer for many years. When this member of the staff solved with little hesitation problems which had baffled the writer, there was a choice of explanations. It could be said that one man had insight and the other none, which seemed the poorer explanation; or it could be pointed out that one man had had previous training and the other none, an explanation much more charitable.[2]

During his latter years at the University of Washington, Guthrie was hampered somewhat in marshalling laboratory evidence for his position by the relative lack of graduate students and the press of his administrative duties as a dean. He countered this handicap quite effectively by his ability to be persuasive in drawing on instances from everyday life that supported his position. There was one major research study conducted with a collaborator[3] which involved cats in a Thorndike-type puzzle box (p. 255). They found the expected trial-and-error behavior but also detected a tendency for each cat to repeat again and again the precise movements leading up to and including the manipulation in the escape mechanism (which, unlike Thorndike's study, was always the same kind and always in the same position). They referred to this behavior as stereotyping. They interpreted the repetition of precise routines as evidence for contiguity, since behavior repeats itself under similar conditions.

It has been our conclusion from our observation of this series of experiments that the prediction of what any animal would do at any moment is most securely based on a record of what the animal was observed to do *in that situation at its last occurrence*. This is obviously prediction in terms of association.[4]

Guthrie regarded reinforcement as something altering a situation and in that situation, contiguity, is the principle of learning.

A final summary statement of his position appeared in 1959, the year of his death,[5] but, following Hilgard's analysis,[6] it is possible to offer here a very short summary in two final excerpts. The first concerns Guthrie's one law of learning:

A combination of stimuli which has accompanied a movement will on its recurrence tend to be followed by that movement.[7]

There is no mention of drives, of rewards, of punishment—only stimuli and movements. But a second statement is needed to account for the undeniable fact of improvement with practice. Later, in the same account, he writes:

A stimulus pattern gains its full associative strength on the occasion of its first pairing with a response.[8]

Here we have what is sometimes referred to as "one-trial learning." Now, if learning occurs completely on one trial, then, as the excerpt on p. 377 indicated, what was last done in the presence of the stimulus-movement combination will most likely be that which occurred "*in that situation at its last occurrence*."

47

HULL ON

THE HYPOTHETICO-DEDUCTIVE APPROACH TO A BEHAVIOR SYSTEM

CLARK HULL (1884–1952), American psychologist, during the years from the 1930s on, at Yale University, made major contributions to the study of learning. The more or less contemporaneous research of Pavlov, Thorndike, Watson, the Gestalt psychologists, Lashley and Tolman, and Guthrie, already familiar to us through previous excerpts, as well as the contributions of Skinner to the same area yet to be reported, show that learning was a dominant problem in the psychology of the immediate past. In these decades, Hull began research in conditioning, which he then extended to rote learning and eventually moved on to the position in which learning is the salient problem of no less than a complete objectified quantitative general psychology. He wished to extend his system to all forms of behavior. The very titles of his later books, *Principles of Behavior* (1943), *Essentials of Behavior* (1951), and *A Behavior System* (1952), show the wide scope to which he would give the study of learning. Indeed, in his later years, he made some tentative beginnings to apply his behavior system to social problems.

His was an hypothetico-deductive approach to "a behavior system." He would start with a small number of empirically based principles and definitions (which, however, were subject to revision as new evidence accumulated, and, hence, hypothetical) and proceed by rigorous deduction to derive testable theorems and corollaries, which could be used to develop predictions to be verified by research. His approach was enormously productive, both on his own part and from work by his colleagues and others.

To bridge the gap between the learning formulations of Pavlov and Thorndike and to show how he would encompass their views in his own system, we have excerpted one of Hull's earlier statements:

ADAPTIVE BEHAVIOR—A SCIENTIFIC THEORETICAL SYSTEM IN
MINIATURE

Definitions

1. *A reinforcing state of affairs* (Postulate 3) is one which acts
    to give to the stimulus-trace component (Postulate 1) of pre-
    ceding or following temporal coincidences consisting of a
    stimulus trace and a reaction, the capacity to evoike the reac-
    tion in question (Postulate 2).
2. *Experimental extinction* is the weakening of a conditioned
    excitatory tendency resulting from frustration or the failure
    of reinforcement (Postulate 4).
3. *Frustration* is said to occur when the situation is such that
    the reaction customarily evoked by a stimulus complex can-
    not take place (Postulate 4).
4. *Seeking* is that behavior of organisms in trial-and-error situa-
    tions which, upon frustration, is characterized by varied al-
    ternative acts all operative under the influence of a common
    drive (S_D).
5. An *attempt* is a segment of behavior the termination of
    which is marked by either reinforcement or extinction.
6. A *simple trial-and-error situation* is one which presents to
    an organism a stimulus complex which tends to give rise to
    multiple reaction tendencies which are mutually incompat-
    ible, one or more of them being susceptible to reinforcement
    and one or more of them not being so susceptible.
7. A *correct* or "right" reaction is a behavior sequence which
    results in reinforcement.
8. An *incorrect* or "wrong" reaction is a behavior sequence
    which results in experimental extinction.
9. *Discouragement* is the diminution in the power of one ex-
    citatory tendency to evoke its normal reaction, this diminu-
    tion resulting from one or more unsuccessful attempts in-
    volving a second reaction.
10. A behavior sequence is said to be *directed* to the attainment
    of a particular state of affairs when there appears throughout
    the sequence a characteristic component (r_G) of the action
    (R_G) closely associated with the state of affairs in question
    and this component action (r_G) as a stimulus tends to evoke

an action sequence leading to the total reaction (R_G) of which the component constitutes a part.

11. Striving is that behavior of organisms which, upon frustration, displays varied alternative action sequences, all *directed* by an intent (r_G) to the attainment of the same reinforcing state of affairs.

12. A *goal* is the reinforcing state of affairs towards the attainment of which a behavior sequence of an organism may be directed by its intent (r_G).

13. An organism is said *to anticipate* a state of affairs when there is active active throughout the behavior sequence leading to the state of affairs a fractional component (r_G) of the action associated with the state of affairs in question.

14. *Success* is the culmination of striving which is characterized by the occurrence of the full reaction (R_G) of which the fractional component (r_G) is a part.

15. *Failure* is the culmination of striving which is characterized by the lack of the enactment of the full reaction $(R\,b6G)$ of which the fractional component (r_G) is a part.

16. *Disappointment* is the diminution in the power of one reinforcing situation to evoke appropriate consummatory reaction, this diminution (Postulate 4) resulting from the failure of a second reaction sequence directed (by an intent, or r_G) to a different reinforcing situation from that to which the first was directed, both being based on the same drive (S_D).

17. A *habit-family hierarchy* consists of a number of habitual behavior sequences having in common the initial stimulus situation and the final reinforcing state of affairs.

18. *Individual freedom* of behavior, so far as it exists, consists in the absence of external restraint.

Postulates

1. The adequate stimulation of a sense organ initiates within the organism a neural reverberation which persists for some time after the stimulus has ceased to act, the absolute amount of the reverberation diminishing progressively to zero but at a progressively slower rate. (Stimulus trace.)

2. When a reaction and a given segment of a stimulus-trace (Postulate 1) repeatedly occur simultaneously and this coinci-

dence occurs during the action of a drive (S_D) and temporally close to a reinforcing state of affairs (Definition 1), this and stronger segments of the stimulus trace tend progressively to acquire the capacity to evoke the reaction, the strength of the association thus acquired manifesting a negatively accelerated diminution with distance of the associates from the reinforcing state of affairs. (Positive association.)

3. A characteristic stimulus-reaction combination ($S_G \longrightarrow R_G$) always marks reinforcing states of affairs (Definition 1). The particular stimulus-response combination marking the reinforcing state of affairs in the case of specific drives is determined empirically, *i.e.*, by observation and experiment. (Mark of reinforcing state of affairs.)

4. When a stimulus evokes a conditioned (associative) reaction (Postulate 2) and this event does not occur within the range of the reinforcing state of affairs (Definition 1 and Postulate 3), or when an excitatory tendency in a behavior sequence encounters a situation which makes the execution of the act impossible (Definition 3), the excitatory tendency in question undergoes a diminution in strength with a limit below the reaction threshold (Definition 2), this diminution extending in considerable part to other excitatory tendencies which may be operative at the same time or for some time thereafter. (Negative association or experimental extinction.)

5. The strength of any given increment of either positive or negative association (Postulates 2 and 3) diminishes with the passage of time, and the portion remaining shows a progressively greater resistance to disintegration with the increase in time since its acquisition, a certain proportion of each increment being permanent. (Negative retention or forgetting.)

6. Each reaction of an organism gives rise to a more or less characteristic internal stimulus. (Internal stimulation.)

Key to Diagrams

S = an adequate stimulus together with the remaining trace (Postulate 1).

S_D = the stimulus associated with a drive, such as hunger.

S_G = the stimulus associated with the goal or reinforcing state of affairs.

s = an internal stimulus resulting from a reaction.

R = a reaction.

R_G = the reaction associated with the goal or reinforcing state of affairs.

r_G = a fractional component of the goal reaction.

$\longrightarrow$ = excitatory tendency from stimulus to reaction.

$\rightsquigarrow$ = causal connection of a non-stimulus-reaction nature.

$\ldots$ = a continuation or persistence of a process, as of a drive (S_D). Distance from left to right represents the passage of time.

Theorems 1

The Pavlovian conditioned reaction and the Thorndikian associative reaction are special cases of the operation of the same principles of learning.

1. Suppose that in the neighborhood of a sensitive organism stimuli S_C and S_G occur in close succession, that these stimuli in conjunction with the drive (S_D) evoke reactions R_C and R_G respectively, that S_m coincides in time with S_C while S_n coincides in time with S_G, and that (Postulate 1) the stimulus trace of S_m extends to R_C, and the stimulus trace of S_n extends to R_G.

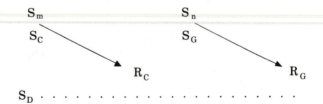

2. From (1) and Postulate 1, it follows that one phase of the stimulus trace of S_m will coincide with R_C and one phase of the stimulus trace of S_n will coincide with R_G.

3. Now, by Postulate 3, the combination $S_G \longrightarrow R_G$ marks a reinforcing state of affairs.

4. From (1), (2), (3), and Postulate 2 it follows, among other things. that the trace of S_n will become conditioned to R_G, and the trace of S_m will be conditioned to R_C, yielding the following excitatory tendencies:

$$S_m \longrightarrow R_C$$
$$S_n \longrightarrow R_G$$

5. But by (3) and (4) the reaction of the newly acquired excitatory tendency $S_n \longrightarrow R_G$ is that intimately associated with the reinforcing state of affairs, which identifies it as a conditioned reaction of the Pavlovian type.

6. On the other hand, by (3) and (4) the reaction of the excitatory tendency $S_m \longrightarrow R_C$ is a reaction distinct from that of the reinforcing state of affairs, which identifies it as an associative reaction of the Thorndikian type.

7. By (5) and (6) both the Pavlovian and the Thorndikian types of reaction have been derived from (1), (2), (3), and (4) jointly, and these in turn from the same principles of learning (Postulates 1, 2, and 3).

8. From (7) the theorem follows.

Q.E.D.[1]

The illustration of his hypothetico-deductive approach, just excerpted, is tightly but precisely stated, demanding much of even the sophisticated reader. Its general intent, however, is clear—to state adaptive behavior as envisioned by Pavlov and Thorndike as an exemplification of the same reinforcement principles of learning. In the same article, he goes on to formulate twelve other theorems in conditioning and trial-and-error learning. In his later work, theorems concerning the learning processes were not stated in terms of the work of a particular researcher, although it continued to be an intricately interwoven system.

Reinforcement is historically related to one aspect of the Thorndike law of effect—that having to do with "reward" and "effect." Although Hull was somewhat reluctant to refer to himself as a behaviorist, there is no question that he considered psychology to be contentually objective, and he wished to expunge from his behavior system anything that smacked of the subjective. Therefore, reinforcement was the term he chose, since "effect" had subjective connotations.

At Yale, Hull developed a following of colleagues and students who have carried on work in this framework to the present day. A different approach to reinforcement will be examined through the work of Skinner (p. 397). The other fundamental basis for learning, that of contiguity, is examined through the work of Guthrie (p. 375).

To bring out the nature of his commitment to psychology as a behavioral science, an excerpt is offered about his consideration of man's capacity for adaptive behavior which had been seen by many before him as demanding the agent of mind. He asserted that a variety of behavioral theorems could be marshalled, which then were supported by observationally known facts without recourse to mind.

By way of introduction to the system we may begin with the consideration of Theorem I. In brief, this theorem purports to show that Pavlov's conditioned reactions and the stimulus-response "bonds" resulting from Thorndike's so-called "law of effect" are in reality special cases of the operation of a single set of principles. The major principle involved is given in Postulate 2. Briefly, this postulate states the assumption of the present system concerning the conditions under which stimuli and reactions become associated. The difference in the two types of reaction thus turns out to depend merely upon the accidental factor of the temporal relationships of the stimuli to the reactions in the learning situation, coupled with the implication that R_G, which in part serves to mark a reinforcing state of affairs, is also susceptible of being associated with a new stimulus.[6] The automatic, stimulus-response approach thus exemplified is characteristic of the remainder of the system.

A consideration of Theorem II will serve still further as an orientation to the system before us. We find this theorem stating that both *correct* and *incorrect* reaction tendencies may be set up by the conditioning or associative process just referred to. Our chief interest in this theorem, as an introduction to the system, concerns the question of whether the terms "correct" and "incorrect" can have any meaning when they refer to reaction tendencies which are the result of a purely automatic process of association such as that presented by Postulate 2. It is believed that they have a very definite meaning. Definitions 7 and 8 state in effect that correctness or incorrectness is determined by whether the reaction tendency under given conditions is, or is not, subject to experimental extinction. Such purely objective or behavioral definitions of numerous terms commonly thought of as applying exclusively to experience, as distinguished from action, are characteristic of the entire system.

With this general orientation we may proceed to the theorems more specifically concerned with adaptive behavior. The proof of the first of these, Theorem III, shows that under certain circumstances organisms will repeatedly and successively make the same incorrect reaction. At first sight this may seem like a most commonplace outcome. However,

---

[6]"In effect this deduction purports to show that the Pavlovian conditioned reflex is a special case under Thorndike's "law of effect," though Thorndike might not recognize his favorite principle as formulated in Postulate 2. For a fuller but less formal discussion of this point see *Psychol. Bull.*, 1935, 32, 817–822."

when considered in the light of the definition of correctness given above it is evident that this theorem differs radically from what might be deduced concerning the behavior of a raindrop or a pebble moving in a gravitational field.[7]

Theorem IV states that after making one or more incorrect reactions an organism will spontaneously vary the response even though the environmental situation remains unchanged. This theorem is noteworthy because it represents the classical case of a form of spontaneity widely assumed, as far back as the Middle Ages, to be inconceivable without presupposing consciousness.

Theorem V states that when an organism originally has both correct and incorrect excitatory tendencies evoked by a single stimulus situation, the correct tendency will at length be automatically selected in preference to stronger incorrect ones.[8] This theorem, also, has been widely regarded as impossible of derivation without the presupposition of consciousness. Otherwise (so it has been argued) how can the organism know which reaction to choose?

Theorem VI represents the deduction that in certain situations the organism will give up seeking, i.e., cease making attempts, and thus fail to perform the correct reaction even when it possesses in its repertoire a perfectly correct excitatory tendency. The substance of this proof lies in the expectation that the extinction resulting from repeated false reactions will cause indirectly a critical weakening of a non-dominant but correct reaction tendency. This theorem is of unusual importance because it represents the deduction of a phenomenon not as yet subjected to experiment. As such it should have special significance as a test of the soundness of the postulates.

With Theorems VII and VIII we turn to the problem of anticipatory or preparatory reactions. The proof of Theorem VII derives, from the

---

[7]"It may be suggested that if water should fall into a hollow cavity on its way to the sea, it might at first oscillate back and forth vigorously and then gradually subside, each oscillation corresponding to an unsuccessful attempt and the gradual cessation, to experimental extinction. In all such cases the discussion as to whether the observed parallelism in behavior represents an essential similarity or a mere superficial analogy requires that both phenomena possess a thorough theoretical basis. *If the two phenomena are deducible from the same postulates and by identical processes of reasoning, they may be regarded as essentially the same, otherwise not.* But if one or both lacks a theoretical basis such a comparison cannot be made and decision can ordinarily not be reached. Much futile argument could be avoid if this principle were generally recognized."

[8]"See Simple trial-and-error learning: A study in psychology theory, Psychol. Rev., 1930, 37, 241–256; especially pp. 243–250."

principles of the stimulus trace and conditioning (Postulates 1 and 2), the phenomenon of the antedating reaction. The substance of this theorem is that after acquisition, learned reactions tend to appear in advance of the point in the original sequence at which they occurred during the conditioning process.[9] Pursuing this line of reasoning, Theorem VIII shows that in the case of situations demanding flight, such antedating reactions become truly anticipatory or preparatory in the sense of being biologically adaptive to situations which are impending but not yet actual. Thus we arrive at behavioral foresight, a phenomenon evidently of very considerable survival significance in animal life and one frequently regarded as eminently psychic, and inconceivable without consciousness.[10]

Passing over Theorem IX, which lays some necessary groundwork, we come to Theorem X. Here we find a deduction of the existence of the fractional anticipatory goal reaction. Of far greater significance from our present point of view, the deduction purports to show that through the action of mere association the fractional anticipatory reaction tends automatically to bring about on later occasions the state of affairs which acted as its reinforcing agent when it was originally set up. For this and other reasons it is believed that the anticipatory goal reaction is the physical basis of expectation, of intent, of purpose, and of guiding ideas.[11]

Theorem XI represents a deduction of the phenomenon of behavioral disappointment[12] as manifested, for example, by Tinklepaugh's monkeys. When these animals had solved a problem with the expectation of one kind of food they would tend to refuse a different kind of food, otherwise acceptable, which had been surreptitiously substituted.[13]

Theorem XII purports to be the deduction of the principle that organisms will strive actively to attain situations or states of affairs which previously have proved to be reinforcing. The automaticity deduced in the proof of Theorem X has here reached a still higher level. This is the capacity to surmount obstacles. But with the ability to attain ends in spite

[9]"See A functional interpretation of the conditioned reflex. Psychol. Rev., 1929, 36, 498–511; especially pp. 507–508."

[10]"See Knowledge and purpose as habit mechanisms, Psychol. Rev., 1930, 37, 511–525; especially pp. 514–516."

[11]"See Goal attraction and directing ideas conceived as habit phenomena. Psychol. Rev., 1931, 38, 487–506."

[12]"It is to be observed from a comparison of Definitions 9 and 16 that *Disappointment* necessarily presupposes a specific expectation or intent (r_G), whereas *Discouragement* does not."

[13]"O. L. Tinklepaugh, An experimental study of representative factors in monkeys, *J. Comp. Psychol.*, 1928, 8, 197–236. See especially p. 224 ff."

of obstacles comes automatically a genuine freedom (Definition 18), of great biological value but in no way incompatible with determinism.[14]

Theorem XIII is also derived with the aid of the fractional anticipatory goal reaction. This theorem represents the phenomenon of the adaptive but automatic transfer of learned reactions to situations having, as regards *external* characteristics, nothing whatever in common with the situations in which the habits were originally acquired. This, once more, is a form of adaptive behavior of the greatest survival significance to the organism, and one supposed in certain quarters to be impossible of derivation from associative principles. This is believed to be a low but genuine form of insight and a fairly high order of the "psychic."

This concludes the list of formally derived theorems. They have been selected from a series of fifty or so which are concerned with the same subject.[2]

The footnotes were retained in this excerpt, because they refer one to sources of research evidence for the particular theorem.

His guiding tenets all are captured in this excerpt.—to be precise and exact in all of his formulations, to present his approach to psychology in behavioral terms, and to relate psychological issues to biological problems.

While interest in testing detailed predictions through Hull's system has waned today, its rigorousness made it the central rallying point for a whole generation of psychologists who specialized in problems of learning.

[14]"An additional element of interest in this theorem is the fact that the fundamental phenomenon of motivation seems to have been derived from the ordinary principle of association (Postulate 2). If this deduction should prove to be sound, it will have reduced the two basic categories of motivation and learning to one, the latter being primary."

48

SKINNER ON

WORK AS A SCIENTIST,
OPERANT CONDITIONING,
AND FREEDOM AND CONTROL

BURHUSS FREDERIC SKINNER, born in 1904, and hence fourteen years younger than any of his eminent fellow contributors to psychology included in this volume, began to carry on significant studies in the early 1930s. From the very beginning of his career, he was committed to descriptive behavioral study without appeal to internal unobservables—such as the nervous system. He prefers to work with what he can manipulate, so he deals with the environmental variables, water deprivation, food and the like, and kinds of behavior, drinking, or eating, which can be controlled, not the unobservable events within the organism.[1]

In the mid-1950s, he was faced with the need to solidify the order he had developed in his work habits as a scientist up to that point in time. He had been asked to contribute a chapter to one of the already familiar Sigmund Koch edited volumes, *Psychology: A Study of a Science*. Routinely, Koch supplied all participants with a lengthy statement of suggested discussion topics—their formalized scientific method and theory—their themes, their independent intervening and the dependent variables in construct terms, their formal organization of the system, their view about principles of the system believed valuable outside the system, and the like. But Skinner had developed his actual practices in a very different manner. He denied using any form of implicit behavioral hypothetical constructs, intervening variables, and such. What could he do? He decided to present a case history—an autobiographical history of how he behaved as a scientist—the problems he had seen in some sample of behavior that interested him, the gadgets he developed, the leads he got from something "going wrong in the apparatus or the planned carrying out of a procedure" and the labor saving devices he found (such as why feed a rat when you can get him to feed himself?). At one summing-up point, he wrote the following:

This account of my scientific behavior up to the point at which I published my results in a book called *The Behavior of Organisms* is as exact in letter and spirit as I can now make it. The notes, data, and publications which I have examined do not show that I ever behaved in the manner of Man Thinking as described by John Stuart Mill or John Dewey or as in reconstructions of scientific behavior by other philosophers of science. I never faced a Problem which was more than the eternal problem of finding order. I never attacked a problem by constructing a Hypothesis. I never deduced Theorems or submitted them to Experimental Check. So far as I can see, I had no preconceived Model of behavior—certainly not a physiological or mentalistic one, and I believe, not a conceptual one. . . . Of course, I was working on a basic Assumption—that there was order in behavior if I could only discover it—but such an assumption is not to be confused with the hypotheses of deductive theory. It is also true that I exercised a certain Selection of Facts, not because of relevance to theory but because one fact was more orderly than another. If I engaged in Experimental Design at all, it was simply to complete or extend some evidence of order already observed.[2]

Just as in his work habits, order in behavior was sought. This was his guiding rule—to find out what happened in the environment and what happened to the organism when order of some sort or other seemed to be present.

    Skinner has published so much on so many topics that excerpt selection is more difficult than usual. The rationale for the following excerpt is that it relates his work in learning to that of two of his predecessors, Thorndike and Pavlov, while at the same time distinguishing his work in operant conditioning from their trial-and-error learning and classical conditioning. It is uncharacteristic only in that he has shown a marked disinterest, due to his very style of work, in concerning how his findings relate to those of others working in different traditions. But, as students of history, we cannot indulge in this single-minded absorption.

    Prior to the excerpt, he had reminded his readers that Thorndike's "Law of Effect" means that a behavior is stamped in when followed by certain consequences as observed from the fact that certain behavior occurred more and more readily in comparison to other behavioral characteristics of the situation, thus providing the Thorndike learning curves.

Learning curves do not, however, describe the basic process of stamping in. Thorndike's measure—the time taken to escape—involved the elimination of other behavior, and his curve depended upon the number of different things a cat might do in a particular box. It also depended upon the behavior which the experimenter or the apparatus happened to select as "successful" and upon whether this was common or rare in comparison with other behavior evoked in the box. A learning curve obtained in this way might be said to reflect the properties of the latch box rather than of the behavior of the cat. The same is true of many other devices developed for the study of learning. The various mazes through which white rats and other animals learn to run, the "choice boxes" in which animals learn to discriminate between properties or patterns of stimuli, the apparatuses which present sequences of material to be learned in the study of human memory—each of these yields its own type of learning curve. . . .

To get at the core of Thorndike's Law of Effect, we need to clarify the notion of "probability of response." This is an extremely important concept; unfortunately, it is also a difficult one. In discussing human behavior, we often refer to "tendencies" or "predispositions" to behave in particular ways. Almost every theory of behavior uses some such term as "excitatory potential," "habit strength," or "determining tendency." But how do we observe a tendency? And how can we measure one?

If a given sample of behavior existed in only two states, in one of which it always occurred and in the other never, we should be almost helpless in following a program of functional analysis. An all-or-none subject matter lends itself only to primitive forms of description. It is a great advantage to suppose instead that the *probability* that a response will occur ranges continuously between these all-or-none extremes. We can then deal with variables which, unlike the eliciting stimulus, do not "cause a given bit of behavior to occur" but simply make the occurrence more probable. We may then proceed to deal, for example, with the combined effect of more than one such variable.

The everyday expressions which carry the notion of probability, tendency, or predisposition describe the frequencies with which bits of behavior occur. We never observe a probability as such. We say that someone is "enthusiastic" about bridge when we observe that he plays bridge often and talks about it often. To be "greatly interested" in music is to play, listen to, and talk about music a good deal. The "inveterate" gambler is one who gambles frequently. The camera "fan" is to be found taking pictures, developing them, and looking at pictures made by himself and others. The "highly sexed" person frequently engages in sexual behavior. The "dipsomaniac" drinks frequently.

In characterizing a man's behavior in terms of frequency, we assume certain standard conditions: he must be able to execute and repeat a given act, and other behavior must not interfere appreciably. We cannot be sure of the extent of a man's interest in music, for example, if he is necessarily busy with other things. When we come to refine the notion of probability of response for scientific use, we find that here, too, our data are frequencies and that the conditions under which they are observed must be specified. The main technical problem in designing a controlled experiment is to provide for the observation and interpretation of frequencies. We eliminate, or at least hold constant, any condition which encourages behavior which competes with the behavior we are to study. An organism is placed in a quiet box where its behavior may be observed through a one-way screen or recorded mechanically. This is by no means an environmental vacuum, for the organism will react to the features of the box in many ways; but its behavior will eventually reach a fairly stable level, against which the frequency of a selected response may be investigated.

To study the process which Thorndike called stamping in, we must have a "consequence." Giving food to a hungry organism will do. We can feed our subject conveniently with a small food tray which is operated electrically. When the tray is first opened, the organism will probably react to it in ways which interfere with the process we plan to observe. Eventually, after being fed from the tray repeatedly, it eats readily, and we are then ready to make this consequence contingent upon behavior and to observe the result.

We select a relatively simple bit of behavior which may be freely and rapidly repeated, and which is easily observed and recorded. If our experimental subject is a pigeon, for example, the behavior of raising the head above a given height is convenient. This may be observed by sighting across the pigeon's head at a scale pinned on the far wall of the box. We first study the height at which the head is normally held and select some line on the scale which is reached only infrequently. Keeping our eye on the scale we then begin to open the food tray very quickly whenever the head rises above the line. If the experiment is conducted according to specifications, the result is invariable: we observe an immediate change in the frequency with which the head crosses the line. We also observe, and this is of some importance theoretically, that higher lines are now being crossed. We may advance almost immediately to a higher line in determining when food is to be presented. In a minute or two, the bird's posture has changed so that the top of the head seldom falls below the line which we first chose.

When we demonstrate the process of stamping in in this relatively simple way, we see that certain common interpretations of Thorndike's experiment are superfluous. The expression "trial-and-error learning," which is frequently associated with the Law of Effect, is clearly out of place here. We are reading something into our observations when we call any upward movement of the head a "trial," and there is no reason to call any movement which does not achieve a specified consequence an "error." Even the term "learning" is misleading. The statement that the bird "learns that it will get food by stretching its neck" is an inaccurate report of what has happened. To say that it has acquired the "habit" of stretching its neck is merely to resort to an explanatory fiction, since our only evidence of the habit is the acquired tendency to perform the act. The barest possible statement of the process is this: we make a given consequence contingent upon certain physical properties of behavior (the upward movement of the head), and the behavior is then observed to increase in frequency.

It is customary to refer to any movement of the organism as a "response." The word is borrowed from the field of reflex action and implies an act which, so to speak, answers a prior event—the stimulus. But we may make an event contingent upon behavior without identifying, or being able to identify, a prior stimulus. We did not alter the environment of the pigeon to *elicit* the upward movement of the head. It is probably impossible to show that any single stimulus invariably precedes this movement. Behavior of this sort may come under the control of stimuli, but the relation is not that of elicitation. The term "response" is therefore not wholly appropriate but is so well established that we shall use it in the following discussion.

A response which has already occurred cannot, of course, be predicted or controlled. We can only predict that *similar* responses will occur in the future. The unit of a predictive science is, therefore, not a response but a class of responses. The word "operant" will be used to describe this class. The term emphasizes the fact that the behavior *operates* upon the environment to generate consequences. The consequences define the properties with respect to which responses are called similar. The term will be used both as an adjective (operant behavior) and as a noun to designate the behavior defined by a given consequence.

A single instance in which a pigeon raises its head is a *response*. It is a bit of history which may be reported in any frame of reference we wish to use. The behavior called "raising the head," regardless of when specific instances occur, is an *operant*. It can be described, not as an accomplished act, but rather as a set of acts defined by the property of the height to which the head is raised. In this sense an operant is defined by an effect which may be specified in physical terms; the "cutoff" at a certain height is a property of behavior.

The term "learning" may profitably be saved in its traditional sense to describe the reassortment of responses in a complex situation. Terms for the process of stamping in may be borrowed from Pavlov's analysis of the conditioned reflex. Pavlov himself called all events which strengthened behavior "reinforcement" and all the resulting changes "conditioning." In the Pavlovian experiment, however, a reinforcer is paired with a *stimulus*; whereas in operant behavior it is contingent upon a *response*. Operant reinforcement is therefore a separate process and requires a separate analysis. In both cases, the strengthening of behavior which results from reinforcement is appropriately called "conditioning." In operant conditioning we "strengthen" an operant in the sense of making a response more probable or, in actual fact, more frequent. In Pavlovian or "respondent" conditioning we simply increase the magnitude of the response elicited by the conditioned stimulus and shorten the time which elapses between stimulus and response. (We note, incidentally, that these two cases exhaust the possibilities: an organism is conditioned when a reinforcer [1] accompanies another stimulus or [2] follows upon the organism's own behavior. Any event which does neither has no effect in changing a probability of response.) In the pigeon experiment, then, food is the *reinforcer* and presenting food when a response is emitted is the *reinforcement*. The *operant* is defined by the property upon which reinforcement is contingent—the height to which the head must be raised. The change in frequency with which the head is lifted to this height is the process of *operant conditioning*.

While we are awake, we act upon the environment constantly, and many of the consequences of our actions are reinforcing. Through operant conditioning the environment builds the basic repertoire with which we keep our balance, walk, play games, handle instruments and tools, talk, write, sail a boat, drive a car, or fly a plane. A change in the environment—a new car, a new friend, a new field of interest, a new job, a new location—may find us unprepared, but our behavior usually adjusts quickly as we acquire new responses and discard old.[3]

In the piece just excerpted, Skinner was showing that his operant conditioning procedure (sometimes referred to by others as instrumental conditioning since the successful act is instrumental in securing food) was related both to classical Pavlovian conditioning and to Thorndikian trial-and-error learning, yet could be distinguished from both. An additional point of description that might help one to understand the relation to Thorndike's procedure and apparatus is to realize that Thorndike's puzzle box supplies many leads to be tried by the animal which accounts for the numerous errors. The "Skinner box" reduced these errors very drastically, because there was little for the animal to manipulate other than the lever that released the food. To summarize, in Pavlovian conditioning, a reinforcer is paired with a stimulus. In operant conditioning, a reinforcer is contingent on the animal's response. Hence, Thorndikian learning, classical conditioning, and operant conditioning all depend on reinforcement. Any external agent, the stimulus, which increases the probability of occurrence of a previous response, is a reinforcement.

His impact on others has been profound. Today, he is probably the most eminent, and certainly best known, of all living psychologists, both to his colleagues and to the general public. Two kinds of subgroups of influence merit attention—one favoring his views, the other in opposition. There were those psychologists who were attracted to his way of doing research, eventuating in the establishment of a group that became "The Division for the Experimental Analysis of Behavior" within the American Psychological Association, and the accompanying foundation of several journals whose research reports were interrelated in such a fashion as to allow relatively little intrusion from sources other than those of the group. His views also stirred general opposition, both from some psychologists and nonpsychologists, sometimes described as taking place only at the level of "Skinner-baiting." Much of this general opposition stemmed from his uncompromising stand concerning the thorough deterministic prediction and control of human behavior that he advocated and lifted to titular status in his book, *Beyond Freedom and Dignity*,[4] his statement for the general public on how we must design our culture to shape the behavior necessary for sheer survival. In short compass, however, the excerpt below from a paper, "Freedom and Control of Men," designed for the scholarly community, will best serve to bring out some aspects of his position.

Perhaps the most crucial part of our democratic philosophy to be reconsidered is our attitude toward freedom—or its reciprocal, the control of human behavior. We do not oppose all forms of control because it is human nature to do so. The reaction is not characteristic of all men under all conditions of life. It is an attitude which has been carefully engineered, in large part by what we call the "literature" of democracy. With respect to some methods of control (for example, the threat of force), very little engineering is needed, for the techniques or their immediate consequences are objectionable. Society has suppressed these methods by branding them "wrong," "illegal," or "sinful." But to encourage these attitudes toward objectionable forms of control, it has been necessary to disguise the real nature of certain indispensable techniques, the commonest examples of which are education, moral discourse, and persuasion. The actual procedures appear harmless enough. They consist of supplying information, presenting opportunities for action, pointing out logical relationships, appealing to reason or "enlightened understanding," and so on. Through a masterful piece of misrepresentation, the illusion is fostered that these procedures do not involve the control of behavior; at most, they are simply ways of "getting someone to change his mind." But analysis not only reveals the presence of well-defined behavioral processes, it demonstrates a kind of control no less inexorable, though in some ways more acceptable, than the bully's threat of force.

Let us suppose that someone in whom we are interested is acting unwisely—he is careless in the way he deals with his friends, he drives too fast, or he holds his golf club the wrong way. We could probably help him by issuing a series of commands: don't nag, don't drive over sixty, don't hold your club that way. Much less objectionable would be "an appeal to reason." We could show him how people are affected by his treatment of them, how accident rates rise sharply at higher speeds, how a particular grip on the club alters the way the ball is struck and corrects a slice. In doing so we resort to verbal mediating devices which emphasize and support certain "contingencies of reinforcement"—that is, certain relations between behavior and its consequences—which strengthen the behavior we wish to set up. The same consequences would possibly set up the behavior without our help, and they eventually take control no matter which form of help we give. The appeal to reason has certain advantages over the authoritative command. A threat of punishment, no matter how subtle, generates emotional reactions and tendencies to escape or revolt. Perhaps the controllee merely "feels resentment" at being made to act in a given way, but even that is to be avoided. When we "appeal to reason," he "feels freer to do as he pleases." The fact is that we have exerted *less* control than in using a threat; since other conditions may contribute to the result, the effect may be delayed or, possibly in a given instance, lacking. But if we have worked a change in his behavior at all, it is because we have altered relevant environmental conditions, and the processes we have set in motion are just as real and just as inexorable, if not as comprehensive, as in the most authoritative coercion.

"Arranging an opportunity for action" is another example of disguised control. The power of the negative form has already been exposed in the analysis of censorship. Restriction of opportunity is recognized as far from harmless. As Ralph Barton Perry said in an article which appeared in the Spring, 1953, *Pacific Spectator,* "Whoever determines what alternatives shall be made known to man controls what that man shall choose *from.* He is deprived of freedom in proportion as he is denied access to *any* ideas, or is confined to any range of ideas short of the totality of relevant possibilities." But there is a positive side as well. When we present a relevant state of affairs, we increase the likelihood that a given form of behavior will be emitted. To the extent that the probability of action has changed, we have made a definite contribution. The teacher of history controls a student's behavior (or, if the reader prefers, "deprives him of freedom") just as much in *presenting* historical facts as in suppressing them. Other conditions will no doubt affect the student, but the contribution made to his behavior by the presentation of materials is fixed and, within its range, irresistible.

The methods of education, moral discourse, and persuasion are acceptable not because they recognize the freedom of the individual or his right to dissent, but because they make only *partial* contributions to the control of his behavior. The freedom they recognize is freedom from a more coercive form of control. The dissent which they tolerate is the possible effect of other determiners of action. Since these sanctioned methods are frequently ineffective, we have been able to convince ourselves that they do not represent control at all. When they show too much strength to permit disguise, we give them other names and suppress them as energetically as we suppress the use of force. Education grown too powerful is rejected as propaganda or "brain-washing," while really effective persuasion is described as "undue influence," "demagoguery," "seduction," and so on.

If we are not to rely solely upon accident for the innovations which give rise to cultural evolution, we must accept the fact that some kind of control of human behavior is inevitable. We cannot use good sense in human affairs unless someone engages in the design and construction of environmental conditions which affect the behavior of men. Environmental changes have always been the condition for the improvement of cultural patterns, and we can hardly use the more effective methods of science without making changes on a grander scale. We are all controlled by the world in which we live, and part of that world has been and will be constructed by men. The question is this: Are we to be controlled by accident, by tyrants, or by ourselves in effective cultural design?

The danger of the misuse of power is possibly greater than ever. It is not allayed by disguising the facts. We cannot make wise decisions if we continue to pretend that human behavior is not controlled, or if we refuse to engage in control when valuable results might be forthcoming. Such measures weaken only ourselves, leaving the strength of science to others. The first step in a defense against tyranny is the fullest possible exposure of controlling techniques. A second step has already been taken successfully in restricting the use of physical force. Slowly, and as yet imperfectly, we have worked out an ethical and governmental design in which the strong man is not allowed to use the power deriving from his strength to control his fellow men. He is restrained by a superior force created for that purpose—the ethical pressure of the group, or more explicit religious and governmental measures. We tend to distrust superior forces, as we currently hesitate to relinquish sovereignty in order to set up an international police force. But it is only through such counter-control that we have achieved what we call peace—a condition in which men are not permitted to control each other through force. In other words, control itself must be controlled.

Science has turned up dangerous processes and materials before. To use the facts and techniques of a science of man to the fullest extent without making some monstrous mistake will be difficult and obviously perilous. It is no time for self-deception, emotional indulgence, or the assumption of attitudes which are no longer useful. Man is facing a difficult test. He must keep his head now, or he must start again—a long way back.[5]

His approach has also had considerable impact on psychological treatment in the form of behavior modification, teaching machines, and programmed learning. The thread of consistency through all of these methods of seeking order in human nature is his operational definition of reinforcement, described before as anything that increases the probability of occurrence of a previous response.

REFERENCES

In some books, the source given is that one judged most readily accessible to a reader who wishes to pursue the matter further, often a reprint. Hence, the date for the publication may be misleading without supplemental comment. So, while the full reference for these books is given, including the date, it is followed by the original date of publication, in parentheses. Other books are cited in terms of chapters, parts, or sections, not pages. What may appear to be a derilection of duty, namely failure to report precise pages is meant, on the contrary, to suggest that almost all editions, including the one the most convenient for you to find, will report this and related material in the fashion thus indicated. If still at a loss to find a source, consult the bibliography that lists all of them, (except the works of Skinner) prepared by this editor: *Eminent Contributors to Psychology* Vol 1. *A Bibliography of Primary References*. New York: Springer, 1974.

For articles, when the original journal is cited, the full citation, including pages, is followed by a parenthetical statement of pages excerpted. For articles reprinted in collections the title is followed by the original date of publication and the pages excerpted are given in parentheses after the full page citation for the article as reprinted.

Galileo

1   Galileo, *Il saggiatore*, (1623), Part 23. Translated in E.A. Burtt, *The metaphysical foundations of modern physical science*. Rev ed. New York: Humanities Press, 1932.

Bacon

1 Bacon, F. *Novum organum.* (1620), in *The physical and metaphysical works of Lord Bacon, including the advancement of learning and the novum organum.* London: Bell, 1886. Book 1, Aphorism 3.
2 *Ibid.,* Aphorism 44.
3 *Ibid.,* Aphorisms 19, 22.
4 *Ibid.,* Aphorism 105.
5 *Ibid.,* Aphorisms 99, 103.

Harvey

1 Harvey, W. *An anatomical disquisition on the motion of the heart and the blood in animals.* (1628), in R. Willis. (Trans.). *The works of William Harvey, M.D.* London: Sydenham Society, 1847. Chap. 8.
2 *Ibid.,* Chap. 9.

Descartes

1 Descartes, R. *Discourse on the method of rightly conducting the reason.* (1637), in *The philosophical works of Descartes.* (2 vols.) Trans. by Elizabeth S. Haldane and G.R.T. Ross. London: Cambridge University Press, 1931, Vol. 1, Part 5.
2 Descartes, R. *Rules for the direction of the mind.* (1701), in *ibid.,* Vol. 1., Part 12.
3 Descartes, R. *Meditations of first philosophy.* (1641), in *ibid.,* Vol. 1., Part 4.
4 *Meditations, op. cit.,* in *ibid.,* Vol. 2. Reply to fifth objections.
5 *Discourse, op. cit.,* in *ibid.,* Vol. 1., Part 4.
6 *Ibid.,* Part 2.
7 *Meditations, op. cit.,* in *ibid.,* Vol. 2, Reply to sixth objections.
8 Descartes, R. *On man.* (1662), as translated in S. Diamond. (Ed.). *The roots of psychology.* New York: Basic Books, 1974, pp. 198, 200. Art. 26.
9 *Discourse.* In *op. cit.,* Vol. 1, Part 5.
10 Descartes, R. *Passions of the soul.* (1649), in *The philosophical works of Descartes. op. cit.,* Vol. 1, Arts. 31–32.

Hobbes

1 Hobbes, T. *Human nature: Or the fundamental elements of policy.* (1650), in W. Molesworth. (ed.). *The English works of Thomas Hobbes.* (11 vols.). London: Bohn, 1839–1845, Vol. 4, Conclusion.
2 Hobbes, T. *Leviathan or the matter, form and power of commonwealth, ecclesiastical and civil.* (1651), in *ibid.,* Vol. 3, Chap. 13.

3 *Ibid.*, Chap. 11.
4 *Human Nature, op. cit.*, Chap. 7, Sec. 1.
5 *Ibid.*, Chap. 2, Secs. 4–8, 10.
6 *Ibid.*, Chap. 4, Sec. 2.

Newton

1 Newton, I. *Sir Isaac Newton's mathematical principles of natural philosophy and his system of the world.* (2 vols.) 3rd ed. Trans. by A. Motte and rev.
   by F. Cajori. Berkeley, Ca.: University of California Press, 1934. Preface to
   the first edition. (1687)
2 Newton, I. *Opticks, or a treatise of the reflections, refractions, inflection
   and colors of light.* 4th ed. New York: Dover, 1952. (1730) Book 1, Part 2,
   Definition.
3 *Ibid.*, Book 1, Part 2, Prop. 5, Theorem 4.

Locke

1 Locke, J. *An essay concerning human understanding.* (2 vols.) A.C. Fraser.
   (Ed.). London: Oxford University Press, 1894. (1690)
2 *Ibid.*, Book 1, Chap. 1, Secs. 1–3, 5, 15.
3 *Ibid.*, Book 2, Chap. 1, Secs. 1–5.
4 *Ibid.*, Book 4, Chap. 4, Sec. 3.
5 *Ibid.*, Book 2, Chap. 8, Secs. 7–17.
6 *Ibid.*, Book 2, Chap. 33, Secs. 1, 3–6, 9–12.

Berkeley

1 Berkeley, G. *A treatise concerning the principles of human knowledge.* 2nd
   ed., in A.A. Luce and T.E. Jessop. (Eds.). *The works of George Berkeley,
   Bishop of Cloyne.* Vol. 2. London: Nelson, 1949, Sec. 1. (1734)
2 *Ibid.*, Sec. 2.
3 *Ibid.*, Sec. 3.
4 *Ibid.*, Secs. 9–10.
5 Berkeley, G. *An essay towards a new theory of vision,* in A.A. Luce and T.E.
   Jessop. (Eds.). *The works of George Berkeley, Bishop of Cloyne.* Vol. 1.
   London: Nelson, 1948, Secs. 1–17, 20–22, 27–27. (1709)

Hume

1 Hume, D. *A treatise of human nature.* Vol. 1. New York: Dutton, 1911,
   Introduction. (1739)
2 *Ibid.*, Part 1, Sec. 1.

3 Hume, D. *Enquiries concerning the human understanding and concerning the principles of morals.* Ed. by L.A. Selby-Bigge. Oxford: Clarendon Press, 1955, *An enquiry concerning human understanding,* Sec. 3, Part 19. (1748)
4 *Ibid.,* Sec. 3, Parts 22–27.
5 *Treatise, op. cit.,* Part 4, Sec. 6.

Hartley

1 Hartley, D. *Observations on man, his frame his duty and his expectations.* Delmar, N.Y.: Scholars' Facsimiles and Reprints, 1966, Chap. 1. Introd.
2 *Ibid.,* Chap. 1, Sec. 2, Prop. 10–11.

The Mills

1 Mill, J. *Analysis of the phenomena of the human mind.* 2nd ed. Ed. by J.S. Mill, with notes by J.S. Mill, A. Bain, A. Findlater, and G. Grote. New York: Kelley, 1967, Chap. 3. (1829)
2 Mill, J. S. *A system of logic, ratiocinative and inductive, being a connected view of the principles of evidence, and the methods of scientific investigation.* 8th ed. New York: Harper, 1874, Book 6, Chap. 4, Sec. 3. (1843)

Kant

1 Kant, I. *Critique of pure reason.* Trans. by J.M.D. Meiklejohn, New York: Dutton, 1964. Sec. 1. (1781)
2 *Ibid.,* Book 1, Introduction, Part 1, Secs. 1–4.
3 Kant, I. *Metaphysical foundations of natural science.* Trans. by J. Ellington. Indianapolis, Ind.: Bobbs-Merrill, 1970, Preface. (1786)

Herbart

1 Herbart, J.F. *A text-book of psychology.* New York: Appleton, 1891, Part 1, Chaps., 1–3, Secs. 10–23.
2 *Ibid.,* Chap. 5, Secs. 39–43.

Müller

1 Müller, J. *Elements of physiology,* Vol. 2. Philadelphia, Pa.: Lea & Blanchard, 1843, Book 4. (1833–1840)
2 *Ibid.,* Book 5, Parts 1–8.

Weber and Fechner

1   Weber, E. H. *The sense of touch and common feeling.* (1846), as translated in B. Rand. (Ed.). *The classical psychologists.* Boston: Houghton Mifflin, 1912, pp. 557–558.
2   Fechner, G. T. *Elements of psychophysics.* (1860), as translated in B. Rand. (Ed.). *The classical psychologists.* Boston: Houghton Mifflin, 1912, Chaps. 7, 14.

Helmholtz

1   Helmholtz, H.v. On the rate of transmission of the nerve impulse. (1850), in W. Dennis. (Ed.). *Readings in the history of psychology.* New York: Appleton-Century-Crofts, 1948, p. 197.
2   Helmholtz, H.v. *Treatise on physiological optics,* Vol. 2. Rochester, N.Y.: Optical Society of America, 1924, Sec. 20. (1860)
3   Helmholtz, H.v. *On the sensations of tone.* 4th German ed. New York: Dover, 1954, Chap. 6. (1863)
4   Helmholtz, H.v. *Treatise, op. cit.,* Vol. 3. Sec. 26.

Wundt

1   Wundt, W. *Principles of physiological psychology.* 5th ed. New York: Macmillan, 1904, Preface first edition. (1873)
2   *Ibid.,* Preface, fifth edition.
3   Wundt, W. *An introduction to psychology.* 2nd ed. New York: Macmillan, 1912, Chapter 2. (1911)
4   Wundt, W. *Outlines of psychology,* 7th ed. Leipzig: Engelmann, 1907, Sec. 23. (1896)

Brentano

1   Brentano, F. *Psychology from an empirical standpoint.* 2nd ed. London: Routledge & Kegan Paul, 1973, Book 2, Chap. 1, Sec. 2, 3, 59 (1874)
2   *Ibid.,* Book 1, Chap. 2, Secs. 2, 3.

Ebbinghaus

1   Ebbinghaus, H. *Memory: A contribution to experimental psychology.* New York: Teachers College, Columbia University, 1913, Sec. 2. (1885)
2   *Ibid.,* Sec. 4.
3   *Ibid.,* Sec. 11.
4   *Ibid.,* Secs. 27–29.

Külpe

1 Külpe, O. *Über die moderne Psychologie des Denkens*. (1912), in Vorlesungen über Psychologie. 2nd ed. Leipzig: Hirzl, 1922. As translated in and by J.M. Mandler and G. Mandler. (Eds.). *Thinking: From Association to Gestalt*. New York: John Wiley, 1964, pp. 208–216.
2 Marbe, K. *Experimentell-psychologische Untersuchungen über das Urteil, eine Einleitung in die Logik*. Leipzig: Engelmann, 1901.

Darwin

1 Darwin, C. *The origin of species by means of natural selection*. New York: Appleton, 1897. Chap. 4, Summary. (1859)
2 Darwin, C. *The expression of the emotions in man and animals*. New York: Philosophical Library, 1955, Chap. 16. (1872)

Galton

1 Galton, F. *Hereditary genius: An inquiry into its laws and consequences*. 2nd ed. New York: Dutton, 1907, Introductory chap. (1869)
2 *Ibid.*, Comparison of results.
3 Galton, F. *Inquiries into human faculty and its development*. 3rd ed. New York: Dutton, 1907, pp. 93–94. (1883)

Spencer

1 Spencer, H. *The principles of psychology*. 4th ed. New York: Appleton, 1897, Vol. 1., Sec. 54. (1855)
2 *Ibid.*, Sec. 203.
3 *Ibid.*, Sec. 189.

Romanes

1 Romanes, G.J. *Animal intelligence*. London: Kegan Paul, Trench, 1882, pp. 1–5.
2 *Ibid.*, p. 291.
3 *Ibid.*, pp. 497–498.

Morgan

1 Morgan, C.L. *An introduction to comparative psychology*. 2nd ed. New York: Scribner's, 1904, pp. 291–293. (1894)

James

1 Perry, R.B. *The thought and character of William James: As revealed in unpublished correspondence and notes, together with his published writings.* (2 vols.) Boston: Little, Brown, 1935.
2 James, W. *The principles of psychology.* (2 vols.) New York: Holt, 1890. Vol. 1, p. 224.
3 *Ibid.,* pp. 237–239, 243, 244–245.
4 *Ibid.,* pp. 138–144.
5 *Ibid.,* pp. 292–296.
6 *Ibid.,* p. 103.
7 *Ibid.,* pp. 121–122, 127.
8 *Ibid.,* Vol. 2, 383–384, 385, 389–391.
9 *Ibid.,* pp. 449–450.
10 *Ibid.,* Vol. 1, 663–664.
11 *Ibid.,* pp. 666–667.

Hall

1 Hall, G.S. The content of children's minds. *Princeton Review,* 1883, 249–272.
2 *Ibid.,* pp. 261–262.
3 Hall, G.S. *Adolescence, its psychology and its relations to physiology, anthropology, sociology, sex, crime, religion and education.* New York: Appleton, 1904, pp. 2–3.
4 *Ibid.,* pp. VII–X.

Cattell

1 Cattell, J. McK. The inertia of the eye and brain. *Brain,* 1885, **8**, 295–312.
2 Cattell, J. McK. Mental tests and measurements. *Mind,* 1890, **15**, 373–380. (pp. 373–374)
3 Cattell, J. McK. Statistics of American psychologists. *American Journal of Psychology,* 1903, **14**, 310–328. (pp. 310–312)
4 Cattell, J. McK. *Psychology in America.* New York: Science Press, 1929.
5 Cattell, J. McK. Retrospect: Psychology as a profession. *Journal of Consulting Psychology,* 1937, **1**, 1–3. (pp. 1–2, 2–3)

Titchener

1 Titchener, E.G. The postulates of a structural psychology. *Philosophical Review,* 1898, **7**, 449–465. (pp. 449–454, 455–457, 458–459, 460, 461–462, 465)

2   Evans, R.B., E.B. Titchener and his lost system. *Journal of the History of the Behavioral Sciences,* 1972, **8**, 168–180.

Dewey

1   Dewey, J. The reflex arc concept in psychology. *Psychological Review,* 1896, **3**, 357–370. (pp. 357–361, 362–370)

Angell

1   Angell, J.R. The province of functional psychology. *Psychological Review,* 1907, **14**, 61–91. (pp. 62–63, 65–66, 66–67, 67–68, 68–70, 73–74, 75–76, 80–82, 85–86, 87–88)

McDougall

1   McDougall, W. *Physiological psychology.* New York: Dutton, 1921, pp. 1–2. (1905)
2   McDougall, W. *An introduction to social psychology.* 16th ed. Boston: Luce, 1923, pp. 2–4. (1908)
3   *Ibid.,* pp. 20–21.

Thorndike

1   Thorndike, E.L. Animal intelligence. *Psychological Review Monograph Supplement,* 1898, No. 2, pp. 1–109. (pp. 13, 45)
2   *Ibid.,* p. 45.
3   Thorndike, E.L. *Educational psychology.* Vol. 2. *The psychology of learning.* New York: Teachers College, Columbia University, 1913, p. 4.
4   Thorndike, E.L. A proof of the law of effect. *Science,* 1933, **77**, 173–175. (pp. 173–175)
5   Thorndike, E.L. Reward and punishment in animal learning. *Comparative Psychology Monographs,* 1932, **8**, No. 39, p. 58.
6   Thorndike, E.L., and Woodworth, R.S. The influence of improvement in one mental function upon the efficiency of other functions. *Psychological Review,* 1901, **8**, 247–261, 384–395, 553–564.
7   Thorndike, E.L. Mental abilities. *Proceedings of the American Philosophical Society,* 1941, **84**, 504–513. (pp. 503–504)

Pavlov

1   Pavlov, I.P. *The conditioned reflex.* (1934), in *Experimental Psychology and other essay.* New York: Philosophical Library, 1957, pp. 245–270. (pp. 245–248, 248–251, 252, 253–255, 260–262).

Watson

1 Watson, J.B. Psychology as a behaviorist views it. *Psychological Review,* 1913, **20**, 158–177. (pp. 158–159, 163–164, 165–166, 166, 167)
2 Watson, J.B. *Psychology from the standpoint of a behaviorist.* 3rd ed. Philadelphia, Pa.: Lippincott, 1929, p. 24. (1919)
3 *Ibid.,* pp. 38–40.
4 Watson, J.B., and Morgan, J.J.B. Emotional reactions and psychological experimentation. *American Journal of Psychology,* 1917, **28**, 163–174. (pp. 165–166, 166–167)
5 Sherman, M. The differentiation of emotional responses in infants. *Journal of Comparative Psychology,* 1927, **7**, 265–284, 335–351.
6 Watson, J.B., and Rayner, R. Conditioned emotional reactions. *Journal of Experimental Psychology,* 1920, **3**, 1–14. (pp. 2–3, 4–5, 5–6, 7–8)
7 Watson, J.B. *Behaviorism.* 2nd ed. Chicago: University of Chicago Press, 1939, p. 104. (1924)

Von Ehrenfels

1 Ehrenfels, C.v., "Ueber Gestaliqualitaten," *Vierteljahrschrift für wissenschaftliche Philosophie,* 1890, **14**, 249–292.
2 Ehrenfels, C.v., On Gestalt-qualities. (1932) *Psychological Review,* 1937, **44**, 521–524. (pp. 521–523)

Wertheimer

1 Wertheimer, M. Experimentelle Studien über das Sehen von Bewegung. *Zeitschrift für Psychologie,* 1912, **61**, 161–265.
2 Wertheimer, M. *The general theoretical situations.* (1922), in W.D. Ellis. Ed. *A source book of Gestalt psychology.* New York: Harcourt, Brace, 1938, pp. 12–16. (pp. 12–16)
3 Wertheimer, M. *Principles of perceptual organization.* (1923), in D.C. Beardslee, and M(ichael) Wertheimer. Eds. *Readings in perception.* Princeton, N.J.: Van Nostrand, 1958, pp. 115–135. (pp. 115–117, 118–121, 134–135)
5 Wertheimer, M. *Productive Thinking.* Enlarged ed. Ed. by M(ichael) Wertheimer. New York: harper, 1959. (1945).

Köhler

1 Köhler, W. *The mentality of apes.* Trans. E. Winter. New York: Humanities Press, 1927. (1917)
2 Köhler, W. *Intelligence in apes,* in C. Murchison. (Ed.). *Psychologies of 1925.* 3rd ed. Worcester, Mass.: Clark University Press, 1928, pp. 145–161. (1926) (pp. 146–147, 158–159)

3   *Ibid.*, p. 149.
4   Köhler, W. *Die physischen Gestalten in Ruhe und im stationären Zusand.* Erlangen: Verlag der philosophischen Akademie, 1924.
5   Köhler, W. *Gestalt psychology.* New York: Liveright, 1947, pp. 36–40. (1929)
6   Köhler, W. *The place of value in a world of facts.* New York: Liveright, 1966, pp. 251–254. (1938)

Koffka

1   Koffka, K. *The growth of the mind: An introduction to child psychology.* Trans. R.M. Ogden, London: Routledge and Kegan Paul, 1928, pp. 53–54. (1921)
2   Koffka, K. *Principles of Gestalt psychology.* New York: Harcourt, Brace and World, 1963, pp. 27–38. (1935)
3   *Ibid.*, pp. 67–68.
4   *Ibid.*, p. 73.

Lewin

1   Lewin, K. *Environmental forces in child behavior and development,* in C. Murchison. (Ed.). *A handbook of child psychology.* 2nd rev. ed. Worcester, Mass.: Clark University Press, 1933, pp. 590–625. (1931) (pp. 598–602)
2   Lewin, K. Action research and minority problems. *Journal of Social Issues,* 1946, **2**, 34–46. (pp. 39–44)

Freud

1   Freud, S. *The psychopathology of everyday life.* (1904), in J. Strachey et al., ed. & trans. *The standard edition of the complete psychological works of Sigmund Freud.* Vol. 4. London: Hogarth Press and the Institute of Psycho-Analysis, 1953, pp. 107–118.
2   Freud, S. *The interpretation of dreams.* (First part) (1900), in J. Strachey et al. ed. & trans. *The standard edition of the complete psychological works of Sigmund Freud.* Vol. 4. London: Hogarth Press and the Institute of Psycho-Analysis, 1953, pp. 107–118.
3   Freud, S. *An outline of psychoanalysis.* (1940), in J. Strachey et al., ed. & trans. *The standard edition of the complete psychological works of Sigmund Freud.* Vol. 23. London: Hogarth Press and the Institute of Psycho-Analysis, 1965, pp. 145–151.

Adler

1   Adler, A. *Die theorie der Organminderwertigkeit und ihre Bedeutung für Philosophie und Psychologie.* (1907) Reprinted in translation in H.S.

Ansbacher and R.R. Ansbacher. (Eds.). *The individual psychology of Alfred Adler: A systematic presentation in selections from his writings.* New York: Basic Books, 1956, p. 24.

2   Adler, A. Trotz und Gehorsam. (1910) *Ibid.,* pp. 53–54.
3   Adler, A. *Über den nervösen Charakter.* (1912) *Ibid.,* pp. 96–97.
4   Adler, A. *Individual psychology: Some of the problems fundamental to all psychology,* in C. Murchison. (Ed.). *Psychologies of 1930.* Worcester, Mass.: Clark University Press, 1930, pp. 395–405. Reprinted in H. Ansbacher, and R. Ansbacher (Eds.). *The Individual Psychology of Alfred Adler, op. cit.,* pp. 103–104.
5   Adler, A. *Über den nervösen Charakter. Ibid.,* pp. 111–112.
6   Adler, A. *What life should mean to you.* Boston: Little, Brown, 1931. (pp. 239, 239–240, 240, 241) Reprinted in H. Ansbacher and R. Ansbacher. (Eds.). *The Individual Psychology of Alfred Adler, op. cit.,* pp. 131–133.
7   Adler, A. *The science of living.* New York: Greenberg Publishers, 1929. (p. 98) Reprinted in H. Ansbacher and R. Ansbacher. (Eds.). *The Individual Psychology of Alfred Adler, op. cit.,* p. 173.

Jung

1   Jung, C., et al. *Man and his symbols.* Garden City, N.Y.: Doubleday, 1964, pp. 20–23.
2   *Ibid.,* pp. 27–28.
3   Jung, C.G. *The concept of the collective unconscious.* (1936), in H. Read et al. (Eds.). *The collected works of C.G. Jung,* Vol. 9, Part 1. *The archetypes and the collective unconscious.* Princeton, N.J.: Princeton University Press, 1959, pp. 42–53. (pp. 42–43)
4   Jung, C.G. *The association method.* (1910), in H. Read et al. (Eds.). *The collected works of C.G. Jung.* Vol. 2. *Experimental Researches.* Princeton, N.J.: Princeton University Press, 1973, pp. 439–465. (pp. 462–463)
5   Jung, C.G. *Psychological typology.* (1936), in H. Read et al. (Eds.). *The collected works of C.G. Jung.* Vol. 6. *Psychological Types.* Princeton, N.J.: Princeton University Press, 1971, pp. 542–555. (pp. 550–555)

Lashley

1   Franz, S.I., and Lashley, K.S. The retention of habits by the rat after destruction of frontal portions of the cerebrum. *Psychobiology,* 1917, 1, 3–18.
2   Lashley, F. In search of the engram. (1950), in F.A. Beach *et al.* (Eds.). *The neuropsychology of Lashley.* New York: McGraw-Hill, 1960, pp. 478–505.
3   Lashley, K. *Brain mechanisms and intelligence: A quantitative study of injuries to the brain.* New York: Dover, 1963, pp. 172–173, 175–176. (1929)
4   Lashley, K.S. In search of the engram, *op. cit.*

Tolman

1 Tolman, E.C. *Purposive behavior in animals and men.* New York: Century, 1932, pp. 7–8, 10–12.
2 *Ibid.,* pp. 12–13.
3 Tolman, E.C. *Principles of purposive behavior,* in S. Koch. (Ed.). *Psychology: A study of a science.* Study 1. *Conceptual and systematic.* Vol. 2. *General systematic formulations, learning and special processes.* New York: McGraw-Hill, 1959, pp. 92–147. (p. 95)
4 Tolman, E.C. The determiners of behavior at a choice point. *Psychological Review,* 1938, **45**, 1–41.
5 Principles, *op. cit.,* pp. 113–114.

Guthrie

1 Smith, S., and Guthrie, E.R. *General psychology in terms of behavior.* New York: Appleton, 1921, pp. 252–253.
2 Guthrie, E.R. Conditioning as a principle of learning. *Psychological Review,* 1930, **37**, 412–428. (pp. 419–425, 426–427)
3 Guthrie, E.R., and Horton, G.P. *Cats in a puzzle box.* New York: Rinehart, 1946.
4 *Ibid.,* p. 42.
5 Guthrie, E.R. *Association by contiguity,* in S. Koch. (Ed.). *Psychology: A study of a science.* Study 1. *Conceptual and systematic.* Vol. 2. *General systematic formulations, learning, and special processes.* New York: McGraw-Hill, 1959, pp. 158–195.
6 Hilgard, E.R. *Theories of learning.* 2nd ed. New York: Appleton-Century-Crofts, 1956. (1948)
7 Guthrie, E.R. *The psychology of learning.* Rev. ed. New York: Harper & Row, 1952, p. 23.
8 Guthrie, E.R. Conditioning: A theory of learning in terms of stimulus, response and association. *Yearbook of the National Society for the Study of Education,* 1942, **41**(2), 17–60. (p. 30)

Hull

1 Hull, C.L. Mind, mechanism and adaptive behavior. *Psychological Review,* 1936, **44**, 1–32. (pp. 15–18)
2 *Ibid.,* pp. 11–15.

Skinner

1 Skinner, B.F. *Science and human behavior.* New York: Macmillan, 1953.

2 Skinner, B.F. *A case history in scientific method,* in S. Koch. (Ed.). *Psychology: A study of a science.* Study 1. *Conceptual and systematic.* Vol. 2. *General systematic formulations, learning, and special processes.* New York: McGraw-Hill, 1959, pp. 359–379. (p. 369)
3 Skinner, B.F. *Science and human behavior, op. cit.,* pp. 60–61, 62–66.
4 Skinner, B.F. *Beyond freedom and dignity.* New York: Alfred Knopf, 1971.
5 Skinner, B.F. Freedom and the control of man. *American Scholar,* 1955–1956, **25**, 47–65. (pp. 54–57)

NAME INDEX

SUBJECT INDEX